QlikView for Enterprises

A Practitioner's Reference

A.Rajendran

2012

QlikView for Enterprises
A Practitioner's Reference
A.Rajendran

Rajendran
Visit website at www.qv4ent.com for more information

Library of Congress Control Number: 2012906795

ISBN-10: 0-9855017-0-7
ISBN-13: 978-0-9855017-0-9

Editing by Mahashree Rajendran
Most illustrations from QlikTech published material

First Edition: April 2012
10 9 8 7 6 5 4 3 2 1

I dedicate this book to

my wonderful family:

loving wife Meena

beloved daughter Mahashree

wonderful son Shreedhar

QlikView for Enterprises

A Special Thanks to

Rob Wunderlich

for his valuable inputs for improvement

and

his unbeatable attention to detail!

QlikView for Enterprises

TABLE OF CONTENTS

QlikView for Enterprises

LIST OF FIGURES

QlikView for Enterprises

LIST OF TABLES

QlikView for Enterprises

FOREWORD

To my knowledge, this is the first book about QlikView being published that is more than an introduction or a beginner's guide. It is written by a Senior BI professional and aimed at an audience that either has recently discovered QlikView or has been working with it for some time and wants to gain a deeper understanding.

Mr. Rajendran has implemented and overseen 160+ QlikView projects in the last 7 years: from small, medium to large; in CPG, Manufacturing, Telecom, Financial Services and Insurance.

He has summarized his experiences to help you position, develop, implement and understand QlikView. It's an ambitious book and ambition is THE key word in the context of Business Intelligence (BI). To become better organizations must encourage innovation and learn from experiences—yours and others—and really take advantage of available information resources.

In 2012, striving to innovate and become better is no longer an option but a must, and to harness relevant data and adapt faster is a challenge every organization must address. Data is our new raw material and how we refine and use it is instrumental.

Business Intelligence is the term used for a group of tools intended to access, manage and analyze data. In enterprise organizations, tools must be reliant, secure and stable (hygiene factors required by IT) while being easy to use and fast to develop and adapt (hygiene factors required by users).

Traditional BI tools has failed in the latter and is now playing catch up with QlikView and other Data Discovery tools that better meet the new needs of information workers—a group that is growing to mean almost everyone in your organization, not just a select few.

I hope you get value from this book and the experiences of a great QlikView practitioner—and that it helps you to stay ahead of the curve.

Johan Averstedt

6 April 2012

PREFACE

Very few people don't get impressed by the capabilities of QlikView. Everyone who has set out to analyze some kind of data and find an answer to a question—immediately recognizes the usefulness of QlikView. I have been in the Data Analytics space, for over 27 years including my Engineering (CIT Coimbatore) and M.Tech (IIT Delhi) days. Both qualitative and quantitative analysis, seeking for patterns to arrive at conclusions, useful patterns, to help find root causes and solve problems of varying magnitudes.

My first tryst with structured analytics was when I got immersed in Data Mining, with the use of MineSet (TM) a product of SGI (Silicon Graphics Inc). That 3-year period gave a tremendous understanding of the various aspects of analytics, appropriateness of techniques for the types of problems and the ability of data analytics to enhance our cognitive abilities. I was an ardent fan of MineSet, its capabilities and I loved the idea of Visual Data Mining as a tribute to the human intelligence. Though MineSet had great capabilities to analyze using the automated Machine Learning algorithms including Bayesian, Decision Trees, K-Means Clustering, and so on, to me, the most impressive feature was the ability to "Visualize" multi-dimensional data—of up to 8 dimensions in a single interactive visualization. I was just SOLD on its capability to enhance and assist human intelligence to "Perceive" hidden relationships—the visual representation of correlations, which is very tough to understand using our natural linear logic / with which we need to construct an internal special model to visualize the relationships.

In 2005, I moved into Team, and was working towards creating a practice for Business Intelligence—evaluating various products and offerings in the market—also got involved in evaluating various BI products for one of the MNCs in India. During this exercise, came across QlikView, and I got the same Eureka moment that I got when I started working with MineSet.

I feel QlikView is another wonderful embodiment of Visual Data Mining —with an ability to substantially increase the Cognitive Value of any data set. The ability to navigate across questions that arise while looking at a data asset, in any order, without being restricted due to the hierarchical structures posed by most other products is the real unique value proposition of QlikView.

The first encounter with QlikView was with total disbelief—something must be really wrong—something is being misrepresented—the skeptical view. How can group by's be executed on the fly, without going back to the SQL Engine, and how can it be so fast? Then I took the product, and evaluated it on our own data—Team's own multiple instances of FACT (Financial Accounting Package) running in different branches—to create a unified view of the entire company Sales and distribution. Voila, that's what helped me understand the power of Navigable Reports—my discovery of QlikView's capabilities started.

I liked when I read "Uncontrollable Smiles" used by QlikTech as a tag line when talking about the impact of QlikView on users. Very few technologies / products create this effect. I always wondered why people smile—I have heard WOWs in most situations, when QlikView is first shown with their own data.

Since then, I have been in the QlikView technology space, for over 6 years, in various capacities—Pre-sales, Sales, Architecting, Developing, Deploying, Testing, Training, well, the appreciation of QlikView is very infectious.

While QlikView evokes an excitement in almost everyone, the next questions are actually genuine concerns to understand if QlikView is a viable alternative to the other well-known solutions in the market. Will it scale? Will it solve all my issues? What is its weakness? How does it compare with other choices? Is it enterprise capable? Will I get the right skills required? And so on.

With over 180 implementations of QlikView done by the team, teaching QlikView and its capabilities to about a significant part of over 200 people who have worked in this technology at Team the appreciation for QlikView and its capabilities has grown; this has transformed into a clear understanding of what it can do and where it can help, and where it cannot.

With some of the most inquisitive, untiring and probing minds who worked with me at Team (whom I have mentioned in the acknowledgements), in the various Customer locations and various specialists in QlikTech India and in the US, my discovery of the product and its usefulness kept progressing.

This book is an attempt to present some of the important understandings, the key capabilities of QlikView, its fitment – business challenges it helps solve and the technical fitment in the various enterprise IT infrastructure configurations. While I am so excited to introduce QlikView and start talking about it, I feel compelled to set a context, set a backdrop of "What and Why", and then place QlikView in the right place. QlikView is no more or no less than a product – it has got its place, where it is the most useful. Understanding this place is a key to putting it to the best use.

The book essentially focuses on "What and Why" of QlikView and strategic "How-To" questions. The "What and Why" questions are very well answered by the various Case Studies published by QlikTech – however they don't help in creating a philosophical framework of conclusive knowledge, to help place QlikView in the larger space of information management.

Tactical "How-To" questions are answered very well by the various blogs, the QlikCommunity apart from the Reference Manuals. I have not attempted to replace or reproduce what the QlikView Reference Manuals and other QlikTech documents / presentations which are being made available recently. However, I have focused on providing the Strategic "How-To" in the form of various frameworks that will allow overall performance improvement of QlikView and reduction of the Total Cost of Ownership while deploying QlikView for the enterprise. Some of the material published by QlikTech is used in various places to explain and evolve the framework.

The book has been organized in three major parts:

Part I: What is QlikView? Why we buy/bought it? What can it do?

Part II: How does QlikView work?

Part III: How to make best use of QlikView?

Beyond what is given in this book, various bits and pieces of knowledge and experience of the QlikView team at TEAM, have been consolidated into the implementation methodology – which is CMM Level 3 certified, making it as one of the unique ways of delivery – derived from the Agile methodology. Some of the key elements of this methodology are also discussed in the book - particularly in Part III. These are great time savers, and customers should try and use these methods during implementations.

QlikView is fast becoming one of the best fit tools for Interactive Analytics – Visual Data Mining. With QlikView becoming more and more appropriate for Enterprises of all sizes, the number of professionals who will make it as their main practice is going to increase.

This book is aimed as a starting point for such professionals, whether working in a presales or a solution architect role with a customer or in an implementation partner organization. I would be very happy if the book adds to the right understanding of the fitment of QlikView for various Enterprises.

Trust this book increases the understanding of QlikView, its relevance in decision making and data analytics. I strongly believe QlikView is one major step forward to making this world better and more efficient, by allowing information-driven decision making. The move of aspiring enterprises and individuals into profitable excellence is made easier by one more degree by QlikView.

Happy increase in Analytical Quotient!

Happy Journey!

Warm regards,
Rajendran Avadaiappan
9 April 2012

QlikView for Enterprises

PART I

QLIKVIEW AND ENTERPRISE NEEDS

QlikView for Enterprises

INTRODUCTION TO PART I

> *"A computer [Information/Analytics] will not make a good manager out of a bad manager. It makes a good manager better faster and a bad manager worse faster"*
> *- Edward M. Esber, CEO, Ashton-Tate*
> *Fortune Magazine, March 2, 1987*

What Ashton Tate mentioned almost 25 yrs ago is so relevant even in today's context of QlikView as well. It is no more or no less than a product – it has got its place, where it's most useful.

Understanding this place is a key to putting it to best use. Good managers decide to see the right things faster and make right changes faster. Bad managers can decide to use the wrong tools, decide to see the wrong things and make changes in the wrong places. QlikView certainly accelerates this process giving an easy and fast tool.

This Part sets the context starting with the overview and various aspects of Enterprise systems. It positions QlikView among the various enterprise software solutions. Starting with a bird's eye view of the Information Systems, the chapter converges to the specific position of QlikView.

Understanding this overview allows one to see the connectivity of it with other systems – logically from a decision support perspective and physically from a data connectivity / flow stand point.

Starting with an overview of enterprise information systems, through information needs, Enterprise Information Framework, categories of information, the chapters move towards exploring the various scenarios where QlikView is a great fit.

With the QlikView product expanding and improving in various fronts, the uses of the product is increasing every day, with more use cases being added - innovation and ingenuity at work.

The overall intent of this part is to establish the needs where QlikView is a natural solution, providing use cases of where it is relevant and useful.

CHAPTER 1

ENTERPRISE INFORMATION NEEDS

BUSINESS DISCOVERY/INTELLIGENCE IS THE PURPOSE OF IT FOR BUSINESS MANAGERS

Introduction to the Chapter

Information plays a very important role in shaping enterprises. With increasing business complexities and speed, the need to make informed decisions is extremely important. While the information systems have multiple needs to meet, the ultimate need is to allow the business to thrive and grow into excellence and profitability.

This chapter explores the various information needs of organizations, and discusses the driving factor that demands information. Starting with the definition of Type-I and Type-II challenges of business, the chapter sets out to show how Information can help address these challenges.

It attempts to provide a systematic framework to classify the requirements so that appropriate solution can be chosen for different needs. The chapter goes on to introduce and discuss the Analytics Quotient that defines the propensity of any organization to use information and take advantage.

This chapter sets the backdrop for the entire book, giving the context in which business analytics, data discovery, reporting, dashboards and scorecards–all make sense. This backdrop helps understand the core purpose of implementing QlikView in an organization.

Business Velocity and Complexity

Businesses are getting more and more complex, with newer innovative interconnections, supported by the global open economy. This is further fuelled by the Internet technologies, making myriad combinations come to life in very short spans of time.

Information is now no more an advantage. Innovation is a middle-class resource, and technology has shrunk time. Everything is social and collaboration now, bringing the consumer technologies into the enterprise.

This has led to two challenges:
First, with changes happening so fast, market being more dynamic and transparent, the entire product and service life cycles are reduced greatly. In most businesses, the parameters of business have not changed, but the window of time required for making decisions has shrunk. Hence the challenge is, "How do we make high quality decisions in a short time?" This is Type I challenge.

Second, with all the transformations happening in the market, new products, new markets and new ways of conducting business are all making life more interesting and enjoyable; this is an exciting period for everyone. The impact is that business managers are posed with increasingly complex decisions with complex interconnections and unexpected changes in patterns of behaviour. This is Type II challenge.

Together, these two types of challenges have left business managers wanting. When these two types of challenges come together, the quality of decision suffers, since the linear logical analysis breaks down, or takes too long.

Added to this, there is another challenge of multiple data capture systems, with different pieces of information about the enterprise stored in different data stores. Unification of these information sources, and creating a unified view of the enterprise with an ability to see the details and various summarized information on demand, is a major challenge.

From a different view, the amount of information that is getting captured both inside the enterprises and outside the enterprise is increasing drastically. The ability to keep up with all this information, and make use of this for effective business decision making is a challenge, more than ever. Any solution that will simplify this assimilation and decision making process is a welcome help, and QlikView is one very important solution.

Enterprise Information Systems

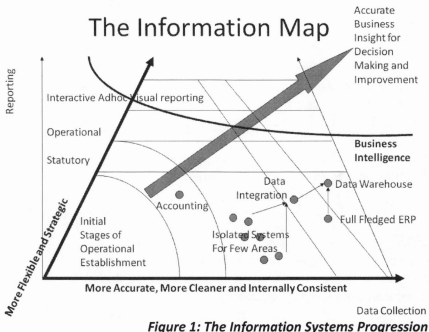

Figure 1: The Information Systems Progression

Enterprise systems involve a large variety of hardware and system software associated. For the context of this discussion, the focus is on the Software Applications only. The software systems have evolved over time, and the following chart captures the various aspects of Capture vs. Reporting influence on the various information systems.

Enterprise Application Systems can be seen broadly as three parts:

1. *Data Capture and Control Systems*: ERP systems, Point of Sales systems, Spreadsheets, and many other applications including the collaboration and social media applications are used today to capture the *transaction* data, and keep historical time-stamped record of the transactions. All these applications are the *senses*—eyes, ears, nose and skin—of the enterprise, that *feel* and collect information from the environment as things happen.

2. *Persistence Systems for Storing and Managing Data*: All Database, File System, Document Management, ETL and User Management Software form the intermediate systems. This is where the enterprise Memory is stored, with all the (business) rules associated with the way in which the data is processed, stored and allowed for consumption. Security and associated restrictions also form part of this persistent data of the enterprise.

3. *Data and Information Output Systems*: All systems providing Reporting, Analytics, Dashboards, Scorecards, Alerts, What-If and Real Time View fall under this category.

Depending on the nature of the business and the particular function in question, different view of data/information is required. Depending on the need, various levels of detail are provided, in different visual representations, with varying degrees of interactivity to handle corollary questions and alternative thinking.

This book focuses completely on this part of the enterprise needs, goes on to explore what QlikView can address in this gambit of requirements for the enterprises. For more elaborate information on EIS, please read the references, particularly the Journal of Enterprise Information Systems (Taylor & Francis) [1] and pages in Wikipedia.

Business Purpose of Enterprise Systems

Every enterprise system has got an important role to play, and there is a context sensitive answer about the need, relevance and importance of each system. There are two key uses and hence important outcomes / benefits expected from the enterprise Systems: i) Improving efficiency of operations, ii) improving decision-making quality.

While data about the business is constantly collected in multiple systems, there are process controls implemented seamlessly within the collection system, by way of integrated process paths and restrictions, workflows and approval systems.

This is one of the key benefits of an enterprise system —making the business and its processes to be person independent and as efficient as possible. This need is taken care of by the *Data Capture and Control Systems* mentioned above.

In addition to increasing the efficiency of operations, there is a need to create organizational memory of all transactions and associated rules. It is interesting to note at this point that there is structured content stored in Database Tables and unstructured content stored in File Systems and Document Management Systems.

Incidentally, such storage systems also help meet the statutory compliance and traceability demands on the enterprise. This need is taken care of by the *Persistence Systems* for Storing and Managing Data.

Most of the IT investments in the last few decades have been only in creating and establishing these capture systems and storage systems. However, this is not the ultimate purpose—one can say these form only necessary conditions.

Business Intelligence (BI): Is it the Business Purpose of IT?

There is an important business purpose for the enterprise Systems: Making the data available to make better decisions, for making the business itself better. The real use of the data collected is when it helps various stake holders to view the data in appropriate ways and gain a cognitive benefit of understanding the business and its characteristics so that they can take decisions to drive the business to better meet its objectives more efficiently. The word Business Intelligence has been used to represent various views.

Business Intelligence was first used as early as September, 1996, in a Gartner Group report:
By 2000, Information Democracy will emerge in forward-thinking enterprises, with *Business Intelligence* information and applications available broadly to employees, consultants, customers, suppliers, and the public. The key to thriving in a competitive marketplace is staying ahead of the competition.

Making sound business decisions based on accurate and current information takes more than intuition. Data analysis, reporting, and query tools can help business users wade through a sea of data to synthesize valuable information from it.

A Technical User Definition

In its technical sense, Business Intelligence (BI) refers to all the processes from taking this data, analyzing and presenting the information. Wikipedia refers to BI as "Computer-based techniques used in identifying, extracting and analyzing business data, such as sales revenue by products and/or departments, or by associated costs and incomes".

Business Intelligence is a term used to include all the processes/tools/techniques used for the following: Extraction, Integration, Transformation and Preparation of data; and Reporting, Analytics, Dashboards, Scorecards, Scenario / What If Analysis, and Real time Analysis.

The starting point of BI processes is the data captured and stored in enterprise databases. Majority of material available on BI focus on just this part and provide the What, Why and How of BI from the stand point of handling data. However it is important to keep in mind that all these technologies, tools and techniques should lead to a better use of the rich information available in this data. Only that allows businesses to improve.

A Business User Definition

From a business user perspective, BI is the collection of all processes for finding the patterns, trends in business—of the products, people, geographies, customers, suppliers, etc.—in a timely fashion, and take advantage of such knowledge by decisions to improve performance of the business. Dashboardinsight.com refers to BI as: "Turning data into knowledge to support informed decision making". In this perspective, BI focuses on visual and automated pattern recognition that provides the ability to understand the exceptions and deviations that are happening on the ground.

Managers primarily need to focus on *causes of pain*—what is not working right & correct it—and *factors that can fuel growth*. Their job is to take advantage of every such understanding to positively influence the business. Hence they turn to BI to get intelligence of both types. To run businesses better and constantly improve, these insights should be available to all managers. With this result in mind, it is appropriate to say: *Business Intelligence is the Purpose of IT.*

Information Needs of Management

In many ways, management is all about finding *what is NOT happening* (or) *GAP* versus *the plan*, and ensuring that they happen. This forms the core of *Performance Analysis* in all the companies. This essentially focuses on finding what is being produced by anyone for every dollar spent. Plan targets and budgets are generally created on Excel sheets, and in more mature organizations on planning and budgeting Systems. Actual information comes from transaction systems. Monitoring the GAP constantly requires reports which combine plan and actual data from different systems.

Beyond plans and budgets, there are compliance/statutory demands for action. From an information standpoint, these are also targets / objectives to be met. Periodic activities, submission of data to statutory and other governance bodies forms part of this. In addition, internal governance needs including renewal of contracts, bank limit management, employee welfare and security initiatives form part of such targets.

In addition to internally generated data, additional benchmark data from outside are used in organizations for performance management: competitive industry benchmarking data, supply / demand projection data, industry statistics, commodity prices, exchange rates, and others.

Regular Reports

Combining these data sources and constantly providing GAPs is the need. Such GAPS are presented and communicated using dashboards and scorecards, in a standard format with key metrics, color coded for easy understanding. Traditionally, scorecards and dashboards are essentially predefined formats, in which reports are generated regularly, and distributed to everyone. These reports are generally created using the following reporting infrastructures:

a.   Transaction Systems like ERP, CRM, SCM, MES, etc.

b.   Excel reports created by combining various outputs

c.   Reporting Systems Crystal Reports, Jasper, etc.

Interactive Analytics

Once the GAPS are identified, more important is the ability to find root causes for the GAPs, allowing managers to take appropriate actions. This analysis is typically ad hoc, to find the root cause and take decisions / actions to remove the GAPS. There are two approaches available:

1. Ad hoc reports are generated—brute-force query method—where programmers write new reports to answer new questions. Every corollary question may lead to new reports and this could be a very involved process with no end. Traditionally, such reports are generated on the transaction systems, or with data extracted into Excel.

2. Interactive Analytic Tools is the other approach – OLAP tools and QlikView belong to this category. Typically, these provide interactive ability to drill through, drill across and see the data in different ways, without any programming required for the same. While OLAP tools provide limited interactivity, QlikView is very powerful for this purpose, providing the necessary flexibility and yet not require any programming. Comparison of OLAP and other technologies along with QlikView is provided in Chapter 3.

Enterprise Information Outputs

The information needs can also be looked at from a functional standpoint. Irrespective of the industry and the size of companies, use of information falls generally into the following categories:

Compliance Reporting

The most important and basic need for reporting comes from statutory reporting requirements. Whether any other advanced reporting / analytics are performed in the company or not, this Compliance Analysis is a must and required for the company to exist legally.

Statutory reporting is primarily for submitting information about the company performance to the government regulatory agencies – Income Tax, Sales Tax, Environment Emission Compliance, etc. Generally, these reports have *pixel perfect* or *character perfect* formatting requirements.

The contents and more often the formats of these outputs are prescribed by the agencies / recipients of the information. Additional compliance reporting requirements are prescribed from time to time, by the compliance bodies, and the need is to quickly respond to such requirements, without spending too much time to create these reports.

For compliance reporting, timely generation of information and the formatting of the data in the predefined format are the most important requirements. Compliance reports also include voluntary disclosures that are submitted to industry associations, associate companies and customers to meet collective governance guidelines.

Performance Analysis

Setting goals and measuring achievements against the goals set is an essential need for any organization. Goals are set with a reference point: What do we want to be. These are the targets, budgets and quotas against which performance of individuals and groups are measured.

These reference points, goals, are chosen from among the following:

- Past Performance: How we did in past—Last Year, Last Month, etc.
- Industry Performance: How others in the industry are doing, how best can we be in comparison to them.
- Own Aspirations: Setting new standards, esp. for completely new products and services or while creating operations of different scale, purely based on perceived market opportunity.

Setting goals is a very important part—typical goals can be:

- Sales (Absolute Sales Target)
- Growth over last year (Growth Percentage Target)
- Market Share (Share Percentage Target)
- Time Taken for a Process (TAT Target)
- Quality of a Product or Service (Customer Satisfaction Index Target)
- Expenses (Absolute Expense Budget)
- Expenses vs. Gross Margin (Ratio Target)

Constantly measuring achievements against goals, understanding the GAP of goal vs. achievement, finding the root causes, making adjustments—course corrections—is the key to management.

Business Analysis

Irrespective of the targets and budgets, there is a need to understand the patterns of business. What is selling more, selling less. Decisions about which product / services should be expanded or discontinued is all taken based on such information.

Key measures that are used for this kind of Analysis are:
- Distribution like Sales: Geography wise, Product wise, etc.
- Contribution like Profits/Expenses: Geography wise, Product wise
- Trend like Sales: Yearly, Monthly, Weekly, etc.
- Rate of Change like Sales, Quality: What is growing positively and negatively?
- Scenario or Impact Analysis like Marketing vs. Sales, Interest Rate vs. Loans: What is the impact of one over the other?

Such analyses are normally required for planning, product management, sales management, distribution management, capacity planning, logistics, research & development, etc. This is also referred to as Discovery Analytics. Typically these are ad hoc in nature, and require interactive analysis capabilities. Traditional reporting on transaction systems and Excel sheets can be very time consuming and restrictive for this kind of analysis.

OLAP solutions have traditionally aimed at addressing this need. QlikView is a better solution for the same due to the flexibility, presentation and scalability benefits. Comparison of OLAP and other technologies along with QlikView is provided in Chapter 3.

Market Analysis

Information about competition, demographics, when compared with internal transaction data, is referred as Market Analysis. The primary intent is to understand how the company performs vis-à-vis the other market players.

The following measures become very relevant in this type of analysis:
- Market Share
- Relative Market Penetration
- Relative Pricing
- Segmentation of Customers

Data about market and competition is collected from various industry associations, government statutory bodies, data collection companies and analysts like Gartner and IDC. Data is also collected from vendors and customers.

All the data collected are typically in different formats. The biggest challenge is to combine all the data into a homogenous form and compare them with the internal transaction data, to create necessary analysis. The solution required has to provide easy ways of combining data from different sources, powerful and flexible ETL and a good visualization / presentation layer.

Various ETL solutions have found this to be a tough problem to solve, due to the relative inflexibility. QlikView's flexible and extensible ETL helps analyze and visualize the data. The most important feature of QlikView useful for this analysis is the simple and easy but powerful slice and dice capability (more in subsequent chapters).

Enterprise Information Analysis Trends

As the various data analysis technologies have become better, and more management techniques have been formulated, the enterprise analysis has taken various shapes and sizes:

- Reporting
- Dashboards
- Scorecards
- Interactive Reports
- Forecasting
- Statistical Analysis
- Data mining
- Predictive Modelling
- Optimization
- Testing and
- Curve Fitting

All the above & more have combined to provide a systematic spectrum of solutions to address various needs. All these solutions are divided into two categories: a) Reporting: visibility information and, b) Analytics: business analytics. Together they form the *Decision Support Systems*.

From a technical standpoint, Chapter 3 discusses various technologies available for reporting, and explores the appropriateness / challenges with each of those options, and highlights how QlikView can address some of the segments.

From a business standpoint, these two serve different segments of requirement. The following diagram provides an overview of the needs of any organization. While there is no tool that completely addresses all requirements entirely, every solution focuses and specializes in some.

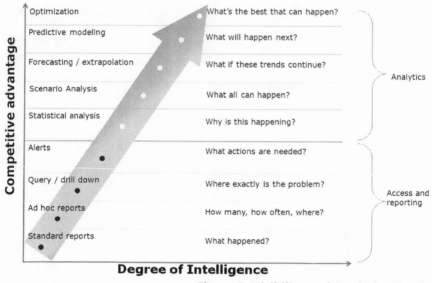

Figure 2: Visibility and Analytics Needs

Visibility Needs – Regular Information Dissemination

The lower four items in the diagram are very clearly needed for day-to-day management; transactional / operational and tactical. Management is like driving a car and it is important to have the windscreen and rear-view mirrors clear. The visibility solutions provide this clarity for business, with enough detail to take informed decisions. Most solutions focus on rear-view showing the past. It is important to design good report formats to get the view ahead and not just the rear-view.

Standard Reports address the transactional / operational information needs. The key capabilities include pre-formatted reports, with compliance and performance reports forming the bulk of this segment. These are generally, as observed earlier, done from the transactional systems or from dedicated report servers. Focus is on generating information in the same format and sending in time to everyone who needs it. Automation of this segment is a key aspect of any information management strategy, since this is a large chunk of time spent by the IT team, if it is to be done manually.

Ad hoc reports are traditionally generated using Report creation tools, like Crystal Reports and Jasper. The approach is to create queries to be run on the backend, with the ability to present data in the front-end using tabular features. These are generally created and run by the IT department members, and then published to the users who require it.

Query Drill down needs have been addressed, over the last decade, by OLAP solutions like Business Objects, Cognos and Hyperion. The market is showing significant move towards new solutions like QlikView, Tableau, and other similar products.

Alerts are small information pieces/messages generated and sent when a particular condition is met. These messages are results of queries or calculations, which are triggered by specified conditions. These result messages are sent across to designated members, either through email, text messages (SMS) or as a pop-up that appears on the screen when the conditions are met.

These tools are like the various meters on the dashboard of a car, showing where one is at present, and showing where we are with respect to the destination / goal. QlikView is a great fit for this, by default, and provides much better capabilities than most of the competitive products—particularly the Ad hoc, Query drill down and across and Alerts.

Analytic Needs – Strategic Insights

"By analytics we mean the extensive use of data, statistical and quantitative analysis, explanatory and predictive models, and fact-based management to drive decisions and actions", declare Thomas

Davenport and Jeanne Harris in Competing on Analytics (Harvard Business School Press, 2007) [2]

While visibility tools show where we are with reference to the destination, there are other needs for the management, which are at the strategic decision making level. Questions which span across various time periods, with interest to look at *root causes and patterns* that exist require more than just presenting data as of NOW. They need trending and predictive capabilities, deciphering patterns beyond what meets the eye and capabilities to segment the data.

The upper five items in the diagram get addressed by strategic decision making tools. There are two types of tools that help analytic needs: a) Visual Analytic Tools and b) Automated Algorithmic Analytical Tools.

Visual Analytic Tools: These are tools that provide interactive analytic capability: with capabilities for flexible slicing and dicing and abilities to visualize the relationship across various data elements. Multi-dimensional visualization tools like QlikView, MineSet, R, SPSS, Dundas fall in this category. They provide more than just a collection of visualization components—an ability to flexibly slice and dice & dynamically visualize the relationships. This extends the cognitive abilities of human brain allowing it to see the otherwise invisible relationships, much easily. This is called *Visual Data Mining*.

Statistical Analytic Tools: The various statistical analysis including Curve Fitting, Regression, Distributions, Statistical Testing using T-test, F-test etc., are used in standard statistical Modelling techniques. Most reporting solutions do not provide all these features. QlikView includes these capabilities out of the box, making it useful for such applications, including statistical quality control reports, box plots and SQC charts.

Automated Analytic Tools: In this category, many machine learning algorithms are implemented, which allow the patterns in data to be automatically detected and presented. Cross-section of such algorithms is available in tools like SAS Intelligent Miner, SPSS, MineSet, IBM Intelligent Miner, Project R, etc. These are essentially learning algorithms broadly classified as: a) Supervised Learning, b) Unsupervised Learning and c) Reinforcement Learning. Please refer to the Wikipedia page on "List of machine learning algorithms" to read more about various techniques under each of these.

To quote the Wikipedia: *Machine learning, a branch of artificial intelligence, is a scientific discipline concerned with the design and development of algorithms that allow computers to evolve behaviors based on empirical data, such as from sensor data or databases. Machine learning is concerned with the development of algorithms allowing the machine to learn via inductive inference based on observing data that represents incomplete information about statistical phenomenon and generalize it to rules and make predictions on missing attributes or future data.*

An important task of machine learning is classification, which is also referred to as pattern recognition, in which machines "learn" to automatically recognize complex patterns, to distinguish between exemplars based on their different patterns, and to make intelligent predictions on their class.

These automated machine learning algorithms are not available out of the box in QlikView. However, the Extensibility API allows the external libraries like R to be integrated to provide the solution. More on this is discussed in Chapter 14: *Deploying QlikView*.

The various analytic requirements in this segment can be broadly classified as Scenario Analysis, Statistical Analysis, Predictive Modelling, Forecasting, Extrapolation and Optimization. These are all extensions that can be added on top of QlikView, using different external solutions like R, SPSS, SAS or other libraries available from various commercial and research projects.

Actionable Information

With the myriad complexities that have arisen in enterprises, consumption of information has gone through a major change over the last decade. Now everyone needs Actionable Information.

Exception Reporting, Evidence Based Management, Deviation Analysis, Target vs. Actuals, Sales Trends, Market Basket Analysis, & more are various attempts to produce actionable information. Some produce, some don't. Some produce better quality information and some just produce trash. *The difference lies in the ability to differentiate what information is actionable and what is not.*

Today's enterprise requires instant, actionable information in times of crisis to accelerate decision making, inform and update personnel and customers, as well as minimize impact of incidents. Earlier businesses focused on manual notification, call trees or automated mass notification services, popular for providing the same message to a large population of recipients. They must consider requirements of today's real-time, mobile enterprise. In this new breed of real-time enterprise employees, customers and other stakeholders need role-specific information that accelerates their ability to act. This requirement reveals a new challenge as enterprises attempt to provide thousands of employees or stakeholders with instant, personalized information.

On the flip-side, an event—whether newsworthy or not—must be noted and acted upon / resolved as quickly as possible, especially if it creates business impact. It is important to understand that while sending the same voice or text message to everyone, may raise awareness but, it does not accelerate an organization's ability to take actions and minimize the impact of the issue.

Hence actionable information delivery needs to move beyond mass notification to deliver instant role-specific information in the form the receiver needs it. This ability to provide personalized information increases the chances of each person making appropriate, real-time decisions. Leading global businesses embrace the use of instant, actionable information, frictionless processes and optimized operations as strategic advantages.

Increased need for Actionable Information

Gartner has characterized these organizations as "real-time enterprises" which (a) utilize accurate, role-specific information to accelerate business processes; (b) identify and eliminate organizational delays; and (c) use speed as a competitive advantage.

In the past, traditional organizations were able to operate without significant interruption during outages or crises. Business processes were *only* enabled by IT; communications were informal and the pace of business was slower. In today's enterprise the availability of instant, actionable information is required and must be supplied by IT or other functions to ensure service, application and business availability.

The enterprises today depend on instant and personalized actionable information, application availability and organizational agility to outpace the competition, avoid outages and minimize the impact of catastrophic events. This new breed of enterprise is event-driven and architected around lean processes.

Identifying Actionable Information

An interesting challenge here is "How to identify actionable information for each member?" This is still an art than a science. Though there are industry specific vertical solutions that are made available for some of the verticals, supplied by companies like IBM, majority of the customers have challenge in finding actionable information for various members of the decision making hierarchy.

The key to success of any Business Intelligence / Business Discovery implementation in any company is identifying the right actionable information and provide them to relevant decision makers of the organization. These are generally the metrics that represent the most problematic or important leverage of the company, by changing/managing which, far reaching improvements can be created in the company's performance.

One interesting technique to find these actionable metrics—Key Performance Metrics (KPIs)—is the use of *Strategic Maps*, to identify the key goals, and their key impacting actions. Then define measures that quantify and/or qualify these key leverage actions that move the company towards the strategic goals.

Another important aspect is that this set of Key Actionable Metrics (KPIs) keep changing depending on the changes in the business and its environment as depicted in the diagram. These KPIs are context sensitive. Once the current key challenges at any point of time are monitored, acted upon and improved, the relevant Metrics become relatively unimportant. The other problems which were relatively less impactful, become more important, and the KPIs related to other problems then need attention and improvement as an organization.

As part of implementation of the BI Solutions, like QlikView, the need is to constantly switch from one set of context sensitive KPIs of relevance as the Actionable Information – to another. The technology chosen should help such adaptation, and support for business dynamism. QlikView is a great technology to support this swiftly and efficiently.

Dashboards, Analytics, Reports and Scorecards (DARS) Model – A Blended Approach to Enterprise Information Dissemination

- Guiding Analytics
  - *KRA/KPI* - Dashboards
  - Balanced Scorecards
  - Analytics – Slicing & Dicing *the Gaps*
  - Reporting – Detailed *Root cause* Understanding

- Actionable Dashboards
  - Performance Maximization
  - Operations Optimization
  - Productivity Improvement
  - Compliance Monitoring
  - Legal / Attorney Monitoring

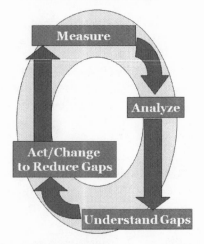

What to do is important than just Analytics!

Figure 3: Management Information Cycle

Organizations have to go through a constant syndication of data, from various sources of data (the lower-most layer) and the four categories of reporting discussed above, are created. These reports need to be now presented using modern information presentation layers, using Actionable Information display techniques / tools like Dashboards, Scorecards, and Strategy Maps.

Such systems created should help Monitor changes with the associated ability to slice and dice, and help review all processes. With such tools root causes for GAPS are identified, and new processes / process adjustments are created. These in turn create the necessary changes in the base layer of processes.

This perpetual cycle of observing GAPS, finding root causes and then creating changes in the basic process layers of the company is the key to making BI systems work for the enterprises. These GAPS or exceptions or actionable items, create the synchronization layer, allowing the entire organization to work closely in unison as a harmonious whole. This is what Alvin Toeffler calls as "Synchronized Enterprises".

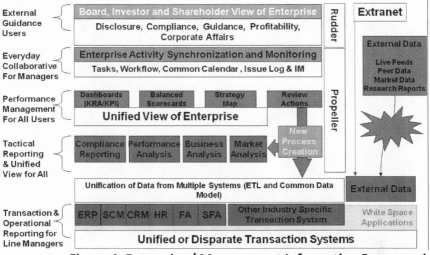

Figure 4: Enterprise / Management Information Framework

Analytics Quotient

Synchronized enterprises have the ability to get data in time, and act on time. This is the ability to take advantage of information. Analytics Quotient is an interesting measure of readiness of every organization to take advantage of Analytics, and create impact in their business by using them to take appropriate decisions. IBM has created a maturity model for this purpose, which is a great way to measure where the company is. A later chapter looks at how this can be applied, along with other best practices that have worked for QlikView implementations.

The IBM micro-site called *Analytics Quotient (AQ)* is a great place to immerse on this topic, more for every customer who is interested in creating a BI strategy for the company—*What's your AQ (Analytics Quotient), IBM* [8].

Conclusions for the Chapter

Understanding the fast paced information needs of organizations and supporting the management with actionable information is the need. Syndication of data to presenting them in various personalized forms will increase the competitiveness of the organizations.

QlikView is a great product which provides all the necessary components to support this entire cycle to a large extent, with least investments both first time, and subsequent maintenance making the

Total Cost of Ownership (TCO) to stay within reasonable limits. QlikView can easily help increase the Analysis Quotient and help improve the competitiveness of the enterprises.

The remainder of the book discusses the appropriateness of QlikView to meet most of these requirements, and how it can work closely with other solutions available already in the Enterprises, to ensure all information needs of the Enterprise are completely met, in the most cost-efficient and time-efficient manner.

References

1. Journal of Enterprise Information Systems, Taylor & Francis, [http://www.tandf.co.uk/journals/journal.asp?issn=1751-7575&linktype=145]

2. Thomas Davenport and Jeanne Harris, Competing on Analytics (Harvard Business School Press, 2007)

3. Decision Support System Trends, DataCleaners, SlideShare.Net, [http://www.slideshare.net/datacleaners11/decision-support-systems-decision-support-trends]

4. Curation in the Enterprise – Actionable Information, ConfusedOfCalcutta.com, [http://confusedofcalcutta.com/2011/08/22/curation-in-the-enterprise-actionable-information/]

5. BI – A Practical Perspective, Team Computers & MAIA Intelligence, Slideshare.Net, [http://www.slideshare.net/businessintelligence/bi-a-practical-perspective-by-team-computers]

6. Business Intelligence – An Infoduction, Team Business Solutions LLC, Slideshare.Net, [http://www.slideshare.net/TBSL/tbsl-business-intelligence-7394842]

7. Outperforming with a higher AQ (Analytics Quotient), IBM, IT ToolBox, [http://businessintelligence.ittoolbox.com/research/outperforming-with-a-higher-aq-24853]

8. What's your AQ (Analytics Quotient), IBM, IBM.COM, [http://www-01.ibm.com/software/analytics/aq/] **(Must Read)

Chapter 2
What is QlikView?

Innovation is No Accident – Active Search Leads To Discoveries

Introduction to the Chapter

As we saw earlier, *Business Intelligence* was first used as early as September, 1996, in a Gartner Group report. Since then various technologies—ETL, Warehouse, OLAP, Reporting, etc.—have all been included into this broad category called BI. BI also includes Advanced Analytics—statistical analysis, machine learning and data mining tools—and OLAP—flexible / quick query tools.

With the advent of tools like QlikView and other in-memory solutions, a new way of slicing and dicing was created, to make the process easier and flexible. For want of better words, QlikView has been traditionally named as a BI tool, though it was distinctly different from other solutions available. QlikTech called it as Business Discovery and in 2011, Gartner came up with a new classification: "Data Discovery" tools.

This chapter discusses the positioning of QlikView. Starting with a discussion on expectations from BI, the need for a better way to use data is discussed. Then the concept of Business Discovery/Data Discovery introduced and shows how QlikView fits the bill. The chapter goes on to share the popularity QlikView has been gaining, discusses the key reasons why QlikView is gaining this popularity.

The chapter then provides pointers to quickly understand and experience QlikView. The discussion then moves to define the use-cases where QlikView is the right fit and introduces a framework to compare various BI tools available for the enterprises.

Lastly, the limitations of QlikView are discussed with a discussion on the various solutions that can help overcome those limitations. The chapter sets the perspective of what, why and how of QlikView for enterprises.

The rest of the book builds on this positioning. Understanding the contents of this chapter will be a basic foundation in understanding QlikView in Enterprises.

Is QlikView a Business Intelligence Tool?

QlikView has been traditionally classified as a Business Intelligence tool. Is QlikView a BI tool? Before answering that, the meaning of Business Intelligence and what it represents needs to be understood. We looked at some of the basic definitions in the last chapter. Some of the more detailed discussions show different expectations from BI. Let us take a look at a few of these expectations:

The current definition of Business Intelligence in Wikipedia [1]:

> Business Intelligence technologies provide historical, current and predictive views of business operations. Common functions of business intelligence technologies are reporting, online analytical processing, analytics, data and process mining, complex event processing, text mining, predictive analytics, business performance management, and benchmarking.

> It aims to support better business decision-making. Thus a BI system can be called a decision support system (DSS). (Though) The term business intelligence is sometimes used as a synonym for competitive intelligence, because it supports decision making. BI uses technologies, processes, and applications to analyze mostly internal, structured data and business processes while competitive intelligence gathers, analyzes and disseminates information with a topical focus on company competitors. Business intelligence understood broadly can include the subset of competitive intelligence.

The definition literally covers everything that was discussed as Enterprise Information Requirements. Another generic definition of Business Intelligence is found in Techtarget [2]:

> Business intelligence applications can be:

- Mission-critical and integral to an enterprise's operations or occasional to meet a special requirement
- Enterprise-wide or local to one division, department, or project
- Centrally initiated or driven by user demand

The above descriptions make BI sound more like a branch of study, covering all aspects of information needs, rather than being a technology or a process or a methodology in itself.

Classifying a product as a BI product actually seems to mean not much, with a wide spectrum of uses and meanings attached to it. This is in some ways is like saying "Bugatti Veyron" is a transportation product. To nail this down it is important to understand the various contexts which are represented by BI.

Redefining Business Intelligence Needs

This feeling is reflected by many in the industry, especially by those who work with the new generation products which have entered into this space. There is a perception of insufficiency of what is represented by classical BI.

In February 2006, Rock Gnatovich, the then CEO of Spotfire observed about this insufficiency [3]:

Neil Raden has said that, "the proper term for interacting with information at the speed of business, analyzing and discovering and following through with the appropriate action, is 'analytics'."

CIOs often assume that business analytics (BA) comes along with BI. The traditional BI market has been associated with providing executive dashboards and reporting to monitor the assumptions and key performance metrics that are part of long term planning cycles. Everybody wants a dashboard.

To the extent that all of us are CEO's of our own business discipline, we want a simple measurement display of how we are doing and an alert mechanism of when something goes wrong. Additionally, dashboards address the growing urgency around Sarbanes Oxley. Monitoring planning assumptions and key performance metrics has now become mission critical from a regulatory and compliance standpoint.

But BI reporting ends with the dashboard, which is sufficient only for some business planning, and BA picks up the rest for the Go-To Guys. Simply, this group must interact with data in a much different way from what traditional BI allows.

As we can see, he had attempted to describe the insufficiency of what BI delivers. For want of any other appropriate term, he used *Business Analytics* as an alternative phrase to represent what is actually required for business managers. It is very interesting to see his conclusion that (conventional) BI is not what is required for what he calls as "Go-To-Guys" or the decision makers / key influencers (full article in references section) :

BI is architected to automate the distribution of standardized reports that monitor pre-determined key performance metrics and planning assumptions. BI's answer to analytics has been to deliver the report to the business user and the business user typically takes the data in the report and dumps it into Microsoft Excel in order to do his own analysis.

This is similar to the scenario that we see in almost all companies today, with so many Excel reports. He goes on to say:

As a result, there are $8B (yes, billion) of internally developed analytic applications with Excel as their front end. BI players treat output to Excel as a feature. But I actually think it's a tremendous failing. **It is proof that you don't get BA when you buy BI**.

The (conventional) BI architecture cannot support the operating needs of the business users to ask & answer their own questions in response to new occurrences & events in the marketplace.

Secondly, Excel is not an answer either. As soon as the data is dumped into Excel, the user is out of the BI system with no way back in. Any insight that the business user gains while interpreting

Excel spreadsheets tends to stay with him—all opportunity for organizational learning or process improvement is lost.

Requirements for analytics are different than requirements for BI & benefits are different too.

This is an excellent summary of the true situation in all the enterprises today, with multiple technologies inducted as BI, not meeting the expectations of the business users. It is interesting to note what Rock professes as the need for the "Go-To-Guys":

Where BI Stops and BA Begins: But BI reporting ends with the dashboard, which is sufficient only for some business planning, and BA picks up the rest for the Go-To Guys. Simply, this group must *interact with data in a much different way* from what traditional BI allows.

The question is what is that different way and what exactly should this provide the users? What characteristics should be borne by this class of new tools that are supposed to help the "Go-To-Guys" or the "Decision Makers & Decision Influencers"? What should they be named? [4]

Business Discovery – The New Name of "Analytics"

In chapter 1, the information needs of businesses were discussed. All these needs require certainly what is already available—the so-called "conventional BI"—with its mass production of reports, and the "Analytics"—with the ability to allow statistical / artificial intelligence based insights. However, the key difference now in the modified situation is the need for speed.

Think about how people get what they need quickly in consumer applications like Google, Facebook, and SalesForce. Now, think business intelligence. Different worlds, right? Companies like QlikTech attempt to help both business users and IT to discover what is possible next in BI. To create tools to support the way people think today—get fast, correct answers to critical business questions.

Fortunately, now there is technology that helps find how the concepts of social networking and business intelligence can be combined for anytime information access, zero-wait analysis and insight for everyone. *Business Discovery* is this new combined force of self service with interactive analytics available at very high speed.

Understanding Business Discovery

An interesting article in QlikPower.com's Blog talks about the genesis of business discovery and its impact on business and IT, and goes on to highlight the value business discovery can produce [5]:

> The emergence of Business Discovery is a response to users' mounting frustrations and unmet needs, according to a recent report by CITO Research. It's a new kind of productivity software putting users in control of exploring and exploiting their own data, allowing IT to focus on core processes rather than attending to their every need.

> Business Discovery bridges the gap between reporting-focused BI solutions and standalone applications like Excel. It enables users at every level of the organization to find tailored insights addressing their individual needs and deadlines. In essence, Business Discovery transforms everyone into a highly informed business analyst.

> In many ways, Business Discovery aims to fulfil the original promise of BI, which proved to be impossible due to the limits of architecture, forcing IT to shoulder the burden. But Business Discovery improves upon reporting-focused BI because there is no predefined path to follow and no questions to formulate ahead of time. Users ask what they need to, and they explore—aggregating up, down, and sideways—rather than simply drilling down.

> Using lightweight tools that marry connectors to the underlying databases with fluid interfaces reminiscent of apps, Business Discovery systems drive down the cost and complexity of aggregating disparate data sources, which can then be combined and correlated in different ways to discover waste or opportunities.

> For example, a question as simple and as random as whether there's a correlation between the size of a product shipment and the number of units placed on backorder may require data from three separate databases. IT knows all too well that combining those three would take six months and cost upwards of $250,000.

So the answer to most questions is usually, "Forget it; it's not worth it."

But what if it cost $5,000 and a day's worth of work? Users would have an answer the next day, with enough money in the budget left over to commission another dozen or more projects just like it. If only one results in significant savings, the scattershot approach will have been worth it. By driving down the opportunity costs for IT and users alike to ask questions and make better-informed decisions, users are in a better position to capture market share, drive revenue growth, and cut costs because they no longer have to wait for the data they need.

The evolution from a reporting-focused BI paradigm to Business Discovery has profound implications for IT, replacing its traditional delivery role with a support and enablement one. Rather than building applications (read as: reports) day-in-day out, they dispense tools & training to users while focusing on larger issues such as data governance, security & underlying enterprise systems.

Gartner calls this revolutionary approach as *Data Discovery* [6] and defines it as a separate category of BI in their 2011 Magic Quadrant which was released in February 2011: "These data discovery alternatives to traditional BI platforms offer highly interactive and graphical user interfaces built on in-memory architectures to address business users' unmet ease-of-use and rapid deployment needs". QlikView is the poster child of data discovery solutions.

The QlikTech whitepaper on this, talks about Business Discovery in a very concise manner [7]:

Business Discovery is user-driven business intelligence that helps people make decisions based on multiple sources of insight: data, people, and the environment. Users can create and share knowledge and analysis in groups and across organizations. Business Discovery platforms help people ask and answer their own questions and follow their own path to insight. Business Discovery platforms deliver insight everywhere, an app model, mobility, re-mix ability and reassembly, and a social and collaborative experience.

So now to define what is QlikView – *It is a Business Discovery Platform that delivers true self-service BI that empowers business users by driving innovative decision-making.*

Business Discovery or as is called by Gartner as Data Discovery, is a new approach to provide the much needed support to the so-called "Go-To-Guys" or what Gartner calls "business users". These are actual decision makers, action guys who need actionable information whenever they need to take a decision.

It is important to understand the various decision making needs and the solutions that can help each need: when (traditional BI) reporting adds value, what are the pockets in which the statistical and AI based automated analytics can help, and when is this new Business Discovery essential for creating value.

QlikView Gets more Popular – Google Trends & Gartner Magic Quadrant

Business Discovery needs has been gaining prominence and is seen as a great productivity boost for decision making. The growth of QlikView around the world is an important indicator of this trend. The most important evidence of popularity of QlikView is from Google Trends. The trend of search on Business Intelligence products from 2004 is provided here as a snapshot (Source: http://google.com/trends):

As one can see, QlikView has been gaining more popularity, and the progress it has had is interesting. Along with this, see the trend of how QlikView has featured in the Gartner Magic Quadrant over the past 4 years. QlikTech has moved from the *Visionaries* quadrant to the *Leaders* quadrant steadily, and gaining market share in the enterprises. In 2011, Gartner has recognized this class of Analytical tools and called them "Data Discovery Tools". QlikView is the leader in those tools. The Gartner report in its opening statement goes to say [7]:

> In 2010, business users had greater influence over BI buying, often choosing data discovery vendors as an alternative to traditional BI tools. But megavendors continued to hold the majority of BI market share, despite ongoing customer dissatisfaction, by selling the stack into their installed base.

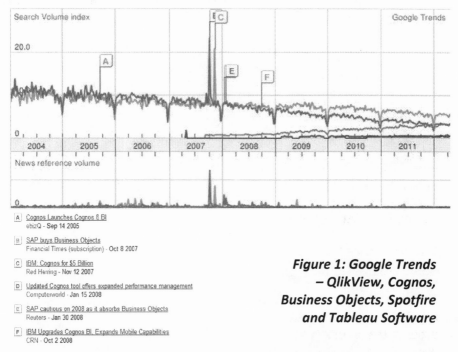

qlikview 1.00 **spotfire** 0.20 cognos   7.80 (business objects)   7.40
(tableau software) 0

A Cognos Launches Cognos 8 BI
   ebizQ - Sep 14 2005

B SAP buys Business Objects
   Financial Times (subscription) - Oct 8 2007

C IBM: Cognos for $5 Billion
   Red Herring - Nov 12 2007

D Updated Cognos tool offers expanded performance management
   Computerworld - Jan 15 2008

E SAP cautious on 2008 as it absorbs Business Objects
   Reuters - Jan 30 2008

F IBM Upgrades Cognos BI, Expands Mobile Capabilities
   CRN - Oct 2 2008

Figure 1: Google Trends
– QlikView, Cognos,
Business Objects, Spotfire
and Tableau Software

And though there are negatives highlighted about the product strategy, support and performance challenges, it is interesting to note their observation about QlikView:

> QlikTech is the poster child for a new end-user-driven approach to BI. Evidence for this can be found in the buzz around it (with a brand many times more prominent than its current market share), its continued growth, and the success of its July 2010 IPO on NASDAQ — the first BI flotation for many years.

Some of the challenges highlighted by the report are essentially impacts due to two important factors: a) Limitations induced by the commercial policy of the company and not so much the limitation of the product, b) Limitations created by not following best practices when implementing QlikView—mostly the same problems that have affected other BI products as well at various times. Later in this chapter there is a section discussing the challenges that Gartner has cautioned about in 2011. In the subsequent chapters some of the issues and possible ways of overcoming these challenges are discussed.

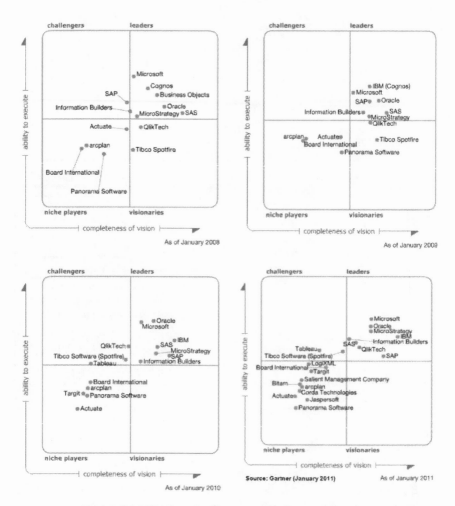

Figure 2: QlikView in Gartner Magic Quadrant over 4 years

The popularity of QlikView has created a lot of effects—more and more partners signing up, more customers buying the software. The pressure is on creating enough implementation skills in the market and making them all deliver with the same skill level. Best practices have been evolved by QlikTech and shared with partners and only a few implementation partners have created a methodology to deliver, with repeatable training and processes. This is changing and some partners like TEAM have led the process of such standardization, and surely the large players stepping into the arena would accelerate the changes.

What is special with QlikView?

Last few years have seen an unprecedented acceptance of QlikView across the world. It is seen as the business users' natural choice. Like how Gartner mentions it, QlikView "address (es) business users' unmet ease-of-use and rapid deployment needs". This rapid adoption of this product has shown in the revenues of QlikTech and also in the Gartner Magic Quadrant.

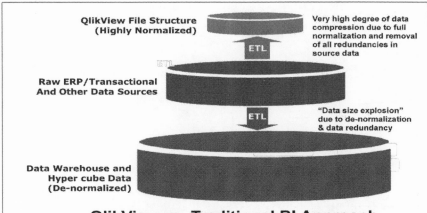

Figure 3: QlikView Vs. Traditional BI Approach

The key special elements of QlikView are:

a) **Data Implosion**: A method of storing data, that results in reduction in data sizes instead of the bloating that is witnessed in other traditional BI technologies (de-normalizing and OLAP cubes). This helps achieve smaller foot prints which could be kept in-memory, making the memory requirement lesser by magnitudes.

b) **Integrated In-Memory Data Model**: Since the data is now reduced in size, all data can be held in memory along with the relationships between various data elements—in the form of a star schema or snow-flake schema—without having to deal with the data explosion that normally happens.

c) **Associative Query Language (AQL)**: QlikView holds all data in memory with every association between data points defined. Think of QlikView as on-demand data access: all joins and calculations are made in real time, as the user clicks.

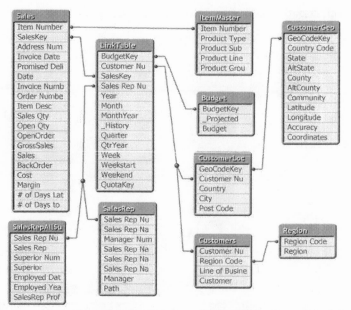

Figure 4: In-Memory Snow-Flake Data Model

The engine created for this is the core marvel created by the creators of QlikView—to hold all data in raw-form in memory, with an ability to dynamically make selections on the fly (apply where clauses), summarize (apply any aggregation function) on any field for the subset of values connected to the selections. To quote Dan English [8]:

> Way back in 1993, the founders of QlikTech had a vision. They believed that anyone making complex business decisions should have full access to their decision support data, and not as isolated and discrete queries without context between one query and the next. Instead, decision makers should be able to interact with their data as an organic whole with all of the associations that make up the living web of data intact. In fact, every data point should have a valid association with every other data point at all times throughout the entire analysis process. Only by having this holistic and multifaceted view of the data and by retaining those associations would decision makers be armed with the information needed to make the most informed business decision possible.

> The desire to associate data does not originate with QlikView. The concept of association has long been seen as the holy grail of business analytics. The real genius of QlikTech's founders can be

seen first in the extent of association, stating that "every data point anywhere in the entire dataset to be analyzed, regardless of how many data fields there are or how complex the underlying schema may be, should always be associated with all other data points at all times." Second, starting with that, they invented a revolutionary new technical architecture to make this vision a reality.

Lot of companies, today have created in-memory models, but are generally seen to be using either of the following approaches:

a. Making raw data in some optimized format stay in Memory using caching or RAM-Disk approach

b. Making the aggregations stay in memory (CUBES)

However, though this has created some form of in-memory implementation, they continue to use the SQL approach to operate on this data. This has allowed taking advantage of quicker processing speeds and more memory by avoiding disk read/writes. Improvements have not been made in the capability of analysis, the experience of the user or for creating new associations in mind. The key difference of QlikView is the ASSOCIATED or CONNECTED Analysis, or for want of any other word, QUERIES.

This naturally creates NAVIGABLE REPORTS / ANALYSIS, where the user moves from one question/answer to another without losing the context of the previous questions/answers in a session of analysis. This is the most unique offering of QlikView. No product has yet come close enough to this unique offering of QlikView.

As an analogy, think of the entire multi-dimensional data space as a multi-dimensional swimming pool; the analyst as a swimmer trying to get to different points to experience/understand the metrics of that spot. All other products allow the swimmer to start from home point, swim to every point of interest in a particular predefined sequence (drill downs). To go to any other point belonging to any other hierarchy, the swimmer needs to come back to the home point and then start the sequence separately, remembering what was chosen in previous traversals. Erica's notes are a good reference [9].

QlikView allows the swimmer to jump into any point, and go to any other point, without having to come back home. The track of the swimmer is retained as the context—without having to take notes and remember—in the form of current selections. The implementation of this lofty idea of allowing unlimited but easy associations is the most important marvel of QlikView.

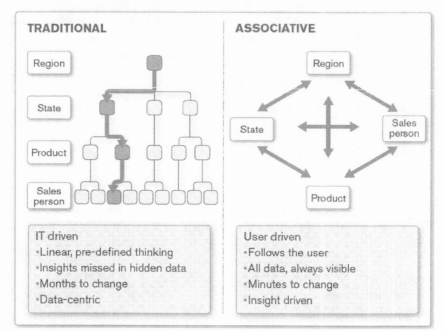

Figure 5: Associative Experience

What is QlikView now?

With these unique capabilities, the core engine was created as back as 1993. Since then more and more features have been added to support, reinforce and take advantage of them. With Version 10 and 11, the new capabilities include Extensible APIs to take advantage of external products to interact with the in-memory associative model of QlikView, social capabilities to blog-on-selection-context, comparative analysis (selection sets and selection states), mobile support for various tablets and smartphones, rapid analytic platform – making every user a "start-user" and removing the notion of "end-users", improved extensibility using Workbench with more granular control of object properties, metadata enhancements and finally, enterprise enhancements for reloading, clustering and security.

With all the characteristics of QlikView a formal definition of what is QlikView, will probably look like this:

QlikView is a Business or Data Discovery Platform that allows:

- ✓ *interactive analysis with navigable reports*
- ✓ *with multi-dimensional analysis on the fly*
- ✓ *on post-facto data from multiple data sources*
- ✓ *squeezed into an efficient compact-storage-imploded-form*
- ✓ *of interconnected fixed-schema-hashes in-memory*
- ✓ *made available through a powerful dynamic selection & rendering engine*
- ✓ *allowing users to interactively query with clicks, slice & dice in new non-hierarchical paths*
- ✓ *to create & follow the new cognitive synaptic connections that are formed dynamically while visualizing appropriate actionable KPIs*
- ✓ *both individually and collaboratively (socially),*
- ✓ *without having to use the painful SQLs or Excel Sheets*
- ✓ *but through the familiar browser interfaces*

While such a definition probably meets an academic need of having a definition, the actual need is to really understand and appreciate the various capabilities that QlikView has.

While this chapter is focused on demystifying QlikView, a subsequent chapter—Enterprise Framework for Combining BI Technologies—delves deep into defining a framework to understand when to use which technology for meeting the information needs of the decision makers.

First Steps to Understand QlikView

The most important steps to understand QlikView is to experience it first-hand. Experiencing QlikView is like experiencing the speed of a car. Any number of words cannot make it equal to the experience.

This can be done by two easy steps: it is strongly recommended to take some time out and experience these two steps immediately before reading further, if you have not already experienced QlikView. The first step takes about 15 minutes on the internet. The second step is probably about 30 minutes on your laptop.

First Exploration: Please visit http://demo.qlikview.com. You should get the main page that looks like the figure below. Open the tab: *How*

QlikView Works and there is a *Movie Database* Application. You can watch the video of the application. After viewing the movie, search for the *Movies Database* in the Search Demos box and open the application. The application, when opened should look like Figure 7.

First explore "How QlikView Works" tab. Then explore this application by walking through the various tabs and selecting different data by clicking on them. Remember to use the CLEAR 🔘 button to explore different permutations of data selection. This application helps intuitively understand how QlikView works. Please see the difference between the Traditional OLAP (Cube based solutions) vs. QlikView.

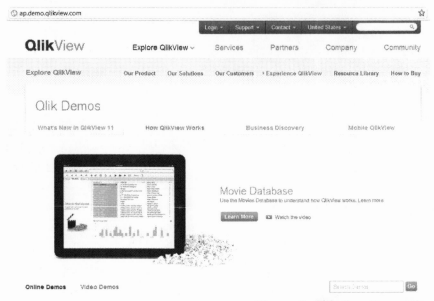

Figure 6: QlikView Demo Site

Second Experience: If you like wetting your hands and developing an application to understand deeper, this is for you. Download the QlikView Personal Edition from the QlikTech website, from the main home page, click Free Download to get your copy and install in your machine. Making the first application will give you an intriguing experience. The tutorials available on the site walk you through a step-by-step development and analysis experience. You can search for TUTORIAL in the site and download the version of Tutorial in a language of your choice. Registering in QlikCommunity is a great way to read various discussions, get peer support and other user opinions.

Figure 7: QlikView Movie Database Example Application

Understanding the Uniqueness of QlikView

Once a first understanding is gained of QlikView, the need is to understand exactly where QlikView can add value, and give unparalleled support to decision making, where other tools and approaches either fail or are far inferior. This also helps understand where other tools should be used.

Following are the aspects of QlikView that make it unique & useful for enterprises. Particularly for a special class of users—who require unrestricted ability to slice & dice data within a fixed schema (much like MOLAP)—QlikView is probably the only right solution because of these unique capabilities:

- *Interactivity*: interactive analytics making data follow *the thought* and vice-versa
- *Event to Information Time*: get necessary information with shortest time elapse from Event to Information
- *Disparate Data Sources*: Integrate data from disparate sources into a single unified view of enterprise—easily
- *Data Sizes*: support large data sizes naturally due to inherent data implosion and large memory & parallel processing support

- **Multi-Dimensional Analysis**: simultaneous multi-dimensional analysis just with clicks
- **On-Demand Reporting**: easy on-demand reporting and analytics on complex *fixed schema*
- **No-Query Language for Users**: no need to know SQL or any specialized pseudo-SQL programming language to get insights
- **Resource Needs**: very efficient use of memory, multi-core processors and network
- **Scalability**: ability to scale as the company grows with more data and complex analytics
- **Mobility**: seamless access to same content across access devices—Desktops, SmartPhones and Tablets—democratizing analysis & decision making, and makes it truly self-service
- **Social**: capabilities with a facility to blog-on-selection-context, making it easy to discuss discoveries and make collective decisions through discussions that are synchronous (like in a room) or asynchronous (like on emails)
- **Users / Usage**: supports tactical and strategic decision making
- **Advanced Analytics**: some statistical analyses are offered by QlikView. For more advanced analytics, other products like R, etc. can be integrated using the Extensibility API

These unique capabilities of QlikView carve out a niche where QlikView is *the perfect* solution. Chapter 4 on "Enterprise Framework for Combining BI Technologies" expands these attributes to evolve a model that can be used to choose which needs could be better addressed by what technologies / products.

QlikView – Uncontrollable Smiles

QlikView is one of the most interesting products available, which give a great data experience to the users. Especially, when users see QlikView for the first time, working on their own data, there is an inevitable joy and smile in their face, which shows that the product has hit the sweet spot, the right one in which it stays best.

The tag line of "Uncontrollable Smiles" was included in all the product campaigns in the years 2007 and 2008. Though it is not used much these days, it seems so relevant in many situations. With this as the special advantage the *Seeing Is Believing (SiB)* events are promoted by QlikTech and its partners.

When the business users are able to see the right KPIs in front of them, from their own data, and are able to make appropriate decisions, the joy that you see in their face is wonderful to watch. Identifying the right KPIs that would make sense and show them in QlikView and display them is the best approach to show the power of QlikView.

When the user is able to slice and dice, and get to the root causes by looking at these KPIs is the real power of QlikView. The speed with which applications can be created and made to come alive is the specialty of QlikView.

Is QlikView a Panacea?

Can QlikView solve every reporting / analytic need? The answer is no. There are requirements which are not handled by QlikView. The Framework in Chapter 4 has attempted to enlist all the needs of a typical enterprise as a checklist and a scoring scale associated with it.

A look at that framework will show the generic needs of any enterprise. As a preview to that Framework, the table below shows the typical scores given to QlikView for each of the framework attributes. The scores for these attributes are given with out-of-the-box features in mind.

All the attributes **highlighted** in the table, together form a unique combination of features not provided by other products. This has made QlikView unique and it has become useful for a set of users with a combination of these needs. QlikView gets maximum value for all attributes scored 10.

Though all other attributes are not supported out of the box by QlikView, they can be addressed very well using the QlikView Automation API and QlikView Extension API. More of such options and possibilities of extensions are discussed in various contexts in Parts II and III.

Table 1: Capability Mapping of BI Tools

Category	Sub-Category	Attribute	Score (for 10)
Capability	Advanced Analytics	Multidimensional Visualization	5
		Scorecarding	5
		Scoring	5
		Statistical Modelling	5
Dissemination	Delivery Mode	Electronic Print	7
		OnScreen	10
		Pixel Perfect Print	4
	Distribution Span	Group Distribution	8
		Mass Distribution	6
		Personalised Distribution	10
Experience	Interactivity	Flexibly Interactive	10
		Limited Interactive	10
		Static	5
	Time of Reponse	Near Real Time	10
		Periodic	10
		Real Time	7
Flexibility	Change of Schema	Fixed Schema	10
		Flexible Schema	5
		Semi-Flexible	7
	Flexibility of Outputs	Fixed Format	7
		Flexible Format	10
		Semi-Fixed	10
Purpose	Business Impact	Perception Impact	10
		Revenue Impact	10
		Time Impact	10
	Business Need	Business	10
		Compliance	7
		Market	10
		Performance	10
		Unified View	10
Timeliness	Regular Production	Quick Production Time	10
	Time for Ad Hoc Creation	Quick Creation Time	10

As can be seen, QlikView is not a panacea, but addresses the needs of Enterprises to support knowledge workers, with an ability to interactively query and do *Visual Data Mining*, quickly and easily. It provides the ease of use that allows business users and subject matter experts, to get benefit from the data they have, without having to go to IT for any support that other products typically require continuously.

The biggest advantage of QlikView is its ability to allow NAVIGATION ACROSS REPORTS WITHOUT LOSING THE CONTEXT. This is the biggest benefit to the business users. The impact of this is not evident at first look; but as they start looking at their own data they discover various slicing & dicing possibilities.

Answers to questions that normally take days or even weeks, get answered across clicks in QlikView. Even more, most users accidentally end up having more questions and answers, than they had intended to ask in the first place—a deeper insight.

What Challenges does QlikView have?

A good summary of the challenges that QlikView has to address are provided in the Gartner Magic Quadrant Report of 2011. An excerpt of just the functional points from the report is provided below for reference [7]:

> **QlikTech offers limited metadata management**. As QlikView grows into larger BI deployments spanning the enterprise, the lack of an enterprise semantic layer becomes a more pressing issue. Filling this gap requires additional cost and effort in the management of metadata to lock down common definitions and calculations, and to conform dimensions for cross-functional analysis across QlikView applications.
>
> QlikTech's focus on analysis and usability for end users delivers significant advantages. However, its **lack of a number of broad BI platform capabilities (high volume enterprise reporting, planning/financially oriented OLAP, Microsoft Office integration, score-carding and predictive modelling)** means that it will almost always need to be used alongside another BI platform.
>
> Interestingly, given QlikView's reputation for blistering speed, **11.6% of its customers reported poor performance as a problem** they'd encountered (vs. the overall sample's exposure to the same issue at 11.9%). In the survey carried out for 2010's Magic Quadrant, only

6.5% of QlikTech customers reported performance as a problem they'd experienced.

The increased incidence of this issue may be associated with the higher numbers of users (it's unlikely to be data—QlikView implementations surveyed have much lower than average data volumes). It should be noted, however, that the general perception of its customers is that QlikView still delivers among the best performance on the market.

Do these problems have solutions?

QlikView has created different products and added more features to address some of the shortcomings. In addition, they have provided, as mentioned above, APIs to expose all the capabilities, and allow imaginative customers to take advantage and integrate its features to create richer functionalities to meet all the Enterprise Needs.

The recent metadata capabilities bring a revolutionary approach to handling the metadata issues. Particularly the ability to incrementally add metadata & traceability information, without having to make significant changes to existing applications is a welcome addition.

Some of the problems are solved by best practices advised by QlikTech or formulated by key partners, with their experience in implementing QlikView in large number of customers of varying sizes. TEAM for example, has evolved a CMM Level 3 certified methodology to deliver, has an Expert Services practice to Audit and Enhance Performance, and a methodology to do Migration from one version of QlikView to the other.

Such methods should become common across the industry and standardized approaches will reduce much of the problems reported related to performance and data management; deeper understanding of QlikView is an important requisite.

The Part II chapters focus on more details related to QlikView, exploring its capabilities in-depth to help understand its enterprise capabilities. Part III focus is on sharing these experiences of solving shortcomings pointed out in the Gartner report and some more which are faced in various customer implementations.

Conclusions - Future of QlikView

For people who have used other BI solutions, particularly for the techies who have implemented other solutions, and spent considerable time in reporting services, QlikView is a breath of fresh air. It helps them to move away from the process of having to generate/dispatch reports and allow business users to have self-service reporting.

Even if reports have to be created from a BI helpdesk and delivered to users on demand, the time and effort taken to create these reports is reduced significantly, almost liberating the helpdesk members from the rigmarole of doing reporting 24x7. They will have time left after reporting, to focus on interactive and advanced analytics; look at more ways of adding value to business using IT.

Particularly, moving entire organization into a more powerful information analytic usage, QlikView can help increase what IBM calls "Analytics Quotient" of the companies and decision makers. QlikView has created a revolution, enhanced self-service and democratized BI and decision making. With QlikView everyone wins, and with time more and more capabilities should get added to cover more ground, remove the current bottlenecks, and probably become more affordable.

One can't forget the vision statement that Mans Hultman made in one of the Qonnection events to make QlikView present on every desktop in the world. I think with the growth of mobility and the initiatives of QlikTech for mobility, one can say "Qlikview probably has the chance of being on every device in the world that provides insight to users".

QlikView has symbolized a disruptive technology, democratized thinking & decision making. It is irreversible. The notion of QlikView is here to stay. "Associative Analysis" is the new thought enabler [10].

References

1. Business Intelligence, Wikipedia.com,
    [http://en.wikipedia.org/wiki/Business_intelligence]
2. Business Intelligence, TechTarget.com,
    [http://searchdatamanagement.techtarget.com/definition/business
    -intelligence]

3. Business Intelligence vs Business Analytics, Rock Gnatovich–CEO of SpotFire, Feb 2006, CIO.com, [http://www.cio.com/article/18095/Business_Intelligence_Versus_Business_Analytics_What_s_the_Difference_?page=3&taxonomyId=3002]

4. Business Intelligence Versus Analytics, Mark Lorion – Vice President Marketing of SpotFire, February 2010, spotfireblog.tibco.com, [http://spotfireblog.tibco.com/?p=1683]

5. From Business Intelligence to Business Discovery, QlikPower Blog, [http://www.qlikpower.com/blog/bid/65269/From-Business-Intelligence-to-Business-Discovery]

6. Magic Quadrant for Business Intelligence Platforms, 2008 to 2011, Gartner Research, http://www.gartner.com

7. Business Discovery – Powerful User Driven BI, Whitepaper, Qlikview.com, [http://www.qlikview.com/us/explore/resources/whitepapers/business-discovery-powerful-user-driven-bi]

8. Understanding QlikView's Associative Architecture, Dan English, May 2010, Whitepaper, Capventis.com, [http://capventis.com/wordpress/wp-content/uploads/2011/09/Whitepaper-Understanding_QlikViews_Associative_Architecture_v1.pdf]

9. MOLAP ROLAP..... SCHMOLAP, Erica Driver, Oct 2010, QlikCommunity, [http://community.qlikview.com/blogs/theqlikviewblog/tags/associative]

10. The Associative Experience: QlikView's Overwhelming Advantage, A QlikView Technology White Paper [http://www.qlikview.com/us/explore/resources/whitepapers/the-associative-experience?SOURCEPARTNER=TEAM

## CHAPTER 3

COMPARISON OF REPORTING & ANALYSIS TECHNOLOGIES

INFORMATION IS OF NO USE UNLESS ITS READILY AND EASILY AVAILABLE WHEN NEEDED

Introduction to the Chapter

As discussed earlier, various techniques of *Reporting and Analysis* have come into existence ever since the RDBMS was invented and built. These technologies attempt to solve some of the problems for the target user groups. None of these is panacea and cannot solve all problems of the enterprises. It is important to understand the scope of benefits each of these technologies can provide, and choose the right solution for the right situation and need. For this, it is important to create a common comparison framework, so that they can be compared apple to apple, and gain understanding across various solutions.

This chapter is an attempt to give in-depth understanding of the historical problems of business analysis technologies and highlight the key significant improvements that QlikView has provided for users and information technologists.

This substantial understanding allows us to make an informed choice: if, when and how to make the switch from other technologies to QlikView. More importantly, which needs of the users should be switched over to QlikView, and which can continue in other technologies.

With this framework of comparison, it is possible to find how to make use of the already made investments and take advantage of every technology / investment, to benefit various parts of the organization.

Many times, it is better to switch over to a newer better technology like QlikView, instead of continuing to use already invested technology: putting good money behind bad money can be avoided. This comparison framework forms the foundation of the subsequent chapters that discuss how to combine multiple reporting / analytic technologies into an enterprise.

Delivering Information to the Decision Makers

Business needs rich analytics. The regular relational databases cannot provide the rich analytics required, in the short time and flexibility that is required. Decision makers have a very short attention span and have a pressure of time to take decisions and act. For tactical & strategic decision making needs, simple dumps provided from operational systems will not cut ice.

Relational Reporting has been in vogue since 1969, ever since Relational Databases were invented by Dr. Codd. Data Mining led by Statistical and Artificial Intelligence have been in vogue since around that time as well in various forms. Through this period all interactive analysis needs, both tactical and strategic, has been implemented using relational reporting. However the real needs of business analysis are not met by relational reporting effectively.

In early 90s, the need for separate specialized systems beyond relational database / reporting systems was recognized and voiced by none other than Dr. Codd the inventor of RELATIONAL DATABASES. He also first coined the phrase OLAP - Online Analytical Processing, to differentiate from relational systems, which were named as OLTP – Online Transaction Processing Systems [1].

Characteristics of an Ideal Decision Support System - FASMI

A common definition of OLAP (DSS) which was independent of any product capability was attempted by many including Dr. Codd himself. One such successful definition created by BI-VERDICT.COM (erstwhile OLAPREPORT.COM) is FASMI (FAST ANALYSIS OF SHARED

MULTIDIMENSIONAL INFORMATION) an acronym that defines in short, what should be the characteristics of an ideal decision support system. A detailed explanation of FASMI is provided in the BI-VERDICT.COM and Nigel Pendse explains this in his article[2]: "This definition was first used by us in early 1995, and we are very pleased that it has not needed revision in the years since. This definition has now been widely adopted and is cited in over 120 Web sites in about 30 countries."

The analysts and customers who compare various products seem to use this as a test to find if a product meets the key requirements of an OLAP or more generically decision support system (DSS). The BI-Verdict report uses this as a test to qualify products to be included in their report.

Following is the short summary of specifications of FASMI:

Fast: Response < 5 seconds in general. Simplest queries in 1 sec & very few taking >20 seconds

Analysis: System can cope with any relevant business logic & statistical analysis for the application and user, keep it easy enough for the target user, requiring no programming

Shared: System implements all the security requirements for confidentiality (possibly down to a cell level) both for reads and writes, if allowed

Multidimensional: If only one item has be picked up to define OLAP, this is it—the system must provide a multidimensional conceptual view of the data, including full support for hierarchies & multiple hierarchies, as this is certainly the most logical way to analyze businesses and organizations

Information (or Insight): It is all of the data and derived information needed, wherever it is and how ever much is relevant for the application / analysis

From this perspective, it is interesting to note that *QlikView is FASMI compliant.*

Genesis of Interactive Analytic Technologies

While the above definition states the essence of the expectations on an interactive analytic solution, there is no prescription for the technology to be used or how the implementation should be done. Every vendor has brought various innovations in their product offerings to meet some subset of these requirements to varying degrees.

Most of the offerings of over the last two decades to address this problem are all based directly or indirectly on SQL. The challenges / limitations of SQL have been solved by techniques for pre-aggregation & pre-joining with their associated problems as discussed below.

The various CUBE based OLAP implementations are compared and presented in Wikipedia [3]. Since most OLAP vendors created pre-aggregated CUBE based solutions, OLAP is generally equated to CUBE solutions, though it was meant as a generic definition of flexible multidimensional analysis.

The BI Verdict compares all the OLAP solutions available in the market. All products covered by this study[4] meet FASMI test criteria. They use either OLAP or other techniques derived from OLAP: ROLAP, MOLAP and HOLAP. Majority of them, however, are fundamentally based on relational SQL query engines, they inherit the standard problems that SQL engines have. But as one can see, OLAP as a concept can be implemented even with non-CUBE based technologies. The BI-Verdict.com includes such non-CUBE products as well, which meet the FASMI Test. Perhaps, to make it even broader, beyond the limitations of the word OLAP, they have changed their name from OLAPREPORTS.COM to BI-VERDICT.COM.

Another interesting set of criteria used by Gartner is very similar to the criteria of FASMI. It includes practical implementation and market share elements of each of the products. Please refer to any of the Gartner reports for a detailed explanation of why any product was included in the Magic Quadrant that they publish every year. Following sections explore the challenges commonly found across many technologies and the various solutions for such issues.

Problems in SQL Based Reporting / Analytic Solutions

Irrespective of the technologies used, the key reporting problems common to enterprises are:

- Sluggish server response & slow development speeds: "It takes forever to get the result", "I need it tomorrow. I am on queue. IT department is saying 2 months wait time to get my report done".

- Inability to flexibly and quickly get answers for new questions easily:"I want to get to the root cause of the problem. I have to wait for another report to be developed and run".

The issues in getting timely and accurate data, to take informed decisions, can be classified into three parts: Development/Performance Issues and Usability Issues.

Development/Performance Issues: *High Loads on Servers/Storage and Time Delay*: While generating reports/analytics, the most challenging issues are a) Response time, b) Intensity of Load on the CPU, Memory and Storage, c) Network loads and d) Development time.

When OLTP systems are used to generate the reports, users performing transactions get a serious impact. Such scalability issues have to be addressed by a combination of better optimization techniques and improvement in hardware.

Very often vendors / service providers recommend an extensive increase in the capacity / configuration of the servers (memory, CPU) and network bandwidth, making the cost per report higher. However these performance symptoms demand immediate resolution.

The fundamental source of these symptoms is SQL technology itself. Most of the solutions created by vendors have focused on improving the situation by some incremental innovations. Better storage with higher read/write speeds, data warehouses (DWH) and cubes are some important initiatives which have taken a strong hold in the entire BI space.

Usability Issues: *Lack of Flexibility*: In addition to this, the flexibility offered to users, to choose the required fields across various tables, with filters of choice combinations, is highly limited. This leads to inability to explore all possible scenarios and understand them clearly, to take informed business decisions; but just be happy with the pre-meditated options created at the time of developing the reports.

Improvements through Technology Evolution

Broadly the challenges have been from different layers of the BI systems in general, and particularly, interactive analysis systems. From the users' point of view, these four layers are: a) Collaboration Layer, b) Presentation Layer, c) Compute Layer, d) Data Layer.

With the improvement of compute power, interface layer technologies and presentation layer technologies have gained more flexibility for all categories of users. With the evolution of internet technologies, collaboration layer capabilities have constantly evolved.

Though there were developments in the data layer, it has not kept up with the speed of the other layers. The focus had been on relational systems, and their improvement. The quest for a separate interactive analytic data store started only in early 90s. Even then, for a long time, it was tried out as incremental improvements of SQL based systems. Without the improvements on the data layer, advances of any of the above layers could not be used beneficially.

The various developments have been summarized in a high level in the following table:

Table 1: Information Management Layers

TECH LAYER	PROGRESSIVE INNOVATIONS	RELATED IMPROVEMENTS
Data Layer	ISAM -> SQL -> NoSQL -> AQL	File based -> Relational -> Star/Snow-flake Schema -> Connected
Compute Layer	Optimized Compute Libs -> Increased Parallelization	Disk Based processing -> In-Memory processing
Presentation Layer	Text Graphics -> Pixel Graphics -> OpenGL -> H/W Accelerated Graphics	Direct Memory Access -> High Speed Buses -> High Speed / Capacity Display Architectures + Cognitive Sciences
Collaboration Layer	Printed Paper -> Spread Sheets -> Emails -> Collaboration Workflows -> Social Technologies	Hierarchical Management -> Group Management -> Matrix Organizations -> Crowdsourcing

Historically, Dr. Edgar F. Codd created the Relational Model in 1970. SQL (Originally named as SEQUEL - Structured English Query Language) was developed in the early 1970s, by IBM's Donald D. Chamberlain and Raymond F. Boyce. Please refer to Wikipedia page [5] on SQL for more information. Through 70s and 80s the relational (storage) technologies and SQL (query) technologies gained ground, and got accepted as the default standard for any data manipulation requirements.

NON-RELATIONAL / NON-SQL INITIATIVES

Interestingly no non-SQL databases have been attempted till 1998, when Carlo Strozzi created a No-REL or No-SQL database, which does not expose a standard SQL interface. A lot of interesting developments have happened in this area since 1998, and the Wikipedia page [6] on NoSQL and the extensive collection of all the NoSQL databases presented in NOSQL site [7] are very interesting.

All these databases have been motivated to overcome the constraints of a) Relational model and, b) SQL Query Engine limitations. The June 2009 article "Should you go Beyond Relational Databases?" by Martin Kleppmann [8] is a great read.

The other good summary of all the various non-relational works at various times is in Christopher Browne's Web Pages[9]. An interesting comparison of structured storage software is available in Wikipedia too [10].

Lastly, there is an initiative to create a Query Language called UnQL. Please read the Wikipedia page on UnQL [11]. It is interesting that UnQL is a superset of SQL, within which SQL is a very constrained type of UnQL for which the queries always return the same fields (same number, names and types). However, UnQL does not cover data definition language (DDL) SQL statements like CREATE TABLE or CREATE INDEX.

During this period, while the limitations of SQL were realized, most vendors and researchers spent time to make the SQL engine itself work incrementally better. They shifted problems from one stage to another, or found batch processing alternatives to solve query-time problems. All these solutions addressed the performance problems associated with the SQL query technology. They did not however, solve the flexibility challenges inherent.

Surprisingly, for a very long time, no-one has actually asked WHY RELATIONAL (or) WHY SQL PROCESSING? Dr. Codd himself raised the need for a different business analysis database, and proposed the OLAP concepts in 1994. Even after that most attempts were done to improve the SQL / RELATIONAL technologies and overcome the shortcomings, to address the business analysis needs.

The common theme across all such initiatives is performance improvements, especially as the data sizes become larger. Even with small size of data, the flexibility is restricted by SQL Queries, which limits the capability to interactively query the data.

Though these improvements did not remove the challenges completely, they made SQL technology *good enough* for some more classes of problems. Having a good understanding of what these problems are, and how they can impact particularly in an Interactive Analytic situation, is very useful to make choices. There were few initiatives which looked at alternative methods (see box).

While such initiatives were happening, as far back as 1993, inventors of QlikView recognized this. It went almost unnoticed through to 2004, but created a very important way by which the limitations of the SQL Query Language can be overcome. The results were the *In-Memory Compact Storage* and *Associative Query Language (AQL)* discussed in the chapter "What is QlikView?"

SQL Characteristics and Limitations

It is important to understand different issues of SQL and various improvements made all around. The key parts of an SQL statement and their purpose are:

Table 2: SQL Characteristics

SELECT	Choosing list of fields & expressions (calculations) for the result
WHERE	Three purposes for which Where clauses are used:
	JOIN - connecting two or more tables using the primary key – foreign key combination
	RELATIONALIZE - connecting two or more (non-relational) tables using the non-relational conditions like

	date or value ranges
	FILTERS - choosing a subset of the rows selected by the JOIN condition
GROUP BY	Aggregating various fields / expressions on various dimensions
ORDER BY	Changing the sort order of the results of all the above

Each of these parts of SQL poses different challenges:

Select clauses produce the final output required from the complete SQL statement.

Problems created: If complex formula/expressions are present involving multiple fields from one or more tables, then they impose a significant compute load on the server.

The need is to increase the CPU capacity to support large number of such calculations.

Join conditions in all the Queries combine all fields from various relational tables chosen, connected through primary and foreign keys.

This works only when the tables are connected with relational integrity fields (one-to-one or one-to-many relationships). The joins lead to Cartesian Product Effect (Cross Joins), restricted only by conditions chosen to varying degrees, creating varying number of RESULTANT records to handle. The load generated also depends on the level of Indexes created on the fields used for joins.

Problems created: a) bloating of data: leading to large memory and storage requirements, and/or b) heavy read/writes: when the memory available is insufficient, the disk is used heavily to join large record sets, c) additional compute load: due to full-table scans whenever there are no related indexes.

Relationalization conditions (*Conditional Join*) are external logical conditions like date or value ranges used to connect records of all the non-relational tables. This works always along with the regular JOIN conditions.

These add another layer of compute in the form of conditional joins (conditional expression evaluations) to ensure integrity of joining across the non-relational tables. This creates the additional rules of joining beyond the relational integrity of actual data itself.

Problems created: a) compute load on the server requiring large CPU and memory, b) bloating of data either in memory or in storage depending on the data being kept transient or permanent.

Filter conditions select the required subset of resulting records from the record set created from the above two JOIN conditions.

Execution of CONDITIONAL EXPRESSIONS on every record is returned as the PRODUCT of JOIN.

Problem created: a large compute load, proportional to the number of records in the JOIN RESULT SET.

Group By conditions in all the queries lead to execution of AGGREGATION functions.

Efficiency of Group By is defined by the indexes created on dimension fields grouped on.

Problem created: A large compute load based on number of unique values of group by fields.

Order By sequences / sorts the result set in the order required for consumption.

Especially for large datasets, the system heavily uses SORTING algorithms, which need SORT BUFFER sizes to be very large.

Problem created: This leads to a huge impact on memory usage and compute load.

Impact of SQL Limitations on Reporting

SQL was designed to quickly retrieve relevant small subset of records during a transaction, perform integrity check and other relevant calculations to support transaction processing. This was required in OLTP systems. When the same SQL technology is used for reporting /

analytic technologies, the limitations of SQL seen above become the show-stoppers.

Data Sizes: When data sizes become large, more than a few records, the impact of this problem becomes larger.

Ad Hoc Analysis: Added to the data sizes, when the need is to run various reports on demand, particularly with variations in the filter conditions, the load on the system is multiplied. The flexibility offered by various tools has not improved due to this.

The direct impact of this comes on servers, making all the processes running to get sluggish. This further makes the response to users too slow. By the time the answers appear, they lose the context of querying. This sends decision makers back to their usual gut-feel based decision making or to Excel-based analysis, rendering the reporting system useless.

The cost of reporting also increases making it uninteresting from an ROI perspective.

Various Solutions for the Problems Above

On the first track, as mentioned before, natural reaction is to try and increase the hardware configurations, Memory/CPU/Storage Speeds/Network Speeds etc. However, all these tend to solve problems for some short time, and the problem comes haunting back again.

In the second track of SQL/Relational improvements, very innovative improvements were done to the SQL Engines themselves for improving query processing performance: Fixed Length Records, Indexing, Hashing, Pre-Fetch Records, Caching, Raw File Systems, Partitioning, Clustering, Parallel Databases, Distributed Databases and more.

On the third track, various solutions have focused on 'somehow' reducing time of response to service requests of end-users. This was achieved by pre-processing different sub-stages of SQL—essentially shifting problems to earlier stages of processing. However, these solutions need more than required processing power and/or exploded data storage than actually justifiable.

The following table summarizes the impact of these solutions which have aimed at improving the end-user response times, by *improvising* SQL based solutions at various stages.

As we can see, these solutions increased the need for CPU, memory and storage infrastructure requirements of the BI implementations. Corresponding to those the effort required also increased, making the Total Cost of Ownership (TCO) to be very high. Though the response times for end-users were made better, it was at a very high cost.

Table 3: Problems of SQL and Solutions

SQL CLAUSE	PROBLEMS CAUSED	BI SOLUTIONS	IMPACT OF SOLUTION
SELECT	Medium Compute	Pre-Calculate and store (or) Stored Procedures	More CPU + Memory + More storage required
WHERE			
JOIN	Data Bloating + Read-write + Medium Compute + Medium Memory	Pre-Fixed Schema, Pre-Join and store – Data Warehouse – Batch ETL	Very Large Amount of Storage + Large Time for pre-process
RELATIONALIZE	Heavy Compute + Medium Memory	Pre-Join and store – Data Warehouse – Batch ETL	More CPU + Memory + Time for pre-process
FILTERS	Medium Compute	Dynamic Filters – Hierarchical Drill Downs	More CPU + Memory + Delayed Response Times for users
GROUP BY	Heavy Compute	Pre-Aggregate and store – OLAP Cubes – Batch Aggregation	More CPU + Memory + Storage +
ORDER BY	Medium Compute + High Memory	Pre-Ordering and store + Dynamic Ordering	More CPU + Memory

Various vendors combined multiple combinations of these SQL sub-system solutions, leading to different possible solutions. These solutions are summarized in the table below.

Table 4: Solutions to Overcome Problems of SQL Technology

Live DB Server [or] Reporting (Staging / Copy) Server	Restricted Schema [or] Full Schema	Relational Source [or] Relational Snapshot [or] Data Warehouse (Pre-Joined)	Real-Time Queries [or] Pre-Aggregated Cubes [or] Non-Aggregated Snapshot	Unrestricted Aggregation [or] Hierarchical OLAP Cube Style (Pre-Aggregated)	Excel-like Output [or] Dynamic Flexible Front-end	Sample Solutions Supporting this Combination
Live DB	Full Schema	Relational Source	Real-Time Queries	Unrestricted Aggregation	Excel-like	Reporting Tools like
Report Server DB	Full Schema	Relational Source	Real-Time Queries	Unrestricted Aggregation	Excel-like	Crystal Reports, SSIS,
	Restricted Schema	Data Warehouse	Real-Time Queries	Unrestricted Aggregation	Excel-like	Jasper, One-Key, AlphaBlox, etc.
Report Server DB	Full Schema	Relational Source	Real-Time Queries	Hierarchical OLAP Style	Excel-like	Business Objects
	Restricted Schema	Data Warehouse	Real-Time Queries	Hierarchical OLAP Style	Excel-like	Business Objects
	Restricted Schema	Data Warehouse	Pre-Aggregated Cubes	Hierarchical OLAP Style	Excel-like	Cognos
	Restricted Schema	*Relational Snapshot*	*Non-Aggregated Snapshot*	*Unrestricted Aggregation*	*Dynamic Flexible Frontend*	QlikView

Solution from QlikView

QlikView is very unique in that, it has completely removed the two layers: 1) pre-joined data warehouse (DWH) layer, 2) pre-aggregated CUBE layer. It has brought the following:

1. *Relational Snapshot of Complete Data Set*: Not having to do any pre-joins, means no need for data warehouses. Even without DWH infrastructure, the query load on the transaction / reporting server can be completely avoided. [If the DWH infrastructure is already available in the company, DWH can become one of the sources of data for further analysis].

2. *Non-Aggregated Unrestricted Aggregation*: Supports Ad Hoc queries since the data is on-line with all its richness, and the flexibility to ask any combination of dimensions and measures, anytime, is in the hands of the End-User.

3. *Restricted Schema*: Provides an element of restriction in flexibility of including any table / field by the end-users. However, as we will see

in future chapters, the data implosion that is built-in the ETL process allows as much data to be included as possible, making this restriction insignificant if the data model is done carefully.

4. *Dynamic Flexible Front-end*: Allows unrestricted slicing and dicing to be performed by users, ensuring that the answers for the questions come immediately without any wait times.

This is possible because QlikView completely removed the SQL core engine requirement, & uses AQL engine, as explained in chapter "What is QlikView?" On top of this, it puts the imploded data in-memory, taking advantage of the processors working at memory speeds instead of disk-read writes. More on these capabilities of QlikView will be discussed in Part II, when we take a deeper look at how QlikView works.

Detailed Look at Some of the Approaches

A detailed look at some of the combinations above, provide a deeper understanding of the choices and their impacts. The distinct approaches most commonly used in enterprises are discussed below:

1. Direct Queries from Live Transaction System
2. Direct Queries from Mirror of Transaction System (Report Servers)
3. Direct Queries from Data Warehouse
4. OLAP over Mirror of Transaction System
5. OLAP over Data Warehouse
6. Direct Queries from QlikView (QV)

In Figure 1, these different paths / methods are shown to obtain reports & analytics. Some possible paths are discussed individually here:

Comparison of the 6 Sample Approaches of Reporting

1. Direct Queries from Live Transaction System (say, Crystal Reports / Jasper etc)

By running the query on the live transaction system, every time a report is requested, we can generate the reports & analyses.

However, this being a live system, repeated report runs can increase the load on the system and time taken to get the output is high. Also response of the system is considerably brought down for the regular transaction users.

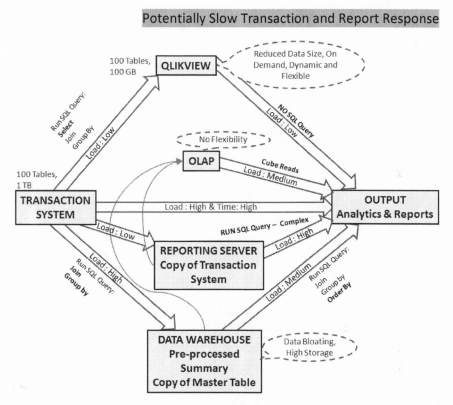

Figure 1: Comparison of Various Reporting Technologies

2. Direct Queries from Mirror of Transaction System (Crystal Reports / Jasper etc):

In this method a copy of the transaction system is created. The copy system does not only hold copy of the live data but also holds all the historical data. Running the query to fetch reports & analyses on this copy system will take a considerable amount of time as the system is already loaded with a huge amount of ever increasing historical data. However, the actual transaction users would be freed from the sluggish response in option 1.

Potentially Slow report response

3. Direct Queries from Data Warehouse

When a data warehouse is created, only the master tables are saved as-is, transaction tables are stored with required fields and summary level information is stored for all the transaction tables. The summarization will have to go through the joins, group by and order by, leading to problems highlighted above.

Potentially Slow summarization and report response

4. OLAP over Mirror of Transaction System

Creating an OLAP cube and fetching the data from the copy of the transaction system: in this method the traditional relational OLAP technology is used wherein the query is pre-aggregated. This however, limits the flexibility of choosing dimensions and measures in any report, making Ad Hoc reporting very cumbersome (every new combination requiring a new CUBE to be made).

Potentially No flexibility and Ad hoc reporting

5. OLAP over Data Warehouse

This approach will reduce the DWH load due to Joins, Group by and Order By, generated repeatedly at the time reports are run by different users at different times. However, this load is shifted to the CUBE refresh phase, where the OLAP engine pre-calculates all the chosen measures across the various predefined permutations of multiple dimension values.

It is important to note, that not all the various permutations would be used by users any time, hence leading to a wasteful effort of exhaustively calculating all permutations and combinations.

Potentially Time Consuming and High Cost

6. Direct Queries from QlikView (QV)

QV extracts the data from the transaction system and saves the extracted data in raw QVD files – which are compressed up to 90% of the original database size by way of normalization. This is a copy of the complete database. Join by, group by and order by queries are run on these QVD files eliminating the load on the live transaction system hence the response time is quick.

QV uses the In-Memory technology, not pre aggregated. This provides the end user flexibility of ad-hoc, dynamic, flexible reporting with user friendly GUI and lesser overall time for report creation.

Potentially Quick response, Flexible and Cost Effective

Appropriateness of Technologies for Different Enterprises

While various products have brought very interesting improvements and innovations, they all work fundamentally with the SQL as the core. Hence the pre-aggregation and pre-joining are used as key techniques. These two choices have rendered all these solutions not to be flexible and ad hoc enough, from the eyes of the business users, who are the real consumers of data.

For operational decision making, traditionally, relational reporting has been used, as we saw in the beginning of the chapter. However, the other SQL based technologies that provide additional limited flexibility can become more useful for this layer of operational decision makers, who want pre-defined formats, pre-aggregated data, available for consumption at any point in time, without any interactive analysis requirement.

All the technologies which were originally meant to be used for OLAP or Interactive Analysis are fit to be moved to handle more operational reporting requirements.

The new solutions, like QlikView, which take advantage of all the newer technology developments all around, can be used for true interactive analysis.

The key items are the immediate comprehensive information access (due to compact small foot print data stores), speed of response (due to in-memory data models) offered by most data discovery tools.

The most unique capability of QlikView is the flexibility of limitless ad hoc querying (due to the modern Associative Query technique).

Conclusions - A Holistic Interactive Analysis System

This chapter has focused on data layer challenges and analyzed the impacts of various technology choices. This was extended to understand how tools like QlikView have introduced fresh thinking to improve data layer limitations traditionally the characteristic of SQL based technologies.

The next chapter is going to focus on comparing Usability, Security and Deployment aspects, and evolve a more elaborate comparative framework. Of course, more than what the technology or products offer, the approach will be to find what the needs are, and define ways to find which technologies can meet those needs.

This framework is also important for defining what technologies should be used for what type of problems. Departing from the traditional vendor approach of showing how one product can replace the other, the attempt in this book is to explore what are the areas where maximum benefit will come by replacing any technology with others. Though QlikView is discussed at the center, the book also gives an approach to find how other technologies, already invested in, can be gainfully employed for information dissemination.

The most important responsibility of a CIO is to ensure that the already made investments are protected, and ensure the future investments to meet the same requirements, are minimized. The most important error is putting good money to make a bad investment work. Care should be taken in ensuring that the organization is not caught in the trap of spending more to protect past investments. A good approach is to take TCO including investments made in the past and required in the future—both capex and opex—to make the right call.

References

1. Online Analytical Processing, Wikipedia,
    [http://en.wikipedia.org/wiki/Online_analytical_processing]
2. What is OLAP? FASMI, Nigel Pendse, March 2008, Bi-Verdict.Com,
    [http://www.google.co.in/url?sa=t&rct=j&q=bi-verdict%20what%20is%20olap%20pendse&source=web&cd=1&ved=0CCYQFjAA&url=http%3A%2F%2Fwww.olapreport.com%2Ffasmi.h

tm&ei=FEO7TuH1L8-
rrAfymLXRBg&usg=AFQjCNHEGaUJZVNfLRnVeTTMr-wN4pHZpA]
3. Comparison of OLAP Servers, Wikipedia,
   [http://en.wikipedia.org/wiki/Comparison_of_OLAP_Servers]
4. Business Intelligence (OLAP – FASMI Compliant) Products
   Evaluation, BI-Verdict.com, [http://www.bi-verdict.com/bi-products/]
5. SQL, Wikipedia, [http://en.wikipedia.org/wiki/SQL]
6. NoSQL, Wikipedia, [http://en.wikipedia.org/wiki/NoSQL]
7. NOSQL site, [http://nosql-database.org/]
8. Should you go Beyond Relational Databases?" , Martin Kleppmann,
   June 2009, ThinkVitamin.com,
   [http://thinkvitamin.com/code/should-you-go-beyond-relational-databases/]
9. NonRDBMS Databases, Christopher Browne's Web Pages,
   [http://linuxfinances.info/info/nonrdbms.html]
10. Comparison of Structured Storage Software, Wikipedia Page,
    [en.wikipedia.org/wiki/Comparison_of_structured_storage_software]
11. UnQL, Wikipedia Page, [en.wikipedia.org/wiki/UnQL]

QlikView for Enterprises

## CHAPTER 4

ENTERPRISE FRAMEWORK FOR COMBINING BI TECHNOLOGIES

EVERY SOLUTION HAS A SWEET SPOT WHERE IT WORKS THE BEST—INCLUDING HUMAN BEINGS

Introduction to the Chapter

Finding the sweet spot for each solution, and using it there is an enterprise challenge. Many times, solutions are deployed to address wrong needs. This adds more problems, and the original need is not solved. The same holds for BI products/solutions, and there is a need to choose right solutions for right problems.

This chapter discusses such a framework for BI, by putting down a NEEDS LED approach instead of FEATURE LED or BENEFITS LED approach often used by vendors in sales situations. The attempt is to define a set of parameters for all the information requirements, and categorize them. Then these categories allow requirements to be grouped and each group can be solved with the right product/solution which is best suited. This framework can also be used to select DSS/BI products at the time of evaluation/purchase.

The traditional TCO based approach can be overlapped on top of this NEEDS LED approach, to ensure that the solution is affordable for the enterprise. Many times, the money that can be spent on a particular solution depends on the value that the solution can bring. While this is an important part of the framework to select the solutions, this has not been included in the discussion here.

It is easy to add commercial considerations and expand this framework. Every organization can make this amendment to the model, based on the specific guiding principles of CAPEX / OPEX / CASH FLOW specific to the company and its current priorities / circumstances.

The chapter goes into details of every parameter defined for the framework, discussing the impact and presenting relevant practical scenarios where possible. The most important need for organizations is leveraging the already made investments, as discussed in the last chapter. Having a common framework to compare various solutions— existing and new—and make the right mix of them to solve the enterprise needs / challenges.

Reference Framework to Compare Dissemination Systems

To understand this in the right perspective, as it was highlighted in an earlier chapter, the need is to define exactly where QlikView can add value, and give unparalleled support to decision making, where other tools and approaches either fail or are inferior.

Establishing such a reference structure to evaluate BI tools, including the Business Discovery tools, is a very useful step. This will help business and IT users to deliberate, create clusters of business problems and associated information needs, and decide which technologies are appropriate for which need cluster.

The key to making QlikView work in enterprises is to properly evaluate the needs, and find where QlikView is the only right solution. Applying QlikView to a wrong problem is going to fundamentally defeat the effort. Not just for QlikView, but for all BI products, this has been one of the most important needs in the industry.

The traditional BI solutions address many pockets of requirements. The emerging business / data discovery solutions address some newer pockets of requirements. More and more new features are getting added in these emerging technologies, to address some of the new demands that are arising. With the evolution of businesses with speed and complexity demands, the need for information has evolved into need for actionable insights.

As we have seen earlier, much of these demands are now possible to be addressed, solved by the earlier unimaginable developments in hardware technologies including networking, processors & memory scalability, software technologies including parallel processing, optimal memory hashes, social network / micro blogging, graphical presentation, mash-ups, real-time integration of systems, incremental web updates, AJAX, multi-dimensional visualization techniques and many more.

A combination of all such techniques has expanded the possibilities around information dissemination, particularly for decision support. The business discovery solutions, like QlikView, take advantage of all such advancements, and start off with completely different paradigms. So have many other tools with different degrees of success. Mobility has particularly created new possibilities of information inclusion.

Making the right choices

Choosing the right tools for the right problem is an important step to be done in evolving an enterprise roadmap for BI. The most common approach is to compare all the *features and capabilities* of products, and choose the products with desired ones. This generally is a wrong approach. This is a FEATURES LED analysis and is generally the approach product companies take to highlight the uniqueness of their products. Many times, while the capabilities themselves may be very impressive, the challenge is to know how they can help the business.

Second approach is to use BENEFITS LED analysis to compare products. In this approach, all the benefits that other implementations have got by using the products are taken as a reference. This gives ideas in terms of how the same product can be deployed in a company. Using this, the choice of the product is made. There are challenges in this approach too since there is a need to really profile the needs that exist in each company, which could be different from the examples.

In addition, there is a need to see how all the various technologies already invested-in can be put to use, including QlikView. Choosing the right deployment, replacements and in the right sequence is important.

For each company there is a unique way based on the extent of problems, already made investments, additional investments possible, time and skills available for implementing any change. An important part is the very change management itself. Making the right choices is extremely important for any BI initiative to be successful. The most important element is to know "WHAT IS THE REQUIREMENT?" This is what gets the least formal treatment in selecting any BI solution. The following sections focus on how to arrive at these needs.

Establishing a NEEDS-LED Reference Framework

To do this in the right perspective, it is important to create a list of NEEDS in a product independent way to consolidate the needs in a single place:

A. Tabulate all the enterprise requirements generically and characterize into clusters.

B. Then assess what generic technology capabilities are required to address every cluster.

C. Once this assessment is done, the various tools at the disposal of the company can be evaluated to see the fit for each cluster. Else buy new ones.

This is not a well established science yet, but the attempt in this chapter is to create a basic NEEDS-LED framework which can be expanded to suit needs. On top of this, the cost benefit analysis can also be superimposed, with FINANCIAL and BUSINESS IMPACTS.

This will help business and IT users to deliberate, create clusters of business problems and associated information needs, and decide which technologies are appropriate for which need-clusters. This will help create a roadmap of deployment of various tools, particularly replacement of various tools with new solutions like QlikView.

Such a framework also clarifies our view about BI—both conventional and the new expanded BI including Business Discovery—and the scope of each of these solutions. This moves towards a scientific approach to select what to use where, to meet all the information needs for decision making in different organizations. The core to all this is the NEEDS-LED thinking, which is explained further in the following section.

The previous chapter focused on data layer and improvements around it. However, the requirements revolve around all four layers introduced: a) Data Layer, b) Compute Layer, c) Access Layer and d) Collaboration Layer. Characteristics that are central to this framework are:

a. There are multiple approaches / technologies / tools available in each of these layers

b. A solution is a combination of one or more of these in each layer

c. A checklist of all options need to be created, for each of these layers

d. Both requirements and solutions need be classified into groups, using attributes

e. Match requirements and solutions by the groups they belong

f. This will help make the right product/solution choices

The most important pre-requisite for this approach to work is, IDENTIFYING REQUIREMENTS. This is one of the difficult activities especially in an enterprise context. The following section gives a quick overview of a couple of possible approaches to help arrive at consolidated requirements for the enterprise in a systematic fashion. This requires experience with synthesis skills.

Understanding and Consolidating Requirements of the Enterprise

The core of the approach is to use Business Analytics successfully for business benefits. The key outcome, as discussed in an earlier chapter, is ACTIONS based on the insights provided by the BI systems. Without that result, all the business intelligence solutions are of no use.

This is the most important point to realize: the reason a BI implementation becomes successful, is not just the tools or technologies, but the analytics quotient of the people involved and more, the culture to use analytics effectively to define actions, and act on the findings positively. A very good in-depth view of the impact of this culture is given in the IBM Business Value Institute-MIT Sloan Review: "Analytics: The Widening Divide, How Companies are achieving competitive advantage through analytics" [1]. In addition, the article of Steve Miller in his blog on Information Management is a great reading as well [2] (more links are also provided in the references [3]).

One of the most common mistakes done in enterprises is the IT department tries to define what the requirements are, and puts a lot of effort to build something to meet those requirements. When this sincere first development is shown to business users, they are generally unable to relate to it, and the project starts off on a negative note.

The key need is to take a strategic approach to this, by ensuring that the requirements are created by the business users. Whether the scope is for a particular department function, or a process (across multiple departments) or the entire enterprise, the need is to take a strategic approach along with the business users and decision makers—involving them to define what their objectives and key issues are. Without this knowledge, making an assumption and proceeding is one of the sure ways of failure.

There are two distinct methods that can be used to consolidate all the requirements:

1. Collect all the reports, and distill the requirements from the same
2. Use best practices of industry leading customers, vendors and standards bodies
3. Conduct a Strategy Map exercise and capture all the requirements

As required, these tools can be combined at appropriate levels to arrive at the requirements. However, doing the Strategy Map exercise with the business users should not be dropped. This is the key step to ensure buy-in comes from the business users.

Consolidating All Existing Reports

Every organization produces a lot of reports from different systems. They are distributed among various members at differing frequencies. Getting hold of a deck of all these reports, and distilling the various dimensions and metrics used in all these reports is a great starting point.

This consolidated list of dimensions and measures, with an indication of which users use each of these measures, is a good way to understand what is required for whom. The only time when this is not possible, is when the organization is completely new.

Best Practices of Industry Leaders

One of the interesting ways to start a BI requirement specification is by starting off with a list of KPIs and Metrics used by other industry-leading companies in the same domain. One can also use the recommendations of consulting organizations and vendors in this domain area. This is a very useful starting point. This can reduce the amount of time spent on creating everything from scratch. This can be used as another way to consolidate requirements for the business, along with the exercise of putting together all the current reports being made.

This can also be one more way to give ideas to the business users about what their requirements could be. This and the current reports being generated should be consolidated together and used as a starting point for the Strategy Map exercise.

Strategy Map Exercise

The list of current information usage and the *best practices* can act as a starting point. For this, the relevant business users should be brought into one room to collectively add/remove/approve this list and define what more they need.

One of the good techniques to collectively do with business users is to go through a Strategy Map exercise. This is an established process and there is a lot of information available about how to create Strategy Maps. One caution however is, this exercise should be done down to the operating layers of the organization.

All levels of users will define metrics / measures that are required for meeting their work needs. There is an interesting discussion available on LinkedIn: Paulo Goncalves—see reference: "What do you think of the Strategy Map exercise, to define and align business unit operation & goals with the organization ones?" [4]

A consolidation of all such metrics and the kind of presentation that is required for these metrics should be the output of such an exercise. Creating a list of actionable insights that the business users will get from these outputs is an important component of this requirement gathering. Specifically defining standard operating procedures around these actionable insights is essential.

This exercise can be done in very different ways and formats. It is extremely important that this exercise is conducted, without fail, to ensure that the BI initiative succeeds and produces tangible results. Irrespective of the method used, creating a document defining the details of various outputs that would be produced is a must—to gain visibility and acceptance among business users.

Generally IT departments tend to shy away from such an exercise, for the fear of setting very high expectations and not being able to deliver. But not doing this exercise could be worse. Defining the total output requirement and defining phased deliverables is the best way to keep expectations appropriate. The most important requirement is, to reiterate, the list of actionable insights that business users will get from the outputs desired.

Categories of Output Desired

The outputs desired by the business users can be broadly classified into following categories:

Detailed Listings	Getting detailed raw / summary of transactions
Target Vs. Actual	Understanding "where are we" vs. "where we want(ed) to be"
Patterns & Trends	Understanding the characteristic patterns and trends of business
What-if Scenarios	Understanding what could happen if something different is done
Predictions	Understanding what is likely to happen and the factors that will affect the outcomes in future

All the requirements consolidated by the Strategy Map exercise should be classified into these categories. This will help understand the data and the technology needs that are grouped under the four layers that were referred earlier: a) Data Layer, b) Compute Layer, c) Access Layer and d) Collaboration Layer.

Formulating the Framework

To create a framework, it is important to establish the various need attributes—a list of attributes of inputs, process, outputs and actions.

Table 1: Layers and their Attributes

Layer	Characteristics	Attributes	Possible Values
Data Layer	Source Data from various sources – ability to *integrate data from multiple sources*	1. Data Granularity	1. Transaction Level 2. Summary Level
		2. Timeliness	1. Real Time 2. Near Real Time 3. Periodic
Compute Layer	Creating *calculated outputs* - various formulae supported by the system	3. Richness of Analysis	1. Aggregations 2. Patterns & Trends 3. Complex predefined analysis of data 4. What-if Scenarios 5. Predictive
		4. User Flexibility	1. Pre-calculated and stored 2. Calculated on user request
Access Layer	Display of information to help gain insights – helping decision makers to find *actionable insights*	5. Access Freedom	1. Static Published 2. Static on-demand 3. Interactive Dynamic 4. Alerts
		6. Presentation	1. Textual 2. Pixel Perfect 3. On-Screen Graphics
		7. Security	1. Authentication 2. Authorization for Data Access 3. Authorization for Analytic Features
Collaboration Layer	Facility for decision makers to share, review together, discuss and decide – *collaborative decision making*	8. Devices	1. Desktop/Laptops 2. Tablets 3. Smartphones 4. Other Mobiles
		9. Sharing	1. Bookmarks 2. User created Graphs 3. User created Reports
		10. Social	1. Microblogs—user created Notes 2. Collaborative Discussions on context 3. Session sharing
THE OUTPUT OF THESE LAYERS TOGETHER IS ACTIONABLE INSIGHTS & ACTIONS			

All the information needs and in the same token, all the products and solutions available can be classified using key attributes related to these four layers. The table summarizes these *need characteristics* against each of the layers. Along with the attributes, the possible options / values for each of these are also presented. Next section talks about how these attributes can be used to characterize the requirements and products using the same framework.

Using the Framework

Every metric / measure defined as a requirement in the Strategy Map exercise, can be qualified using these 10 attributes. Each attribute can assume one or more of possible values given in the last column. Some of the attributes may assume the same values in all the requirements. This generally characterizes a common need across all the requirements. These common characteristics across requirements will define what kind of solution could be useful for the company.

Creating clusters of all attribute values define the characteristics of the needs in the enterprise. Any particular format for collecting these inputs and adding the attributes is not provided here, since this is very simple and intuitive. A standard Excel sheet format can solve the purpose.

Understanding all attributes in the right perspective and using them to describe the needs is very important to arrive at the specifications for solution required. Following individual sections explain each of these layers, their attributes and define briefly when various possible options of each attribute are applicable. Wherever relevant, characteristics of QlikView are provided along with the description of attributes.

Data Layer

The last chapter primarily focused on this layer, while comparing various reporting/analytic technologies. The mechanics of how each technology works at the data layer was reviewed in-depth, particularly taking the structure of SQL as a frame of reference.

As we saw in that comparison, the SQL based technologies will introduce a bigger time-lag in the processing, as the size and complexity of data increases, for a given investment on hardware. Hence the data layer is key to the time elapsed from the capture of data to making it available for actual analytics. With larger data sizes, system delay is even more pronounced particularly on SQL based technologies.

One way to lower this impact of data layer is to keep the scope of deployment lesser. With this perspective, there are three scopes typically chosen for BI deployments: 1) Departmental / Specialized, 2) Process Level—maybe across multiple departments and 3) Enterprise wise—across all departments/processes. Along with this choice, there is also a need to define the sluggishness permissible.

With larger scope, SQL based technologies introduce additional processes which increase this elapsed time and require a larger system configuration. Hence, two attributes collectively dictate the sizing, processes and investments required: Data Granularity and Timeliness.

Data Granularity

Most businesses / analyses benefit from a highly granular (more detail) data at the level of each transaction or event happening, with sub-second timestamps being preserved. However, due to the challenges posed by data sizes and the SQL impact on such data sets, businesses settle down for a lower granularity of data, agreeing to do analysis on aggregated levels of data. The choices are: a) Transaction Level, b) Summary Level.

In the summary level choice, ETL layer is used to extract actual data and perform a pre-aggregation. Only the summarized information is made available for the subsequent layers of access and collaboration. Hence pre-aggregation solutions using CUBEs impose a limit depending on the design of the aggregation choices made.

Tools like Business Objects, which do not pre-aggregate but execute SQL queries dynamically on request from a user, put a heavy load on the system, and hence a separate copy of the data is kept in a pre-joined data warehouse to minimize execution loads, with large system configurations.

QlikView on the contrary, extracts the data in raw transaction form, and keeps it in the memory allowing dynamic aggregations driven by the slicing and dicing of the users. Solutions like QlikView, due to their dynamic interactive capabilities and their efficient handling of data by significant normalization and reduction, can support transaction level data to be taken all the way up to the access and collaboration layers. This allows literally unlimited amount of slicing and dicing, allowing the analyst to find the root causes at a much more granular level.

Timeliness *

Capture to Analysis Time

The amount of time *elapsed* from the time of actual data capture to the time data is available for analysis is a critical element. As we have seen, with higher complexity and competition, the time to respond is very low.

Depending on the nature of business and the need for quicker decisions, the data needs can be: 1) Real-time, 2) Near Real Time and 3) Periodic (intervals).

Real-Time systems need the data to be captured from the transaction system, stored, processed with the analytic algorithms and displayed within a couple of seconds. The use of intermediate storage and extracting into analytic platforms is not a choice that will work. Hence solutions like Datawarehouse or QlikView Data (QVD) files and OLAP Cubes cannot be used in such a scenario. The need is to look for real time components embedded in the transaction system itself, or another system like QlikView Real-Time server, which will receive data from the source as a stream, and put it through the analytic engine in real-time.

Near-Real Time reporting requires least amount of pre-processing requirements. Tools like QlikView provide this nimbleness to do incremental extracts of data in intervals desired (as low as 5 mins) and the data is integrated into the data model by very quick reloads facilitated by the compact data footprints. CUBE based systems naturally have difficulties in this, longer time or higher investments on hardware. Other direct SQL query based systems have the challenge of high-loads discussed in the last chapter.

Periodic (interval based) reporting systems typically refresh data once a day / once a week. Such requirements can be addressed by any of the solutions available. Particularly, if there are already invested systems like Cognos and Business Objects, etc., they can be used for meeting such reporting requirements. These systems typically distribute static published reports either in a portal or through emails, allowing users to access them when needed. With these systems, there are inherent delays in the daily runs, due to data sizes and process delays. Hence business users have challenges in getting even regular reports in time.

QlikView has brought a lot of comfort to earlier users of Cognos and/or BO by helping them get reports much quicker with lesser load and more flexibility. With the QlikView publisher option and its APIs for data output, the publishing of data is also done very well. If deployed appropriately, cost & time per production report is kept low with technologies like QlikView.

New Reports/Analyses Creation Time

The time required for getting a new report, from definition, creation to submission, is the other attribute that is important. An important value-add of solutions like QlikView is the AGILE approach. Requirement definition to realization of reports can be done in a very short time. This adds to the overall nimbleness of the organization and the cost per new report is brought down significantly. Times—both production run times and creation times—are important in deciding which technology is appropriate.

Data Layer plays a very important part in enabling the timely information availability to decision makers. Choice should be made with the implications of various technologies given in the previous chapter.

Right technology choice for this layer can ensure the following: a) Quicker Concept to Report times, b) Lesser loads on transaction systems, c) Reduction of storage and intermediate processing costs, d) Reduction of intermediate processing times and e) Reduction of daily report production times.

Compute Layer

This layer consists of all the computation elements which are required for processing, both in the backend data layer pre-processing and in the on-line processing requirements when requested by the user.

The computational layer is where the real processing of information happens. The formulae that are required for various information needs are used in the compute layer. Computations are done either offline during the data preparation stage, or at the time of actual user interactions. This defines the flexibility for users. In addition, various solutions can provide different richness of analytics. These form the two key attributes in the compute layer.

Richness of Analysis

Various analytical needs of users can all be combined into following broad categories:

a. Aggregations
b. Patterns & Trends
c. Complex predefined analysis of data (domain specific formulae)
d. What-if Scenarios
e. Predictive Analysis

Aggregations: Most commonly used functions are aggregation functions like sum, average, and count. The performance of aggregations decides the time taken for report generation in general. Most of the KPIs that we use in businesses are essentially aggregates or ratios of aggregates of key measures of the business.

Trends: Trends are essentially changes of any KPI or Measure over time. These are measured as time series or as gradients / peaks / valleys / high-lows over time. All businesses need to understand time based variance of KPIs. In addition to visual plotting over time, Rate-of-change of any KPI (Velocity) and Rate-of-change-of-Velocity (Acceleration) are two interesting measures that help understand improvements and degradations in business.

Patterns: Patterns are essentially variation of the KPIs or Measures over any dimension other than Time. Geography-wise, Product-wise, People-wise, Vendor-wise, Customer-wise and such representation of distribution over other dimensions, help understand the behavioral patterns and affinities between different data elements. A very large percentage of business reporting is done with just the above three categories of compute capabilities.

Most pre-defined / pre-formatted reports use simple aggregations over time and other dimensions.

Complex Predefined Formulae: Statistical, probability, trigonometric, financial, inter-record, and other domain specific functions form this part of the compute layer. These are necessarily defined by the subject-matter-experts with understanding of their usage.

What-if Scenarios: Most businesses are required to make some guesses about what is likely to happen, if we do something. For doing such forecasts or impact analysis, one needs to use the past data along with the formulae of relationship, and some mechanism of projecting the past to the future like a linear extrapolation. These capabilities allow What-if Scenarios to be built. These are extremely useful tools for planning.

Predictive Analytics: In many situations, we have past data, but we do not really have a set of equations defining their relationship, or any extrapolation mechanism. In such situations relationship between various data elements have to be identified automatically. Automated Machine Learning Algorithms allow such Modelling to be done automatically. Using these models, it is possible to make predictions about future situations and use them for planning or taking decisions. Very few companies and businesses are really in a position to take advantage of this Predictive Analytics. In fact this is called commonly as Advanced Analytics, and is considered in some schools of thought as superior analytics.

Most tools provide the first four extensively. The key challenges are: a) whether these formulae are given in the hands of the end user or they have to be pre-calculated, b) whether these algorithms are optimized for performance.

QlikView provides one of the best implementations of various aggregations and a rich set of functions. It provides Excel style formulae and it also provides a facility to create user functions, making it extensible. Functions can be written using Javascript / VBScript.

Extensibility API of QlikView, introduced in version 10 allows using external library and program functions by making calls. Such external functions can be allowed to use the data in-memory within QlikView. Solutions like R can be integrated inside QlikView using this method.

Such integrations of course require IT to add these functions into the application so that users can then use it as a self-service solution.

Compute Flexibility for Users

Computation is allowed in systems either 1) Pre-calculated, stored and retrieved when user requests reports or 2) Calculations On-Line as the user interacts and requests for the reports/information.

Most of the DWH and OLAP based systems use the first approach. Very limited amount of flexibility is offered to the data users. This is to avoid the load generated by online calculations done at the time of user request for reports / information.

Few tools provide facility to directly query the source data or a copy of the source data. When they use SQL or similar calculation / processing engines, the load they put on the CPU and I/O is quite high. QlikView supports calculations on-line with data in-memory. This allows very quick on-line response times, with maximum flexibility to compute while the user slices and dices the data.

Compute layer provides the processing capabilities that are required for the analysis. This is the core component of all analytical systems. The variety, flexibility and power provided in this layer forms the true strength of the analytical solution. QlikView provides a very powerful, fast and flexible implementation of the Compute Layer.

Access Layer

This layer makes the products useful in the business setup. The most important aspect is the need to have the information when needed in the desired form, so that it could be useful for taking timely decisions. Information access is characterized by the following four attributes: 1) Access Freedom, 2) Information Delivery, 3) Presentation and 4) Security. The most successful platforms provide multiple access options, particularly the delivery and freedom of access.

Access Freedom

The way in which end users are allowed to receive and use the content is what defines the effectiveness of BI solutions. The necessary information can be distributed in the following ways: a) Static Published, b) Static on-demand, c) Interactive Dynamic and d) Alerts.

Static Published: This has been the oldest method, with all the reports generated in a backend server, and pushed out to the users, either by email or to a directory designated for them. One of the issues in this approach is, though the system automatically pushes the reports out every day, there is no assurance that every user would use the reports they receive.

Publishing in XLS format is the most common with most systems supporting it. This is done to support further downstream ad hoc analysis on the data supplied on the Excel. Of late, publishing in PDF format has become more common since it allows the data integrity to be maintained in the reports.

Publishing reports to large number of users, through the SQL based technologies creates a major load condition on the servers during the generation—also a heavy load on network during distribution. Even OLAP based technologies have a serious performance challenge due to this approach. But this was the best way to avoid delays and outages at the time when the user needs the information. This used to be the sweet spot for all the popular technologies along with their pixel perfect reporting capabilities.

Now, QlikView provides PDF publishing through one of its additional components called PDF Publisher. To publish data in XLS format, the Automation API available on the product needs to be used and custom solutions need to be created. There are third party solutions available for this XLS distribution of data to large number of users. Though the formatting of the reports is not as pixel perfect as other solutions, the reports generated are of a good quality to meet functional requirements—can be improved by custom code.

Fixed Format On-Demand: To avoid the problem of wasteful generation of reports every day for users who don't use the reports, the on-demand report generation is a solution. However this can pose problems of outages if many users request for their reports at the same time.

With the SQL based technologies this becomes an acute problem and in fact, only to solve this all the DWH / OLAP technologies have been created. Even with DWH and OLAP technologies this becomes a problem since the amount of pre-processing required is significantly high.

QlikView, with its in-memory technology and AQL, along with the dynamic report generation functionalities included in version 11, has made this an extremely easy way of generating ad hoc reports. They are not pixel perfect in the sense of printing by default, but they meet the off the cuff information requirements. With external customization with Workbench, these reports can be made to comply with the pixel perfect rendering as well. Soon we can expect components, from QlikTech and third-party, which will take advantage of this feature and support real-time pixel perfect reporting for end-users directly.

Interactive Dynamic: This is the real requirement that was set out by Dr. Codd in his explanation about the OLAP tools. However, like we discussed in the previous chapter, all the challenges from the SQL world did not allow this to take the best shape possible. Not until the in-memory technologies came in.

QlikView with its combination of in-memory and AQL technologies allows users to interactively work with data, slice and dice at will, using practically unlimited hierarchies and selections. This leads to a powerful analytic capability, allowing users to get insights beyond what they can otherwise imagine and seek.

QlikView has re-defined ad hoc reporting due to this capability, and has left all other product companies to find ways to replicate this as much as possible. However, AQL of QlikView is still unbeaten with its tremendous potential to not only provide answers, but also to allow new questions to come up.

Alerts: When the user needs to pro-actively get informed about unique situations—both positive and negative—as soon as such a state is reached, the user needs to be informed proactively, so that action can be taken.

Instead of just sending post-facto reports of a result, one can also use alerts to send pre-alerts before the actual problem occurs. This gives a heads up for the business users to prevent or enhance the occurrence of an event according to business needs.

QlikView provides alerts which can be set by the developers / administrators. The Automation API of QlikView can be used to allow users to create user-defined alerts as well.

Presentation

Information can be presented in various ways for the consumption of decision makers. Following are the three ways in which they can be presented: a) Textual, b) Pixel Perfect Reporting and c) On-Screen Graphics.

Textual reporting has been the traditional presentation of data for decision making. With character & high-speed line printers, this form of reporting almost ruled the world. Pre-formatted reports distributed are mostly created with Textual / Tabular outputs.

Pixel Perfect Reporting is the successor of textual reporting. This is done through modern (laser / inkjet) printers for mandatory compliance reporting, to prepare statutory reports for filing in the company and for some of the management reporting. These use high resolution printing and displays available and format the reports with exact pixel perfect alignments. QlikView has added limited pixel perfect capabilities through the PDF report generation functionality. There are third party tools available for printing and distribution of reports.

On-Screen Graphics provides rich visualizations for the users. With interactive analytics and by allowing slicing & dicing for users, the on-screen visualizations add a tremendous depth to the insights. While there are three-dimensional and multi-dimensional data representations available, two-dimensional representations have given the most useful insights due to their simplicity and ease of creation/usage.

QlikView uses two-dimensional charts and graphs, and since all the charts are connected to the data model, which uses AQL, all charts and graphs are interconnected seamlessly. This gives a multi-dimensional analysis capability that is unparalleled. The on-screen graphics can be used in QlikView PDF generation facility to be embedded as charts and graphs in print. This combines the on-screen and pixel-perfect printing capabilities seamlessly, allowing lots of interesting access restriction possibilities.

Security

The core security concern is to see if the solution components have any vulnerability and if any malicious software / hacker can break into the system and cause damage or steal data. Most of the software today are carefully tested for such vulnerabilities and ensured they are strongly fortified. However, it will be a good idea to verify and ensure this.

The deployment architecture should be chosen in such a way that the solution components are deployed behind firewalls for extra protection. This is basic security hygiene which needs to be ensured.

In addition to this basic fortification, security features should protect data from unauthorized access and allow people who have the right permissions to access data permitted for them. To perform this, following features are required: a) Authentication, b) Authorization for Data Access and c) Authorization for Objects (Reports/Sheets/Charts) Access.

Authentication

This is verifying the users' credentials and establishing their identity. This is done by using Username/Password, Security Tokens, Biometric, etc.

Generally the user database is kept in the identity management systems of the enterprise. The most popular ones are the ADS and LDAP. The need is to have the BI solution allow authentication using one of these already existing user DBs.

In addition, there is also Federated Authentication services like the ADFS, Ping Identity Server, etc., which allow users to reach a single server for authentication, but depending on the group they belong to, use different authentication databases as appropriate. This becomes very useful, particularly when there are extranet portals using analytics, and both internal users and extranet (partner and customer) users require to be authenticated.

QlikView supports multiple authentication mechanisms—with ADS, LDAP integration as the most common methods. In addition, Integrated Windows Authentication is also allowed to authenticate against the users database of a single machine. To use custom user DBs, QlikView provides a DMS based solution. This is discussed in detail in the security chapter in Part II.

Authorization

Once the identity of a user is established clearly, the various areas which the user can be allowed to visit or look at are defined by Authorization. While the data available in the system—Data Models or Cubes—is the entire data from the various source systems, the users need to have access only to the data related to their scope of work.

Product managers need to have access to the data to their products only, but across all geographies. Sales Managers of particular geographies require access to all information related to their region, across all products of interest. Similarly function-wise restrictions and role-wise restrictions are all required to be enforced according to the business policies.

This is achieved by the Authorization capability of the solutions. The following multiple layers of Authorization are required:

1. Access to the applications or cluster of reports related to the Function / Department / Geography
2. Access to the particular Reports / Charts / Graphs / Sheets within the application
3. Access to the data that is related to the scope of work / role—of particular product or region or people relevant.

These are implemented in different ways in various solutions. It is important to explore what capabilities are required and ensure the needs of the company are met appropriately.

QlikView implements all these capabilities using what is known as Section Access functionality. This is a very unique way in which security is implemented.

Powerful and flexible, this security solution can allow implementation of very complex security needs of an enterprise (more in chapter on *QlikView Security*).

Collaboration Layer

The purpose of BI is to ensure that the data available is used to create actionable insights. And more importantly, ensure that actions are taken based on those insights. Making use of Actionable Insights, taking informed decisions and actions are the real benefits of BI solutions.

With the complexities increasing, businesses demand far more collaboration than ever before. More minds work together to take decisions, even in small companies. When data is processed and multiple actionable insights are shared, teams of people have to collaboratively analyze these insights, understand, discuss and take conclusive decisions for actions. This requires collaboration as a very important element in the BI solutions. Collaborative Decision Making (CDM) is identified separately by Gartner [5]:

"CDM combines social software with business intelligence. This combination can dramatically improve the quality of decision-making by directly linking the information contained in BI systems with collaborative input gleaned through the use of social software," says a recent Gartner report.

The Computer Weekly article first written in July 2009 speaks about "Business Intelligence: Collaborative Decision-Making" [6].

Collaboration is enabled in companies by three broad capabilities: a) Information Access Devices, b) Sharing Mechanisms and c) Social Features. These three have evolved over time in multiple ways.

Over many decades, even before computers came into being, these capabilities existed and were strongly leveraged in making collaborative decisions. Paper based reporting for information access, notice boards for sharing and socializing / meetings for collaborative decision making are classical solutions.

With the advent of computers, and more importantly, the advent of internet based technologies, the solutions have expanded to provide more alternative ways to collaborate.

Information Access Devices

The number of devices available for accessing information has expanded drastically in the past few years. Though they started off in the consumer information space, enterprises have started taking advantage of such variety of devices.

Desktops, Laptops, Notebooks, Tablets, SmartPhones have all got the capabilities to share information through emails and social networking sites— from wherever people are—not just the knowledge workers, but even line managers.

Even mobiles of minimal capabilities are included into this knowledge network, allowing 2-way communications using SMS (Texting) with the corporate applications.

Any BI solution should provide support to all these devices. Gone are the days when the corporate IT procurement dictated what devices should be bought and provided to employees. Now the employees are bringing their own devices and need to be connected to the enterprise network, and have access to all the capabilities similar to the Internet.

Various software solutions for collaboration, including micro blogging is available across all such devices. Support to all these devices is the basic need to enable collaborative decision making.

Sharing Mechanisms

Sharing information just as a print out or as a document removes the context, and also the thoughts around it. Printouts delivered without the personal presence to discuss it makes it a difficult mechanism to share.

Key to collaboration is the ability to share the information along with the context. Since the BI applications are server based, users from different locations can connect to the server and take a look at the same datasets and collaborate together.

To do this more efficiently, there are new user-created views and snapshots, which can be shared with other users to work together in the same context. This is achieved by using elements like: User-Created Bookmarks, User-Created Graphs and Reports.

Users can capture the current state of analysis as a bookmark and share it with other users, and then get on a call to discuss the state with the context. While analyzing, users can create other ways of looking at the data, of a different metric of interest and formulate a graph or a report to represent that.

These newly created objects need to be shared with other users to collaboratively look at the new findings and seek actionable insights collectively.

These sharing mechanisms are provided by QlikView without any extra components required for the purpose. Out of the box, these features are available for all users, and more details on this are available in the chapter on QlikView Components in Part II.

Social Features

Online shared data model systems, bookmarks and shared objects allow the users to share the context. However, the discussions that they have around such contexts are not captured in these systems.

Conclusions about why the deviations happen between targets and actual get discussed but these Deviation Analyses are not recorded for future reference inside the system. This is allowed by the social features that are now provided in some of the advanced business intelligence systems. Adding notes and annotations, and leaving them for reference of other users is a very important feature required in BI solutions.

In addition, features of micro-blogging like Facebook or Google+ or private enterprise micro-blogging solutions can be integrated with the context of interest, using a bookmark as a unique identifier of the context. This allows multiple threads of discussions to be associated with a context. This can lead to richer discussions that lead to the decision, with a record of all such decisions for future reference and traceability. These are very powerful additions, allowing business users to work together actively on a particular point of concern.

QlikView implements these very well—Notes, Annotations and Social Networking inside the Enterprise—as part of the BI Dashboard / Analytic / Reporting (& Scorecard) / Scenario (What-if) Application. As a powerful combination, this creates the framework for business users to actively collaborate on decision making.

A typical collaborative decision making scenario can be: The CFO receives an alert that one of the biggest projected deals is not happening so he knows the P&L is going to be negatively impacted. At the same time the Sales Manager gets the same alert and both of them jump into action. They get on a conference call, and open the QlikView application that contains the relevant information. The Sales Manager creates a bookmark to capture the context of the scenario. He then shares the bookmark with the CFO and they both look at the same scenario. More people can be invited to open the same application / bookmark, and can participate in the conference. They can now create a Notes / Microblog and start capturing each other's thoughts, and probably arrive at a few alternative choices of actions to take. This can now be sent as a link to the CEO, and can be requested to suggest which of the possible choices can be decided as the next plan of action.

All this can happen irrespective of the devices, where they are currently present and yet take a decision by active collaboration and joint decision making.

Using the Framework to Compare and Combine BI Solutions

What features need to be used? What all are possible to be achieved through the discussions above? Knowing these the solution needs can be defined for the organization clearly. The needs should not stop with the business statements, but should get translated into operational needs. Then the IT department should use the operational needs to prescribe what technical capabilities are essential to meet those needs across the organization.

Organizations need to use this NEEDS-LED approach to define what functionalities are required. This common set of requirements can be used to compare all the products/solutions available in the organization and in the market.

If there are existing solutions in the company, their features can be mapped with this requirement set, to see what requirements can be met by these existing solutions. Some solutions may meet the requirements partially. There is a trade-off required between the investments / ROI vs. the fulfillment of the requirements.

The key factor that needs to be kept in mind in all such considerations is: THE FINANCIAL IMPACT OF DECISIONS which will be enhanced by fulfilling the requirement. If this is significantly high, then replacement of the current solution with a more appropriate and modern solution like QlikView at least for important business functions is recommended and justified.

This approach can be used to define which of the existing products can be used gainfully for which cluster of existing requirements. The remaining requirements not met by existing solutions can be clustered together as requirements for a new system. This way, the already made investments can be protected and put into some more use. And the new investment will be clearly justified with crystal clear view of what improvements they will bring. This will help in satisfying the Return on Investment demands and make BI investment decisions easier.

In some business situations, the requirements are extremely important to improve the business performance. Hence even though there are existing solutions in the company, it may be a much better choice to displace them with new solutions that will give a significant boost to better decision making. A classic analogy that is given is "A cycle takes us anywhere we want. However, to reach early, it is worth considering buying a car, or taking a flight ticket and travelling".

Procedure to Combine BI Technologies

The following process can be used to combine multiple BI technologies:

1. Collect all reports produced currently, with frequencies, # recipients and business impact (time & value)
2. Find out what reports can be retired—not used by anyone
3. Identify all the dimensions and metrics used across all the reports
4. For each metric, fill out the need attributes as shown in the table above
5. Cluster all requirements on these attributes
6. Map existing products for each of these clusters—what is used now, and what is desired
7. Choose new products to fill clusters where improvement is required or not served right now
8. Based on business impact of these clusters, prioritize and sequence them
9. Formulate the BI Roadmap—phased with investment and time needs for each

This approach will bring in a NEEDS-LED analysis of what is required for the enterprise. This will enable the objectivity required to service all the requirements, with the various solutions existing and new.

Challenges in Combining Multiple BI Technologies

While combining various technologies is a natural choice from a business optimization perspective, there are some caveats that need to be kept in mind:

1. Duplication of Data: If the various technologies are going to have different stores of data, each instance of the same data needs to be in sync. The need is to have a single central copy of all the data, and allow all the reporting solutions to use this as the single unified source.
2. Duplication of Rules / Formulae: If all formulae used for various calculations, generally referred to as Business Rules, are distributed across various systems, maintaining consistency across all of them is

a challenge. Finding a way to keep all the rules / formulae in an early stage of the data path is important, preferably in one place where the data is stored.

Conclusions - Effective Decision Making and Creating Wealth

In his book "Revolutionary Wealth", Alvin Toffler talks about *Synchronized Organizations* that will create wealth in a revolutionary way. Synchronization in everything is the key to the growth of world in its current form. From GPS satellites to Cellular Phones to Collaboration Software, everything is about how synchronized we are—the family, the groups, the organizations and the nations. He goes on to mention that only those enterprises which are synchronized will survive from now onwards.

Given this context, Enterprises need to ensure benefits are brought to business users, getting them synchronized, so the value of the company can be taken to higher levels. Make best use of every investment in BI and bring in tools like QlikView to create the interactive synchronization that is required to create Synchronized Organizations. Be Synchronized.

References

1. Analytics: The Widening Divide, How Companies are achieving competitive advantage through analytics, (David Kiron, Rebecca Shockley, Nina Krushwitz, Glenn Finch and Dr. Michael Haydock), MIT Sloan Management Review Research Report FALL 2011, [http://www-935.ibm.com/services/us/gbs/thoughtleadership/ibv-embedding-analytics.html]
2. Business Value with Analytics, Stever Miller, Blog on Information Management, [http://www.information-management.com/blogs/analytics_BI_ROI_MIT_information_management-10021285-1.html]
3. Various whitepapers on Business Strategy / Planning, IT Toolbox.com, [http://businessintelligence.ittoolbox.com/research/biz-str-pl/]

4. What do you think of the Strategy Map exercise, to define and align Business Unit operation & goals with the organisation ones?, Paulo Goncalves & others, [http://www.linkedin.com/answers/management/planning/MGM_PLN/535707-4985197]

5. Collaborative Decision Making (CDM), Gartner Report, [http://mediaproducts.gartner.com/reprints/microsoft/vol6/article8/article8.html]

6. "Business Intelligence: Collaborative Decision-Making", Computer Weekly, July 2009, [http://www.computerweekly.com/feature/Business-intelligence-Collaborative-decision-making]

## CHAPTER 5

WHAT BENEFITS CAN BE EXPECTED FROM QLIKVIEW?

ONE BENEFIT OF BEING POOR IS IT DOES NOT TAKE MUCH TO IMPROVE THE SITUATION

Introduction to the Chapter

Investments in QlikView are done with expectations of returns, in the form of business benefits which can be derived by deploying QlikView, including savings in license, hardware, skills and opportunity costs.

The question "What benefits can QlikView give?" forms the center of the investment decision. The fact is that the benefits are really specific to where the company is, with reference to the current IT setup. Also depending on who is looking at it, benefits are different.

Business users look at benefits that impact the business and processes, while IT users look at what technical and time challenges are solved. Most of the times they are two sides of the same coin: the improvement that QlikView introduces fundamentally into the information dissemination system.

This chapter explores various benefits QlikView can bring into an organization, and discusses what it takes to realize these benefits. It also explores what can prevent organizations from realizing these benefits. A checklist of what benefits can be achieved is included in the end of this chapter. This can be used to set goals and then measure the results that QlikView brings about. Such a list provides a good means to manage expectations objectively, and pursue to achieve them.

Benefits – A practical perspective

Often organizations are unclear about where they are currently. Once we get used to what we have, we take it for granted, and consider it not enough. We believe it can improve or get better in some ways. This happens particularly in information dissemination. Benefit is when we get something completely new, or when we get something more than we have today.

Talking of QlikView, the most important benefit that users can aim to get is *actionable insights*. Only actionable insights can allow businesses to *Improve* and become high-performing to demonstrate constant gain/benefits to the business stake holders. All existing business information systems attempt to provide such actionable insights.

The amount of information that is currently provided by existing information systems to business users is not trivial. However the extent to which these information pieces evoke actionable insights is questionable.

Other benefits expected include improvement in response times, quality of data, integration of data from various sources, access from anywhere, flexibility of analytics, and collaboration. Such benefits are perceived differently by IT and business users. The following two sections focus on these two perspectives before we formulate the checklist for benefits that should be aimed from QlikView.

Need Profile of IT

Taking the layers discussed in the earlier chapter, IT Users spend all their time and energy in ensuring the following:

1. Data and Compute Layers are entirely handled behind the scenes or "back-end". The amount of time spent in the "back-end" is quite significant. There always is a "dead-line" before which all the information or insights have to be provided to the business users. If it is delayed beyond that time limit, then the business cannot use them for that purpose.

2. In the Presentation and Collaboration Layers, when the business users view and interact with the data they require a particular

response time and flexibility. This means that the infrastructure, technology and skills input into the systems should be such that the business needs are met *in-time*.

3. In addition they work to providing "functionalities" for the other two layers—Presentation and Collaboration. To meet the "functionality" requirements, the IT department has to ensure a lot of things: a) highly granular data for flexible analysis, b) various analytic capabilities, c) constant upgrade of the systems with new features.

To meet the timeliness and flexibility needs together, IT makes investments on powerful back-end systems and manages to prepare the data required. Such prepared data is provided to business users generally in Excel or similar packets, so that the business users can do their own analysis in silos of their departments.

Hence the need for IT is to acquire better technologies at a cheaper cost, so that the Data and Compute layers are made more efficient and also flexible. In addition, bring a presentation layer that allows business users to use them flexibly without having to get into silos.

However, the reality is that there are constraints on the amount of investments that can be made for infrastructure, technology and skills. Within the constraints of economic viability, time available and existing technologies, business user needs are taken care of at a compromised level. QlikView eases these challenges and provides an option that needs a lesser Total Cost of Ownership (TCO). The benefits section highlights all the benefits that QlikView can bring about for the IT team.

Business Needs Profile

With complexity and speed of businesses increasing, the need to innovate ways to improve profitability and performance efficiency is the need for business users. Ability to get more such actionable insights is the need from information systems.

For the operational users, the reports and listings they get should be in time, and in more frequency to gain fine-grain monitoring and control of their processes.

For middle-managers and above, information / report systems have to become insight / analysis systems. Ability to find core-need or root-cause and take actions to improve or take advantage of them is the need.

To take such advantage and make businesses become more profitable, four pre-requisites exist: 1) *Timely and accurate* detailed and summarized *information*, 2) *Tools to* flexibly *analyze and discover* data relationships, 3) *Skills to* use the tools and *develop actionable Insights* and 4) *Organizational culture to* collaboratively *take decisions* using insights *and positively act* on them.

The first two are important benefits that are expected of the information systems—IT can help to mature in these. These form the foundation for the business users. The third one has to happen at individual business users' level and fourth at organizational level. Both third and fourth are capabilities that every user should acquire and polish.

Benefiting from BI is more a Culture

It is significant to see how The IBM Research and MIT Sloan Study, The Widening Divide [1], published in fall 2011, presents three required competencies for gaining competitive advantage (2 and 3 above are combined into the second one):

Table 1: Analytics Quotient Contributing Factors

MANAGE THE DATA	UNDERSTAND THE DATA	ACT ON THE DATA
Information Management	Analytics Skills and Tools	Data-oriented Culture
• Solid information foundation • Standardized data management practices • Insights accessible and available	• Skills developed as a core discipline • Enabled by a robust set of tools and solutions • Develop action-oriented insights	• Fact-driven leadership • Analytics used as a strategic asset • Strategy and operations guided by insights

*Managing the data—Information Management—*is the foundation and it is expected from IT, as discussed (in point 1) above. *Understanding the data—Analytics Skills and Tools—*has been discussed as (points 2 and 3) Tools and Skills above. *Act on the Data—Data-Oriented Culture—*is equivalent to point 4 above—led by Fact-Driven Leadership.

Data-oriented culture is the most challenging element and this requires change in all levels of the company. But luckily it's also a by-product more than a pre-requisite across the company. In fact, making data available, and key leaders becoming fact-driven, actually brings data-oriented culture in organizations quickly.

QlikView can straightaway provide benefits in 1 & 2: Timely Data Availability and Tools for Insights. In addition it provides support to cultivate a collaborative data culture by multiple ways of sharing insights and work collectively using them. With this as the background, the following sections explain in more detail what benefits QlikView can provide, for business and for IT users.

There is a lot of interest in making culture work for BI implementations. In a video, included in the references, Howard Dresner talks about importance of culture for successful BI [2]. Howard, now the founder of Dresner Advisory Services, was Chief Strategy Officer of Hyperion (2005 to 2007) after his 13 yrs stint at Gartner—he coined the word "Business Intelligence" in 1989. Other articles are provided in the references for discerning readers. The Nov 2011, ITBusinessEdge.com article on "Creating a Business Intelligence Culture" by Ann All [3], collates some trends happening.

Benefits of QlikView

Benefits of Business Intelligence have been discussed in various articles and books extensively. There are a few references which are interesting that are added in the references section below [5, 6, 7, 8, 9, 10]. Particularly, the article "Measuring the benefits of Business Intelligence" by Peter James Thomas [4], posted Feb 2009, is a good read as a background—discussions have been going on this article even up to Aug 2011. Also the Enterprise Apps Today article "Ten Benefits of Business Intelligence Software" of Nov 2010 by Jennifer Schiff [3] is a good read.

The crux of them all: *Eliminate Guesswork and Get Fast Actionable Insights to Business Questions*. These have the potential to improve business performance and are expected as key benefits from BI. Particularly with QlikView, some of its capabilities make these benefits more pronounced and the impacts can be much more than with other tools. In the Chapter on "What is QlikView?" the unique capabilities of

QlikView were discussed. (Please view that chapter, if you have not already, before proceeding to understand the benefits of QlikView).

The following sections discuss about benefits that QlikView can bring about for business and IT users in separate sections. This will help in monitoring and measuring how QlikView can bring benefits.

QlikView is like a kitchen set. For the cooks, the benefits it offers are so obvious. It makes cooking a pleasure, makes it faster, easier and richer. They can apply multiple techniques of cooking, to create different tasty dishes in shorter times. Quicker, Faster, Easier, Richer and Tastier dishes—in short describes what a cook will experience. However, from the perspective of consumers, who come to appreciate food, the tool does not make any difference. However, shades of taste produced, the textures produced in the food will be felt and appreciated sincerely. They need to experience it. Some of the attributes of experience include: time for serving, consistency of quality across serves, balance of tastes, quantity to fulfill and fragrance.

The same holds true with the business users when it comes to QlikView. The following section highlights the benefits that business users can derive and experience on a daily basis.

Benefits for Business Users

What is accepted as benefits by business users is very different from what IT perceives as benefits for the business users. Business users are interested in how their information needs are taken care of and how quickly they are able to take decisions and actions.

QlikView can bring the following benefits for business users:
1. Less Dependency on IT for data and insights
   a. Data and reports of multiple systems can be integrated into one report set / application
   b. No need for data-warehouses—however they can be leveraged if they exist
   c. Static reports automatically delivered in mail or folder
   d. Access interactive reports on browser interface with quick response

    e.   Easy to implement security with flexibility of access in the hands of business units

    f.   Summary and detailed information can exist in the same application in a unified view

    g.   Move towards self-service of data/information/insights

2. Automated Timely Availability of Insights

    a.   Once IT creates dashboards, daily data refresh is automated

    b.   Reports / analytics can be made available near-real-time

    c.   Efficient distribution of analytics / reports—delivered in time— as Interactive / Static / Text based updates

    d.   Compliance reports, scorecards can be generated quickly & dispatched with least effort

    e.   Mass generation of reports for large number of users is possible – can be transmitted as mails, files and messages.

3. Lesser Time Spent on Data Preparation / Reconciliation

    a.   Lesser time spent on local processing of data that IT provides

    b.   More time on analysis / decision making / actions

    c.   Lesser time for reconciliations—mostly not required

    d.   Quick ability to find root-cause for differences without help of IT

4. Available Anywhere – Analyze on Demand

    a.   Single front-end once created is accessible from multiple devices

    b.   Access from any device, anywhere on Laptops, Desktops, Tablets (iPad, Android and others), Smart-phones (iPhone, Android phones and others)

    c.   Static Distribution of Reports (PDFs / XLS / etc) and Interactive Analysis On-Demand (through Browser on any device)

5. More Reports in Less Time

    a.   QlikView gives a much faster time to reports—conception to completion of new ones

    b.   Lesser time required for IT and providers

    c.   Many reports can be created by business users—as required—even on mobile devices

6.   Ease of Adding New Data

    a.   Adding data from external sources / Excel Sheets / Access Files / Web sites is very easy

    b.   Can add new fields to existing tables directly—calculated dimensions & measures

    c.   New classification of data can happen very quickly—even without IT involvement (or with very less IT involvement)

    d.   Actual vs. Target/budget reports / analytics can be created very easily even if target/budgets don't exist in the back-end systems (with lesser or no IT involvement)

7.   Quicker Richer Insights - Discover New Relationships within Data

    a.   Dashboards, Scorecards, What-if Analyses and Rich Interactive Reports can be made available for business users easily

    b.   Navigability across different reports in a report set / application without losing the context of analysis in flexible ways

    c.   Scorecards, Charts / Graphs, What-if Analysis and Dashboards allow quick understanding of patterns

    d.   Trends and Distributions on any chosen dimension

    e.   Comparative Analysis across dynamic segments/groups of data—periods, products, people, customers, geographies, etc.

    f.   Integrated GIS analysis (using Google Maps etc)

    g.   Quick formulation of new hypothesis using all the interactive features

8.   Quicker Hypothesis Testing

    a.   Validate any hypothesis of data relationships very quickly

    b.   Slicing and dicing from any level to any level—highest aggregated level down to the lowest detail level & back—just with few clicks

    c.   Dynamically defined hierarchy of dimensions and metrics

d. Drill Across from any dimension to any other dimension and back in a few clicks

e. Supports statistical tests to validate hypotheses easily

f. Find root-causes for patterns/relationships and define actions

9. Easier and Better Sharing / Collaboration

a. Export and share data / observations in Excel, pictures or XML as files / emails

b. New Charts / Graphs and reports created can be shared with others selectively

c. Bookmark the current status of analysis and share with other users asynchronously

d. Collaborate with others through a discussion around bookmarks, trends and patterns

e. Share a session of analysis / navigation with any other user (even non-licensed) anywhere synchronously

10. Get Pro-active Information for Action

a. Get automated alerts on alarm conditions—easy to get intimated even when not in office through emails and Text (SMS) messages

b. Add new reports and KPIs on the fly as required—driven by the internal and/or external events. Majority of the new requirements can be done without having to go to IT

11. Better Extensibility

a. All new chart types from Google Charts, and similar charting engines can be used easily

b. With appropriate training, custom formulae can be implemented quickly by business users to create new metrics/measures

c. Predictive Analytics, Scoring Models and Optimization tools like R can be integrated seamlessly (with little one time help from IT)

12. Lower Total Cost of Ownership (TCO) and Greater ROI

a. Lesser lost time of business users to find right answers
b. Lesser time to find root causes for problems and fix
c. Lower TCO
d. More self-service reduces additional IT and support required
e. Lesser time and costs for services

All these benefits can contribute towards getting actionable insights quicker, cheaper and taking better decisions. This will help the company have incremental improvements continuously, and build a strong competitiveness and grow.

Benefits for IT Users

The benefits of IT users are basically based on the features discussed in the chapter on "What is QlikView?" In a nutshell, IT users can spend lesser time on the day-to-day data management activities and save their time for more strategic work. They can now focus on data integrity and quality of the data layer and more powerful back-end analytics; move the compute and presentation layers to be managed by the Business Analysts (Power Users); and make the usage easy for the Business Users—more of self-service rather than centralized IT bottlenecks.

In detail, following are the benefits that IT users can gain:

1. Lesser Time for Development
   a. Lesser time for development of reports
   b. Rapid agile application development process
   c. Easier validation for individual reports—required only at the Data Model Level

2. Lesser Storage Space Required
   a. No pre-joining required, hence no data bloating
   b. No pre-aggregation and cubes required
   c. Data size reduces in QlikView by over 80% and hence lesser space required

3. Lesser day-to-day support / administration
   a. Lesser time spent on daily report processing and delivery
   b. Can enable more automation for existing reports

    c.   Self-service for most new reports as well

4. Powerful and Flexible Security
   a. Security settings can be flexible
   b. Lesser time spent to manage security
   c. Authentication can be integrated / SSO
   d. Authorization rights can be delegated
   e. Extensive auditing and tracking of usage

5. Better Data and Rules Integrity
   a. Single point data and rules storage / processing
   b. Lesser time for reloading and processing
   c. No pre-joining, hence lesser time for pre-processing
   d. No pre-aggregation, hence lesser time for pre-processing
   e. Lesser time for validation and reconciliations
   f. Simplified Metadata management

6. Self Service for Business Users reduces IT time
   a. Access from Desktops / Laptops / Tablets and Smart phones without separate development for all of them
   b. Multiple features for sharing among users
   c. Features for collaboration among various users
   d. Tracking of collaboration and sharing among users

7. Lower Total Cost of Ownership (TCO) and Greater ROI
   a. Lower hardware and software costs
   b. More self-service reduces IT intervention required
   c. Lesser time and costs for services
   d. Reduced IT TCO
   e. Overall reduction in Cost Per Report and Time Per Report

8. Easy Scalability and Enterprise Support
   a. Unified Enterprise Deployment Administration
   b. Single Sign On—integration with any directory service / custom DB
   c. Clustering—load balancing and high-availability
   d. Version control integration in the development layer

9. Better Extensibility and Automation
   a. Easy integration and automation with Automation APIs
   b. Finer control over Automating Reload, User Management and Other Admin functions using Server and Publisher APIs
   c. Extensibility APIs for extensions to include features from other products like R
   d. Can easily use external services / products like Google Maps, Google Charts, etc.

10. Better Responses to Business
   a. Accurate & timely reports help increase the good will for IT
   b. IT will be free to focus on business and technical process improvements, and increase profitability of the company
   c. Visibility and transparency in the company can improve working conditions and will be truly IT enabled

All these benefits for IT users can make their lives easier. Free them from the daily drudge of MIS and Reporting/Analytics. The trend across the world is to have IT leaders take on Supply Chain, Process Improvement and other responsibilities. They also play a more central role in strategy, since they have a 360 degree view of the business due to the data integration and familiarity.

Checklist for Benefits

The above list of benefits defined for both business users and IT users can be taken as a reference check list. The approach used for measuring benefits can be in the following steps:

At the start of the QlikView project (creating a reference checklist)

1. Take the above lists for business and IT users as a starting point
2. For each benefit listed, identify the relevance of that benefit in the company on a 10 point scale, scoring the relative importance of each of the benefits
3. Higher scores are items that are more required. They can be planned to be done earlier on the roadmap (80/20 rule). Also solutions should be chosen to meet these key requirements.

At any point during implementation/use of QlikView

4. Take the list and score the achievement on the same 10 point scale, reflecting how much of the expectation is satisfied

5. The difference between the original expectation scores and the current score is the gap between the need and achievement

6. Based on these differences the actual implementation priorities can be changed

Repeating this exercise often and keeping close watch on the achievement of benefits using QlikView is necessary to continuously gain benefits with QlikView.

The method suggested is a quick and approximate measurement system, instead of very accurate and elaborate measurement systems. These measurements cannot be used for standardized comparisons of benefits achieved with other QlikView customers. Hopefully standardized test / measurements would be created in future for such comparisons across companies using different Data Discovery tools including QlikView.

What Can Prevent Achieving these Benefits?

While QlikView is a good product, and can provide all the above benefits, there are many bottlenecks due to which the desired benefits are not achieved. Some such experiences are presented below to be aware of and avoid while QlikView is implemented in enterprises:

1. Insufficient investments can delay / prevent benefits

   Hardware investments are postponed to much later in a project. Hence development and first experience of users are severely affected. For less risk, insufficient number of licenses is taken, but not enough users get access to the solution, during and after development.

2. Affinity/attachment to old technology conventions

   QlikView is a radically different technology compared to other SQL based solutions. Most existing BI and other IT department members do not understand this, and try to solve problems using SQL queries inside QlikView. This reduces the effectiveness of the solution and postpones the benefits greatly. Habits die hard.

3. Lack of Needs-Led Strategy

With the excitement about features of QlikView, problems that are not so important are chosen to solve first. It is important to choose the problems that are of serious importance for the business users, giving a good impact on the bottom-line or top-line of the company. As discussed in the previous chapter, defining a NEEDS-LED requirement with priorities defined is important.

4. Not choosing the right level of granularity for right windows of time

QlikView allows use of data at all granularities for all periods. However, the memory and CPU requirements will increase as granular transaction level data is used for all the periods. Business may not need such granularity across all periods. In other situations, already aggregated data is chosen, like from BW cubes, to create QlikView applications. This does not provide the ability to drill-down to find root-causes. Hence it is important to choose right granularities as a good trade-off to choose the right sized hardware and application relevance.

5. Not Saying No To QlikView sometimes

QlikView cannot possibly solve all the problems. Particularly problems that are in the Advanced Analytic space may not get completely solved just with QlikView. Maybe there is a need to combine QlikView with other tools like R, or just get them solved outside of QlikView.

6. Not Taking advantage of already made investments

Most companies have invested in data warehouse, cube technologies etc. Particularly companies using product of stack vendors like SAP (BW, BO, SAP Query, BEX, etc), Oracle (OWH, Discoverer, OBIE, etc), IBM (DB2, Cognos, etc) and recently Microsoft (BI solutions) may have made significant investments into those technologies. It is important to architect QlikView solutions in such a way that already made investments are taken advantage of.

7. Not taking appropriate training on QlikView

Since QlikView is a very different technology, and it uses AQL instead of SQL, the developers and modelers have to be trained afresh in new Modelling approach. Deploying developers from SQL without appropriate training will make them create applications that do not take advantage of QlikView's features. This can also lead to negative experiences for the business users.

8. Not taking Expert Advice on Architecture and Deployment

QlikView turns the data management upside down from a sizing perspective—less storage and more memory in general. Sizing for servers, licensing choices are all unique to QlikView and taking expert guidance on these is a good idea. Security, data Modelling and deployment techniques are also unique with QlikView.

9. Not doing periodic application performance tuning

Since QlikView is flexible and easy to develop/use, the models and presentation layer are created using agile development model. This leads to deployments with technical inefficiencies while the business questions are answered quickly. It helps to invite expert service professionals, get applications reviewed / audited and take advice on what improvements can help. Such an exercise is typically useful two times a year. If there are multiple developers and modelers managing the applications, such inefficiencies creep in, requiring tuning more often.

Conclusions - Maximizing Benefits from QlikView

QlikView keeps improving with newer releases. Some of the improvements are radical in nature. Getting the developers trained on these improvements and ensuring they are used in the updated applications is a key to maximizing benefits from QlikView.

Encouraging all the stake holders involved in QlikView projects to participate in the QlikCommunity, and various other forums that exist, is a good idea. Some of the forums are provided in the references section.

Regularly visiting the QlikView.com site and checking out the success stories presented there is another idea to get inputs on what new benefits can be aimed at. Particularly, case studies of companies in similar businesses can give a lot of good ideas.

QlikView can bring benefits much quicker than most other tools. The challenge that is commonly seen is the "Hockey Stick Effect" where all of a sudden more users want to have QlikView for their analysis, and there is a sudden surge of requests. Please ensure all requests are carefully evaluated, checked against the initial roadmap, and make changes only if the new request is of higher importance and impact, to help the company.

Enabling users to create their own charts, share and collaborate is the most important way to maximize the benefits of QlikView. Collaborative decision making, and actions based on actionable insights is the key to successful future organizations.

References

1. Analytics: The Widening Divide, How Companies are achieving competitive advantage through analytics, (David Kiron, Rebecca Shockley, Nina Krushwitz, Glenn Finch and Dr. Michael Haydock), MIT Sloan Management Review Research Report FALL 2011, [http://www-935.ibm.com/services/us/gbs/thoughtleadership/ibv-embedding-analytics.html]

2. For business intelligence success, culture counts as much as technology, Howard Dresner, Sep 2009, [http://searchbusinessanalytics.techtarget.com/podcast/For-business-intelligence-success-culture-counts-as-much-as-technology]

3. Ten Benefits of Creating a Business Intelligence Software Culture, Jennifer Schiff, Ann All, Nov 2010, Enterprise Apps Today2011, ITBusinessEdge.com, [http://www.enterpriseappstodayitbusinessedge.com/cm/blogs/all/creating-a-business-intelligence/ten-benefits-of-business-intelligence-software-1.html-culture/?cs=48976]

4. Measuring the benefits of Aligning Business Intelligence, Peter James Thomas, Feb to Organizational Culture, Jerry Kurtyka, Information Management Special Reports, March 2009, [http://peterjamesthomaswww.information-

management.com/specialreports/2009/02/26/measuring-the-benefits-of-business-intelligence/ 131/10015066-1.html]

5. QlikView Maven, QlikView Blog, [http://qlikviewmaven.blogspot.com]
6. QlikView Notes, QlikView Blog, [http://qlikviewnotes.blogspot.com]
7. Quick – Qlear – Qool, QlikView Blog, [http://www.quickqlearqool.nl]
8. QlikMetrics, QlikView Marketing Intelligence Blog, [http://qlikmetrics.com]
9. QlikSter, The QlikView Integration & Mashup Blog, [http://www.qlikster.com]
10. And Points Beyond, QlikView Blog, [http://andpointsbeyond.com/]

## CHAPTER 6

What Should Be The QlikView Strategy For My Company?

Even Elephants Can Be Eaten One Spoon At a Time

Introduction to the Chapter

Every organization is unique. *Information* is a key common factor that enables every organization to be high-performing, makes them continuously improve and grow. Making necessary information available to more people inside the organization is necessary to improve efficiency and create profitable growth.

QlikView precisely addresses this need to make information available to more people in the company—both in static and interactive forms. This increases the efficiency of organizations since they are able to zero-in on the root-cause of problems and levers of growth. Use of QlikView is intended to allow actionable insights and increase of efficiency.

There are various abstract and tangible factors that affect the way in which QlikView will bring benefits to the company. The abstract factors are all cultural in nature, and tangible factors are data and technology related. This chapter enlists all these factors and also other strategic points that need to be kept in mind while defining a roadmap for QlikView implementation in the company.

Around each of the factors, the company needs to understand where they stand, make choices, set goals and define a roadmap. Such decisions become cornerstones for deployment, and characterize the usefulness of QlikView for the company. These decisions define the path and success of QlikView usage in the company throughout the life cycle.

In the beginning information inclusion is introduced as a measure to represent the sum total of the background factors like culture, policies and belief systems. Readiness for QlikView is discussed next, including various factors that affect/influence its deployment. With this readiness assessment, the size of the first deployment is discussed with options and their implications. Taking these factors into account, an approach for a successful implementation is defined irrespective of the size of the deployment.

Then the chapter develops a checklist of all strategic items which need to be specifically addressed appropriately, and right choices to be made, for a successful deployment of QlikView. Not just for the first time, but to shape as an enterprise wide solution producing continuous improvement.

Assessing Culture - *Information Inclusion*

From 2003, *Financial Inclusion* has been a buzz of the world economies, particularly the developing countries. To quote Wikipedia, "Financial Inclusion is the delivery of financial services at affordable costs to sections of disadvantaged and low income segments of society".

Similar to Financial Inclusion, one can define *Information Inclusion:* "to deliver information at affordable costs to all sections of a company, including the disadvantaged (i.e., not in the power ring of 'C' Level people). This will enable everyone in the company to make Data-Driven-Decisions (DDD)—informed choices at every level".

> *Two interesting readings on Data Driven Decision Making are included in the references section of this chapter: 1) Bayesian Data-Driven Decision Making by Jim Harris in his blog[1], 2) Intuition Vs. Data-Driven Decision-Making: Some Rough Ideas by Bob Sutton [2] in his blog. Discerning users who look for proof of benefits of DDD can read the research paper: "How Does Data-Driven Decision Making Affect Firm Performance" by Erik Brynjolfsson, et al [3]- talks about his research paper that publishes field research results on how DDD correlates to productivity and better asset utilization in companies.*

Such data-driven companies show a great propensity to higher productivity and greater competitiveness. This is a sum total of what the company practices at various levels, and how data driven the company is. It is the essential culture of the company and how it manifests itself.

The extent of information inclusion in a company is a result of the following factors:

Depth of Management is a reflection of the organizational structure, and the vision with which the company was formed and is run. This is typically driven by the board and the core management teams. Delegation is a good indicator of management depth— higher the delegation in a company greater the information inclusion in the company.

Data-Based Collaborative Decision making culture is a very important factor in taking advantage of QlikView. To use the visibility and insights it provides the culture of the organization should promote data-based and insight-driven decision making. Collaboration should be practiced in the management group as a core discipline.

Policy of sharing information is an indicator of democratization of data. This allows anyone who can take advantage of a piece of data to use it and take better decisions that will allow the company to become better. In certain industries and situations democratization is not the best way, and recognition of this is very important in defining the right strategy and approach for QlikView implementation.

Lastly, level of *Enablement with Data and Technology* in the company is a very important factor in information inclusion. If data and necessary technology components don't exist in the company, the ideals of information inclusion stay theoretical.

Extent of information inclusion in a company decides the demand for information as well. The culture to use the data / information / insights is present only in companies where the information inclusion is high. The MIT Sloan and IBM research study is once again a great reference to know about the impact Data-Driven-Decision-Making can have.

> Two practical indicators of Information Inclusion can be:
> *Inclusion Ratio = # Levels that get reports sent to / # Levels that exist*
> *Reports Per Manager = Total reports generated / # Managers in the company*
> Such indicators can give a broad idea of how much of an information culture the organization has. Higher information inclusion shows the need in the organization for dissemination of information across the company. Companies with higher Information Inclusion will greatly benefit from QlikView. And QlikView will further contribute to high levels of data driven decision making.

Success of any QlikView deployment is determined greatly by the information inclusion existing among the designated users of QlikView. QlikView strategy should enable increase in information inclusion of the company, and allow more data-driven decisions across all levels.

Forming the QlikView Strategy

When bringing a new solution like QlikView, the questions that normally come up in the discussions include the following:

How ready is the organization for QlikView?

What needs QlikView will address? What benefits to expect?

How large our QlikView deployment should be?

Where do we get our funds from?

What happens to existing BI investments?

What QlikView cannot do or is not expected to do?

What should be our approach and roadmap?

What are the important preparatory steps we need to take?

What are the choices we need to make?

What is the list of things that we need to do?

It is necessary to answer all such questions, and make the necessary choices and plan. Such answers, along with the details of the plan together form the QlikView Strategy document of the company. The following sections discuss the various elements of such a document.

Readiness for QlikView

In formulating the QlikView Strategy for the company, the first and most important factor is to understand the readiness of the organization. The readiness is a resultant inter-play of the following key factors:

Policy of Information	Organizational Readiness to enable more levels of employees to use information and take decisions—more open the policy, higher the usefulness of QlikView
Data Availability	Amount of data captured and available for analysis—any data available small, large or very large—can be best used by QlikView
Data Quality	Quality of data to be used for reliable decision making—even if lower quality, QlikView can be used to create visibility and help improve data quality gradually
Technology	Already made technology investments— especially for process support & decision making. Higher the investments, more the benefits from QlikView
Skills	Skills available in various levels (not just CxO) to use data/analysis develop insights—QlikView benefits from these skills & improves them too
Data-driven Decision	Extent to which data-driven decisions are taken—more the data-driven culture higher the use of QlikView and in-turn, increase in Data Driven Decision culture
Existing DSS Costs	Higher cost and complexity of existing decision support systems—can be reduced by QlikView

Documenting the current status of each of these readiness factors and scoring them on a weighted scale given below is a great way to clearly assess the Readiness for QlikView (table below).

Scoring process: For each item, assign scores on a scale of 10, and multiply by the weight % in the above table. Take the total of the results and divide by 100 to get the score of the QlikView Readiness. If an organization scores high on all these factors, then the organization is more ready to absorb QlikView inside the company, and create maximum returns for the organization.

Table 1: Readiness for QlikView Implementation

READINESS FACTOR	WEIGHT %	SCORING GUIDE
Policy of Information	10	1 – Less Open, 10 – More Open
Data Availability	20	1 – Little Data, 10 – Large Data Available
Data Quality	10	1 – Low Quality, 10 – Good Quality
Technology	10	1 – Less Technology Investments, 10 – High Technology Investments
Skills	20	1 – Low Data Analytic Skills, 10 – High Data Analytic Skills
Data-driven Decision	10	1 – Low Data Driven Decisions (more intuitive), 10 – High # Data Driven Decisions
Existing DSS Costs	20	1 – Low DSS Costs right now, 10 – High DSS Costs Right Now

Scoring on the above factors preferably needs to be done at the organizational level. However, in large organizations particularly, where the deployment needs to happen for a department or a region, scoring can be done for the chosen section of the organization.

Based on the above readiness score, one can choose to take different approaches to deploy QlikView. In general, higher the readiness score, quicker the results from QlikView can be, and roll-out can pay-off quicker. Higher scores also indicate that more investments can be planned by the organization, and returns can be faster. As a general guideline, the items that have got lower scores in the table above need to be given higher importance and focus during the implementation.

Defining the Needs / Benefits and Choosing a Sponsor

The last chapter focused on defining the needs of the users and creating a Benefits Checklist. Such a list is an important part of the strategy of QlikView for the organization. This sets the expectations clearly, and allows the priorities to be set, as to which benefits need to be focused in the beginning and which ones later. This list also becomes a reference target, which needs to be achieved by the QlikView project.

Based on the needs and benefits list, one can identify the key departments / functions which are going to be benefited from the initiative. The head of one of the departments, who is also a key influencer in the overall organization progress needs to be taken as a Sponsor for the project. Different sponsors can be identified for different phases of the entire project.

Choosing a powerful sponsor is one of the most important needs for making a QlikView project successful like any other BI project. This sponsor should clearly appreciate and support Data-Driven Decision-Making (DDD) in the company. Any education required for this sponsor for this purpose needs to be given well before the start of the project. Ideally, the strategy should be formulated under the aegis of such a sponsor. The higher the level of such a sponsor, better it is for the success of the QlikView initiative.

Size of Deployment

One of the classical questions is "How large my QlikView deployment should be?" This also implicitly keeps the cost factor in it. The answer to this depends on all the readiness factors, and also the budget that is available in hand for the solution to be implemented. The readiness score is a very good measure to determine the scale of deployment.

The typical choices available for Scale of Deployment: a) Individual, b) Function Level, c) Department Level, d) Process Level and e) Enterprise Level.

Individual deployment is generally done for personal usage or in an enterprise during the early stages of evaluation. A single user downloads QlikView from the website and performs all the functions on his/her own desktop/laptop. However if the evaluation gets more extensive, then the involvement of QlikTech partners is necessary to get the trial server licenses and also get necessary help.

Most of the early deployments in an enterprise are done either for a *single function / department*. This requires very little investment, and helps demonstrate the use of QlikView very well. While these allow quick wins, in the long term the enterprise wide deployment becomes challenging. With enterprise wide design of ETL + Data Models, the departmental approach also can be made to fit into the long term enterprise wide deployment.

While functions / departments are intuitively considered as units of BI, the true units of BI deployment should be *Processes*. Order to Cash is an example of a process. Metrics representing each stage of the process can be put into same dashboards / analytic reports to understand the interplay of one over the other. Even for process wide deployments, ETL + Data Models should be made with enterprise wide thinking.

Enterprise wide deployment will be like creating a palace straight away, instead of combining multiple huts and houses into a palace gradually. The entire design needs to be for a palace, though different portions are constructed in stages to create the final palace.

QlikView as a technology does not put any restriction on where to start, and how large should be the deployment. It offers flexibility in choosing the size of deployment according to the need. It can expand as the need grows. One can start small (Departmental / Process level) incrementally grow (to include more departments / processes) and end in an enterprise deployment. Such step-by-step growth is more common. Other alternative is to have a big bang deployment for the entire enterprise in a single go, particularly suitable for relatively smaller organizations.

Land and Expand is a recommended strategy for the QlikView deployment. This essentially means start with one high impact need, realize benefits and then deploy for other needs—A Quick Win Approach. How large the first initiative should be, in terms of users and investments, is determined by the readiness score and value of the returns or benefits identified.

If the readiness score of the organization is high, the entire organization will gain from all the benefits that QlikView can provide. Hence the deployment can be taken at the organization level.

Funds for the QlikView Project

The traditional BI initiatives generally have the entire project funded as an IT initiative. Hence the IT budgets are really large and are difficult to justify returns. This also does not put enough pressure on the business users to try and take advantages of the BI initiative. With a clear list of needs and expectation of benefits for both business and IT, it is possible to get the funds allocated from both functions. While IT can focus and invest in the core layers of Data and Compute, respective businesses can be made to invest in making the presentation and collaboration layers available for the various business users.

The costs for ETL (Data Layer) and Data Model (Compute Layer) aspects can be taken care of by IT while the user based licensing can be taken care of by the businesses.

What happens to our Existing BI Investments?

All investments done in the Data and Compute layers can be taken advantage of to a large extent. If a data warehouse is already implemented, with lots of calculations already done there, then QlikView can simply use that output and primarily work on Presentation and Collaboration layers.

If the investment has been done on CUBE based technologies, then the benefits should be continued. QlikView should be deployed in areas where the earlier solution is not catering to, and then over time, all such requirements can be migrated to QlikView platform, in case the advantages are significant.

To be specific, if the earlier solutions meet the operational static report distribution, then they can be continued as is. If additional interactive analytic capabilities are required on top of the static reports, then QlikView can replace the old solution. As an example, a large manufacturing group has SAP with BW/BO for producing Financial Reports and distribute to all the constituent company finance departments. The Finance team wanted a capability to drill down to individual transaction records, to reconcile the accounts and ensure the reports are indeed reflecting all the adjustments. Such a requirement needs an interactive analytic capability. Hence the company has chosen QlikView for the purpose.

What QlikView cannot do or is not expected to do?

QlikView does not provide the following out of the box (refer Gartner Magic Quadrant 2011). However there are ways by which these can be taken care of by extending QlikView appropriately:

a. *Enterprise Wide MetaData Layer*: Creation of common definitions and calculations is made very important by this need. Also the need is to use a Unified Data Model as an intermediate staging, from where all the data is pulled into the various QlikView applications (Presentation / Collaboration Layer).

b. *High Volume Enterprise Reporting is not available out of the box*: The PDF publisher addresses this need to a large extent. Additionally, if more flexibility is required including multiple formats other than PDF, then the QlikView Automation API can be easily used to service the needs.

c. *Planning module*: There is no planning module available along with QlikView. The need is to use a best of breed planning application. In fact this can be an advantage rather than a disadvantage—planning applications appropriate for the company and its business can be chosen and used. QlikView helps in seamlessly integrating multiple data sources into the Unified Data Model, and hence any planning application can be used with equal ease.

d. *Predictive Modelling*: Advanced Analytics as discussed in an earlier chapter is an iterative back-office process, which is used to define the models by using Modelling techniques like Data Mining, Statistical Scoring and Segmentation. Such models can be seamlessly integrated into the QlikView Presentation / Collaboration Layers using the Extensible API.

Approach for QlikView Deployment

Choosing the right approach to deploy QlikView is extremely important—QlikView can change the way in which companies function, particularly the management. The approach should keep in mind the need for change management, and should choose the right momentum to ensure that the change is managed systematically.

The outline of approach that has produced success in QlikView implementations:

- Past Data Analysis as a first step

  - Get meaningful insights about past and understand patterns

  - Compare today with "What we were" (Last Year, Last Month, Last Qtr, etc)

- Integrate Budget, Planning and Forecasting with Actuals

  - Compare CONTINUALLY with "What We want to be" (Targets/Budgets)

- Measure Performance at every level

  - Define KPIs of performance

  - Mirror on everyone's desk and Create "Creative Pressure"

- Integrate Market Data

  - Compare with Industry and Competition

- Create an Enterprise Collaboration Framework

  - Workflow, Shared Calendar, Common Issue Log

- Analyze and Predict Future

  - Data Models, Statistics and Scoring

If there is a BI solution already in the company, some of the above may be addressed already. Based on the stage in which the company is currently, and the challenges it is facing wherever it is now, the above approach can be adjusted and adopted. If there is no pressure to focus straight-away on the later steps, it is strongly recommended to follow the approach outlined above for the QlikView deployment.

Formulating a QlikView Roadmap

In any organization, the information needs are addressed to some degree and is currently fitted into the decision making process of the company. This forms the working culture of the organization currently. Introducing QlikView will bring new ways of getting data, and also analyzing. Some of this will replace older ways of getting information and the way analysis was done in the past. Many times, new metrics are introduced which did not exist in the company earlier.

In all these situations, the need is to figure out how the new information available shall be used by various stake holders. What information means what to them, and what should be their actions / reactions to such information? More importantly how their current decision making process will change. This is at the core of introducing QlikView into the company.

With this understanding, changes have to be introduced step-by-step from a business user stand point. Choice of such stage-wise changes will help determine the roadmap.

In addition to the business process changes, Data and Compute layer improvements can happen with QlikView. All the current IT processes used in the company for ETL, consolidation, computations and report generation can be improved by using QlikView. This essentially improves the efficiency of these IT processes. Depending on the complexity of the existing IT processes, a stage-wise migration plan is to be devised to systematically move the older setup to the new setup with QlikView to realize the benefits envisaged.

The best method is to define different Phases. In each phase identify and define what will be done for the IT processes and what will be done for the business users. Also define the various change management initiatives that will be taken up in each of the phases. This will ensure that the plans for training and development can be taken in sync with these phases.

The approach provided in the previous section can be used as the different phases, and these can be further split by time periods, budgets and subset of needs. In every phase, the following aspects should be covered:

Data & Compute Layer	ETL processes, business rules, people and systems involved, intended changes and benefits
Presentation Layer	Reports / Analytics / Dashboards involved, people and processes involved, intended changes and benefits
Timelines	Phases divided into stages, various players and their roles

Budgets	Expected costs: stage wise, source of funds, capex / opex
Change Management	Plan for process changes and associated training needs
Benefits	List of benefits expected at the end of each phase

With the above aspects covered, a phase wise roadmap for the entire QlikView deployment should be created, and set as the overall plan. Such a roadmap, with intended benefits should be shared with a governing body—having representatives from both Business and IT.

Implementing the Strategy

Creating the roadmap is the first step to implement the strategy and approach discussed above. Setting time lines for each of the phases, defining owners and stating expected benefits in measureable terms is the next important need.

Agreeing on the change process and including them as part of the KRAs of various members of the IT and business members is a very effective way to implement.

Creation of a steering committee and including the key stake holders of the beneficiary groups, and also the sponsor is a very important step. This committee should periodically review the progress and ensure the implementation progresses in the planned way.

Cost of Not Implementing QlikView

In a very innovative approach, some of the enthusiasts inside QlikTech have created an interesting application to calculate the ROI of deploying QlikView. It actually uses unique *ROI and Cost of Delay Model*. This model is explained in the whitepaper titled "Right Decisions Matter the Most – Now" (see references). This is also extensively quoted in various articles and pointed to by most websites talking about QlikView. The QlikView application created for this model allows companies to project the benefits that the company can derive by using QlikView. It is a very good idea to request for this model application from the QlikTech partners / reps and get a monetary indication of what value of benefits can be achieved. Interestingly, it also gives an idea of how much would the company lose or spend more, in case QlikView is not installed. This is found to be one of the good tools to accelerate the process of adoption of QlikView inside the company.

Some Guiding Principles

Define Needs Precisely and Elaborately: As written in the earlier chapters, the needs of the organization, in the form of metrics and measures, should be put down very elaborately. Using Strategy Maps, formulating the KPIs required and then arriving at the user-information need mapping is very important. This will ensure that the organizational needs are clearly understood, and are put into priorities as part of the various phases of the QlikView deployment.

Explicitly Define Outcomes Expected: The expectations from QlikView have to be defined very clearly. Broadly the benefit expectations fall in two categories:
   a.   User Experience, and
   b.   IT Process efficiency

Defining these clearly by using the references provided in the earlier chapter on Benefits of QlikView is extremely important. This gives a way to specifically plan activities and also to measure the success.

Use "Agile" as the philosophy: With the dynamic and complex business climate, that is the reality today, defining all requirements in one shot is next to impossible. Agile Development model is the most appropriate model for QlikView. This means the requirements as understood are immediately implemented, and then as requirements are refined, the solution is improved. This goes very well with the flexibility that the product offers. Quick prototyping is a great benefit of QlikView.

Plan Quick Wins and Execute with Focus: Stages and phases should be chosen so that we have quick wins. There is nothing that helps projects more than success seen on the ground. Clearly defined steps, with stated expectation of benefits is the key to have these quick wins. Many distractions with varying requests will keep coming from various quarters, but need to be sequenced carefully.

Communicate Success Constantly: As and when any milestone is achieved, communicate it among the stake holders. In addition, let all others in the organization know about the success and benefits achieved by the milestone achieved. This increases the interest to get benefited by QlikView when their turn comes.

Common Definitions: Most metrics and dimensions are used across various functions inside the organization. However, the definition of these metrics and dimensions are perceived to be different by those different parts of the organization—hence they get defined multiple times and calculated multiple times. Evolving common definitions across the company will remove these redundancies, and make the information systems more efficient. With such common definitions, various other departments could potentially benefit from every milestone achieved. If not directly, they can re-use these data elements when their turn comes and add only those specific data elements that are unique for them.

Follow Best Practices: QlikTech and its partners keep communicating best practices that need to be used with QlikView. Ensure that these best practices are followed carefully, and that the governing leaders ensure that these are verified. A summary of all the best practices is provided in Part III for ready reference.

A Checklist of Things to do

Defining a QlikView Strategy and converting it into action requires systematic execution. The discussions above should be summarized into a checklist of items that need to be completed for implementing QlikView successfully and realize all the benefits that it can provide. Considerable discussions have happened on this topic of what should be done to make BI successful. Some of the interesting references are included in the references section below.

Following is a high level list of activities. Each of these can go into QlikView Strategy Document:

Strategic Activities

1. Create a list of Current Problems to be solved by QlikView
2. Create a list of Expected Benefits from QlikView
3. Prioritize the problems to be solved with QlikView
4. Identify the sponsor(s)

5. Form the steering committee
6. Take stock of Existing HW/SW Inventory related to reporting / analytics – ROI periods
7. Choose a Right Partner organization
8. Formulate the Roadmap – Plan quick wins
9. Perform the ROI and Cost of Delay calculations and share with each department

Tactical Activities

10. Budget the expenses and plan for funds
11. Form the Data Extraction and Storage Approach to be followed
12. Define Analytical approaches to be built or bought
13. Set down the list of best practices to be followed
14. Divide the QlikView implementation into Phases and set goals
15. Create Common Definitions of Data

Operational Activities

16. Break down the Phases into Stages and individual task items
17. Assign owners and monitor progress
18. Integrate QlikView into Business Processes
19. Constantly Train and help Change Management
20. Review and Measure progress constantly
21. Communicate progress constantly

Conclusions - QlikView can be the change agent

QlikView is a disruptive technology, which can bring about significant change and growth to the organization. Not just once, but can create the culture of Continuous Performance Improvement. For further reading on this topic, please refer to the various references included [5, 6, 7, 8].

The need is to ensure that the complete strategic roadmap is in place and a sustained implementation methodology is deployed. This is a key to the success with QlikView.

Success with QlikView can translate easily into improved business efficiencies. The culture of using data and taking data-driven decisions needs to be evolved constantly. Right from the board to everyone in the company needs to be educated and trained constantly about the benefits that DDD can bring about. This culture is at the core of any BI Initiative, and of course is more relevant with QlikView.

References

1. Bayesian Data-Driven Decision Making, Jim Harris, OCDQ Blog, Dec 2011, [http://www.ocdqblog.com/home/bayesian-data-driven-decision-making.html]

2. Intuition Vs. Data-Driven Decision-Making: Some Rough Ideas, Bob Sutton, Work Matters, Nov 2009, [http://bobsutton.typepad.com/my_weblog/2009/11/intuition-vs-datadriven-decisionmaking-some-rough-ideas.html]

3. Strength in Numbers: How Does Data-Driven Decision Making Affect Firm Performance?, Erik Brynjolfsson, MIT and NBER Lorin Hitt, University of Pennsylvania Heekyung Kim, MIT, [http://www.a51.nl/storage/pdf/SSRN_id1819486.pdf]

4. Analytics: The Widening Divide, How Companies are achieving competitive advantage through analytics, (David Kiron, Rebecca Shockley, Nina Krushwitz, Glenn Finch and Dr. Michael Haydock), MIT Sloan Management Review Research Report FALL 2011, [http://www-935.ibm.com/services/us/gbs/thoughtleadership/ibv-embedding-analytics.html]

5. 10 Keys to a Successful Business Intelligence Strategy, Diann Daniel, Oct 2007, CIO.COM, [http://www.cio.com/article/148000/10_Keys_to_a_Successful_Business_Intelligence_Strategy]

6. Creating Business Value with Analytics, David Kiron and Rebecca Shockley, Sep 2011, MIT Sloan Management Review, [http://sloanreview.mit.edu/the-magazine/2011-fall/53112/creating-business-value-with-analytics/]

7. The Need for a Business Intelligence Strategy: A Critical Analysis for the Insurance Industry, Timothy L. Raab, Jun 2000, Information Management Magazine, [http://www.information-management.com/issues/20000601/2291-1.html]

8. The Right Decisions Matter Most – Now, White Paper, QlikTech, 2008, [http://www.softwaremag.com/linkservid/AB2FABA2-089F-A428-EDA34335AB403B50/showMeta/0/]

PART II

QLIKVIEW - HOW DOES IT WORK?

Introduction to Part II

> *"The price of light is less than the cost of darkness"*
> - Arthur C. Nielsen

> *"Most people use statistics the way a drunkard uses a lamp post, more for support than illumination"*
> - Mark Twain

QlikView is a great tool, with phenomenal capabilities to make a significant difference in the way businesses function. QlikView can bring light at very affordable expense. QlikView should be put to the best use to throw more light on business and the affects. While it is important to put QlikView to maximum use, there is a limit to what QlikView can do.

Like Mark Twain says, use of the tool should not be left to the drunkards – should be used to the optimum level – neither less nor more. The use of QlikView should be with a lot of thought, defined purpose, giving ability to discern, differentiate, collaborate, decide and act. Knowing what can be done paints the possibilities in front of us. Knowing how it works gives us the strength to make the choice of usage, knowing well the possible outcomes with certainty.

Part II explores how QlikView works, how it interacts with the various enterprise solutions that are already in place or is going to be added into the enterprise. Understanding how QlikView works allows companies to make best use of it in every possible way. Also it allows the companies to decide the right usage and formulate the most optimal cost-benefit plan for usage of QlikView.

In addition, knowing how it integrates with other enterprise systems allows best deployment and connectivity with other systems, enhancing the overall business value of information across various systems. The most appropriate usage of QlikView enables the enterprise wide information eco-system to add value to the data-driven decision making using QlikView.

Security, Databases, Data Quality and Data storage in relation with QlikView is discussed at length. In addition, the chapters also discuss how QlikView works along with SAP, Cloud and other popular systems that are found most commonly in Enterprises.

The overall intent of this Part is to help understand the nuances of QlikView, the way it works, and how it can integrate with the rest of the enterprise information system. This will increase the value derived by the use of QlikView across the enterprise.

CHAPTER 7
QLIKVIEW IN DEPTH

EVERY RADICALLY DIFFERENT DISRUPTIVE TECHNOLOGY CHANGES THE WAY BUSINESSES ARE RUN

Introduction to the Chapter

QlikView gained its special position among the data discovery tools, due to the three key differentiators that we discussed earlier in the chapter *What is QlikView?*: Data Implosion, Integrated In-Memory Data Model and Associative Query Language. While these are the core elements, QlikView has many more capabilities and features added over the last many years. The evolution has led to creation of new QlikView components and changes to existing components consistently.

To plan and execute an enterprise wide deployment of QlikView, it is important to get a deeper understanding of the technology, architecture, process and components of the QlikView solution. A complete appreciation of QlikView does not come without actually understanding the inner details of the product, including the development process as well.

It is incomplete without an understanding of the various components and files that are involved all across, the process of development, deployment, security and the related best practices.

This chapter starts setting an agenda for an in-depth tour of QlikView. The best way to get a feel for QlikView is to experience it, both as a user and as a developer. With an example, in-memory associative technology is explained, to help appreciate the way in which QlikView functions. Then the architecture is discussed, explaining various components— both conceptually and physically. This gives an under-the-hood view of QlikView to help understand the various components.

Next sections talk about the typical development process and explain the QlikView Application file and its journey through the development to deployment—the entire life-cycle of a QVW.

The chapter then goes on to talk about the resources required for QlikView—storage, memory, CPU and network bandwidth—and elaborate on the efficiencies that come along with QlikView.

Lastly, a brief introduction is given on the various components that constitute the QlikView technology. This sets the stage for a more detailed discussion on the components of QlikView in the next chapter.

Understanding QlikView in Depth

An in-depth understanding of QlikView has to include the following:
1. Experiencing the QlikView Application
2. Architecture of the Solution
3. Understanding the QlikView Application (QVW) File
4. Developing QlikView Applications
5. Components of the QlikView Solution
6. Various Files used by the QlikView products
7. Security Model
8. How QlikView works with other Enterprise solutions

This and the following chapters of Part II focus on these topics and help deepen the understanding of QlikView. Many documents and white papers are available from QlikTech and its partners about the architecture and how it works. This chapter attempts at consolidating many of those in a single place for easy reference. The references section gives the list of various sources from where the content for this chapter has been syndicated from. Additional notes are added based on the experience and understanding of the author.

The next chapter gives an in-depth view of each of the components, including security model. Other chapters of Part II provide insights on how QlikView works with other enterprise solutions.

Part III develops this understanding further and helps understand the various deployment options, licensing, managing the various gaps that exist and integration of the QlikView Platform with other enterprise solutions.

Experiencing the QlikView Applications

Before getting into any technical discussion, there is a need to experience QlikView firsthand, as a user, to appreciate the benefits that it can provide for business. As was highlighted in the chapter on "What is QlikView", visiting http://demo.qlikview.com [1] and downloading the Personal Edition of QlikView along with the Free Training [2]/ Tutorial files are great ways to get a deep appreciation of the product.

There are various applications in the QlikView Live Demo site with many samples from multiple businesses. There are also application samples that can be opened on mobile devices including iPads, Android Tablets and Smartphones. Check them out to experience the difference QlikView can create for users and how they can navigate across so-called 'reports' without leaving the application.

In addition, visit the Video Demos that are available in the Demo Site, to get a taste of all the various capabilities that can be made useful for the users in the company. Collaborating with others and the Developer Toolkit Videos are a very useful watch. These set a sound backdrop for the various in-depth discussions this chapter and subsequent chapters will cover. All the leisure applications help good understanding of the product, and the business applications give the various possibilities that can be employed in your own company.

While looking at these applications, please look for the effects of *The Associative Experience (refer to the QlikTech Whitepaper)* and experience them:

- *Works the way the human mind works*. Users can navigate and interact with data any way they want to—they are not limited to just following predefined drill paths or using preconfigured dashboards. Users can ask and answer questions on their own and in groups and teams, forging new paths to insight and decision. With QlikView, discovery can be flexible. Business users can see hidden trends and make discoveries like with no other BI platform on the market.

- *Delivers direct and indirect search.* With Google-like search, using the Global Search Bar, users can type relevant words or phrases, in any order, and get instant, associative results. With search boxes affiliated with individual list boxes, users can confine the search to just that list box. They can both conduct direct and indirect searches. For example, if a user wanted to identify a sales rep but can't remember the sales rep's name, but only some details about the rep, such as that he sells fish to customers in the Nordic region. The user can search on the sales rep list box for "Nordic" and "fish" to get the names of sales reps who meet those criteria.

- *Delivers answers as fast as users can think up questions.* Users can ask a question in QlikView in many different ways, such as drag-selecting (lassoing) data in charts, graphs and maps, clicking on items in list boxes, manipulating sliders, and selecting dates in calendars. Instantly, all the data in the entire application filters itself around the selections. Users can quickly and easily see relationships and find meaning in the data, for a quick path to insight. The user can continue to click and un-click (toggle selection) on field values in the application, further filtering the data based on questions that come to mind.

- *Benefit from the power of gray.* While visiting demo site, the most important thing to look and understand is the benefit of GREEN-WHITE-GRAY. As an example, all items selected by the users are shown in Green (Country: Japan). Those items related or associated with the selected items are all shown in White (Product Group: Baked Goods | Year: 2008, 2009, 2010). This helps understand associations clearly. In addition, the items that are not connected or related to the selections are shown in GRAY (Month: Jan). This helps understand non-associations too.

- This has a very important impact: the ability to see what is not associated with selections gives an additional dimension to understand the business. This GRAY item shows that there are no sales in JAPAN in the Month Jan across all the three years. Ability to realize this is a great capability—gives an insight which is not explicit but profound. This could lead to questions of Why, and maybe expose a problem with data entry or that the product is actually not selling in Japan in January. This is an unexpected, new Insight, potentially actionable immediately.

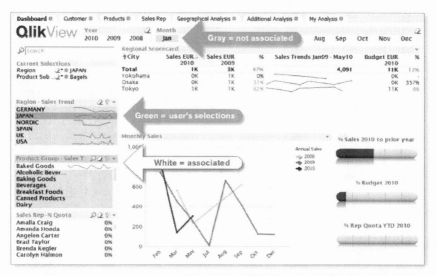

Figure 1: QlikView Associative Experience

The powerful user features and interactive analysis capabilities of QlikView are very impressive. Understanding the technology, architecture and various components of QlikView is important to make the best use of it. The core of the entire solution is the Associative In-Memory Technology.

Associative In-Memory Technology

A QlikView architecture discussion is incomplete without a discussion on the Associative In-Memory Technology. A detailed explanation of this is provided in the Chapter "What is QlikView?"

To summarize and quote the QlikTech Whitepaper (given in the references section), "QlikView uses an associative in-memory technology to allow users to analyze and process data very quickly. Unique entries are stored only once in-memory; everything else is stored as pointers to the parent data. That's why QlikView is faster and stores more data in memory than traditional cubes. Memory and CPU sizing is very important for QlikView, end user experience is directly connected to the hardware QlikView is running on. The main performance factors are data model complexity, amount of unique data, UI design and concurrent users."

Architecturally, it is important to remember that the AQL technology is at the core of the success of QlikView, along with the optimized storage of the data in-memory. This core technology is implemented as the QlikView Associative Engine which is present in the QlikView Local Client (Developer) as well as the QlikView Server. The Associative capability of QlikView is explained in different ways in a few blog posts on QlikCommunity, tagged as "Associative Architecture" [3].

Developing QlikView Applications

Learning QlikView development is an easy 3 to 4 week process. Existing IT professionals, Developers and Business analysts in any enterprise can gain good expertise in this short period. This book does not focus on the How to develop QlikView applications. The following resources can be used to quickly learn development:

- QlikTech has excellent material in their website using which existing IT professionals can learn how to develop QlikView Applications. The QlikCommunity has got the training section where self-paced learning tools are available for free. A collation of all these courses is provided in: http://www.qlikview.com/us/services/training/free-training [2].

- Using the Personal Edition along with the Tutorial documents is the best place to start. The QlikView Reference Manual [4] is a great place to get deeper knowledge about the QlikView capabilities and functions.

- In addition, QlikTech conducts classroom training programs regularly. Typically, developers can come to speed in about 3 to 4 weeks by a systematic learning process around these materials.

- QlikCommunity and other QlikView blogs provide very useful tips & tricks to help pick up advanced concepts and techniques of QlikView Development [9 to 21].

While learning QlikView is relatively easy and quick, it is important to follow a process beyond just creating QlikView applications. Chapter 4, 5 and 6 of this book have laid out the fundamentals based on which such a process can be evolved. The Part III chapters focus on the technical processes. These skills are required for IT Professionals, Business Analysts and QlikView Developers.

Here is a quick summary of the process steps that need to be used for successful QlikView development and deployment:

1. Requirements Analysis: understanding the needs and choosing what to solve through a roadmap of different phases.
2. Setting Benefit Expectations: based on the discussions in chapter on "What Benefits can be expected from QlikView?"
3. Defining various measures, dimensions and the formulae / logic required for various calculations
4. Identifying data sources, tables and fields from each of the sources—to get all the dimensions and measures required
5. Creating the QlikView Source Documents: QVW files with Scripts to extract from data sources - writing the ETL Scripts to connect to data sources, extract and transform necessary data elements and store them in intermediate QVDs
6. Creating the QlikView Intermediate Documents: QVW files with Scripts to process intermediate QVDs to create more QVDs
7. Creating the QlikView User Applications: QVW files with Front-end UI elements to allow interactive analytics for users—to be deployed on the Publisher / Server combination

Steps 1 to 4 are preparatory steps. Typically these are done by the Data Analysts and DBAs. Steps 5 and 6 are done by QlikView Modelers / Deployment specialists / Architects. Step 7 is done by QlikView Developers. Steps 5 to 7 are done using the QlikView Desktop Local Client, also called as the Development Version. More extensive process definition from a business gains perspective is discussed in Part III in the chapter on "Making QlikView Work".

Understanding QlikView Application (QVW File)

The QlikView Associative Engine processes the data and allows users to interactively take advantage of the Associative Algorithm implemented. All the ingredients necessary for this AQL engine to work are present in the QlikView File (QVW).

The QVW file stores all the user data, the logic/algorithms and the front-end visualization components. It is the core of rich user experience that is provided by QlikView Technology. QlikView Application is stored in disk as a QVW file - this is the end-point of development.

All components of the QlikView Solution interact with the QlikView Applications (QVW Files) either directly or indirectly. Hence to understand the entire solution well, it is important to get a deeper understanding of the QlikView File also called the QlikView Application. This file is created by the Business Analysts or QlikView Developers. The QVW file contains the following:

1. ETL Scripts to extract, load and transform the data from respective sources
2. Data Model—schema of the transformed data—definition of tables, fields and their relationships. This is a relational structure, with a snow-flake schema
3. Data—the entire data transformed in its final form—stored highly optimized
4. UI Elements—the entire front-end definition, in the form of objects and their properties, with formulae defined for calculations and rendering at the time of user interaction
5. Access Control List—the list of user ids, passwords for authentication—with their authorizations: the access rights they have while interacting with the data
6. VB Script / JavaScript code for programmatic control of objects and data using the Automation API of QlikView

The QlikView file is loaded by the QlikView Aggregation Engine in the computer's RAM, which together with the QlikView Associative Engine (AQL technology) provide excellent performance when executing ad hoc data analysis.

The ETL Script contains instructions for connecting to data sources (ODBC, OLEDB, etc.) and for defining what tables and fields are to be read into the QlikView application. Once executed, a copy of the source data is read into and stored in the QlikView application. The connection of tables is handled by appropriately using the automatic table linking feature. The result is QlikView in-memory data structure which can hold data from many different sources and systems in a unified data model. When a QVW file is open in memory, the ETL script is executed only when an explicit RELOAD command is issued by one of the following: 1) Manually Pressing Reload Button on development client with QVW application open, 2) Programmatically executing a Reload Task in the publisher or 3) Command Line execution of Development Client with a /R switch.

The QlikView data structure is flat, non-aggregated, non-hierarchical, and can hold a virtually unlimited number of dimensions. The typical QlikView data structure holds data up to transactional level and since it is non-hierarchical, any value of the application can be a starting point of analysis.

QlikView's feature for compressing data is very powerful. The possibility of storing huge non-aggregated datasets in a single in-memory application is immense. The size of data is reduced to as low as 10% of the original data size. Storing data this way helps portability and facilitates off-line analysis for a travelling work force, when data sizes are small. QVW file stores the data in its highly compressed form.

The data stored in a QlikView application is made accessible for analysis through an intuitive point-and-click user interface. The features for making layouts with list boxes, graphs, and tables have been developed for optimum developer performance. The QlikView application layout is easy to create and configure. The various graphs, based on QlikView's patented graph engine, provide an excellent overview of results and trends. QVW file stores all the visual layout information.

The security model in QlikView makes it possible to protect data residing on the file. At the development stage, access restriction can be built into the QVW file giving different users access to different data or parts of the application. Security definitions are also included in the QVW file.

QlikView is equipped with an Automation interface which can be accessed by external programs or internal triggers/macros for programmatically controlling the application or specific parts of the application functionality. These JavaScript/VBScript macros are also included in the QVW file itself.

When a QVW file is opened, the QlikView Engine keeps the un-aggregated raw data in memory, and allows the user to analyze the data interactively at near-instantaneous speeds of aggregation and analysis. The next two sections talk in detail about how this works.

This file can be opened and allowed for use only in one of the two ways:

a)   QlikView Local Client (also called Developer) in a single machine used by a single user,

b)   QlikView Server (QVS) to allow multiple users to interact with the QlikView Application through a browser and interactively analyze and collaborate

QlikView Engine elements are embedded in three products of QlikView: QlikView Local Client, QlikView Server and QlikView Publisher. The section on QlikView Architecture explains how this functions and more information is provided in the next chapter on QlikView Components.

How QlikView Works?

QlikView is snapshot based: at predefined intervals a snapshot (copy) of all relevant tables/data is extracted from the data sources. Wherever possible, incremental data is extracted instead of the entire tables to keep extraction loads and times to be minimal. (A subsequent section talks about incremental loads and the pre-requisites in detail).

This fresh / update data is refreshed into the QVW file through a process known as reloading a QlikView document. When a QlikView document is reloaded QlikView will establish connectivity to the data source(s) to be analyzed and will extract all the un-aggregated granular data from the data source and then compresses this data. The un-aggregated compressed dataset is then saved to disk for persistent storage as a .QVW file.

If there is a need for extensive transformations to be done before loading data into QVW file (data model), the data can be stored in intermediate data-only format called QVD (QlikView data file) between such processes. QVD is a 'headless' (i.e. UI-less) optimized application containing just the data. This stores the data in a binary form, a direct dump of the way in which data is optimally stored in memory. Hence the size of these data files is very small compared to the original storage of the same data in the data sources.

At the beginning of an analytic session, when a user opens a document, the QlikView Engine loads it from persistent disk based storage (i.e. a QVW file from hard disk) and places the entire dataset into RAM (random access memory).

When using a QlikView Server, this in-memory repository serves as base dataset for the initial user and all other users requesting the same document share this data instance. This repository stays in memory until no user activity has occurred within a defined time-out period.

During an analytic session QlikView will not make a call out to the database or access any other disk based data repository: It will only rely on the dataset present in RAM giving QlikView the unlimited flexibility and near instantaneous response times (all data aggregated in RAM).

Users explore data via selections. Central to QlikView is the concept of a user-defined selection state. As users click around in a QlikView document, they indicate which subsets of data they are interested in analyzing and which should be ignored. QlikView takes advantage of the in-memory hash tables to produce quick responses. It dynamically presents a subset of all the data available in the QlikView document based on the selection state. This happens in 'real time' on every user click as the user clicks.

Every click is a where clause—from the traditional SQL perspective—applied on the entire data set. In SQL world, the query needs to be re-executed with the new where clause every time. In QlikView, the new filter (where clause) is applied on the fly, and all the objects are refreshed with the effective subset of data created by all the selections.

Upon selection on the fly, QlikView renders aggregates as intuitive and interactive user interface objects: charts, graphs, tables, etc. Users interact with objects in QlikView documents through any supported client.

Going back to the applications in the Demo Site, the applications are loaded by a QlikView Server (running on Amazon infrastructure) and held in memory. For every user who connects and accesses the application, a separate user session space is allocated, where the selections and other information related to the user session are maintained.

On every click, the server receives the selections, records the selections in the user session space and applies it on the dataset held in memory and renders the results only to the user who clicked. Every user has a separate view of the data.

Only one copy of the main data set is kept in memory. All processing is done on that same data set based on the selections of the users. All objects in the users view are updated with the selections.

All the objects created by QlikView Developers are available for the users subject to the permissions / section access rights set in the application. In addition, users can create their own objects using the collaboration features of QlikView. Such objects created by users can be shared with other users using the sharing features available.

QlikView Architecture

The entire QlikView technology revolves around the core functions, each of which can be viewed as a sub-engine:

a) *ETL Script Engine* for Loading Data and building the Data Model
b) *In-Memory Data Engine* for Managing In-Memory Data
c) *Associative Search Engine* to implement Associative Technology
d) *Aggregation Engine* to perform aggregations on the fly

e) *Presentation Engine* which renders the UI definitions on to the client interfaces

f) *Authorization Engine* which defines what is accessible for which user

g) *Export Engine* to output data in the required formats to other downstream systems and users.

A QlikView application has a life-cycle in which it works through these engines and produces the necessary data experience for the users. The typical QlikView file goes through three phases through its life-cycle: Development, Reloading and Deployed for Users:

Development Phase: The developers create a QVW file, with 3 important parts: a) Load Script, b) Data Model to store un-aggregated Data and, c) User interface definitions. Once developed, the application is stored in the disk as a file (shown in the lower part).

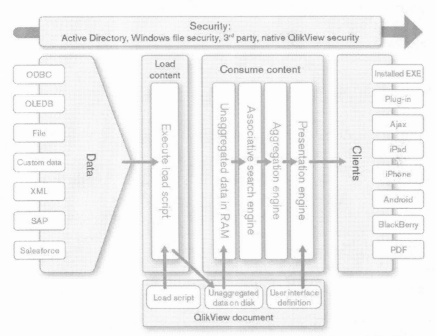

Figure 2: Overview of QlikView Platform

Reloading Phase: The QVW file is loaded and the Load Script is executed to extract the data, perform the necessary transformations and load the data to create the data model defined. The load script execution happens in the development phase as well.

Deployment Phase: The QVW file is loaded in memory into two parts: a) Un-aggregated Data, b) User Interface Definitions. The Associative Search Engine and the Aggregation Engine use the un-aggregated data to perform the calculations based on user selections. The Presentation Engine uses the UI definitions and presents the objects with data and results to the users.

Clients: The visual front-end runs on client machine, either inside a browser or in a standalone EXE program.

For convenience of understanding, the QlikView solution can be divided into Front-End and Back-End components as shown in the Figure below.

Back End (Including Infrastructure Resources)

This is where the Extraction QlikView Applications (QVW Files) also called QlikView Source Documents, created using the QlikView Developer, reside. From a backend perspective, these source files can be one of the following:

a) Scripts within Source Documents (Extraction QVW files) to extract data from the various data sources (e.g. data warehouses, Excel files, SAP, Salesforce.com)

b) The actual binary data extracts themselves within QVD files (intermediate QV Data Storage files) created by Source Documents

The main QlikView component that resides on the back end is the QlikView Publisher: this is responsible for data loads and distribution. Within the back end, the Windows file system is always in charge of authorization (i.e. QlikView is not responsible for access privileges).

The back end depicted in the following Figure is suitable for development, testing and deployment environments.

Front End

This is where end users interact with the documents and data that they are authorized to see via the QlikView Server. It contains QlikView user documents created via QlikView Publisher in the back end. File types seen on the Front End are QVW, .meta & .shared documents.

Communications between the client and server occurs here. It is handled either via HTTPS (in the case of AJAX client) or via the QlikView proprietary QVP protocol (in the case of plug-in or Windows client). Within the Front End, the QVS is responsible for client security.

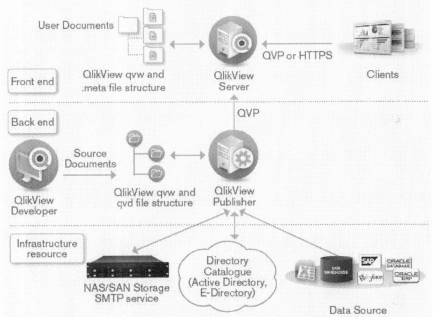

Figure 3: A Simple QlikView Architecture Overview

Deployment Approaches

The above diagram shows the simplest way of deploying QlikView in an enterprise. QlikView platform over years has become highly scalable with options to scale different layers/components independent of the others, based on the load conditions. The various deployment methodologies / options are all discussed in Part III.

Resources Required for QlikView

QlikView uses resources in the most effective fashion. Lot of optimization techniques and performance optimization steps are inherently built into the QlikView engine. In addition many best practices allow constant improvement of performance of applications, as more data and logic are added. The key resources that are of interest are: a) Storage on Disk, b) Memory, c) CPU and d) Network Bandwidth.

Storage on Disk

QlikView extracts data from the back-end systems and stores in a highly optimized, reduced storage. It was explained earlier, how data implosion happens with QlikView. Data extracted is reduced to about 10 to 20% of the original size consistently for every table.

Data can be stored separately in QVD files without any UI or Scripts. This is a compact form of storage. In many installations, instead of taking a back up of the data from the warehouse, it is extracted into QlikView and then backed up since it takes much less space.

QlikView file contains the UI, the data, the scripts and the various session buffers while in memory. When it is saved, by default, the QlikView Desktop Client stores the QVW file in a compressed format. The size reduction is about 20% while such compression is used. When the compressed QVW file is opened, it takes a longer time to open and bloats in memory as well when it is uncompressed and loaded. This can be set to "none" in the User Preferences (Dialog) -> Save (Tab) -> Compression -> None. Now, the memory size and the disk size are exactly the same when compression is set to none. Time taken is lesser for loading, and the QVW expansion in memory does not happen.

Memory Usage of QlikView

To take advantage of the benefits QlikView provides, all data to be analyzed must fit in RAM—all data to be analyzed by QlikView: the un-aggregated dataset to be analyzed as well as the aggregated data and session state for each user viewing the document.

RAM is the single biggest factor determining the quantity of data that can be analyzed in a QlikView environment. There are, however, many factors that determine how much RAM the analysis of a given dataset will require. The illustration below is a simplified diagram of various usages of RAM that would be found on a typical QlikView Server.

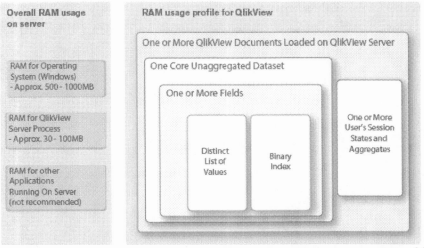

Figure 4: QlikView Memory Usage[7]

CPU Usage of QlikView

As seen above, QlikView does all the aggregations on the fly in memory, as the user makes selections. Calculations happen faster, since no disk-read is required to do the calculations. No data movement required from one place to another. However, the calculations of aggregation or any other expressions used in various display elements—charts, graphs, tables etc—are performed as the user makes the selections.

With more number of users, the need for CPU for the same application is higher. CPU cycles are used whenever a user makes a selection for a new aggregation, new drill-down path, redraw of the UI based on a new chart interaction and so on. As a result, CPU capacity needs to be added when more concurrent users are expected. Fortunately QlikView scales linearly with the CPUs and Memory for additional users. The following chart shows the linear scaling that happens with QlikView.

Figure 5 highlights that as more concurrent users are requesting access to an application, a uniform increase in both CPU and RAM capacity will ensure that performance levels are maintained at an acceptable level.

In many cases the machine running the QlikView server cannot be vertically scaled by adding more CPUs or cores. As an increasing number of users make requests to an application with a finite number of cores or CPU's available, performance degradation occurs. This is most commonly offset by scaling horizontally using a clustering and load balancing technique (Part III covers these more).

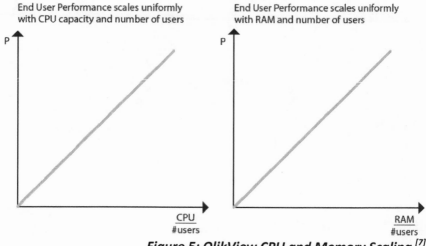

Figure 5: QlikView CPU and Memory Scaling [7]

Factors Contributing to QlikView Usage of RAM

There are many factors that determine how much RAM the analysis of a given dataset will require. The illustration above is a simplified diagram of some of the various usages of RAM that would be found on a typical QlikView Server.

A major function of the QVS is to load QlikView applications (.qvw's) into memory. The memory size needed depends on:
- QlikView application size (in uncompressed format)
- The application size in memory, it is often bigger than the actual application size
- How the application is designed. A poorly designed application could utilize unnecessary memory amounts
- How the data model is designed (e.g. avoiding using synthetic keys can reduce the memory footprint needed)
- Number of users accessing applications on the server. Typically a % extra memory is required for each additional user: this extra memory is for user state and caching. The cache memory will be reused if needed. The % depends on different applications and can

be found approximately using Optimization application available from QlikView.

A detailed discussion of how memory usage is dependent on these and other factors is provided in depth in the whitepaper from QlikTech: QlikView Scalability Overview, April 2011 [6]. This paper also explains various factors affecting CPU usage of QlikView. There is also a Video Series of John Callian in the QlikCommunity site [8].

Best practice guidelines are available to keep a check on both memory and CPU based bottlenecks created in badly designed and deployed QlikView applications. These best practices are summarized additionally in the Part III chapter on "Making QlikView Work".

Scalability Strategies

While more memory will certainly help larger growth in data, there are other strategies which can be used to handle large data sets, with relatively lesser increase in memory added:

- Telescopic Summarization
- Keeping only limited number of fields at transaction level
- Creating compact data models, by using the various optimization techniques available
- Document Chaining

Client Machine Loads

When the plug-in or AJAX clients are used, it works more like a remote display and the actual processing happens on the QlikView Server. Very similar to Citrix and other virtual client tools, just the screen updates are transferred over the network on the Client Machine.

As a result of this, irrespective of the size of data in the applications, the client machines need not have any expansion of memory; only the server needs to be upgraded anytime there is a need for additional memory due to data increase or new applications. This is a very important feature.

Network Usage

As shown above, QlikView holds data and application on the server memory only. Only the screen update happens over WAN (similar to

Citrix/Remote Desktop) making use of only limited bandwidth per user. Data does not travel entirely. Only the screen changes—update of graphs/charts / list boxes—are sent across the network. QlikView uses AJAX, to update only the objects that change.

With large companies spread across various Geographies, not every up-country area has sufficient bandwidth to support transmission of large amounts of data over the line (internet or MPLS). There is a need for effectively managing large data and ensure minimal bandwidth usage.

In a typical customer situation, the average effective bandwidth requirement is approximately 2kbps per user. On every click by users, bandwidth usage can have bursts of up to 12kbps for brief times.

In another instance, QlikView applications are locally deployed in remote branches, and daily central incremental data in QVDs is transferred to the branches and the user facing QVW applications are refreshed in the branches. This is another effective way to handle unstable bandwidth situations.

Like mentioned in the architecture section, *QlikView Desktop* contains all core QlikView engines: a) ETL Script Engine, b) Associative Search Engine, c) Aggregation Engine, d) Presentation (Graph) Engine, e) Authorization Engine and f) Export Engine

Components of QlikView

Extract	Develop &	Serve & Manage	User Access & Integration
	Development of QlikView Applications (1)	Management of Architecture, Configuration, Enterprise Integration and Scalability (6)	APIs to Connect to Enterprise Systems: Directory, Portals, Network, Other Applications
ETL for Refreshing Data in Applications (2)	Management of Application, Data Freshness, Security and Back-end Actions (3)	Serving Applications for Interactive Analytics and Collaboration (4)	Browser based Interactive User Front-End for Analytics and Collaboration (8)
		Distribution of Interactive Applications and Static Data (5)	Standalone QlikView Applications (7)
			PDF Viewers and Static File Viewers

Figure 6: Architecture Schematic

Hence all the functions of QlikView can be done just with the Desktop Version by a single user. QlikView solution consists of various distinct elements as shown in this functional schematic:

1. Tool for QlikView Application Development – DEVELOPER CLIENT – **QLIKVIEW DESKTOP**	2. ETL Components for reloading from Data sources – *ETL SCRIPT ENGINE, CONNECTORS, QVX and QVD FILES*
3. *Managing and Reloading Applications –* **QLIKVIEW PUBLISHER**	4. Serving to Users – **QLIKVIEW SERVER**
5. Distribute Information as Files – **QLIKVIEW PDF PUBLISHER / DISTRIBUTOR**	6. Managing Deployment and Configuration – **QLIKVIEW MANAGEMENT CONSOLE**
7. Interactive Analytics on Desktop –LOCAL CLIENT – **QLIKVIEW DESKTOP**	8. Device Independent Browser Front-end – QLIKVIEW AJAX / HTML5 CLIENT – **ACCESS POINT**

All these components are explained in more detail in the next chapter. All the elements colored Green in Figure 6 are part of the offerings of QlikView. Of these elements, three are main infrastructure components: QlikView Developer (1, 7), QlikView Server (4) and QlikView Publisher (3, 4).

To enable enterprise deployments, these engines are separately packaged into separate products:

- Of these engines, *ETL Script Engine* and *Authorization Engines* are packaged into the *QlikView Publisher* to perform reloads and refresh the QVW applications with fresh data updates.
- The four engines: *Associative, Aggregation, Presentation* and *Authorization* are included in the *QlikView Server* to load the QVW files in the server memory and allow users to have interactive analytics through a browser. In addition there is an optimized *Communication Engine* that manages the Client communications.
- *Export Engine* is packaged into the *PDF Publisher/Distributor*.

QlikView Management Console is an integrated administration console that allows management of the QV Server, QV Publisher and QV PDF Distributor.

The *QlikView Access Point* is the entry point for business users with the Browser Client. This component runs on a Web Server separate from the QlikView Server.

In addition to the above, there are other sub-components of above products, or provided as external development add-ons:

- Directory Services Connector (DSC) and Document Management Service (DMS) are sub-components of the QlikView Server
- Event Driven eXecution Engine (EDX) is an extension of QlikView Publisher
- QlikView Management Service (QMS) is an extension of the QlikView Management Console
- QlikView WorkBench is a development add-on to be used with Visual Studio Development Environment, to integrate QlikView objects into external websites.

Conclusions – Setting the stage for more

QlikView catapults most of the traditional beliefs and conventions and sets a new path for data analytics. Like any other technology, understanding QlikView in-depth increases the chance of success of the QlikView implementation. It allows the right components to be used to their best capabilities for the right purposes. The next chapter provides in-depth information about each of these components, and also maps the users and the functions they perform with each of these components.

References

1. How QlikView Works, Qlik Demos, [http://demos.qlikview.com]
2. Free Training, QlikView Web Site, [http://www.qlikview.com/us/services/training/free-training]

3. New to QlikView, QlikCommunity Section,
   [http://community.qlikview.com/community/new-to-qlikview]5
   Associative Architecture Posts, QlikView Blog, Aug 2010 to Feb
   2011,
   [http://community.qlikview.com/blogs/theqlikviewblog/tags/associ
   ative_architecture]
4. QlikView Introduction, Oak Management Website,
   [http://www.oakmgt.com/resources/QlikView.pdf]
5. QlikView Architectural Overview, A QlikView Technology White
   Paper, Oct 2010, QlikView.com,
   [http://www.qlikview.com/us/explore/resources/whitepapers/qlikv
   iew-architectural-overview]
6. QlikView Scalability Overview, A QlikView Technology White Paper,
   Apr 2011, QlikView.com,
   [http://www.qlikview.com/us/explore/resources/whitepapers/qlikv
   iew-scalability-overview]
7. QlikView Architecture and System Resource Usage, A QlikView
   Technology White Paper, Apr 2011, QlikView.com,
   [http://www.qlikview.com/us/~/media/Files/resource-
   library/global-us/direct/datasheets/DS-Technical-Brief-QlikView-
   Architecture-and-System-Resource-Usage-EN.ashx]
8. New Five-Part Video Series on QlikView Scalability, The QlikView
   Blog, Apr 2011, QlikCommunity.QlikTech.com,
   [http://qlikcommunity.qliktech.com/blogs/theqlikviewblog/2011/04
   /21/new-five-part-video-series-on-qlikview-scalability]
9. QlikView Maven, QlikView Blog, Tim Benoit,
   [http://qlikviewmaven.blogspot.com]
10. QlikView Notes, QlikView Blog, Rob Wunderlich,
    [http://qlikviewnotes.blogspot.com]
11. Quick–Qlear–Qool, QlikView Blog, Gilles Pol, William Van Lith and
    Juan Martin, [http://www.quickqlearqool.nl]
12. QlikMetrics, QlikView Marketing Intelligence Blog, Renco Smeding,
    [http://qlikmetrics.com]

13. QlikSter, The QlikView Integration & Mashup Blog, Industrial Code Box, [http://www.qlikster.com]

14. And Points Beyond, QlikView Blog, Jay Jakosky, [http://andpointsbeyond.com/]

15. iQlik – Everything QlikView, QlikView Blog, Mike, [http://iqlik.wordpress.com/]

16. QlikFix – QlikView tips, tricks and tutorials, QlikView Blog, Barry Harmsen, [http://www.qlikfix.com]

17. QlikBlog, QlikView Blog, Stefan Walther, [http://www.qlikblog.at/]

18. The Qlik Board! , Practical Posts for QlikView fanatics!, Bill Lay, [http://qlikboard.com/]

19. Qlik Tips, QlikView Blog, Stephen Redmond, [http://qliktips.blogspot.com/]

20. QlikDecision, QlikView Blog, Ed Bobrin, [http://qlikdecision.blogspot.com/]

21. Beyond Business Intelligence, QlikView Blog, Vlad Gutkovsky, [http://www.qlikvlad.com/

## CHAPTER 8

QLIKVIEW COMPONENTS AND USER ROLES

THE WHOLE IS GREATER THAN THE SUM OF ITS PARTS

Introduction to the Chapter

This chapter delves deep into the QlikView platform and explores the various granular functions useful for enterprise implementations. The intention is to allow practitioners to appreciate the platform in all its intricate structure, exposing how they can take advantage of these fine elements to architect enterprise solutions.

The chapter starts with the view of the platform from the perspective of QlikTech, as represented in some of the whitepapers and the marketing literature. Subsequently, the platform is explored in a granular functional perspective, to discuss the inner functions of QlikView components in greater detail, more like Lego parts.

Some of this attempt may lead to gross approximation of some of the fine features of QlikView. However, the intent is to give an approach to explore the capabilities in more detail. The author however has found this to be a successful way to explain the functionalities of QlikView to on-board new comers into this technology.

QlikView Components

A typical deployment of QlikView in an enterprise uses some or all of the following components that are available from QlikTech:

- QlikView Desktop (Developer/Local Client, *Personal Edition*)

- QlikView Server (Small Business Edition, Enterprise Edition, Extranet Server, Internet Access Server, Cluster Server, Test/UAT Server in addition to one SBE/EE editions)
- QlikView Publisher
- QlikView PDF Distributor
- *QlikView Access Point*
- *QlikView Clients (AJAX, Local Client, Personal Edition, IE Plug-in)*
- Client Access Licenses (Named User CALs, Document CALs, Session CALs and Usage CALs)
- *QlikView Management Console (Clustering Support)*
- *QlikView Directory Services Connector*
- *QlikView Web Server*
- *Standard Connectors (ETL for OLEDB, ODBC, Various File formats, QVX, Salesforce, etc)*
- Optional Connectors for SAP, Informatica
- Sharepoint Web Part
- QlikView Workbench
- QlikView OCX
- The various APIs (Automation, Custom ETL Connector, Extension, QMS, EDX)

While some of these are commercially priced products, some are included as sub-components in other products. At the time of writing this book, the components which are available free are shown in *italics* above. Also the QlikView Server has different commercial avatars, but all versions of QlikView servers have the same core. From a commercial license pricing standpoint, each server edition has different limitations of servicing particular use-cases or users of defined characteristics.

The typical bare minimum components required to deploy QlikView in an enterprise are:

- QlikView Developer
- QlikView Server (one of the editions)
- QlikView Publisher
- QlikView Access Point

- Client Access Licenses (# as applicable – minimum # restrictions exist based on Server editions)

Depending on the organization, the deployment can get more complex, with the number of QVW applications, the stages of Development, UAT and Production, the load requiring horizontal scaling, etc. A detailed discussion on various scenarios and possible configurations are discussed in Part III.

QlikTech whitepaper gives this overview of key QlikView products:

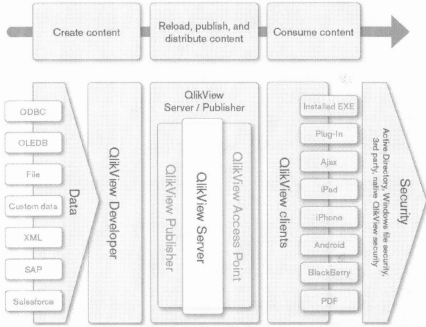

Figure 1: All Components of QlikView Platform

Development Components

QlikView Developer is a Windows-based desktop tool that is used by QlikView designers and developers to: 1) create a data extract and transform in to data model and 2) create the graphical user interface (presentation and collaboration layer). The QlikView applications created by this process are saved as QlikView files with QVW extension. These applications are then placed in a shared location accessible to both QlikView Publisher and QlikView Server.

QlikView Personal Edition is available from QlikTech website for free download. It is a complete non-expiring Desktop version, with the only limitation that the QVW applications created using the personal edition cannot be shared with other users using personal editions. This can be used by any user, for any amount of time to do analytics for individual use. This helps create QlikView skills around the world.

Once again, this is a step to put QlikView in everyone's desktop, making it as the default interactive analytic application for the world. This has no doubt increased the adoption of QlikView and more importantly evaluate without any commitment to invest.

Infrastructure Components

QlikView Server (QVS) loads QlikView applications into memory and ensures everyone has access to the latest data and analysis. It handles the communication between clients and the QlikView applications, calculates and presents based on user selections in real time. QlikView Server delivers support with role-based access to ensure that only those who have permissions can access data. QlikView Server plugs into existing security infrastructure to keep data fully protected. Users can access apps hosted on QlikView Server through any of the supported Windows, browser, or mobile clients.

QlikView Publisher opens the QlikView Applications (QVW Files) and refreshes them with fresh data by extracting and loading data from different data sources (OLE DB/ODBC Sources, QVX, XML, XLS, etc). At defined schedules, Publisher saves QVW files with fresh data, and distributes them to the QlikView Server document directory. It also creates reduced versions of QVW files for different users according to their access restrictions and distributes to the QlikView Server.

QlikView PDF Publisher/Distributor is a separately priced add-on to the QlikView Publisher. This allows publishing of selected charts and graphs into a formatted PDF report and distribute as static non-interactive reports to designated users in designated schedules.

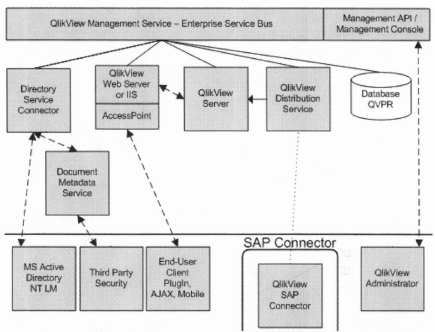

Figure 2: Infrastructure Components of QlikView Platform

Access Point is the front-end for users. This is a .Net web application that runs on an IIS Server, or the web server provided by QlikTech called *QlikView Web Server*. This becomes the intermediate layer between users and the QlikView Server. Users access through a browser, similar to how we access http://demo.qlikview.com. Access Point manages the authentication, establishes a session and connects the user with QlikView Server using the credentials established. This also provides flexibility to users to access from different types of clients and devices.

QlikView Directory Services Connector is used by QlikView Server, Publisher and Access Point to perform authentication of the users and establish their credentials. The Access Point then determines which QVW Applications users can access and provides only the allowed list of applications to the user. QV Server uses identity of the user established and allows dynamic data reduction, which is a unique capability of QlikView. The security aspects related to this are discussed separately in detail in the Chapter on "QlikView Security".

Instances of QlikView Server, Publisher and Access Point can all run on same Windows machine. However, since they have different roles and handle CPU and memory differently it's considered a best practice to keep them on different servers as separate layers. Also each of these layers can scale independently based on loads. To scale horizontally, each of these services can be clustered on more than one machine.

EXAMPLE DEPLOYMENT IN AN N-TIER ENVIRONMENT

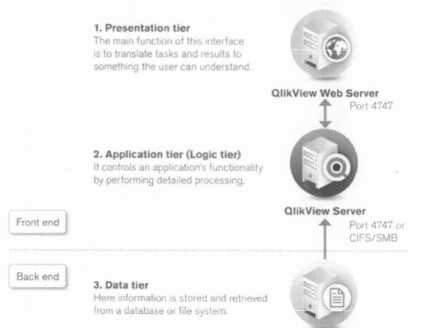

1. Presentation tier
The main function of this interface is to translate tasks and results to something the user can understand.

QlikView Web Server
Port 4747

2. Application tier (Logic tier)
It controls an application's functionality by performing detailed processing.

QlikView Server
Port 4747 or
CIFS/SMB

Front end

Back end

3. Data tier
Here information is stored and retrieved from a database or file system.

QlikView Publisher

Figure 3: 3-Tier Deployment Architecture

QlikView Management Console is used by administrators to manage the distributed environment through web-based interface. Using this console, separate instances (or clusters) of QlikView Server, Publisher, PDF Distributor, QlikView Web Servers (Access Points) can all be managed in an integrated fashion. This eases enterprise administration. All configuration files of the Management Console can be saved in a central location. This allows ease of business continuity and disaster management—more on this in the deployment discussions in Part III.

User Components

QlikView Clients: There are multiple options for users to access the allowed applications: AJAX (or Zero Foot Print / ZFP), IE Plugin or through a thick QlikView Local Client installed on the user desktop. Even

Personal Edition Desktop clients can be used as a local client but it requires a Client Access License (CAL). There were separate clients for iPhone and BlackBerry in the earlier versions of QlikView. In the recent versions, AJAX front-end works universally on browsers on all the front-end devices: Desktops, Laptops, iPads, iPhones, Android Phones/Tablets, Blackberrys.

CAL Type	Features	Typical Use Cases	Order Used
Named User	• Tethered to a single person • Unlimited QVW usage • Can be developer, designer and/or user	• VIP User (i.e. Execs) • Heavy Usage (i.e. 3 times/day or 1 hour at a time) • Developer or Designer of QV	1
Document	• Tethered to a single person • Tethered to a single QVW • Note: document chaining will require more than one Document CAL	• 2 or less QVWs needed • Manageable # of users (i.e. less than 200)	2
Session (pool)	• Not tethered to individuals • Unlimited QVW usage • CAL returned to "pool" after use	• 3 or more QVWs needed AND • Casual User (1-2 sessions/day, less than 30 minutes)	3
Usage (pool)	• Not tethered to individuals • Each session uses one CAL • 1/28th of total CALs returned to "pool" each day	• Natural monthly spike (month-end heavy use of an app) • Early warning for depleted session pool	4

Figure 4: Various Licensing Options [5,6]

All clients connect to the Access Point to be authenticated and get a list of applications that they can access. On selecting any QVW application, user is connected to the QlikView server to allow access to the application. Connection of the client to QV Server can be either direct, or through IIS Server as a tunneled connection (more on this in the chapter on "QlikView Security").

Every user connecting to the QlikView Server needs Client Access License (CAL). The different CAL options at the time of writing are: Named CAL, Document CAL, Session CAL and Usage CAL. Various CAL types are explained by this illustration by QlikTech

On a QlikView Server, all these licenses can be deployed together, in a mix that is appropriate for the user distribution. In such a case, the following process is used to allocate the licenses for the users as they connect to the QV Server:

1. If there is a dedicated Named User CAL for the connecting Client, it will be used

2. If there is a Doc Cal for this user, it will be used

3. If there is an available Session CAL, it will be used

4. If there is an available Usage CAL, it will be used

5. If none of the above are available, access is denied

The exact mix of appropriate licenses should be worked out with a detailed understanding of the applications: user vs. access frequency mix. QlikView Solution Architects from QlikTech or its partners can help arrive at this.

ETL Components

Standard Connectors (ETL for OLEDB, ODBC, Various File formats, Salesforce, etc) – The QlikView core ETL Script Engine comes with an in-built ability to connect to the standard OLEDB, ODBC and various file formats. Salesforce connector is also provided by QlikTech as a standard.

Optional Connectors for SAP and Informatica are provided by QlikTech. These are separate priced components that are required only if SAP or Informatica is present in the company and data needs to be extracted by QlikView directly from them. Additional information on the ETL Components and the processes/practices around these are provided in the chapter on "QlikView ETL".

Deployment Components

QlikView Web Part for Sharepoint® enables users to embed QlikView content in SharePoint portals and applications. It's as easy as choosing the QlikView object web part from SharePoint web parts library and point it to the QlikView document and object (e.g., specific chart, graph, list box, etc.). With QlikView web parts for Microsoft SharePoint, users can create Mashups that place analytics and related content side by side in a collaborative environment familiar to users.

Integration and Extension Components

QlikView Workbench is a Microsoft Visual Studio® plug-in that developers use to create powerful, web-based QlikView extensions. It is a drag-and-drop web integration toolkit that combines the flexibility of QlikView API with the easy-to-use, drag-and-drop Visual Studio integrated development environment. QlikView Workbench also includes a Visual Studio template to help content developers quickly and easily get started with building QlikView extensions.

QlikView OCX is an ActiveX component containing the QlikView application that can be embedded into host application programs developed by 3rd party software manufacturers. It is provided on an OEM basis to provide a 'white labelled' version of QlikView. This component provides full QlikView UI functionality and can be controlled and manipulated by the host application. The host application can be either a web or a desktop application.

QlikTech has exposed many *APIs (Automation, Custom ETL Connector, Extension, QMS, EDX)* that can be used to:

- Integrate QlikView seamlessly and tightly with other products (e.g., Mashups, Portals, Embedded QlikView)
- Extend capabilities of QlikView by adding new functions (e.g., create a new chart/graph or a programmatic interaction capability)
- Making other products to work seamlessly with QlikView by sharing the data in-memory (e.g., invoke R algorithms work on data in-memory in a QlikView instance)
- Automate the processes enveloping QlikView in an enterprise deployment (e.g., integrating user management to an HR system or daisy chain ETL with external End of Day processes)

More information is provided about these APIs in the QlikCommunity Thread: QlikView Version 11 SDK, Dan English [4].

Parts of the QlikView Platform

Like explained in the architecture section in the last chapter, the fundamental elements of QlikView Platform are the core engines that embody the patented technologies:

a) ETL Script Engine for Loading Data and building the Data Model
b) In-Memory Data Engine for Managing In-Memory Data
c) Associative Search Engine to implement Associative Technology
d) Aggregation Engine to perform aggregations on the fly
e) Presentation Engine which renders the UI definitions on to the client interfaces
f) Authorization Engine which defines who can access what
g) Export Engine to output data in required formats to downstream systems and users.

In addition to these core engines, the following logical engines help enterprise deployment:
h) Server Side Session Communication Engine to manage user sessions
i) Authentication Engine with Directory Services Connector & Document Management Service
j) Scheduling Engine to manage reloads
k) Client Side Communication Engine
l) Client UI Engine (AJAX, ActiveX)
m) Configuration Management Engine – includes QlikView Management Console (QMC) which covers Authorization (Access Control) Administration, Schedule definition, Configuration and Management of all components of QlikView

Apart from these, the ability to extend QlikView functionality has been added by the following parts:
n) Data Connectors for various data sources
o) QlikView Workbench
p) QlikView Web Parts for Sharepoint
q) APIs to allow programmatic administration & control of all Engines

With all these components, QlikView provides a modular approach to architect enterprise solutions. The original developers of QlikView may not have segregated the different functionalities into such discrete parts. However creating logical blocks for each function and understanding how they assemble into each product helps understand and appreciate the functions of these products.

Group	Functional Parts	QlikView Component						
		Publisher	Server	Desktop	OCX	AJAX Client	WorkBench	WebParts
Core	Data Connectors	Y		Y	Y			
	ETL Script Engine	Y		Y	Y			
	In-Memory Data Engine	Y	Y	Y	Y			
	Association Search Engine		Y	Y	Y			
	Aggregation Engine		Y	Y	Y			
	Presentation Engine		Y	Y	Y			
	Authentication Engine	Y	Y	Y	Y			
	Authorization Engine	Y	Y	Y	Y			
	Export Engine	Y	Y	Y	Y			
Extend	Extension API		Y	Y	Y	Y	Y	
	Automation API	Y	Y	Y	Y	Y	Y	
Client	Client UI Engine			Y	Y	Y	Y	Y
	Client Communication Engine		Y	Y	Y	Y	Y	Y
	Server Session & Communication Engine		Y					
Admin & Integrate	Scheduling Engine	Y						
	Configuration Management Engine	Y	Y					
	EDX	Y						
	QMS API	Y	Y					
	Version Management			Y				

Figure 5: QlikView – Functional Parts vs. QlikView Components

Users and Components of QlikView

The most important step to make QlikView deployment a success is defining the work flow processes around QlikView. To achieve this successfully, it is necessary to understand the various types of users involved and understand who will work with which components of QlikView. The following diagram shows a typical QlikView work distribution in the enterprise:

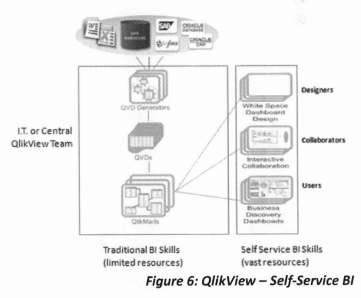

Figure 6: QlikView – Self-Service BI

There are three broad types of users:

- Business Users: Regular Users, Power Users and Travelling Users
- QlikView Front-End Developers: Business Analysts or BI Developers or Designers
- IT Professionals: Enterprise Architects, Data Analysts/Modelers, Security Specialists and IT Administrators

QlikView Product Family brochure [1] gives an overview of users vs. products as given in the figure below. The following sub-sections provide a discussion about each of the user types and the QV Components they use. This gives an idea of what functions are performed by which user category.

QlikView and the Business Users

Business users are essentially consumers of data who analyze data, sometimes do new analysis by creating tabular reports, charts and graphs, annotate and collaborate with other users. These business users primarily use QlikView over the Browser clients, Mobile clients and sometimes QlikView Desktop.

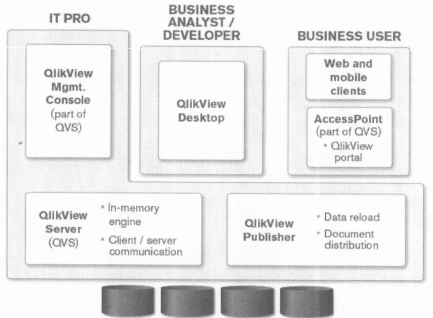

Figure 7: Components and Users of QlikView

Browser Clients

They interact with QlikView applications exclusively with any browser using an AJAX client requiring no downloads/installs or with an Internet Explorer Plugin. Users simply open their AccessPoint portal (or, in the case of integrated solutions, their organization's own enterprise portal) and select the QlikView application they wish to use.

The desire in every QlikView deployment (for that matter in any BI deployment) is to have the CxOs, Managers and Analysts use the solution to benefit the business by better decisions. The traditional BI deployments with other technologies have made the usage so restrictive and monotonous that the senior business users lose interest quickly and delegate usage to the line managers under them, or to the personal assistants. Sometimes, QlikView applications are also created just by reproducing reports that already exist, without making use of the Associative Analytics capabilities. Then these line managers and personal assistants perform the regular information browsing. Once they find anything that is of interest and significance they share such information / insights to the senior business users. With appropriate use of QlikView's capabilities, and careful choice of metrics and measures, the business user adoption is seen to be higher.

Once the user's security credentials are verified, they can work with the application, get the in-memory associative experience to explore and interact with the data, ask and answer their own stream of questions in a self-service mode.

In spite of all such interactive analytic capabilities of QlikView, the real adoption and sustained usage of QlikView by senior business users happens only if the benefits are planned, needs are mapped and questions are appropriately answered as the needs arise. For this, the questions that arise dynamically have to be answered, and more importantly, allow discussions around answers and help formulate newer questions consistently inside the same interface. With QlikView browser clients, users can ask a business question, use a chart to find the answer, make selections to see associations, and then change the chart or create a new one instantaneously.

QlikView's latest collaboration capabilities will help create this stickiness. Users can collaborate with other users in the organization, sharing insights and exploring data together, in real time or asynchronously. They can collaborate with others and preserve a record of decisions with in-app annotations. They can conduct direct and indirect searches—globally or within a field.

Because users are working against server image of a QlikView app, rather than downloading an app to their local machine, all are working with same app and data. Any modifications a user makes to that document (e.g., a new graph or chart) can be shared with others, but tied to server image—not a local image of document.

QlikView on Mobile

QlikView on mobile delivers true Business Discovery and the full power of QlikView to the mobile executive—including the associative experience, interactive analysis, access to live data, and search. In addition the location sense also adds to the experience, with "location" automatically reflected in insights.

At no additional cost, QlikView 11 delivers full mobile functionality for iPad and Android tablets and small-screen devices such as Apple iPhone and Android phones. Using a browser-based, build once/deploy anywhere approach, QlikView takes full advantage of native mobile gestures and features with centralized security, scalability, and manageability.

However, QlikView applications need to be developed by keeping the device form factors and mobile gestures like pinching etc. Though same applications developed for mobile devices can be deployed on desktops / laptops, the layout could create inconveniences for non-mobile users.

QlikView Desktop

Business users who travel a lot need to have access to the QVW applications while on the road. They can carry copy of QVW files (reduced only with their data) in their laptops and open these with the QlikView Desktop Client. They cannot use the collaboration features like object sharing, sharing sessions and live annotations while offline. Once back in the office, they can connect using the QlikView Desktop itself to connect to QV Servers and open documents on the server.

Business users who are savvy analysts can also use the QlikView Desktop to create new applications, with both new data models and visualizations. Once they finalize the same, it can be copied onto the server by the IT Administrators and pushed to production servers after appropriate UAT.

QlikView Front-End Developers—Business Analyst / QlikView Developers

Business Analysts and BI Developers create new QlikView Applications. To create these apps they primarily use QlikView Desktop.

QlikView Desktop

It is a Windows application for extracting and transforming data, designing analytics, and building dashboards and reports. Using QlikView Desktop's intuitive interface, developers create SQL-like scripts (augmented by wizards) that power the collation and transformation of data from multiple sources into an associative model. QlikView Developers generally reuse existing extracted and pre-modeled data from the QVD layer by pulling "off-the-shelf" data from the QVD, when relevant for their application. For pulling data, separate applications are created—*QlikView Source Documents*. These are essentially QVW files without any visualization, but to only store the extracted data into intermediate QVDs.

QlikView Applications created are the *QlikView User Documents.* The pre-processed QVDs and other lookup files are loaded finally into a Data Model and the user interface is laid out. These QlikView User Documents are deployed on QlikView Server and users are allowed to use them through browser and mobile clients. Designers choose the best visual representations of data from a wide array of available options—including custom-built/third-party visualizations.

QlikView enables rapid construction of apps ranging from simple, single-graph depictions of data to secure, multi-tabbed, multi-user and multi-dimensional views of an enterprise. QlikView analysis can be packaged according to the user's needs: Slice & dice analytics, intuitive dashboards, pointed score-cards, what-if scenarios and broad-based reporting. With QlikView, users can test and prototype with their data, learning all the while, without taking their eyes off the data or interrupting their thought process.

By implementing Section Access rights, QlikView Developers also ensure QlikView business applications are distributed to the correct business user community.

Automation API

Using Automation APIs triggers and macros can be written to programmatically perform various automated functions inside QlikView Applications. Dynamic features that are not available by default in QlikView interface can be created by these APIs. The standard application called APIGuide.QVW distributed with QlikView contains the details of all the API Functions available.

More complex and extensive integration with external enterprise applications, Mashups and other portals can be done using the Automation API. For this, help may be required from IT Professionals—Programmers with VBScript / JavaScript experience.

IT Professionals

QlikView's approach to BI allows for a self-service model for business users on the front end while maintaining strict data security and governance on the back end. Because of this approach, IT professionals—from enterprise architects to data analysts—can remain focused on their core competencies: data security, data and application provisioning, data governance and system maintenance. They no longer have to spend time writing and re-writing reports for business users.

In a typical QlikView deployment, IT professionals focus on:

- Managing data extracts, data and system security
- Creating and maintaining source QlikView files (QVWs and QVDs)
- Controlling data refresh and application distribution through QlikView Publisher
- Administering QlikView deployments via the QlikView Management Console (part of QVS)

- Integration of QlikView with other Enterprise systems and web applications/sites
- Extend QlikView functionalities using APIs
- Security management – Perimeter management, Authentication and Access Control

Different specialist roles played by different groups of IT Professionals and the products they use for their purposes as discussed below.

IT Professionals—QlikView Data Modellers

QlikView Data Modellers and Data Analysts are part of the IT Professionals. They work on extracting necessary data, clean them, transform and store them for re-use. All the transformations are performed to apply the business and data rules of the company.

QlikView Desktop, Connectors and Scripting

QlikView Modellers use this Windows desktop application to write ETL scripts, extract data from source systems, create data models, and transform. Here, they describe all metadata and create QVD data storage layers. During such development, they connect to data sources using standard interfaces (ODBC / OLE DB / File Formats), QVX (an open QlikView format for non-standard sources), and specific connectors to systems like SAP, Salesforce and Informatica.

QlikView Applications or QVWs which contain just the ETL scripts, extract data and store them into QVD files are *QlikView Source Documents*. Those applications that read the QVD files and perform further transformations and store them back into processed QVD files are *QlikView Intermediate Documents*.

To create functions that are not natively supported by QlikView for performing custom calculations, VBScript or JavaScript functions are created with the ETL script. Such extensions are made available as script libraries. Such common shared open source libraries could be very powerful in extending the capabilities of QlikView. One such initiative has been taken up by Rob Wunderlich and he maintains libraries as an open source project in Google Code – QVC – QlikView Components [7].

The next chapter "QlikView ETL" delves more deeply into ETL capabilities of QlikView, associated tools, processes and practices.

IT Professionals—Production, Security and Configuration Administrators

QlikView solution requires the same regular administrative functions like any other IT solution. The IT Administrators need to perform these functions on a regular basis. These are part of user and data processes, required to be done on pre-defined schedules or on-demand.

User DB—Directory Administration

Users, who require access to different components of the QlikView solution, need to be created and assigned appropriate permissions. On appropriate approvals, the users are created an ID in standard enterprise identity management / directory services. QlikView will connect to these systems & authenticate users when they access QlikView applications.

Publisher – Through QlikView Management Console

Authorization: Users first need access to appropriate QVW applications. Then in applications, they further need access to the permitted sheets, objects and data sub-sets. These are authorized for every permitted user—Access Control Lists (ACLs). These permissions need to be defined in the user administration process based on approvals. This is done in Publisher by IT administrators who own this process. If PDF Distributor is used, this process also defines reports that need to be distributed for users.

Publisher administration pages allow this through browser. Rights are assigned to specific administration users using the distributed administration capability of the QlikView Management Console.

Scheduling of Reloads: Reloads have to be performed for the QlikView User Applications on the QV Server (both test and production), the QlikView Source Applications and the QlikView Intermediate Applications. This is scheduled on the Publisher by Administrators. In addition, on a regular basis these scheduled processes are also audited for error-free execution. This is to ensure that business users see right current data in all the applications.

Up-Stream Data Preparation and Processing

Various data sources require periodic closing processes (daily / weekly / monthly / yearly) to prepare data before the QlikView extraction process schedule executes. These processes, though not directly part of the QlikView administration, are pre-requisites which become the starting point for the healthy operation of QlikView solution. Creation of EDX tasks to trigger /integrate with external ETL processes also are managed by the administrators.

IT Professionals—QlikView Solution Architects and Integrators

These are professionals who integrate various enterprise solutions along with QlikView solution elements. Refer QlikTech Whitepaper: QlikView Integration Overview, June 2011 from QlikTech [3].

Directory Services Connector

The enterprise repository of users is kept in the global directory services / identity management systems. Connecting these systems with QlikView components to allow integrated user administration is a key requirement.

In general such integration is done to be part of Single-Sign-On implemented in the enterprise. This is done using the Directory Services Connector by the Solution Architects.

Perimeter Security Control

QlikView Server and QlikView Web Server (of IIS) can be configured to work in a tight combination using Tunneling. It was mentioned briefly earlier in this chapter and will be discussed in detail in the chapter "QlikView Security".

WorkBench

For integrating QlikView Apps into other websites QlikView Workbench can be used. The QV API JavaScript reference provides necessary integrating WorkBench features through direct AJAX. This is a JavaScript class library and is used to build QlikView extensions or to build websites with QlikView Workbench.

QlikView OCX

QlikView OCX is used to integrate QlikView functionality as an embedded feature in the 3rd Party client-server applications.

QlikView Web Parts for Microsoft SharePoint®
QlikView Web Parts for Microsoft SharePoint® integrates QlikView front-end with SharePoint-based portals and collaboration sites.

Custom Connector API

For all the non-conventional, legacy and special data sources, where ODBC/OLE DB connectors are not available, there is a need to create custom connectors. There is an API available and the integration team can create such custom connectors as required. Using these connectors, QlikView ETL Engine can make a connection and extract the data directly into in-memory tables during the ETL session.

QVX

Sometimes with old systems, it is not possible to have them available directly over the network for direct extraction of data. In such cases, programs can be written in the native systems to export data into a QlikView Exchange format (QVX) files. These files can be directly loaded into QlikView like QVD files. QVX is an XML format defined by XSD and sample code is provided by QlikTech.

APIs

QlikView platform is rich with multiple APIs. These can be used for extending the capabilities of various QlikView components. They can also be used for integration of QlikView with other Enterprise Systems.

Automation API: More complex and extensive integration with external enterprise applications, Mashups and other portals can be done using the Automation API. For this, help may be required from the IT Professionals – Programmers who have VBScript / JavaScript experience. APIGuide.qvw provides extensive reference for all the API functions.

Extensibility API: QlikView provides a range of visualization objects out of the box, but there are many cases where customers want a customized way of displaying their data or content from another system. Some examples include maps, Gantt charts, or domain specific visualizations. In QlikView a capability called Extension Objects allows a developer to develop their own ways of visualizing their data but still making use of the powerful associative data engine in QlikView.

Developers can choose from a range of web technologies to build an extension object such as Flash, JavaScript or plain HTML, and have them interact within a QlikView document just like native QlikView charts and objects.

QMS API: QlikView provides common management tasks via a web service API called QMS API. This allows administrators to automate common tasks and apply customized business logic required using a range of technologies.

An example of management automation includes extending the scope of an employee on-boarding system to automatically add permissions and a license for QlikView or to ensure a license for a departing employee to be freed up for a new user. This would remove the need to manually perform such tasks.

EDX - Event Driven Execution: QlikView reloading processes are normally automated within Publisher. Sometimes before the QlikView reload is started, there may be other processes required to be completed.

There may be a need for triggering QlikView reload processes from another enterprise data management / ETL software, like Informatica or MSIS. This is done by using EDX API. This can be combined with the QMS API to create complex business- rules-driven event execution capabilities.

Power Tools

Recently QlikTech released a set of utilities that are very useful for administering QlikView deployments. Primarily meant for Troubleshooting, these tools handle a variety of tasks and are very useful for experienced QlikView administrators. The list of utilities provided in this kit is given below for a quick reference:

Shared File Viewer: Provides insight into the QlikView Server .shared files belonging to .qvw documents. The .shared file stores server data such as server/shared bookmarks, server objects (charts and objects created by a client via the server), annotations and other data that is specific to the document.

The tool visualizes the content of the binary .shared file and provides options to "Repair" legacy files and defrags large .shared files.

QlikView Server Agent: A small service utility that allows easy management of QlikView services. Also allows for quick change of credentials across multiple services at same time.

QMS API Client: A highly useful tool that gives the possibility to interact with the complete setup of QMS API functions in QlikView Server without typing a line of code. Helps visualize data structures and enables the user to parameterize and test every function call based on their own data or data from the QMS API.

QV User Manager: A command-line tool to list / add / remove and edit CAL and user information in a QlikView Server remotely.

QVS Detector: Scans the current subnet for other QlikView Servers and visualizes information like license, root folder, version and such. Also enables certain administrative functions.

Reload Schedule Migration Tool: A small step-by-step instruction tool that helps migrate reload schedules from non-Publisher databases in 9 to Publisher databases in 10 or 11, by manipulating the QVPR database (XML repository required) directly.

Server Object Handler: Enables listing, ownership changing and deletion of server objects in documents hosted on a QlikView Server remotely. It allows ownership to be changed on a selected number of server objects matching a given name pattern.

Server Object Handler Batch: The command-line little brother of the Server Object Handler, that does all the same, but from any command prompt or batch script.

XML DB Viewer: Visualizes and enables searching in and editing of QlikView Publisher Repository database (QVPR), when in XML.

Please refer to the PowerTools thread on QlikCommunity [8] for further details. The PowerTools 1.0 is available for download from QlikTech website as of the time of this writing.

Summary of Users vs. Functions vs. QlikView Components

Figure 8 maps the users and functions vs. the QlikView components. These users play specific roles and interact with the QlikView solution all through. The different functions that are performed by these users are tabulated below. Some of these functions are performed by multiple user types, using different components:

Function	User Group		
	IT Professionals	QV Developer / Analyst	Business Users
Analytics on Client	*Desktop*		
App Creation			*Web & Mobile*
Analytics on Browser			
User Admin	*Publisher*	*Desktop*	
Reload Admin			
Distribution Admin	*Publisher, PDF Publisher*		
ETL	*Connectors, QVX*		
Deployment Admin	*Management Console, PowerTools, QMS, DSC, DMS*		
Test Server	*QVS*		
Production Server			
Integration	*Web Parts, Workbench, OCX*		
APIs	*Automation, Extension, EDX, QMS*		

Figure 8: User Types, Functions Vs. QlikView Component

These users play specific roles and interact with the QlikView solution all through. The different functions that are performed by these users are tabulated below.

Some of these functions are performed by multiple user types, using different components:

Table 1: QlikView Components and Their Functions

Function	Description
Analytics on Desktop Client	Business users who are Power users and Travelling users use the Desktop client
Analytics on Browser	All users use the Browser client to Analyze, Share and Collaborate
Content Creation	Complete QVW with Desktop and Objects with AJAX/IE Plugin)
User Admin	Developers use Desktop to define Access Control (Section Access) rules, IT Administrators define rules on Publisher and users decide whom to share new objects with
Reload Admin	IT administrators define reload schedules and manage them
Distribution Admin	Publisher and PDF Distributor are used configured by IT Professionals to automatically export data in PDF formats and sent to Business users
ETL	Connectors and QVX are used by Developers (during development) and IT professionals (for production deployment)
Deployment Admin	Management Console, PowerTools and other components are used by IT Professionals for deployment management
Test Server	All users access QV Test Servers during the Testing/UAT phase
Production Server	Business Users access the production QV Servers. IT Professionals access them to administer
Integration Components	IT professionals and Developers use these components to create Mashups, embedded QV applications or custom websites using QlikView objects
APIs	Automation, Extension, EDX and QMS APIs are used by Developers and IT Professionals. These are essentially used for extending the capabilities of QlikView platform and for enterprise integration

Conclusions

The core application—QlikView Developer—is the mother of all applications. It generates the QVW Applications that deliver all the promises of QlikView Technology to the users. QlikView Server and QlikView Publisher form the most important infrastructure elements in a QlikView Deployment.

With the variety of capabilities existing in all the QlikView components, any enterprise need can be easily met by appropriate combination of components and configuring them in the right deployment pattern. If any particular need is not readily met by the existing components, then APIs and tools are available to extend the capabilities of QlikView and service those needs.

Integration with existing Enterprise Applications is an important need for making QlikView work seamlessly with other solutions already present or being added in the companies. The most important integrations are a) ETL, b) Web Integration, c) Automation Integration, d) Embedding. Every one of these needs can be taken care of by appropriate use of the components and extension capabilities of the QlikView Platform.

Understanding the platform becomes much easier when we are able to break down the components into the actual functional parts—engines. It will be a good idea to spend enough time visualizing the flow of data and actions, across all the engines and hence the components. The subsequent chapters in this Part II are going to delve deep into each of the key sub-systems of QlikView technology.

References

1. QlikView - The Product Family, 6 Page Brochure, QlikView.com
2. QlikView Architectural Overview, A QlikView Technology White Paper, Oct 2010, QlikView.com, [http://www.qlikview.com/us/explore/resources/whitepapers/qlikview-architectural-overview]
3. QlikView Integration Overview, QlikTech Technology Whitepaper, June 2011 from QlikTech,

[http://www.qlikview.com/us/explore/resources/whitepapers/qlikv iew-integration-overview]

4. QlikView Version 11 SDK, Dan English, Discussion Thread on QlikCommunity, QlikView.com, [http://community.qlikview.com/docs/DOC-2639]

5. QlikView User CAL overview, QlikTech White Paper, May 2011, QlikView.com

6. QlikView Licensing Overview, QlikTech Presentation

7. QVC – QlikView Components , Rob Wunderlich, Open source project in Google Code, [http://code.google.com/p/qlikview-components]

8. Power Tools discussion thread, QlikCommunity, QlikCommunity.com, [http://community.qlikview.com/thread/38461]

CHAPTER 9
QLIKVIEW ETL

SYNTHESIS IS A GREATER BUSINESS VIRTUE THAN ANALYSIS

Introduction to the Chapter

Traditionally BI solutions depended on separate ETL tools, with a need for extensive investments around the same. Due to the dependence on SQL technology, all these solutions required large storages, powerful machines to handle heavy loads generated with large enterprise data.

QlikView has ETL function integrated into the product—it exhibits great capability in handling many complex ETL requirements in an enterprise. There have been arguments about whether it is a good ETL solution or not, particularly the QlikCommunity Thread: QlikView vs. ETL [1]. It will be interesting to browse those discussions to get a background.

This chapter attempts to give a bird's eye view of the QlikView ETL functionality from an architectural standpoint. Arguably, there are still various challenges and solutions that exist with QlikView which are covered in the next chapter.

This chapter explores all the capabilities in a few broad parts: a) ETL Script Engine features, b) Data Source / Connectors, c) Scripting Language scope and d) ETL Integration. The next chapter covers a) Data Quality, b) ETL optimization, c) Real-Time Loads, d) Loading data into other systems using QlikView and finally e) ETL integration capabilities.

QlikView has been consistently growing as an ETL tool. The latest addition being QVX files and export to CSV format from QlikView are important capabilities that made a big difference on the ETL side. The QlikView ETL Script Engine alone can be used separately, independent of its other engines.

The most complaints about QlikView as an ETL tool have been the ability to create, schedule and manage the ETL jobs, using an administrative framework. With the recent Publisher versions this capability has been implemented with scalability and integration capabilities.

Before delving deep into what QlikView does with ETL, it will be good to set some reference points as to what are expected from any ETL tool. With this the chapter first sets some ground expectations on QlikView as an ETL tool. Then various capabilities of QlikView that help meet such ETL expectations are discussed throughout the chapter.

Is ETL Required?

Before discussing the principles of ETL and its implementation in QlikView, it is important to understand the relevance of ETL. A January 2006 article in Information Management, *"ETL is a symptom of the problem, not the solution"*, Ken Karacsony [2] goes on to show that extensive ETL is required only if data is not managed as an enterprise asset, since redundant data is completely eliminated. He goes on to say, "Performing extensive extract, transform and load (ETL) may be a sign of poorly managed data and a fundamental lack of a cogently developed data strategy. I realize this is a provocative statement; but, in my experience, there is a direct correlation between the extent of redundant data, which is a serious problem, and the amount of ETL processes." It is interesting to read this argument and understand the suggestions and pointers he has provided.

The key problem that necessitates ETL is the "silo" approach to having different applications for different functional areas. The solution is to create "Information Hubs" allowing data to be shared with all other beneficiaries instead of "owning" it as "my data". This is frequently referred to as "The Hub-And-Spoke Architecture". In this data-centric paradigm, the database, not the application, is the center of the universe. Once such a data approach is formed, QlikView can simply connect to all the relevant data stores and produce the data model and the necessary analytics/reports without too much of ETL needed. With hardware, particularly storage and network, getting continuously cheaper, this is where the world is moving towards, however slowly.

Till such fundamental change happens in enterprises, splintered existence of data is a reality, with silos and need to integrate them for a unified view. With this perspective, rest of the chapter focuses on the necessary ETL principles and how QlikView takes care of the ETL needs.

ETL Principles Revisited

Data has been always captured in different transaction systems inside an enterprise and stored separately in different data storage systems. The need to integrate data from various systems became stronger with increased need for integrated decision support systems. Data warehouses were created as homogeneous data repositories to combine data from these multiple sources.

ETL evolved as the process used to populate data warehouses with the extracted and pre-processed data from various source systems. Extract and Load are data reading and data writing functions, specific to the source and destination systems respectively.

Transform is "resolving the differences between the two, preserving (or adding to) the value of the data from the source extractor, normalizing it for general usage and delivering it to the target loader". A detailed discussion on ETL is available in the Wikipedia page: on Extract, Transform and Load [3].

Extract

It is essentially a relatively simple read function—but the need is to support as many source system types as possible. Each separate system may also use a different data organization/format. Common data source formats are relational databases and flat files, but may include non-relational database structures or even fetching from outside online sources by web extraction or screen-scraping. QlikView extracts from all possible systems using an appropriate connection mechanism.

An intrinsic part of the extraction involves the parsing of extracted data, resulting in a check if the data meets an expected pattern or structure. If not, the data may be rejected entirely or in part.

In general, the goal of extraction phase is to convert data into a single format that is appropriate for subsequent transformations before loading into the target system. With QlikView, implicitly this target system is the QlikView in-memory data model.

Load

It is a relatively simple write function. The need is to be able to push data into any target system. However, Load function can be standardized by supporting standard interchange file formats like CSV or XML and allowing target systems to import. Another common approach is to push data into a standard RDBMS using SQL inserts or Native import functions of the respective target system. Streaming of extracted data source and load on-the-fly to the destination database is another way of performing ETL when no intermediate data storage is required.

QlikView also provides facilities to push data into common formats like CSV and XML. It is also possible to use QlikView Automation API to push data into standard RDBMS targets.

Transform

Transform poses the toughest of needs. Capabilities of all ETL tools are evaluated on this. Fundamentally it is necessary to apply a series of simple to complex rules or functions to the extracted data from the source to derive the data for loading into the end target.

Following is a list of such transformations commonly required (Wikipedia: ETL):

- Selecting only certain columns to load (or selecting null columns not to load)
- Translating coded values (*e.g.*, if the source system stores 1 for male and 2 for female, but the target stores M for male and F for female), this calls for automated data translation; no manual cleansing occurs during ETL
- Encoding free-form values (*e.g.*, mapping "Male" to "1")
- Deriving new calculated value (*e.g.*, sale_amount = qty * unit_price)
- Sorting
- Joining data from multiple sources (e.g., lookup, merge) and de-duplicating (eliminating redundant) the data
- Aggregation (for example, rollup—summarizing multiple rows of data—total sales for each store, and for each region, etc.)
- Generating surrogate-key values (unique key to be used as primary)
- Transposing or pivoting (turning multiple columns into multiple rows or vice versa)

- Splitting a column into multiple columns (e.g., putting a comma-separated list specified as a string in one column as individual values in different columns)
- Disaggregation of repeating columns into a separate detail table (e.g., moving a series of addresses in one record into single addresses in a set of records in a linked address table)
- Lookup & validate relevant data from tables or referential files for slowly changing dimensions
- Applying any form of simple or complex data validation. If validation fails, it may result in a full, partial or no rejection of the data. Some, no or all data is handed over to the next step, depending on the rule design and exception handling. Many of the above transformations may result in exceptions, for example, when a code translation parses an unknown code in the extracted data.

In addition the following addition needs also exist:
- Concatenating data from multiple tables/sources
- Apply statistical, financial and specialized functions of the domain
- Statistical tests and create new fields of scores evaluated
- inter-record comparisons & calculations to perform conditional evaluations across records
- Perform conditional joins across data tables based on range conditions that exist in one for the keys in the other. For example, to relationalize non-relational data (e.g., combine invoices table with invoice date with pricing options table giving a from-date & to-date for price validity)

Challenges of ETL and Possible Solutions

ETL needs to be understood with a background of the various challenges that exist in a typical Enterprise environment. Can QlikView take care of the common challenges?

Key challenges in the Extract Stage—*Source System*—are:
- Formats of different data sources
- Retrieval methods required for source data (SQL and Non-SQL methods)
- Volumes of data

This is solved by data connectors that bring data from various source systems of different formats into the transform engine. The solution needs a flexible extensible architecture so that any new data source can be easily integrated by a specific data connector. High volumes of data can be handled easily by parallel processing of various data elements from same or different sources, instead of processing them sequentially. Of course appropriate hardware is required for the same.

Key challenges in the Load Stage—*Target System*—are:
- Format of target data storage
- Interface method used for pushing data into the target (SQL and non-SQL methods)

This challenge is solved by choosing some standard target systems and creating output for the same. To support multiple target technologies, common data storage formats are chosen into which the data is pumped in. This can be interchange formats like CSV / XML data files, or a standard RDBMS into which data is populated so that the target system can read the data from this data source.

Key challenges associated with *Transform* are:
- Data bloating that happens due to the intermediate joins
- Compute and memory needs to process this bloated volume of data

This is the most important problem that affects ETL solutions available in the industry. Practically all of these technologies use some form of SQL engine as the core for processing, and the standard problems of SQL are inherited by these tools (refer chapter "Comparison of Reporting Technologies" of Part I for a detailed discussion on the problems of SQL as a reporting / processing language).

Data Quality Challenges: Apart from the above process challenges, there are data quality challenges while performing ETL functions. To quote the Wikipedia ETL page:

> "The range of data values or data quality in an operational system may exceed the expectations of designers at the time validation and transformation rules are specified. *Data profiling* of a source during data analysis can identify the data conditions that will need to be

managed by transform rules specifications. This will lead to an amendment of validation rules explicitly and implicitly implemented in the ETL process."

Scalability and Performance: These are the classic problems of any data processing system, and ETL is probably most susceptible to this challenge due to the batch processing that normally happens. The capacity of network and systems should be made large enough to extract within the time windows during which backend systems are available for extraction. Wikipedia page best states this:

"Design analysts should establish the scalability of an ETL system across the lifetime of its usage. This includes understanding the volumes of data that will have to be processed within service level agreements. The time available to extract from source systems may change, which may mean the same amount of data may have to be processed in less time. Some ETL systems have to scale to process terabytes of data to update data warehouses with tens of terabytes of data. Increasing volumes of data may require designs that can scale from daily batch to multiple (intra)-day micro batches to integration with message queues or real-time change-data capture for continuous transformation and update."

The most important solution to scalability and performance issue is Parallel Processing.

Error Handling and Recoverability: ETL processes are divided into smaller pieces running sequentially or parallel. Ability to identify all data elements and ETL processes uniquely is important. On any error, it helps to roll-back and re-run the failed piece after correcting error conditions. Use of "checkpoints" and log files are helpful for this purpose.

Physical location of Source and Target Systems: With geographically distributed organizations, data centers are present across the globe. Moving data from one location to another is affected by the effective bandwidth available for data transfers. Solutions for this are: a) use compression techniques to reduce the data, b) perform incremental updates only and c) use replication systems to update transactions as they happen in multiple locations.

Dealing with keys: The use of primary keys and foreign keys across data from multiple data sources. Keys in one system may not be compatible with another—this requires new lookups which map them. Also the uniqueness of a record may be established using multiple fields of a record—in such cases, there is a need to create surrogate keys. These surrogate keys are mostly auto-generated integer values which are used only for the database purposes and have no meaning to the business entity / process being represented by the data.

Time Consumption: Typically ETL processes consume a lot of time based on the quantity of data, aggregation and computations. One major reason is due to SQL based processing and the other major reason is due to the extensive multi-stage dependencies among ETL jobs.

The first problem is solved by database tuning, indexing & partitioning of big tables, hardware enhancements particularly of I/O speeds, distributed processing and parallel processing are done to shorten the time taken for the ETL processes.

The second problem is solved by visualizing all processes on a graph, and reducing depth of graph levels by making maximum use of parallelism—making process "chains" as short as possible.

Any ETL solution, including QlikView, should address all of the above needs and find ways to solve the challenges posed above.

ETL with QlikView

The good news is, QlikView ETL infrastructure helps take care of all the above—either by readymade capabilities or by giving a framework where extensions are easy to implement. QlikView has some unique features which make the QlikView ETL powerful and flexible:

In-Memory Data Engine: As discussed earlier, once the data is extracted from the sources, this data is held in memory by the QlikView in-memory data engine in a highly optimized form. Even intermediate data is stored in memory during multi-stage transforms as much as possible. This reduces Disk I/O drastically, hence very less processing time.

Data Compacting: As discussed before, QlikView In-Memory data engine holds data of every column with hash indexes in memory. Hence all data tables are compacted to 10%-20% of original size on average. This reduces the amount of space used by the same data, both in memory and in disk when stored as a binary file.

How data reduces in QlikView: When data is extracted into QlikView, for every field from all tables, unique values are stored into a list. Actual field data are replaced with pointers pointing to distinct list of values. This reduces the number of copies of same value stored, and instead replacing every instance with a much smaller size pointer. This leads to a significant reduction of data sizes in QlikView—typically to 10-20% of the original data size (refer chapter "What is QlikView).

In-Memory ETL Script Engine: All this data is operated upon by the ETL script engine that transforms in-memory (very little or no disk I/O), with faster execution times compared to other disk-based transform systems. All the functions (over 200 functions) are highly optimized to work with the compact data format and also use parallel execution to take advantage of multi-core CPUs.

Non-SQL Data Transforms: QlikView uses a non-SQL transform technology. Combined with the compact data store, SQL engine based problems of data bloating due to Cartesian explosion and full table scans are avoided.

With all this, the amount of time taken for the entire ETL process can be reduced. The need for indexing & partitioning of data, database tuning and I/O enhancements which are typically required for better SQL performance can be avoided with QlikView. The result: an end-to-end ETL capabilities using a non-SQL engine. Other capabilities of QlikView explained below help solve many of the ETL challenges highlighted in the earlier section.

Key Components of QlikView ETL

The key components of the QlikView ETL layer are:
- Non-SQL ETL Engine and a rich Script with flow-control constructs for Transform
- Highly compact stores for intermediate storage (in-memory and as QVDs on disk) between complex Transform stages

- Data Connectors (SQL, File, non-SQL and custom) and QVX (for legacy and specialized data sources) for Extract
- Export Engine for writing data into CSV and XML files for Load
- Publisher for Scheduling and managing QVD extraction and multi-stage ETL jobs
- Error-Handling script constructs for Managing ETL Errors
- Batch files, in-script execution of external programs and EDX for Integration
- Transform script constructs for Data Cleansing

The following sections explain more about QlikView ETL.

QlikView Script

Script is a user program that is run by QlikView ETL Script Engine. It is a description of the location of source data, what fields to load and, if needed, how data is to be processed. This is executed when RELOAD is pressed in Desktop version or when a task is executed in Publisher.

When executed, it connects the QlikView document to one or several data sources and opens tables, reading specified fields. On completion of execution of all the script statements, the tables loaded are automatically connected into an associative data model. These connections are made through keys—fields having same *FieldName* in two or more tables.

Script Statements and Syntax

Like any scripting language, QlikView script has a number of statements. A statement can be either a Regular script statement or Control statement. Certain statements can be preceded by prefixes.

Regular statements are typically used for manipulating data in one way or another. These statements may be written over any number of lines in script and must always be terminated by a semicolon (;).

Control statements are typically used for controlling flow of script execution. Each clause of control statement must be kept inside one script line and may be terminated by a semicolon or an end-of-line.

Prefixes (used for naming resultant intermediate data tables) may be applied to applicable regular statements but never to control statements. The *when* and *unless* prefixes can however be used as suffixes to a few specific control statement clauses.

QlikView ETL Functions: QlikView has over 200 functions in the following categories:

Table 1: Functions Available in QlikView

Aggregation Functions (only in script)	General Numeric Functions
	Interpretation Functions
Statistical Aggregation Functions	Inter Record Functions
Financial Aggregation Functions	Logical Functions
Other Functions	Mapping Functions
Conditional Functions	Mathematical Constants
Counter Functions	Parameter-Free Functions
Date and Time Functions	NULL Functions
Statistical Distribution Functions	Script Range Functions
Exponential Functions	String Functions
Logarithmic Functions	System Functions
File Functions in Script	Table Functions
Financial Functions	Trigonometric Functions
Formatting Functions	Hyperbolic Functions

QlikView help is invoked anytime by F1 and is context sensitive. All the syntaxes are given in the BNF format in help. QlikView Reference Manual is the best place to learn all the nuances about scripting. Also the various blogs give cases and examples of scripting. All programmers with a good understanding of SQL and a bit of programming experience can easily write ETL scripts in QlikView.

Special Capabilities of QlikView ETL Script

Some classical features of specialized ETL tools are included in QlikView, and also some new innovations. Understanding/using these functions will help take true advantage of QlikView for efficient ETL. Please refer to QlikView Reference Manual for more information on these:

Null Value Handling: Specialized mechanisms are provided for handling NULL values separately a) at the time of loading from ODBC or TXT files, b) at the time of evaluating in the expressions. QlikView NULL VALUE handling is one of the best approaches and is easy on developers and data analysts.

Maps: Mapping is a process where lookup tables are used for replacing field values with valid / preferred values during the loading process itself, before the extracted table is stored either in a resulting QVD or in the data model. This allows maintaining a transient *cleansing* step to be done without performing the expensive JOINS required normally for the purpose. The tables loaded as MAP TABLES are automatically dropped from the memory at the end of the ETL Script execution.

Inter Record Functions: Specialized functions are provided to access values of chosen fields in other records (before or after current record) to make comparisons and take dynamic data load-time decisions. PEEK and PREVIOUS are excellent functions which make life easy.

Script Variables: There are many script variables predefined in QlikView to handle various requirements. The variables available are broadly in four categories: Error Variables, Number Interpretation Variables, System Variables and Value Handling Variables. Please refer to the Reference Manual and QlikView Help to understand more about these variables. They are very powerful and give an excellent control of the default behavior of the ETL Engine.

Table Labels: All the tables, as they are loaded in-memory, can be given an identifier in memory. This helps in referring to these tables and fields from other script statements like PEEK and in RESIDENT loads. Developers should make it a practice to use table labels.

Data Connectors

These provide the ability to connect to most data sources, and pull data into the QlikView solution. QlikView makes a copy of the back-end data and stores a copy in a highly optimized reduced data store as QVD / QVX files or QVW files. QlikView requires a much smaller data size than the other systems. The most important advantage is, when the users query the data in QlikView, there is no load on backend databases, freeing them up for transaction processing with better performance.

Data Connectors for standard data sources

Standard Data Connectors: Out of the box, the QlikView core ETL Script Engine comes with the default ability to connect to the standard OLEDB,

ODBC, XML, Microsoft Excel and various other file formats. Salesforce connector is also provided by QlikTech as a standard.

Data from commercial and open source database systems is loaded into QlikView via the Microsoft OLE DB / ODBC interface. For this install the necessary ODBC/OLE DB drivers and configure the database as an ODBC / OLE DB data source. QlikView can also read data from table files, in which fields are separated by a delimiter like commas, tabs or semicolons. Other possible formats are dif files (Data Interchange Format), fix files (fixed record length), HTML tables, Excel files, XML files and native QVD & QVX files.

QlikView JDBC Connector: Recently, in Sep 2011, a new JDBC Connector DLL has been released [4]. This will enable a lot of non-ODBC/OLEDB sources for load into QlikView. Also, it would give much more performance on QV 9 loads (Oracle, mysql etc.) and could speed up on complex network environments (like VPN, firewalls, WAN). This is much better than using JDBC-ODBC Bridge. This allows tuning driver properties by using connection URLs like:
jdbc:oracle:thin:@sampleserver:1521:db?defaultRowPrefetch=1000

This works very well on large data sets.

Custom Data Connectors: For all data sources which do not follow these standards, there is a Custom Connector API that is offered as a standard component with QlikView. Using this, a Salesforce connector has been built by QlikView and provided free. This gets installed when QlikView development version is installed.

Optional Connectors, for SAP and Informatica, are provided by QlikTech. These are separate priced components which are required only if SAP and Informatica are present in the company and data needs to be extracted by QlikView directly from them.

QlikView Connector for Informatica: Many organizations use a data warehouse to secure a single source of data and meet compliance and governance requirements. To facilitate agile and high-performance reporting requirements, organizations can use the QlikView Informatica Connector to extend the value of the data warehouse by producing QVX files that can be directly read into QlikView. This alleviates the need for a reporting data mart.

QlikView for SAP

QlikView SAP Connector for Netweaver: Using QlikView, organizations complement their centralized SAP reporting capabilities with instant, user-driven analysis, allowing decision-making at the speed of business. QlikView Connector for Use with SAP NetWeaver® enables SAP users to perform quick, flexible, visual, ad hoc analysis and reporting.

QlikView combines data from SAP® R/3®, mySAP™, SAP BW & BEX queries with data from non-SAP systems. All of this unified data is available to users.

QlikView also offers out-of-the-box QlikStart templates for a range of SAP modules including Sales and Distribution (SD), Materials Management (MM), Project Systems (PS), Production Planning (PP), Human Resources (HR), Controlling (CO), and Finance (Account Receivable (AR), Accounts Payable (AP), and General Ledger (GL). More on this is given separately in the Chapter on "QlikView for SAP".

Reading CUBE datasets into QlikView

Reading from any existing CUBE is probably not the best thing to do. Instead if the actual raw data can be brought into QlikView, the amount of slicing and dicing that is possible is quite wide. However, there may be some situations in which CUBE data needs to be read & used.

This thread on QlikCommunity talks about the way in which MDX querying can be done on MS Analysis services to extract data[5]. There are related posts in QlikCommunity which provide in-depth information about the same.

Essentially, there is no direct support for building or executing MDX-queries in QlikView. By using openrowset() in SQL, it is possible to encapsulate MDX-query in a standard SELECT statement. Here is an example of how this works:

// Connection string to standard SQL Server instance (note initial

catalog to SQL database not required)

CONNECT TO [Provider=SQLOLEDB.1;Integrated

Security=SSPI;Persist Security Info=False;Data Source=biserver;Use

Procedure for Prepare=1;Auto Translate=True;Packet

Size=4096;Workstation ID=biserver;Use Encryption for

Data=False;Tag with column collation when possible=False];

// Query to extract MDX as relational data set

SQL SELECT * FROM OPENROWSET

('MSOLAP.3',

'Provide=MSOLAP.3;Integrated Security=SSPI;Persist Security

Info=False;Data Source=biserver;Initial Catalog=Analysis Services

Tutorial;',

'SELECT {[Measures].[Unit Price]} ON COLUMNS,

{[Customer].[Customer].MEMBERS} ON ROWS FROM [Adventure

Works DW]')

Similarly, using appropriate OLAP providers, the CUBE data from other cubes like TM1, SAP OLAP etc. can be extracted into QlikView. To connect to BO Universe and other such sources, check out DataRoket Data Connector Suite page [6].

Cloud Data Sources

Custom Data source API can be used to construct connectors for any data source. A custom data connector has been created for Salesforce.com and bundled freely along with QlikView.

QlikView Connector for Salesforce.com: The QlikView Connector for use with Salesforce.com® enables content developers to create QlikView apps that utilize Salesforce.com data, and to merge this data with data from other systems. This connector works on the desktop or with apps deployed on QlikView Server and accessed through the browser — including on mobile devices.

Google Spreadsheet: Google Apps Spreadsheets can be directly used as data sources, and content can be extracted directly into a QlikView table. A discussion on this and a sample application is available from QlikCommunity Thread 1628 [7].

Social Media Sites: QVSource.com has released an API and an SDK for development around it. This allows connectivity of QlikView directly to pull data from: Facebook, Twitter, LinkedIn, OData, MongoDB and of course Google Spreadsheets and Google Analytics, and many others [8].

Non-Standard Data Connectors: Also included is QVX (for legacy and specialized data sources) explained separately below.

QlikView Data Storage Formats

QlikView Data (QVD) File Format

QVD is a native QlikView file format. A QVD file contains one data table, no layout and no security. It could be seen as a "binary csv file", optimized for fast loading. Any data read from any source, including QVX can be stored in QVD format.

A QVD (QlikView Data) file is a dump of table data as it is optimally stored in memory in QlikView, exported for storage in disk. QVD is a native QlikView format and can only be written to and read by QlikView.

The file format is optimized for speed when reading data from a QlikView script but it is still very compact. Reading data from a QVD file is typically 10 to 100 times faster than reading from other data sources.

QVD files can be read in two modes, a) standard (fast) and b) super-fast. The selected mode is determined automatically by the QlikView script engine. Super-fast mode can be utilized only when all fields or a subset thereof are read without any transformations (formulas acting upon the fields). Renaming of fields is not considered a transformation hence is allowed in super-fast mode.

A QVD file holds exactly one data table and consists of three parts:

- A well formed XML header (in UTF-8 char set) describing the fields in the table, layout of the subsequent information and some other meta-data
- Symbol tables in a byte stuffed format
- Actual table data in a bit-stuffed format

Purpose of QVD Files: QVD files can be used for many purposes. At least four major uses can be easily identified. More than one may apply in any given situation:

- *Increasing Load Speed:* By buffering non-changing or slowly changing blocks of input data in QVD files, script execution becomes considerably faster for large data sets.
- *Decreasing Load on Database Servers:* The amount of data fetched from external data sources can also be greatly reduced. This reduces work load on external databases and network traffic. Furthermore, when several QlikView scripts share the same data it is only necessary to load it once from the source database. The other applications can make use of the same data via a QVD file.
- *Consolidating Data from Multiple QlikView Applications:* With the Binary script statement it is limited to loading data from a single QlikView application into another one, but with QVD files a QlikView script can combine data from any number of QlikView applications.

  Data tables from QVW files can be loaded in memory by a binary load, and the tables can be output into separate QVD files. This opens up possibilities of consolidation, e.g. for applications consolidating similar data from different business units, locations, periods, etc.
- *Incremental Load*: In many common cases the QVD functionality can be used for facilitating incremental load, i.e. exclusively loading new records from a growing database - more on incremental loading with QVDs in the section on Optimizing ETL.

QlikView Exchange (QVX) File Format

QVX is a highly optimized data format that QlikView understands natively. QVX provides both a file format specification and a network pipe message format specification for communication between QlikView Script and a Custom data Connector.

This is essentially a mechanism by which legacy and/or non-traditional data sources may be accessed. QVX works alongside other QlikView connections.

QVX File Format: When data sources cannot be directly connected, the data can be exported from the source systems into QVX format.

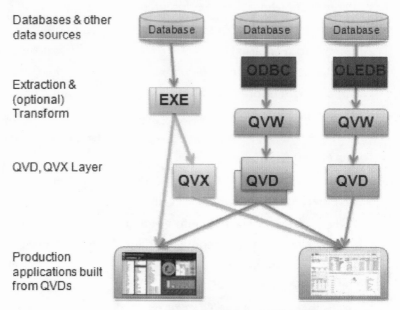

Figure 1: QVX and QVD formats

QlikView can then read the QVX format directly into memory faster than other formats. This format is specified in a detailed fashion, so that data can be easily written to this format. An SDK is also provided for writing EXE files to export into QVX.

It is an XML format defined by an XSD provided by QlikTech—sample code is also available. While using QVX for data exchange, a program using QVX API in the source system generates QVX files directly; QlikView reads them just like QVD files.

QVX Exchange through Network Pipe: A custom application is created as an EXE file listening for connection requests from QlikView Script. This custom application is invoked via the Load Script.

Commands are sent from QlikView to the Custom Application (using QVX_CONNECT, QVX_EXECUTE and QVX_TERMINATE com-mands).

The application interprets the query strings passed and executes custom code to pull data. This data is formatted into QVX messages and transmitted back to QlikView.

Sample code for the same is provided as part of the QVX SDK from QlikTech. Please refer to the QlikCommunity Thread "QVX SDK Libraries and Examples" by Dan English, Dec 2011 [9, 10].

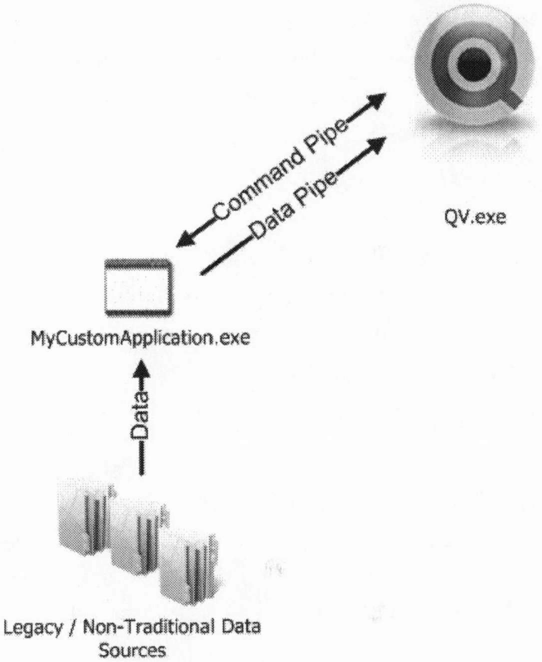

Figure 2: QVX EXE for Data Exchange

Consider QVX for the following situations:
For following Data sets:

- Not accessible by standard connections
- Load optimization or high volume is a factor
- Complex processing needs to be kept in the source system itself to use existing programs already written (without redoing the work)

For following Data Sources (not exhaustive):

- Legacy data sources
  - Mainframe
- Massively parallel processing systems
  - Hadoop
- API / Code based data sets
  - Team Foundation Server
  - Windows Event Viewer
  - Jason API based systems

- NoSQL Databases (http://nosql-database.org)
  - Wide Column Store / Column Family: HBase, Casandra, HyperTable, Amazon SimpleDB
  - Document Stores: MongoDB, CouchDB (JSON API), OrientDB, RavenDB, Citrus Leaf, ClusterPoint Server, Thru DB, Terrastore, SISO DB, SDB
  - Key Value / Tuple Store: Azure Table Storage, MemBase, RIAK, Redis, LevelDB, Cordless, Genie DB, Scalaris, Tokyo Cabinet / Tyrant, GT.M, Scallion, Berkeley DB, Mem Cache DB
  - Eventually Consistent Key-Value Stores, Graph Databases and other Soft NoSQL Databases

Connecting to non-standard data sources using QVX

Developers can use the open QVX (QlikView data exchange) format for importing non-standard data sources into QlikView. QlikView also provides direct connectors to some of today's most popular business applications and platforms.

Sometimes with old systems, it is not possible to have them available directly over the network for direct extraction of data. Sometimes connectors cannot be created for any other reason like security or platform support. In such cases, programs can be written in the native systems to export data into a QlikView Exchange format (QVX) files. These files can be directly loaded into QlikView like QVDs.

Stages and Processes of QlikView ETL

Enterprise needs to be solved using Data Layers

When data is extracted from various sources to create multiple business analytic applications with QlikView, there are some key points that need to be kept in mind:

1. Same data may be required for multiple QlikView Applications— hence its efficient to store on first extract and re-use again
2. Common definitions / processing required for various data elements like Slowly Changing Dimensions, Master Data and for some transaction data—*extracting and transforming* them once and using wherever required is more efficient

3. Pre-processing some of the data and storing them is more efficient:
   a. Pre-join to reduce number of tables
   b. Create aggregates
   c. Create calculated fields (both common calculations across enterprise & special calculations for individual departments)
4. Storing data for each period on a separate QVD is more efficient than updating large QVDs with fresh data every time incremental extract is performed is more efficient

QlikView provides the facility to hold data in the intermediate stages in memory itself or on disk in the form of QVDs. Refer to the short article on Slowly Changing Dimensions in QlikView on GuerillaBI.com. As seen before, QVDs need much lesser space than the source systems. Also, storing and retrieving QVDs is much faster than any other format files. Due to these advantages, QVDs can be used as intermediate layers and an enterprise wide approach of ETL flow can be created. One such broad approach is outlined in the figure below. Horizontally, the figure shows 5 stages / tiers / layers of data. Vertically the various processes required to be performed during the ETL process.

Data Layers (Horizontal) produced by ETL Processes (Vertical)

Stage 1   Source Data systems. This could be any data source as seen in the previous sections. This can also be data warehouses and specialized data sources.

Stage 2   Raw QVDs: on completing the extraction, data is stored as QVDs at the most granular levels. Incremental extraction and basic cleansing processes are done at the time of this extraction by Process 1. This produces Masters, Slowly Changing Dimensions and Transaction tables. Transaction tables of incremental periods can be stored in this stage as separate tables for each period using a filename pattern <filename: fileprefix-YYYY-MM-DD-hh-mm>. Since QlikView is capable of loading multiple tables using a filename pattern into a single QVD in-memory this is a great way to optimize.
Stage 1 is transformed by Process 1 to Stage 2. This Process 1 is done by QVW files with just ETL script, without any objects. Such QVW files are called *QlikView Source Documents*. They

are also called as *QVD Generators*. With QlikView 11 Publisher, this step does not explicitly require a QVW file—instead the *QVD Generation Tasks* are supported directly in the Publisher administration pages. This reduces the need to maintain separate QVW files for Raw QVD generation, unless there is complex processing done in the extraction stage itself.

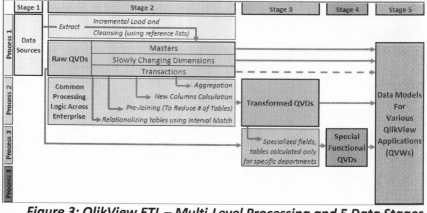

Figure 3: QlikView ETL – Multi-Level Processing and 5 Data Stages (Layers or Tiers)

Stage 3   Transformed QVDs: As an output of the Process 2, the new tables created are stored in this stage/layer. Generally in this level, all the processing which does not depend on the user selections in the front-end should be done. This process optimizes and reduces the front-end load when users interact with the application. Stage 2 is transformed by Process 2 to Stage 3. Process 2, 3 and 4 are performed by QVW files with just ETL scripts, however, they don't make connections to the source systems, but use Raw QVDs and other intermediate QVDs as their input. These are referred to as *QlikView Intermediate Documents,* also as *QVD Aggregators*.

Stage 4   Special Functional QVDs: In Process 3, data required for specialized functions for particular departments/functions is created and stored as additional QVD files. These are also generated by *QlikView Intermediate Documents*. The output created by Stages 3 and 4 are referred to as QlikMarts as well. They actually mimic the way data-marts behave in conventional data warehouse systems.

Stage 5   QVW files: Process 4 loads the various QVDs generated by the previous processes, as required, in various *QVW User Documents*, also known as *QVW User Applications*. All the various stage QVW files that run the Processes 1 to 4 are all defined as Tasks in Publisher Jobs. This is the ETL scheduling and reload job management layer of QlikView.

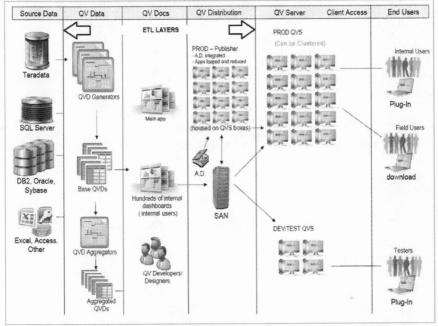

Figure 4: Typical QlikView ETL Stages in a Sample Deployment

Figure 4 shows a sample implementation of QlikView in a very large manufacturing company. This involves 1000s of users and 100s of applications. This is a 4 stage deployment instead of a 5 stage. In practical implementations, the stages 3 and 4 are combined into a single stage of Intermediate QVD generation. However, differentiating them as two different stages helps in assigning responsibilities of ownership for the logic and data in these two layers.

Generally the stages 1, 2 and 3 are owned by Core IT. Stage 4 and 5 can be owned by the Business Analysts, Business Users and QV developers.

QlikView ETL output into Data Model

At the end of ETL Script execution of stage 4 / process 3, a set of tables are left as the final transformed output. Typically these tables are all connected through keys, to form a star or a snow-flake schema. In this form, they are readily available to be loaded in stage 5 / process 4, into the QlikView In-Memory Data Engine, and allow QlikView Associative & Aggregation Engine to operate on them. This in-memory data model is the target into which QlikView ETL by default pushes all data.

Since all the data tables are connected in-memory during analysis, it is important that the data model follows some standard guidelines. One important factor is there should be no circular references - throughout the various transformations, particularly in the final stage, the field names are all renamed in such a way that the table keys do not connect three or more tables in a cyclic fashion.

A detailed discussion on this Data Model is given in the chapter on "QlikView Data Model" and the chapter on "Making QlikView Work" in Part III.

Scheduling of ETL Jobs

With multi-stage ETL discussed above, the sequence of loading can get complex and need to be run as batches. Various tasks inside a batch will have a dependency tree. One needs to follow or trigger another based on this relationship. This task/batch management is done in Publisher.

Publisher Job Scheduling

Publisher is primarily meant for executing scripts (reloading) of all the Source, Intermediate and User QVW Documents—used in Processes 1 to 3 and final user applications in Process 4. To perform this function, the ETL Script Engine is embedded into publisher, along with a Schedule Execution Engine. Schedules are defined using web-based admin console, which is part of the QlikView Management Console. New types of tasks / jobs are available with QlikView 11 onwards, like explained already: QVD Extraction Tasks and External Command Execution Tasks. First is used to perform Process 1 jobs without having to write separate QlikView Source Documents.

Second is used to execute external programs before or during execution of the QlikView ETL scripts—could be used for preparing data for extract or to clean up data after extraction, or to run external tools like R,

MatLab, or other software to perform specialized calculations before/during extraction into QlikView.

Publisher PDF Distributor component contains an Export Engine, and runs the schedules required for exporting various reports into PDF. They are distributed via Emails or published into predefined directories. These jobs are executed after QlikView User Documents are refreshed.

Batch Files and Windows Scheduler for Scheduling Reloads

In simple implementations, where number of QVW applications is just a few, the reload process can be managed by using Windows Batch Files or Scripts. The QlikView Desktop Application accepts a command-line switch /R.

```
<installpath>\QlikView.exe /R <application>.QVW
```

With this switch, the QlikView executable just opens the application specified, runs the ETL script as if RELOAD button was pressed, and once data is refreshed, saves the data into QVW file and quits. Before the recent versions of Publisher, in many large implementations, batch file based reload processes were implemented, but with the new Publisher most of these batches can be executed within Publisher itself.

An additional capability is provided using EDX to integrate Publisher Tasks with external ETL processes in large enterprises, more on this in the next section. Read through this QlikCommunity Thread for further insights of the significant improvements that have been done on Publisher version 11: QV11 - Server and Publisher Getting Started Guides [11].

Enterprise Integration of QlikView ETL

Integration overview

Data from source systems often go through a significant processing before available for extraction into QlikView. Normally these are End-Of-Day (EOD) processes run either on source systems, or in intermediate staging systems already implemented.

Scheduling of QlikView ETL needs to be weaved along with these existing processes. Having a parallel non-connected QlikView ETL schedule will create synchronization issues. The need is to keep one side scheduled, with a trigger to initiate the intermediate tasks on the other when appropriate, wait for their completion and then continue to execute the remaining tasks.

Depending on whether QlikView has to be the leading process or other systems, two approaches are possible: a) QlikView Led ETL and b) Externally Led ETL.

External jobs based on QlikView events—QlikView Led ETL

In enterprises that use only QlikView for ETL from source systems directly, there may be a few external programs that need to be run to perform some transformations / processing before the data is extracted into QlikView. This may be required to be done in between two QlikView Source Applications or as an intermediate process in between QlikView ETL tasks. This is possible by executing an external program from inside the QlikView ETL Script and wait for its completion before proceeding with the subsequent lines of the script.

The *Execute* statement is used for this purpose. With the execute statement it is possible to run other programs during every execution of QlikView script, e.g. conversions that are necessary:

```
execute commandline
```

Where *commandline* is a text that can be interpreted by the operating system as a command line, as shown in the following examples:

```
Execute C:\Program Files\Office12\Excel.exe;
Execute winword macro.doc;
Execute cmd.exe /C C:\BatFiles\Log.bat
Note: The /C needs to be included as it is a
parameter to cmd.exe.
```

E*rror condition* is not returned by Execute statement. If error condition check is required, the external program should write the error condition to a file as name=value pair and it should be loaded in the next script statement as an include file to check the value of the variable in it.

To execute external programs in remote machines, any remote invocation method needs to be used and called through a batch file or a client program written for the purpose. Making web service calls is the most common method. The Source QlikView Application can then be scheduled as a process on Publisher or using Windows scheduler.

Externally Led ETL—EDX

If the need is to have QlikView ETL Jobs triggered based on External Events, this is accomplished by using the EDX (Event Driven Execution)— an API interface. The primary usage of EDX is to have an external scheduler or an ETL tool (like Trillium or Informatica) to initiate QlikView batch jobs as part of a larger batch process. Triggering a QlikView batch may also need to be done on arrival of a file or on user request.

EDX is a programmatic extension to the Management Console through a QMS API extension called QMSEDX. This allows programmatic control over the Publisher (QDS) tasks. A detailed overview of this can be found in QlikView Whitepaper by Arthur Lee: Using EDX in QV 11 [12, 13].

Mostly, ETL batches are all long-running, and hence are triggered typically by batch processes written in operating system scripting languages. This helps scheduling the batch, monitoring its progress and tracking failure/success of the complete batch. However all component ETL processes need to run in the same platform / same machine.

When QlikView runs on Windows machines and other ETL runs on non-windows platforms, or on other windows machines, the common solution is to run individual tasks as web-requests and monitor their progress by repeatedly polling the status of the task. This is the core approach of the EDX API as well.

EDX with QMS API

The QMS API, and hence EDX API, is a web service API that uses the Simple Object Access Protocol (SOAP). From Version 11 onwards, EDX is a part of QMS API and runs through QlikView Management Service (QMS) though in earlier versions it ran as part of the QlikView Distribution Service (QDS).

Client EDX API Applications: EDX API is implemented to be invoked by applications written in .NET particularly due to the security model used (explained in detail in the section on Security with EDX). The .NET Client applications make HTTP (web) requests to QMS on port 4799. A sample application is provided to demonstrate EDX in the QlikCommunity Thread: "Using EDX in QV 11" by Arthur Lee [12, 13].

The EDX operates in a sequence signified by the below steps:

- The client application makes calls to instruct QMS to start a task and in return receives an error code indicating success or failure, as well as an execution ID.

- The execution ID uniquely identifies the execution of the task as opposed to the task itself.

- The client application then periodically polls QMS to check the progress of the task execution.

- This poll request returns a data structure that contains, among other things, the execution status, start time, stop time (if already finished), and a list of new execution IDs.

- These subsequent execution IDs represent the execution of tasks that are triggered because the initial task has finished.

- The client application can then follow an entire set of inter-related tasks that together make up a full parallelized batch flow.

QMSEDX Command Line Tool: In addition to writing separate EDX client applications, there is a command line version of the QMSEDX made available in the same thread given above. This QMSEDX.EXE can be run as part of another batch file. This executes a single task using the task name or task id, and waits for the result. This application has got the following commandline options:

```
qmsedx      -task=name        [-qms=qmsaddress][-
       password=pwd][-variablename=vname][-
       ariablevalues=vvalues][-
       timeout=timeout][-
       pollinterval=interval][-
       verbosity=verbosity]


  Arguments:
```

- *task [REQUIRED]: The name or id of the task to execute*

- *qms [OPTIONAL]: The address of the qms. Default is the local host*

- *password (-pwd) [OPTIONAL]: The password required to execute the task, if set*

- *variablename (-vn) [OPTIONAL]: The name of the variable to pass on to the task, if set*

- *variablevalues (-vv) [OPTIONAL]: A semicolon separated list of values of the variable to pass on to the task*

- *timeout (-to) [OPTIONAL]: How many seconds to wait for the task to finish. Default value is one minute*

- *pollinterval (-pi) [OPTIONAL]: How often to check the status of the task. Default value is every five seconds*

- *verbosity [OPTIONAL]: The level of output, 0-5. 0 will not produce any output and 5 is the most verbose*

The custom clients and the *qmsedx* return an error code to the operating system. This can be retrieved in a standard way by using %ERRORLEVEL% environment variable in a BAT or a CMD file.

User Initiated ETL jobs

When there is a need to allow some privileged users to initiate some ETL jobs, this can be done by allowing them to run custom QMSEDX applications developed for the purpose. These applications can be given special rights to allow the user to run the ETL job, from their logins and machines designated for the purpose. The security model of EDX allows such a fine grained control.

Security with EDX

The requests are made by the EDX client applications as HTTP (Web) requests on port number 4799. An elaborate security mechanism is setup to control such execution of any task through an EDX call as described below:

- The system is secured by NT LAN Manager (NTLM) as well as special protective measures to avoid certain types of hijacking attacks known as "time limited service key".
- This combination of security means the client application must be written in .NET and an example code is provided in .NET projects/solutions developed in Microsoft Visual Studio 2010.
- The client application uses NTLM to authenticate a Windows account to QMS. QMS then checks which Windows groups the Windows account for the client application is member of to determine the function calls the user is allowed to make.
- Most of the QMS API requires membership in a local group called "QlikView Management API", but to run EDX, a separate group, "QlikView EDX", should be used. Both groups are local Windows groups on the server where QMS runs.
- The client application makes calls to instruct QMS to start a task and in return receives an error code indicating success or failure, as well as an execution ID. The execution ID uniquely identifies the execution of the task as opposed to the task itself.
- The client application then periodically polls QMS to check the progress of the task execution. This poll request returns a data structure that contains, among other things, execution status, start time, stop time (if already finished), and a list of new execution IDs.
- These subsequent execution IDs represent the execution of tasks that are triggered because the initial task has finished.
- The client application can then follow an entire set of inter-related tasks that together make up a full parallelized batch flow.

A lot of additional information and use-cases are provided in various threads in QlikCommunity. Particularly one thread talks about how SSIS Script Task can invoke QlikView reloads using EDX.

Load balancing and high-availability: Because communication is with QMS instead of QDS, a QDS cluster can be used to load balance EDX calls. If high availability is required for the batch environment, QMS is a single point of failure. Consider either virtualization of QMS or an active/passive system.

One of the important things about EDX is, it can be used without a Publisher License. Simply pass the name of the QVW instead of a task name and the reload schedule of the QVW will run. Of course, the QVW reload schedule should be defined already in the QV Server Management Console.

Conclusions - Enterprise Grade ETL with QlikView

With EDX on QMS, the QlikView has moved into the slot of enterprise grade ETL solutions. The many options for enterprise integration, automation and flexibility have helped QlikView ETL gain the much desired enterprise solution status.

In addition to all this, there is a need to have a process driven approach to ETL. Due to the quick win capabilities of QlikView normally the approach is not well thought out and systematic. The need is to follow the standard ETL guidelines set in the beginning of this chapter. Some of the advanced capabilities of QlikView ETL can help improve the process significantly. The next chapter focuses on these aspects to derive a more powerful ETL solution using those powerful approaches, methodologies and features.

References

1. QlikView vs. ETL, Discussion Thread on QlikCommunity, QlikView.com, [http://community.qlikview.com/message/79628]
2. ETL is a Symptom of the Problem not the Solution, Ken Karacsony , Jan 2006, Information Management, [http://www.information-management.com/issues/20060101/1044329-1.html]
3. Extract Transform and Load, Wikipedia Page, [http://en.wikipedia.org/wiki/Extract,_transform,_load]
4. QlikView JDBC Connector DLL, QlikCommunity Pages, QlikView.com, [http://community.qlikview.com/docs/DOC-2438#comment-3285]

5. Pull data from Analysis Services Cube, QlikCommunity Thread, [http://community.qlikview.com/message/47588#47588]

6. Data Connector Suite, DataRoket, Dataroket.com, [http://dataroket.com/products/data-connector-suite]

7. Google Spreadsheet Connectivity, QlikCommunity Thread, [http://community.qlikview.com/thread/1628]

8. QlikView Connectors, Qvsource.com, [http://www.qvsource.com/Connectors-For-QlikView]

9. QVX SDK Libraries and Examples, Dan English, Discussion Thread on QlikCommunity, QlikView.com, [http://community.qlikview.com/docs/DOC-2689]

10. QlikView Version 11 SDK, Dan English, Discussion Thread on QlikCommunity, QlikView.com, [http://community.qlikview.com/docs/DOC-2639]

11. QlikView 11 – Server & Publisher Getting Started Guides, Version 3, Arthur Lee, QlikCommunity, [http://community.qlikview.com/docs/DOC-2668]

12. Using EDX in QV 11, A Technology White Paper, QlikCommunity, QlikView.com, [http://community.qlikview.com/servlet/JiveServlet/download/265 0-10-27292/Using_EDX_in_QV11_1.pdf]

13. Using EDX in QV 11, Arthur Lee, Thread in QlikCommunity, QlikView.com, [http://community.qlikview.com/docs/DOC-2650]

## CHAPTER 10

ADVANCED ETL WITH QLIKVIEW

ANALYSIS = SEE FACTS. SYNTHESIS = GET INSIGHTS. ANALYSIS + SYNTHESIS = GOOD DECISIONS [1, 2]

Introduction to the Chapter

QlikView ETL is enterprise ready, can push the envelope and go beyond many other popular ETL solutions. QlikView inherently provides better ways of extraction and transformation, works very uniquely due to the in-memory approach and a non-SQL engine.

In addition to just tools, in an enterprise situation, there are processes and practices that are important to ensure data quality. To meet these requirements some of QlikView's functionalities can be successfully used. Knowing the nuances of QlikView and designing ETL to take advantage of its unique positive features, and avoid non-optimal paths is important to get the best out of QlikView.

The chapter delves deep into every aspect of QlikView ETL and sets the stage for experimenting with QlikView as a powerful ETL platform for the enterprise.

It discusses various ways to Optimize ETL with QlikView, approaches for Data Quality Management with QlikView and Integration of QlikView with the rest of the enterprise ETL systems. Data Quality is a very important need from ETL solutions. The section on Data Profiling shows how QlikView can be used for advanced profiling needs. There may still be limitations for various unique needs, but with extensibility of the platform these can be addressed.

This chapter focuses on providing possible solutions rather than the HOW-TO. Please refer to the references section for resources which discuss the solutions in detail and provide the how-to. QlikCommunity is certainly a great place to get guidance and support.

Optimizing ETL with QlikView

Using QlikView for enterprises needs large data sets to be handled. The window of time available for data extraction is generally short, after the day-end processes. The ETL process has to be optimized to ensure that the extraction happens within this window. QlikView provides some interesting ways to optimize the ETL processes and are discussed in detail below.

General ETL Optimization Considerations in QlikView

Before using the individual methods, the following broad guidelines are to be kept in mind:

1. Extract every table only once and use the copy for other processes requiring the same
2. Use Incremental Loading or Partial Loading wherever possible and process the incremental data before adding to historical store
3. Reduce the number of tables and fields by removing unnecessary items
4. Reduce the number of stages required for ETL processes
5. Parallelize ETL processes to reduce total time taken—reduce the depth of the ETL tree graph
6. Partition large data tables into small chunks based on time and other key dimensions (products, geography, etc.) to gain flexibility of loading as required
7. Use Telescopic summaries to reduce data sizes in the final applications
8. Perform data reducing processes like INNER JOINS before other calculations / transformations that are compute intensive—this reduces the overall ETL time

9. Do every calculation only once as soon as possible in the ETL tree graph and store as QVDs
10. Pickup transformed data from backend if already exists. Perform new transformations in QlikView layer
11. Perform all field trims & calculations in-memory after loading QVDs with optimized load
12. Make use of ETL script features available instead of using standard SQL to transform and join
13. Write QVDs with any transformation required for use in the next layer. This allows super-fast mode to be used for QVD loading and save more time.
14. Write QVDs with only fields required for the subsequent stages. This will reduce the memory requirement in the subsequent layers and in the final application.

Incremental Load using QVD files

Incremental load is a very common requirement—loading nothing but new or changed records from the database. All other data should already be available, in one way or another. QlikView Online Help provides a lot of good information (some reproduced here).

With QVD Files it is possible to perform incremental load in most cases. The reading of QVD files can be done in either "super-fast mode" or "standard mode". (The method employed is automatically selected by the QlikView script engine depending on the complexity of the operation.) "Super-fast mode" is approximately 10 times faster than "standard mode" or about 100 times faster than loading the database through ODBC/OLE DB.

The basic process outline is as described below:
1. Load new data from database (a slow process, but loading a limited number of records).
2. Append old data from QVD file (loading many records, but a much faster process).
3. Create a new QVD file.
4. Repeat the procedure for every table loaded.

5. Sometimes, the incremental new data can be stored in separate QVD files with consistent filename format, later loaded with a wildcard load into QlikView as required.

The complexity of the actual solution depends on the nature of source database, but the following basic cases can be identified:

Case 1: Append Only (Log files)
Case 2: Insert Only (No Update or Delete) (No Update or Delete)
Case 3: Insert and Update (No Delete) (No Delete)
Case 4: Insert, Update and Delete

Quick outline for each of these cases is given below.

Case 1: Append Only

The simplest case: Log files that are only appended. The following conditions apply:

1. The database must be a log file which is contained in a text file (no ODBC/no OLE DB)
2. QlikView keeps track of the number of records that have been previously read and loads only records added at the end of the file

Figure 1: Append Only

Script Example:

```
Buffer (Incremental) Load * From
LogFile.txt (ansi, txt, delimiter is '\t',
embedded labels);
```

Case 2: Insert Only (No Update or Delete)

If the data resides in a database instead of a simple log file the case 1 approach will not work.

However, the problem can still be solved with minimum extra work. The following conditions apply:

1. Data source can be any database
2. QlikView loads records inserted after the last script execution
3. A field ModificationTime (or similar) is required for QlikView to recognize which records are new

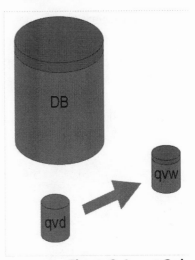

Figure 2: Insert Only

Script Example:
```
QV_Table:
SQL SELECT PrimaryKey, X, Y FROM DB_TABLE
WHERE
ModificationTime >= #$(LastExecTime)#
AND ModificationTime <
#$(BeginningThisExecTime)#;
Concatenate LOAD PrimaryKey, X, Y FROM File.QVD;
STORE QV_Table INTO File.QVD;
```

Case 3: Insert and Update (No Delete)

The next case is applicable when data in previously loaded records may have changed between script executions. Following conditions apply:

1. The data source can be any database
2. QlikView loads records inserted into the database or updated in the database after the last script execution
3. A field ModificationTime (or similar) is required for QlikView to recognize which records are new
4. A primary key field is required for QlikView to sort out updated records from the QVD file
5. This solution will force the reading of the QVD file to "standard

mode" (rather than "super-fast mode"), which is still considerably faster than loading the entire database

Script Example:
```
QV_Table:
SQL SELECT PrimaryKey,
X, Y FROM DB_TABLE
WHERE ModificationTime
>= #$(LastExecTime)#;
Concatenate LOAD
PrimaryKey, X, Y FROM
File.QVD
WHERE NOT
Exists(PrimaryKey);
STORE QV_Table INTO File.QVD;
```

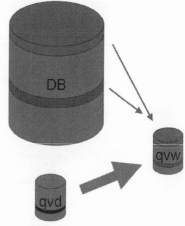

Figure 3: Insert and Update

Case 4: Insert, Update and Delete

The most difficult case to handle is when records are actually deleted from the source database between script executions. Following conditions apply:

1. Data source can be any database
2. QlikView loads records inserted into the database or updated in the database after the last script execution
3. QlikView removes records deleted from the database after the last script execution
4. A field ModificationDate (or similar) is required for QlikView to recognize which records are new

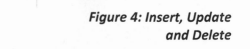

Figure 4: Insert, Update and Delete

5. A primary key field is required for QlikView to sort out updated records from the QVD file

6. This solution will force the reading of the QVD file to "standard mode" (rather than "super-fast mode"), which is still considerably faster than loading the entire database

7. The other alternative is to load the old data QVD in "super-fast mode" and do a resident load with the condition as shown below if enough memory is available

Script Example:

```
Let ThisExecTime = Now( );
QV_Table:
SQL SELECT PrimaryKey, X, Y FROM DB_TABLE
WHERE ModificationTime >= #$(LastExecTime)#
AND ModificationTime < #$(ThisExecTime)#;
Concatenate LOAD PrimaryKey, X, Y FROM File.QVD
WHERE NOT EXISTS(PrimaryKey);
Inner Join SQL SELECT PrimaryKey FROM DB_TABLE;
If ScriptErrorCount = 0 then
        STORE QV_Table INTO File.QVD;
Let LastExecTime = ThisExecTime;
End If
```

Partial Loading

In some situations, only incremental data of tables may be available for extraction—particularly when ONLY ADD is allowed in the source tables. QlikView provides a special Load process called Partial Loading useful for this. When a partial load command is issued on the ETL Script, only the Load and SQL statements that are preceded by a REPLACE or ADD prefix are executed. Other tables remain unaffected by the command.

The add prefix can be added to any *Load, Select (SQL)* or *Map ... using* statement in the script. It is only meaningful during Partial Reload. During a partial reload, an already existing QlikView table will be appended with the result of the *add load / add select* statement. No check for duplicates is performed.

Therefore, a statement using the add prefix will normally include either a distinct qualifier or a where clause guarding duplicates. The *add map...using* statement causes mapping to take place also during partial script execution. Please refer to QlikView Reference Manual and QlikView Help for examples. A comparison of Partial and Incremental Loads is provided in the QlikCommunity thread on Partial Load / Incremental Load [3].

Parallel Loading with Graph Optimization

Multiple instances of QlikView ETL Script can be run at the same time using Publisher. Each instance will run on separate cores up to a maximum of 10 reloads in parallel. However it is important to ensure the dependencies across these jobs are taken care of.

It is common to see a big number of dependencies among ETL jobs. For example, job "B" cannot start until job "A" is finished. Usually better performance can be achieved by visualizing all processes on a graph and reducing the graph with maximum use of parallelism; making "chains" of consecutive processing as short as possible. There are many threads on QlikCommunity on this topic—for e.g. Parallel Process [4], Parallel Reloads in Publisher [5]. Further improvement on Parallel and Distributed Processing is also being discussed as a new idea (Thread #173182).

Each process segment can be made into a separate ETL Script (QlikView Source Document) and run in parallel. Also, Publisher version 9.0 onwards, dependencies are supported—completion of one or more tasks can be used as a trigger to start the next set of processes. Using this feature to implement the optimized graph is a great way to take advantage of the parallelism available in the hardware. This reduces load times significantly. In one situation, the process that took over 8 hours was reduced to less than 1.5 hrs by such an exercise.

Synchronizing data from different sources

With QlikView, since each table is extracted separately, various data tables from different sources can be loaded in different frequencies / intervals. Some tables get updated very rarely—like quarterly budgets/targets—and others get updated more regularly. The rarely updated tables can be extracted / loaded in longer intervals while others can get extracted / loaded more frequently. This can be done by separating extractions into separate tasks in Publisher and set different schedules for them. However, one important issue that comes up in such loading is the relative consistency of data in these independent tables needs to be ensured. Because multiple source databases may have different update cycles (some may be updated every few minutes, while others may take days or weeks), an ETL system may be required to hold back certain data until all sources are synchronized. Likewise, where a warehouse may have to be reconciled to the contents in a source system or with the general ledger, establishing synchronization and reconciliation points becomes necessary.

QlikView jobs/tasks should be designed to take care of such task dependencies, update cycle intervals for different data tables and ensure consistency across all when used in a data model / application.

Splitting Data into Partition Files

While extracting large tables, incremental load, partial load could help in places where modified date-timestamps are available. When there are no such timestamps available, or when the transaction tables are imported for the first time, the extraction of the entire table is required.

In situations like this, the tables can be split into multiple chunks using number range, year / month / date range, products, channels, geography / zip codes, etc. Later these QVD files can be either merged or kept as separate files to be merged when needed to be analyzed together. File naming conventions need to be used reflecting the range to identify the chunks uniquely.

Telescopic Summarization

In addition to incremental loads and splitting into partition files, the older data can be summarized to a lower level of granularity and stored. For example, the latest data of, say current twelve months, can be kept in transaction level, previous 12 months in a daily summarized level, previous 12 months in a weekly summary and so on. In all the summaries, the same number of period fields shall be kept (Year, Month, Week, Day, Hour, Minute and Second). In the summary, for every level of aggregation, the default value for lower period fields can all be kept as the highest possible value (for example: month as December, date as 30, hour as 23, minutes as 59, seconds as 59).

Due to these summaries, the long term trends can be shown. When selections are done and drilled-down, the details are available up to the transaction level for the current 12 months, and up to respective levels of aggregation for the previous periods. Selected dimensions other than time can be included in the aggregation (group by) on all the telescopic granularity levels.

This summarization allows reduction of data sizes to be included into the QlikView User Application. The non-summarized detail data can still be kept in separate detail applications, and through a button can be launched (daisy chained) to show the details for the selections.

Data Freshness and Update Frequencies

The time elapsed between creation of data and update into the QVW application decides how close to real-time the application is and how fresh the data is: Data Freshness. Contrast this with the ability to get answers as and when questions are posed; sometimes referred to as real-time capability. However, it is more to do with dynamic "live" interactivity—the data may be old or new.

The freshness of data is a need based on dynamics of every business. In some businesses the elapsed time cannot be more than a few seconds while in others the business may not change for days.

Based on the business needs, the data on the reporting platform can be updated in three broad ways: periodic updates, near real-time updates and real time updates. Selecting one of these update strategies is important. This determines many aspects of the ETL including the infrastructure, integration, front-end design, and data propagation strategies as well.

Periodic Updates

The regular post facto reporting requirements are met by periodic extracts/updates—generally once a day—but can be more or less frequent. This meets most of the reporting requirements of an organization. The entire infrastructure of Publisher is created to easily address this requirement, with predefined schedules, task dependencies and triggered ETL tasks.

Once a QlikView application is updated with new data by Publisher, the instance that is already loaded in the QlikView Server still contains the old data version. There is a need to update the in-memory copy of the application. Generally, at the end of the Publisher task to reload the data, the application running in QlikView Server is unloaded, and reloaded afresh to reflect the new data. How it is done is controlled by document time-out settings on the QlikView Server and refresh settings in each document: transparent refresh, refresh with confirmation or explicit refresh.

Near-Real Time Updates

There are situations when more frequent updates are required on the QlikView applications. Examples can be month-end monitoring of order booking. The only requirement is that the QlikView ETL Script should be run every time such an update is required, and the document should be refreshed into the in-memory copy on the QlikView Server.

Such frequent updates are possible with tighter extract schedules as frequent as once in few (say 2 or 5) minutes. However, the time taken to execute the extraction and update the QlikView application should be less than the interval chosen for updates.

During such updates, the change in data needs to be immediately reflected to the currently interacting users. This cannot be done by unloading and reloading the QlikView applications on the QV Server. To support this, there is a QVS feature called "Graceful Document Refresh". It is controlled by two aspects:

1. QVS Server option: "Allow only one copy of document in memory" must be checked
2. In individual document, Document Settings -> Server Tab, the options to control if the user should be prompted when new data is available or user's session should just be refreshed transparently.

Update of data happens only when at least one user is interacting with the application in-memory. A discussion on this is at QlikCommunity Thread: Refresh Document Near-Real Time [6].

Real Time Updates

If the need is to have zero elapsed time between the source data update and reflecting data in the in-memory instance of the application, then reloads cannot be a good option. The need is to feed data, as it happens, into the in-memory instance of QlikView. Such changes should be directly updated in the in-memory model, and the various front-end elements should reflect the changes dynamically—as the data happens.

From version 9 of QlikView, a Real Time Update or Dynamic Data Update feature has been introduced. With this feature, it is possible to programmatically update field data in an in-memory table in real-time without having to run the script. Via a new API and almost standard SQL Insert, Update and Delete commands, any QlikView field data can be updated directly in RAM. This functionality is available in stand-alone QlikView and on Real-Time QlikView Server.

This is performed by one function: DyamicUpdateCommand ("SQL Statement"). This function is provided as part of the Automation API. This means it can be used in following two ways:

1. From inside the QlikView application in a VBScript macro to update data in real-time as user clicks/interacts with the QlikView application. A sample is as below:

```
Rem Dynamic Data Update
sub Update
  SET                    Result           =
  ActiveDocument.DynamicUpdateCommand
  ("UPDATE * SET Discount = if(Discount >=
  35, 0, if (City='Stockholm', Discount + 5,
  Discount + 2)) WHERE Country = 'SE'")
  if Result = false then
      MsgBox Result.ErrorMessage
  end if
end sub
```

INSERT and DELETE also can be used like UPDATE. As an example use-case, this can be used for the real-time logging of activities of users inside a memory table and display dynamically the behavior of the users. Though unintended for the purpose, this feature can also be used to create a planning mechanism along with INPUT FIELDS that allows users to input new data into the QlikView data fields.

The resulting in-memory table can be stored as a separate QVD file by using the store command in the macro script.

2. It is also possible to use these dynamic update statements from outside the QlikView application using the Automation API from an external application. The external application can open the QlikView document and call DynamicUpdateCommand to send SQL commands to be executed by the QlikView document open currently. A sample called Call Center.qvw released with Version 9 [7] shows how a VBA script can get data from the excel sheets and insert directly into the QlikView application using the Automation API. When the Excel Macro is executed, the Real Time Dashboard displays new records

| Real Time Dashboard | Call Center Dash |

QlikView

New Calls and Orders

All Calls (Avg)		New	+/-
On Hold	0:00:53	0:00:10	↓
Wait	0:00:53	0:00:10	↓
Talk Time	0:04:00	0:04:05	↑

Call Outcome		
Outcome	All Calls	New Calls
Answered	120,588	1
Abandon	146	0

*Arrow indicators based on threshold value for new

New Orders: 1		
OrderID	Customer	ProductName
16936	Das Alpen Shoe	AAA Running Shoe

Figure 5: Real Time Update

as they get added and also shows changes in aggregates due to new records. This could be very useful for pushing real time updates from any other data source into a running QlikView application. On a QlikView desktop, the application will get updates for the user directly. On a QV Server, the application updates will automatically be propagated to the various on-line users automatically.

Data Quality Management

Having incorrect data used for reporting and analytics will lead to misguided insights and hence can result in wrong decisions and misdirected investments. Data should be a) Correct, and b) Consistent. Data Quality is ensured by combining three different approaches:

1. Capture Correct Data at Source

   Most capture time errors are due to manual entry problems. These problems are solved by

a) Using automated / standardized data capture systems—BarCode, RFID and other standards created by bodies like GS1.

b) Using proper validation processes applying business rules at the time of data capture

These are the most preferred ways to ensure data quality in the enterprises. More and more initiatives are taken world over to implement better quality data capture with Barcodes, RFIDs and appropriate data acquisition infrastructures. Till the time all data sources are standardized, the incorrect data capture will continue and will need to be handled in subsequent stages. QlikView or any ETL system can help little at this stage.

2. Correct and Store Consistent data in the central storage

The data captured at various front-end systems may contain wrong data entered. As a very common case, same data captured in different systems, or at different times may be different (for e.g., date of birth and age may not be consistent with each other). Creating consistency across all the data elements is an important requirement. This is essentially done centrally when data is consolidated for common use. This is where most of the ETL requirements arise. QlikView ETL can help in these situations. The section on Data Profiling & Cleansing with QlikView discusses how.

To avoid this consistency issue, when captured, data needs get into central storage, with appropriate updates all across. This is the intent of the "Hub-And-Spoke Information Hubs" evolving in front-running organizations, as we discussed in the previous chapter.

3. Correct while viewing

Applying business rules (e.g., pick the latest or the earliest data captured) at the time of presenting data to the users is another common approach. This leads to extensive processing load since the same report maybe requested by different users multiple times. This is the most common problem that exists in most enterprises, and a huge amount of time and money is spent on creating reports.

These three approaches normally get combined in every organization based on the current stage of data quality evolution; the need is to have a process structure as follows:

- Capturing data right at source: Standardized, automated Capture
- Understanding data & its meaning for business: Data Analysis and Data Definitions
- Identifying data patterns, correct and wrong: Data Profiling
- Identifying duplicates and removing them: De-duplication
- Correcting wrong data with right data, at least approximately: Data Cleansing

The first aspect of Automating Data Capture is not in the scope of a BI solution as discussed above.

Data Analysis and Data Definitions

Understanding data, defining the data need across the life-cycle of each process, and its meaning as it changes is the core to data analysis. This is a step that is most commonly ignored, with an implicit feeling that "we understand data". Creating common definitions across the enterprise and creating a common data language is an extremely important step. It is said "While making data fit for purpose, deciding what *fit for purpose* means across the business is a bigger challenge".

Data analysis is a process of understanding the data elements associated with business, and making conscious definitions of what they mean to everyone. To sustainably succeed in keeping data fit for purpose, the following key data governance steps should be done *in an on-going basis* [11]:

- A standard data dictionary across the entire enterprise, continuously updated Common definitions for various dimensions, measures and KPIs
- Keep and differentiate different department definitions if one definition of a KPI cannot suffice every need
- Capture all calculation logic employed for various measures and KPIs (Data Rules including Business Rules, Data for Test and Quality)
- Share and make all these common data language available in a central location for everyone's easy access and reference
- Capture and monitor process quality metrics for all the data quality processes

These are more of strategy and discipline elements rather than any tools or technologies used. These are extremely important needs and any QlikView implementation without enough care and attention to these aspects will not get the best possible results, over the long term.

QlikView can provide all the necessary support required for systematic maintenance of all the data definitions, metadata and data quality metrics, with some purpose-built code. With the new out-of-box automated support for metadata, process metric capture & analysis and ETL log files analysis, QlikView has become a better platform to manage data to be *fit for purpose*.

One of the most interesting and valuable approaches is to create a QlikView Application showing the Enterprise Data Dictionary using the metadata about all the tables, fields and KPIs along with their formulae. With a list of all the tables, fields from multiple sources, and the various intermediate and final calculations/transformations they go through, the entire data trace can be included in this application. With the new metadata features provided by QlikView recent versions, it will be much easier to build applications like these for data management with QlikView. The experience of building such an application for an insurance company was excellent—the application was exposed to all business analysts and developers, making it easy for everyone to understand and use the data relationships.

When complexity & dynamism of data definitions is more, using a readymade data quality management application platform could be helpful. Products for this purpose can be fully dedicated to data quality like Trillium, Talend, Pervasive, IxSight, DataMartist [8], etc. They can also be data quality tools that are part of broad based ETL solutions like Informatica. These tools help in all aspects of Data Quality Management, from Data Definitions to maintaining consistency.

While using QlikView or any other data quality solution, the common data definitions are a must. Forming groups to create data definitions in the enterprise is a great catalyst to create data-driven decision making culture in the company. The metadata capabilities of QlikView can be used to include all such definitions and related explanations / comments into the QlikView Data Model. The metadata features of QlikView include: Tags, Comments, MetaModel and MetaMonitor Applications. MetaModel and MetaMonitor are discussed in detail in Part III.

Data Profiling

Data profiling is done while performing Data Analysis and Data Definitions. Typically data profiling is the process of statistically examining data available in existing data sources (e.g. a database or a file), collecting metrics and information about that data. This is done primarily to decipher problem prone areas in data organization and plan for necessary revamp. For more information on this, please refer to the IT Toolbox article on Data Profiling [10] and also the Wiki of Gerard Nico [12].

The purpose of these statistics may be to:

- Find out whether existing data can easily be used for other purposes
- Improve ability to search data by tagging it with keywords, descriptions, or assigning it to a category
- Give metrics on data quality, including whether it conforms to particular standards or patterns
- Assess risk involved in integrating data for new applications, including challenges of joins
- Assess whether metadata accurately describes the actual values in the source database
- Understanding data challenges early in any data intensive project— finding data problems late in the project can lead to delays and cost overruns.
- Have an enterprise view of all data, for uses such as master data management where key data is needed, or data governance for improving data quality.

Profiling helps not only to understand anomalies and to assess data quality, but also to discover, register, and assess enterprise metadata. This helps to clarify the structure, content, relationships and derivation rules. Profiling is done also to identify candidate data sources for a central storage (a traditional data warehouse or Unified QlikView Repository).

How to do Data Profiling: Data profiling utilizes different kinds of descriptive statistics such as minimum, maximum, mean, mode, percentile, standard deviation, frequency, and variation as well as other aggregates such as count and sum. Additional information obtained during data profiling could be data type, length, discrete values, and unique values, occurrence of null values, typical string patterns, and abstract type recognition. This metadata can then be used to discover problems such as illegal values, misspelling, missing values, varying value representation, and duplicates.

Different analyses are performed for different structural levels:

a) Single Column Profiling to individually get an understanding of frequency distribution of different values, type, and use of each table/column—then compare with the metadata definitions for value limits

b) Cross Column and Inter-Table Analysis to find overlapping sets:
   i. Possibly representing foreign key relationships between entities
   ii. Possibly redundant fields (tables) that can be merged (concatenated) and/or subset be dropped

Data Profiling with QlikView

A more extensive overview of data profiling for the practitioner can be found in the DataFlux Whitepaper: Practitioners Guide to Data Profiling, by David Loshin [13]. Understanding the concepts of Data Profiling is of paramount importance to ensure success for a QlikView project and the author urges the readers to refer to this excellent document on data profiling concepts. One key point in the paper is to be kept in mind:

> Data profiling techniques can help the analyst understand the empirical truth associated with enterprise data, and the breadth of analysis techniques can help the analyst draw many conclusions. However, without directing the analyst processes that use profiling technologies, there is a risk of continued review, drill-down, and ultimate "analysis paralysis" in which the specific business objectives are never achieved.

Normally, purpose-built tools are used for data profiling to ease the process. Computation complexity increases when going from single column, to single table, to cross-table structural profiling—hence performance is an important criterion for profiling tools.

QlikView does not provide any such automated mechanism as of now. However QlikView provides some support for profiling with the In-Memory & AQL model. With the enhancements of metadata and simple data profiling information embedded in the QlikView data model, it is not impossible to build some tools for this. With the kind of information that is already available in the data model, providing profiling extensions should not be too difficult for QlikTech or its partners. While such extensions continue to be created, currently the following basic QlikView capabilities help Data Profiling in a limited way.

Automatic Basic Profiling

On loading data into QlikView, once data model is ready, the following are created automatically:

1. *System Fields*: In addition to the fields extracted from the data source, system fields are also produced by QlikView. These all begin with "$" and can be displayed in list boxes much like ordinary fields. System fields which are typically created during Script execution are primarily used as an aid in document design and can be displayed.

Table 1: QlikView System Fields

Field	Description
$Table	Displays all internal tables loaded by the script. When a single table is selected, an information symbol will activate in the caption area of the list box. By clicking here, it is possible to view the table, if it comes from a file.
$Field	Displays the fields that are read from the tables. By setting this list box to Show Frequency in the List Box Properties: General page, it is simple to detect key fields that occur in several internal tables.
$Fields	The numbers in this list box represent the number of fields in different tables.
$FieldNo	This list box shows the position of the fields in the tables.
$Rows	This list box shows the number of rows in the tables.
$Info	If info tables have been included in the document, their names will be displayed here.

2. *System Table*: A very useful tool is the System table, a pivot table with the two dimensions $Field and $Table and the expression only($Field). This can be automatically created by QlikView: Layout: New Sheet Object, System Table.

Table 2: QlikView System Table

$Field ▾	$Table	Region	MetricsOptio...	MetricPickOne	S
Customer N...	-	-	-	-
Sales Rep N...	-	-	-	-
Region Code	Region Code	-	-	-
Item Number	-	-	-	It
SalesKey	-	-	-	S
BudgetKey	-	-	-	-
GeoCodeKey	-	-	-	-
Region	Region	-	-	-
_metricsNo	-	_metricsNo	-	-
_metrics	-	_metrics	-	-
_metricPick...	-	-	_metricPick...	-
Address Nu...	-	-	-	A
Invoice Date	-	-	-	Ir
Promised D...	-	-	-	P

3. *Attributes for each Table and Field:* All the tables and fields are automatically profiled and tagged with profile attributes. The attributes added to each table are: Name, Loosely Coupled, #Records, #Fields, #Keys, Comment.

Table 3: System Table Attributes

Attribute	Description
Name	The name of the internal table.
Loosely Coupled	If the alternative is checked, the table is loosely coupled. It is possible to deliberately set this alternative for a table here.
# Records	The number of records (rows) of the table.
# Fields	The number of fields (columns) of the table.
# Keys	The number of key (connecting) fields (columns) of the table.
Comment	Displays the comments read from the data source and the *Comment Field* made on the field.

The key attributes added for each field are: Dimension, Measure, Tags, Comment, #Tables, #Values, #Distinct Values and Type.

Table 4: Key Attributes of each QlikView Field

Attribute	Description
#	The internal number of the field. Numbers 0 to 5 are used by the QlikView system fields, which are not displayed in this list.
Name	The name of the field.
Dimensions	Mark the check box to the right of the field name to add the system tag $dimension to the field. This tag denotes a field recommended for use in chart dimensions, list boxes etc. A field tagged with dimension will be displayed at the top of all field selection controls in QlikView except in the *Edit Expression* dialog.
Measures	Mark the check box to the right of the field name to add the system tag $measure to the field.. This tag denotes a field recommended for use in expressions. A field tagged with measure will be displayed at the top of all field selection controls in the *Edit Expression* dialog.
Tags	Displays the *Field Tags*. $ denotes a system tag. Please see the note on TAG below this table for more details.
Comment	Displays the comments read from the data source and an indicator for any special status of the field, such as Semantic, AndMode, AlwaysOneSelected, Info, Locked or Hidden.
# Tables	The number of tables in which the field occurs.
# Values	The total number of field values, disregarding selections. This information is not available for key (connecting) fields.
# Distinct	The total number of distinct field values, disregarding selections.
Type	Displays an indicator for any special status of the field, such as Semantic, AndMode, AlwaysOneSelected, Locked or Hidden.

4. *Field Tags in QlikView:* There are three different types of system tags: script generated system tags that cannot be altered by the user, script generated system tags that can be altered in the script and system tags that are set interactively by the user. System tags are always preceded by a $ sign.

The following system tags are automatically generated at the end of script generation. These cannot be changed by the user:

- $system - denotes a system field
- $key - denotes a key field
- $keypart - denotes that the field is part of one or more synthetic keys
- $synthetic - denotes a synthetic key

The following tags are also automatically generated at the end of script generation, but may be altered or overridden using script syntax (see Tag Field and Untag Field).

- $hidden - denotes a hidden field
- $numeric - all (non-null) values in the field are numeric
- $integer - all (non-null) values in the field are integers
- $text - no values in the field are numeric
- $ascii - field values contain only standard ascii characters
- $date - all (non-null) values in the field can be interpreted as dates (integers)
- $timestamp - all (non-null) values in the field can be interpreted as time stamps

The following tags are set in the Document Properties: Tables dialog. They can be enabled or disabled by the user:

- $dimension - denotes a field recommended for use in chart dimensions, list boxes, etc.
- $measure - denotes a field recommended for use in expressions

Single Column Profiling

The most important pre-requisite for data profiling is having data definitions with metadata describing the fields. Of particular interest are: a) Data Type, b) Allowed values (Min / Max for numeric fields and list of allowed values for text fields). With these definitions, it is easy to use QlikView to profile each field of interest. This is done in QlikView by using a) List Boxes with Frequency count, b) Statistics Box and c) Table Charts with Color Coded fields.

Listbox with Frequencies: Every field can be shown as a listbox to profile individual columns.

1. View Distinct Values: The listbox shows all the distinct values as held in the in-memory model. Any unexpected values present can be visually identified.

AltState		Sales	
	637	0	28109
M	35	102.33	222
AB	14	98.24	220
O	12	128.44	211
CA	11	64.44	196
PA	11	67.13	186
VC	9	138.24	181
NW	8	86.33	178

Figure 6: List Boxes

2. Frequency of Occurrence: The listbox can display the number of instances of every value to identify duplicates particularly for master fields and remove them. Along with distinct values the frequencies provide support.

3. It is possible to add more expressions on the same list boxes to create more profiling data.

Table Charts with Color Codes: This helps finding outliers and wrong data in the various fields.

Customer	City	Product Group	Sales Rep N...	Cost	Sales
Output Enab...	Zell am Ham...	Deli	Lee Chin	280.75	455.49
Output Enab...	Zell am Ham...	Baking Goods	Sharon Carver	48.69	108.16
Gemini Cont...	York	Frozen Foods	Edward Smith	84.79	239.56
Gemini Cont...	York	Beverages	Edward Smith	10.4	99.86
Gemini Cont...	York	Baking Goods	Edward Smith	3.44	14.34

Figure 7: Color Coded Table Charts

The min and max conditions of fields can be used to create expressions that decide the color coding of the fields. In the chart shown, the cost field is colored RED when over the upper limit (200), BLUE when below the lower limit (40) and GREEN when in allowed range.

Sales		QuotaKey	
Numeric count	221,233.00	Numeric count	0.00
Null count	238	Null count	66
Text count	0	Text count	174438
Total count	221233	Total count	174438
Missing count	238	Missing count	174504
Sum	203976763.54	Sum	0
Average	922.00	Average	n/a
Std dev	8,833.19	Std dev	n/a
Skewness	32.7908	Skewness	n/a
Kurtosis	1,495.30	Kurtosis	n/a
Min	-107127	Min	n/a
Max	555376	Max	n/a
Only value		Only value	
25%	14.03	25%	n/a
Median	85.62	Median	n/a
75%	271.9	75%	n/a

Figure 8: Statistics Box

Statistics Box (Figure 8): This can be created for any field of interest especially useful for numeric fields. It gives the statistics about the fields. In the figure the field: Sales is profiled. Particularly, Max, Min & Null Count are very useful. Also useful are the Text Count & Numeric Count. Other values like Kurtosis, StdDev, Skewness, Median and Quartiles are all useful to understand data better. For Text Fields
(Quotakey) Null Count & Missing Counts provide important insights, along with Total Count.

Cross Column Analysis and Inter-Table Analysis – Primary / Foreign Keys

Finding if two columns have redundant data is the purpose of the cross-domain / cross-column analysis. Identifying which columns in tables can be used as primary-key / foreign-key combinations, or find redundant columns—ones that can be dropped or merged. Normally such activity is performed using advanced profiling tools like IBM Information Analyzer or Trillium or some such tool —they automatically compare multiple fields with one another to derive such hidden relationships. Though such automated discovery tools are very useful, they are meant for technical resources that normally do not have complete understanding of the underlying business relationship.

Even as it is now, QlikView Table Viewer provides an insight into the relationship between two columns with the same name in the QlikView model. As shown in the figure, on mouse-over, data profile of one field is displayed (multiple profile popup images are pasted together in this pic for illustration). By looking at the *subset ratio*, one can easily say that CustomerLoc is the master table containing the Full List of Customers

[Customer]—SubSet Ratio: 100%. Both Customers & LinkTable contain the foreign key [Customer]—SubSet Ratio: 99.71%. In addition, information density can also provide insight into completeness of data.

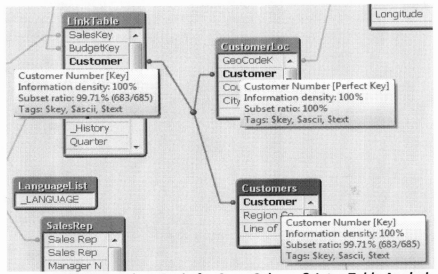

Figure 9: Subset Ratio for Cross Column & Inter-Table Analysis

Those fields named as primary and foreign keys can be found to be faulty, in case the primary key does not have 100% Subset ratio. If both keys have less than 100% Subset ratio, then neither of them is complete and both need to be merged for completeness—after removing duplicates of course. When both are 100% then the redundant one can be removed by appropriately joining the tables.

QlikView MetaData

QlikView handles three forms of metadata: descriptive, administrative and structural. The whitepaper "QlikView's Pragmatic Approach to Metadata" provides a detailed overview of the meta model of QlikView. This is further discussed in detail in Part III.

Key tools for implementing the metamodel are: MetaScanner, MetaMonitor and a template. MetaScanner is an automatic profiling component of this model and is introduced here briefly. This is the metadata "collector" application. The MetaModel of QlikView includes information about QV Data files, QV Publisher, QV Server, QV Applications and QV Log Files. While all other profiling will be discussed in Part III, the Data Profiling is worth mentioning here.

The Meta Scanner application reads headers of all the QVD and QVW files that exist in the repository and creates a record of the size and details of these files. If present, the lineage information is also included along with the automatically gathered information about the QVW / QVD data. Meta Presentation Layer applications use this data to analyze and understand data. More detailed information about this is in Part III chapter "Making QlikView Work".

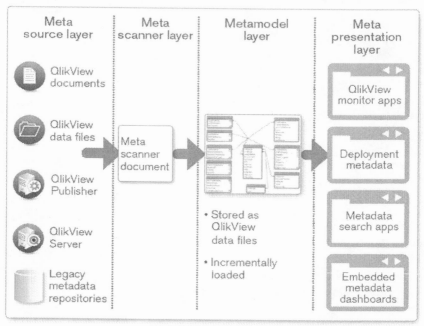

Figure 10: Overview of QlikView Meta Model

TIQView QVD Profiling Solution

While the QlikView Meta Model focuses on the relationship between the different QVD and QVW tables structurally, advanced single field profiling capabilities are made available by an interesting solution from TIQSolutions. Of particular interest is the TIQView, the first profiling solution for QVD files. A sample application can be found in QVapps site: [http://www.qvapps.com/en/qlikview-applications/helper/tiqview-qvd-limited-free-version.html].

This tool allows selecting any QVD file and automatically does the following analyses: 1) Field Analysis, 2) Value Frequency, 3) Format Frequency, 4) Pattern Frequency, 5) Metaphone Frequency. Format

Frequency, Pattern Frequency and Metaphone Frequency give great insights about data, particularly to manage data quality of Master Data.

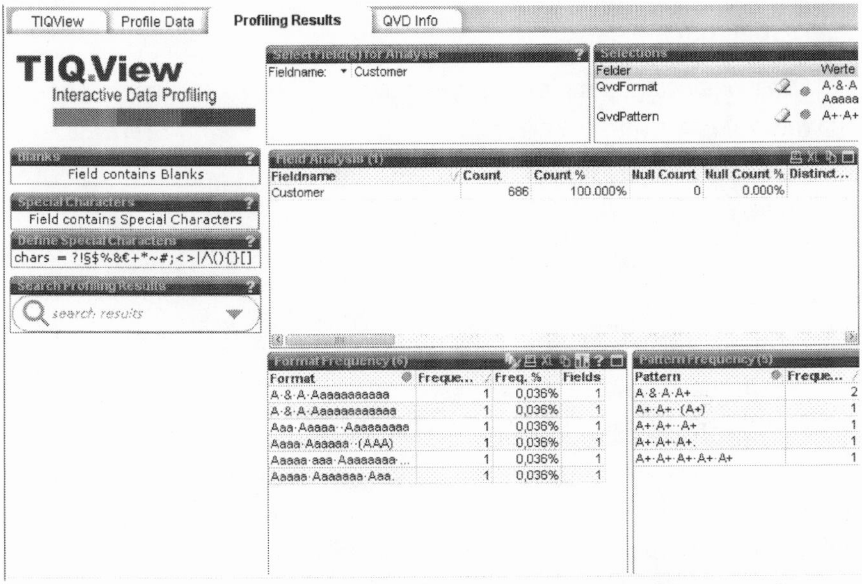

Figure 11: TIQView Application Data Profiling Result Page

What is important is that the entire profiling application of TIQView has been developed right with QlikView script and macros. This is a preview of things to come in the QlikView space.

Extending and Adding Profiling Capabilities

Using the Automation API (VBScript, Javascript), QlikView OCX and Extension API combinations, Data Profiling with QlikView can be extended. All the data profiling features available in specialized products like Trillium etc. can be invoked by using the above APIs.

Data Cleansing

While Profiling helps understand the data better and improve the data design, profiling also throws up all the anomalies that exist in the data. Such anomalies need to be fixed and data should be corrected. This is done using Data Cleansing techniques. Particularly master data like addresses, contact details, other attributes of customers, product data and vendor data should all be accurate to help take and implement accurate decisions.

Wikipedia page on Data Cleansing gives an elaborate discussion on this topic. To quote the key points:

- Data cleansing, data cleaning, or data scrubbing is the process of detecting and correcting (or removing) corrupt or inaccurate records from a record set, table, or database. Used mainly in databases, the term refers to identifying incomplete, incorrect, inaccurate, irrelevant parts of the data and then replacing, modifying, or deleting this dirty data.
- After cleansing, a data set will be consistent with other similar data sets in the system.
- The inconsistencies detected or removed may have been originally caused by user entry errors, by corruption in transmission or storage, or by different data dictionary definitions of similar entities in different stores.
- Data cleansing differs from data validation. Validation almost invariably means data is rejected from system at entry and is performed at entry time, rather than on data batches.
- The actual process of data cleansing may involve removing typographical errors or validating and correcting values against a known list of entities.
- The validation may be strict (such as rejecting any address that does not have a valid postal code) or fuzzy (such as correcting records that partially match existing, known records).

An ETL solution should help perform these functions with relative ease, manage the quality and consistency of data as part of the data acquisition and integration process.

Data Cleansing with QlikView

Data cleansing transformations are done to take care of the following:
- Typographical errors committed during entry (wrong spelling or value from list)

- Format Errors in storing data or inclusion of unwanted characters
- Errors created by wrong programming logic (inappropriate replacements/calculations)
- Incorrect recording of slowly changing dimensions due to process flaw (age recorded instead of date of birth at different times)
- Conversion of Codes to Values
- Encoding freeform values
- Generating Surrogate Keys

Typographical Error Correction: Typically starts with manually creating list of Incorrect and Correct values for every field. Then with the *Map…using* statement, the incorrect field values can be replaced with the right values. While this is normally required for Dimension fields, sometimes the Numeric Measures may also require this approach to correct values entered wrong. If replacement needs to be done using Keys, then a correction table can be created typically as separate Excel sheets for each source table and then JOIN to use correct values.

Format Errors or Inclusion of Unwanted Characters: Dates, Phone Numbers, Zip Codes, Part Numbers, etc. have multiple correct formats to be recorded. However, for easier processing logic, their format needs to be harmonized & stored in one format. This can be done by format check and replace with right format with appropriate conversion. Typically these are similar to Typographical errors, but a special case allowing more automation & re-use. Such script functions can be good candidates for common functions included in Open Source QlikView Components (QVC).

Errors by Wrong Programming Logic: This can be corrected by recalculating these derived values afresh inside QlikView during the ETL process. Any complex logic can be created as a user function and used inside the Load statements. Simple logic can be implemented as nested *IF.. THEN.. ELSE.. ENDIF* statement inside the Load statement itself.

Incorrect Recording of Slowly Changing Dimensions: This also can be corrected by re-calculating the relative values (like age) from the absolute values (like date of birth).

Conversion of Codes: If one system uses a particular code for field values but another uses different codes, the need is to harmonize them into one. For example, if one system stores 1 for male and 2 for female, but the other system users M for male and F for female, there is a need to convert data from both systems into one chosen coding. This can be done by using IF..THEN..ELSE or map table.

Encoding Freeform Values: While the source field may have text data entered as values, the need may be to convert them into codes—either numeric or string. While in QlikView this is not a must, such a replacement can save space used in the in-memory data model.

Generating Surrogate Keys: Multiple fields need to be used together to generate composite keys. Hash functions (hash128, hash160 and hash256) can convert these multi-string keys into a single compact string. This reduces memory used—hash fields can be used instead of original key field(s).

All data cleansing steps done in QlikView should be done as early as possible during ETL. In most situations, error corrections, harmonization and memory reduction are the reasons for the various Data Cleansing exercises done. These can be successfully done in QlikView.

Verifying Query/Transmission Accuracy

One of the important data quality verification methods is using Checksums: Totals and Counts can be separately retrieved from the source systems and set in tables/variables. Same totals and counts can be calculated from the QlikView model as well.

Then these totals and counts can be compared to ensure that the data quality has not degraded during the transfer. This can be used to decide success or failure of every ETL stage, and decide to execute the next stage or not.

On the final production applications, a separate sheet can be provided where these totals are displayed together. Any difference between such key totals and counts can be highlighted by color coding and also by Popup and Alerts to the data owners and business users. This gives a way in which users can verify the reliability of the data they are looking at and also explain differences if any. Input fields can be provided to capture such variance capture.

QlikView Applications provide Continuous Profiling and Data Cleansing

An important aspect to keep in mind is—QlikView is designed to make it a collaborative platform for developers, analysts and business users to work together. The regular QlikView Applications in production, with the unlimited slicing & dicing capabilities, provide the best profiling applications. Business users while using the applications can easily identify anomalies and collaborate with the developers and analysts to get the data fixed.

Collaboration features like Session Sharing, Bookmarks and Linked Notes/Annotations can help enabling continuous data profiling and improvements to data. Understanding data using intuitive and tool-based data profiling processes is to ultimately improve the quality of data before putting it into business use. For the anomalies identified, cleansing becomes an integral part of data management process.

De-Duplication

De-Duplication is a special case of data cleansing—essentially identifying duplicates of data and removing them. This is primarily done to avoid redundancy, increase internal consistency and also optimize the storage/memory required for the data.

QlikView by default removes redundancy of values by storing only one copy of any value of a field. This provides the natural data reduction which is characteristic of QlikView that gives up to 90% data reduction as discussed earlier while discussing benefits of QlikView.

The duplicates that exist in the data set bubble up during data profiling, cross-domain and cross-column analyses. Once these are found, the following techniques can be used to perform the de-duplication:

1. Load Distinct: when same field values repeat in multiple records, the distinct load keeps only one copy of multiple occurrences of the same record. This also avoids data duplication during the joins.
2. Combine duplicate fields across two tables
   a. When one table contains a subset of values for the same primary keys, *joining* these two tables will reduce the number of copies of the primary keys.

b. When two tables contain different subsets of values of the same primary key, *Forced Concatenate* is useful. It is a feature available in QlikView which allows concatenating two tables even if they have different set of fields in each. Fields with same names will get combined into one field. All independent fields from both tables will be included in the resulting table. NULL values will be filled in the new fields for rows of the table that do not contain the field. This reduces the memory usage due to reduction in the number of fields.

Finding the duplicates across multiple tables is actually an involved process. Manually doing it will be cumbersome especially in data sources having large number of tables and fields. Tools like SAS ETL, Trillium or IBM Information Analyzer provide capabilities for the same.

Creating a common data definition and evolving a Unified Data Model is the best way to implement and manage data de-duplication as a continuous process. Data De-duplication is defined as "intelligent compression" or "single-instance storage". More detailed information on de-duplication is available in the article "Data Deduplication" in TechTarget [14].

Exporting Data from QlikView ETL

The QlikView ETL primarily combines data from various sources and produces in-memory QlikView data tables. As seen above, QlikView ETL Script allows complex transformations and integration to be done with relative ease, to create processed data as final tables. These tables are then processed by the Association, Aggregation and Presentation Engines. While various script statements are executed, the data at every stage is kept as memory tables unless explicitly dropped using DROP.

CSV File Repositories

The in-memory tables can be exported into CSV files in designated directories. The STORE command is used for exporting any logical table in-memory into disk files (QVD or CSV format). CSV files are stored in UTF-8 Text format. Either full table or a selected subset of fields from the table can be exported. Joins or Concatenation of tables cannot be done while storing, but before storing such processes can be done to create new tables and then stored or exported. Using incremental loading, partial loading, partitioning and other techniques, various data tables and summary tables can be created to form necessary schema.

Other data systems, like a warehouse or another application can use this data as the source and import this data and store as tables. Particularly if all the unification, normalization and star or snow-flake schema generation are done in QlikView, the CSV files will naturally create a perfect snow-flake schema repository. This can be used as a readymade data warehouse, for reporting and further analytics.

QlikView as an ETL tool

Using the Automation API and Extension API, the data tables created in-memory can also be directly read record by record, and inserted into external database tables. This will remove the need to export into CSV files and then import into the warehouses and other stores. With this enhancement, the ability to push data into other systems—LOADING into other target/destination systems—can be implemented as an integral part of the QlikView ETL solution.

With the Publisher/EDX integration, the entire process of ETL can be seamlessly implemented.

In case in-process export is not possible due to security or data size reasons, then stand alone QVD export can be implemented. This can be done by using the QlikView OCX and Automation APIs. VB.NET applications can be written using these, to read QVDs in a central unified QVD store and LOAD into another RDBMS or warehouse setup as tables.

Exporting Data from Inside a QV Application

In addition to exporting data from the QlikView ETL Script, contents of any QlikView object can be exported out as CSV, TAB (Tab delimited), SKV (semicolon delimited), QVD, HTML, XLS, XML and QVO (QlikView Output – actually TAB delimited) files. This is very useful to export data that is filtered based on selections, and also calculated using the front-end features of QlikView.

Even JOINs can be performed on various in-memory tables to create a fresh table, without actually performing a JOIN in the script. Then this new table can be exported using this front-end export feature.

This export can be done manually by bringing up the popup menu by right-click and choosing EXPORT option. This can also be done programmatically from within a QlikView macro or a QlikView OCX program using the Automation API.

These export macros can be combined with the Loop and Reduce feature of Publisher. The macro triggered in each reduced document at the end of reload produce the necessary export content in a predefined directory.

Conclusions – QlikView can be a viable ETL alternative

One of the general objections about QlikView is its ETL capability. Interestingly, the yardsticks used for ETL comparisons are actually skewed in favor of SQL based technologies. It is not necessary that only SQL based solutions should be implemented in enterprises. QlikView offers a very different and efficient mechanism of ETL.

One of the most important points of contention: QlikView stores all the data in QVDs, which are proprietary; hence other downstream systems cannot make use of these QVDs. In fact, QlikView offers the option to export QVDs into CSV files, which can then be imported into any open RDBMS system. This gives an alternative way of creating processed, Dimensional Models of the enterprise data—Star or Snow-Flake Schema. There are partners who have created tools which read the QVD files and push them into open RDBMS storage solutions, to enable this in a more sophisticated and manageable way.

References

1. Analysis Plus Synthesis: Turning Data into Insights, Lindsay Ellerby, UX Matters, [http://www.uxmatters.com/mt/archives/2009/04/analysis-plus-synthesis-turning-data-into-insights.php]
2. Analysis vs. Synthesis or Analysis and Synthesis, Dr. Ernest Forman, The A-B-C's of Decision Making, July 2007, [http://expertchoice.blogspot.com/2007/07/analysis-vs-synthesis-or-analysis-and.html]

3. Partial Load / Incremental Load, Thread on QlikCommunity, QlikView.com, [http://community.qlikview.com/thread/1303]

4. Parallel Processes (with Batch Files), Thread on QlikCommunity, QlikView.com, http://community.qlikview.com/message/36706 #36706

5. Parallel Reloads in Publisher, Thread on QlikCommunity, QlikView.com, http://community.qlikview.com/message/69435 #69435

6. Refresh Document Near Real Time, Thread on QlikCommunity, QlikView.com, [http://community.qlikview.com/message/30857 #30857]

7. Call Center.QVW Application and RealTimeUpdates.xls, QlikView 9 Distribution, QlikView.com, [http://qv4ent.com/QlikViewETL/ RealTime]

8. Preparing Data for QlikView, Cam Quinn, Nov 2010, Datamartist.com, [http://www.datamartist.com/preparing-data-for-qlikview]

9. Data Profiling, Infosolve Technologies, [http://dataprofiling.net/http://dataprofiling.net/]

10. Data Profiling, IT Tool Box, Jul 2008, ITToolBox.com, [http://it.toolbox.com/wiki/index.php/Data_profiling]

11. Master Data Management, Book, David Loshin, Morgan Kaufmann Publishers, 2009

12. Data Profiling, Wiki on Business Intelligence, Gerard Nico, [http://gerardnico.com/wiki/data_Modelling/data_profiling]

13. DataFlux Whitepaper: Practitioners Guide to Data Profiling, David Loshin [http://hosteddocs.ittoolbox.com/datafluxwp070thepractitionesgui detodataprofiling01112011.pdf]

14. Data Deduplication (intelligence compression or single-instance storage), Stephen Bigelow and Jeff Hawkins, Sep 2008, Search Storage, TechTarget, [http://searchstorage.techtarget.com/definition/data-deduplication

QlikView for Enterprises

## CHAPTER 11

QLIKVIEW FOR SAP

BEST DATA CAPTURE AND PROCESS MANAGEMENT TOOLS MAY NOT BE THE BEST FOR ANALYTICS

Introduction to the Chapter

SAP is one of the most commonly used platforms for ERP and other specialized process management systems. While IBM, Oracle & Microsoft provide solutions of good magnitude & penetration, SAP is different in the way it allows other systems to connect and extract data.

With other systems it is possible to directly connect to the back-end databases and individual tables can be extracted from QlikView. But for SAP, such direct extraction from back-end tables is next to impossible due to the business rules layer present in the SAP platform. The need is to connect to SAP data stores only through business rules layer.

To facilitate this, SAP provides a set of APIs and connection methods through which any external system can connect and retrieve data. Due to the various SAP modules, and the multiple connection methods available for SAP, options available are many and complex. The on-going investments done on reporting and analytics on SAP systems can get prohibitive if appropriate strategies are not used. Not to mention the enormous amount of time required for daily processing and reporting.

QlikView has taken an innovative approach to address this need. QlikView can optimize investments over the SAP system, particularly from Dashboarding, from an Analytics and Reporting perspective.

If SAP is running in an organization, using QlikView on top of it will yield some unexpected benefits. In one of the large auto manufacturers, the need was to do financial closure within the 3rd of every month. On SAP the challenge was, BW gave summary data after processing. The controllers wanted to add adjustments on top of it, and before finally releasing the financials, needed the ability to drill down and browse the detailed accounting entries, to ensure that they explain the variances and also ensure correctness. To enable this on BW was a challenge, but with QlikView this could be done immediately. They also got the ability to slice & dice, and explore detailed information without any limitations.

This chapter discusses the philosophy and approaches of QlikView to connect to various modules of SAP. The discussion also covers how to take advantage of all the investments already done in SAP platform products and intellectual property created by the professional services / development. The information provided is based on material available from QlikTech on the QlikView SAP Connector version 5.6 as of the writing of this book.

Challenges with SAP Reporting

With SAP evolving over many years, the number of reporting components has increased steadily, along with the difficulty and complexity to get information. While SAP has been attempting to harmonize all these solutions in an integrated framework, the system continues to be complex due to the backward compatibility needs for all the systems. Acquisition of Business Objects by SAP has further increased the complexity of reporting / analytics / dashboard solutions for SAP customers.

Details of the current SAP Business Analytics Solutions are provided in the SAP website: "Business Analytics Solutions from SAP" [1], "Data Warehousing Solutions from SAP" [2] and related Technology frameworks and principles in another page: "Platform: Improving Flexibility and Responsiveness" [3]. The SAP reporting architecture provides summary and detail level reports through various reporting interfaces. Most reports available in SAP platform are all pre-defined, probably the most exhaustive in industry. Creation of new reports is still majorly the job of IT folks managing SAP.

SAP's OLAP-based business intelligence (BI) is complex and predicated on an all-SAP cube structure. ABAP queries, SAP BW, and module reports can be difficult to use. These solutions somewhat take users towards the insights they need but have serious shortcomings. The most important shortcomings are: a) Time taken to find the necessary report for the data required, b) Time taken to run these reports and c) Navigability between various reports without losing the context.

It is difficult to interact with the SAP system across its entire dataset, or even across multiple dimensions within tables. Conducting reporting and analysis across tables, and integrating data from other systems, are challenging. Built for centralized reporting, SAP and most third-party add-on tools lack the flexibility to meet business users' requirements for tools they can use to explore data and ask and answer their own questions. The challenge increases when the need is to combine SAP data with data from other sources, and when large data volumes cripple performance. As a result, SAP users lack visibility into their business processes and critical insights remain hidden away inside SAP data.

Traditional OLAP technology used in some new SAP solutions requires executives to anticipate every question and have IT build the analyses. Executives need fast answers to critical, often complex, business questions. They need insights inspiring new questions and deliver answers that weren't considered before. But today such flexibility doesn't exist in SAP reporting and analytic solutions.

This has led to what is termed as *Buyer's Remorse* as highlighted by the CITO Research Paper: "Harness Your SAP Data with User-Driven Dashboards" [4]. The most important power for innovation is with Business Users. Allowing them to explore and find new patterns, relationships from rich data in SAP will unlock a huge potential for organizations. The existing SAP reporting / analytic solutions do not make this possible since most of the work requires IT experts trained on SAP technologies [5].

QlikView for SAP

Broadly, QlikView solution for SAP works in the following lines [6]:

- Extract data from various SAP sub-systems: R3 (with OpenSQL, SAP Query, SAP Report and Extractor), BW/BI (with OLAP, ODS, DSO, BEX) using appropriate connectors
- Use the business logic already built in the SAP sub-systems during extract by executing Reports and Extractors already defined in SAP
- Syndicate data from various sub-systems into a unified data model
- Syndicate and unify data from other non-SAP systems also
- Use QlikView Associative Analytics to analyze the unified data

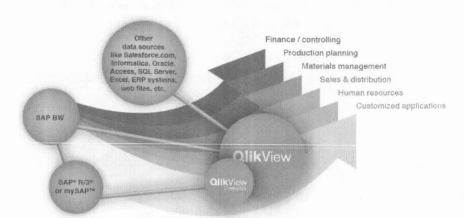

Other data sources like Salesforce.com, Informatica, Oracle, Access, SQL Server, Excel, ERP systems, web files, etc.

Finance / controlling
Production planning
Materials management
Sales & distribution
Human resources
Customized applications

SAP BW

QlikView

SAP® R/3® or mySAP™

QlikView

Figure 1: Overview of QlikView for SAP solution

The key components of QlikView solution for SAP include: a) QlikView SAP Connector for Netweaver, b) QlikStart Templates for key modules of SAP and c) SAP Extraction Script Generators.

QlikView SAP Connector for Netweaver: The QlikView Connector for use with SAP NetWeaver® enables SAP users to extract data from SAP and perform quick, flexible, visual, ad hoc analysis and reporting. QlikView combines data from SAP® R/3®, mySAP™, SAP BW, and BEX queries with data from non-SAP systems. All this data is available to users in the analytic QlikView platform.

Key features of the SAP Connector are:

- Uses Integration based on SAP standards ABAP/4 and RFC API
- QlikView connects to SAP's transactional system, BW/BI or any Netweaver based product

More information about SAP Connector Administration and Usage is provided in the QlikCommunity document: QlikView Connector for Use with SAP Netweaver, Installation and Usage Guide.

QlikStart Templates: QlikView also offers out-of-the-box QlikStart templates for SAP modules including Sales & Distribution (SD), Materials Management (MM), Project Systems (PS), Production Planning (PP),

Human Resources (HR), Controlling (CO), and Finance (Account Receivable (AR), Accounts Payable (AP), and General Ledger (GL).

QlikView SAP Connector Components

The SAP-certified connector works as a read-only remote function call and enables direct access to SAP data. The QlikView SAP Connector consists of 6 connectors: 1) SQL Connector, 2) SAP Queries Connector, 3) ABAP Report Connector, 4) SAP Extractor Connector, 5) OLAP Connector and 6) DSO/ODS Connector. With all these connectors, SAP becomes a "standard" data source for QlikView.

All these connectors have two parts: one is a transport installed in the SAP system, and the other is the custom connector which is generally installed on the QlikView Publisher Server. Transport is installed in each of the SAP server instances. Connector application instance can connect to any number of SAP Servers. Similarly any number of QlikView Developer or Publisher instances can connect to the Connector, to fetch data from any of the backend SAP servers. Each of these connectors provides access to data from specific SAP backend sub-system.

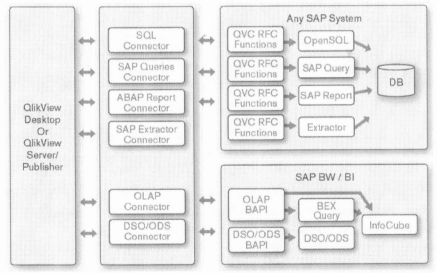

Figure 2: QlikView SAP Connectors

R/3 Connectors:

First four fetch data from any R/3 system (DEV / TEST / PRODUCTION). All these four connectors use QVC RFC functions present in the transport installed on the R/3 Basis system. These RFCs are read-only functions, which do not make any changes to the backend tables.

SQL Connector: This allows access to the SAP R/3 data using OpenSQL. This reads Cluster, Pool and Transparent Tables including SAP Metadata & also extracts tables/views from SAP (standard or custom Z* & Y* tables). An overview of using SQL Connector is provided in the YouTube Video: QlikView for Use with SAP–SQL Connector [7].

SAP Query Connector: Allows execution of existing SAP Queries and get result into a QlikView table.

SAP Report Connector: Allows execution of existing SAP Reports (ABAP) and get result directly.

Extractor Connector: This is a new addition in version 5.6 onwards. In the SAP ERP system there are pre-defined data sources to be used for BI systems (Extractors). The Extractor connector makes it easier to re-use these pre-defined data sources developed for SAP BI systems.

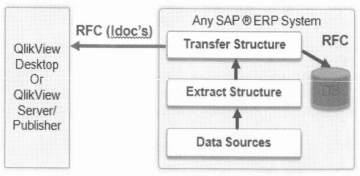

Figure 3: Extractor Connector

Extractor connector can use Standard SAP extraction methods using RFC and IDocs—available as a standard for other SAP® BI products. It provides following additional advantages:

- Minimal needs of skills/knowledge of the table structure in SAP ERP system and how to combine tables for different purpose. Such skills are required when using the SQL Connector.
- Several extractors have delta mechanism—quicker daily extracts.

- Yet another advantage is using the SAP standard functions and programs

BI/BW Connectors:

The last two connectors allow extraction from BI/BW systems. These connectors also are read-only and do not make any changes to the backend structures:

OLAP Connector: The OLAP connector uses the OLAP BAPI calls provided by the BW system. Using OLAP BAPIs data can be extracted directly from the InfoCubes, or BEX Queries can be executed. Both these methods can be used to fetch the InfoCube data.

DSO/ODS Connector: DSO/ODS Connector allows access to DSO/ODS objects allowing re-use of already existing business logic.

With these connectors QlikView can use each sub-system of SAP as a possible data source and provide integrated interactive analytics along with data from non-SAP systems as well.

Business Benefits of QlikView SAP

QlikView delivers power and simplicity without the cost or complexity of traditional BI tools. All the benefits discussed in the chapter on "What Benefits Can Be Expected from QlikView" will be naturally applicable for QlikView with SAP.

In addition, the following are the additional business benefits:
- *Empower Business Users with Self-Service*: The most important benefit that QlikView will provide for the company using SAP.
- *Ease of use*: QlikView is easy for business people to use and IT pros to manage. Most users become productive with QlikView after less than one hour of training.
- *Speed of deployment*: Deploy individual analyses and reporting solutions in weeks or days using the QlikView script builder. Expedite and simplify the process of analyzing relevant data from SAP using the QlikView SAP Data Dictionary.

- *Quick Application Development*: Automatic ETL script generation based on easy point and click selection using Script Builder application—very useful for QlikView Application Developers.
- *Commercially Efficient*: Administratively, one connector to multiple SAP servers (DEV, QAS, PRD)—generally coexists with QV Development and Publisher (no extra hardware)—cheaper.
- *Fast Data Loads and Quicker Daily Processing*: Delta Load Capable and allows Parallel downloads from any SAP server
- *Reuse of reports and queries*: The QlikView BW OLAP connector enables organizations to reuse business logic and leverage investments they have already made in BEX queries. Likewise, QlikView provides rapid and easy access to DSO / ODS objects, ABAP reports, and SAP queries.
- *Reuse of SAP Extractors*: The QlikView Extractor connector makes it easier to re-use pre-defined data sources developed by SAP for their BI systems—allows use of SAP Standard iDocs interface.

Technical Benefits of QlikView SAP

The various technical benefits provided by QlikView for SAP are:

- *Data warehouse not a must*: QlikView combines data from SAP and other sources in memory, with or without an existing data warehouse, for simple and fast reporting, development, and updates. If a data warehouse exists, it can be used to maximum potential and get ROI.
- *Standard and Independent*: Access to SAP data using SAP latest NetWeaver RFC, iDocs (Extractors) and OLAP. No dependencies on other SAP products (e.g. SAPGUI, Bex).
- *Certified interface*: The QlikView Connector for use with SAP NetWeaver gives customers added assurance of SAP certification when using QlikView to visualize critical information from SAP.
- *Multi-threaded and streaming Connector:* While extracting data from SAP, buffers are allocated for holding data before it is transferred out to the requesting client. These buffers can get really

big, demanding large memory allocations on the SAP Server. The QlikView SAP Connector is very light, and it acts like a transparent pipe, streaming data immediately to the requesting QlikView ETL engine. So there is no need for large buffers to be allocated in the SAP Server to support the extraction process. However, if the connector executes an RFC or a BAPI (both R/3 and OLAP) that pre-processes and sends data to the extractor, the memory / compute resources required for those RFCs and BAPIs need to be available.

- *Flexibility to combine data sources*: QlikView combines data from SAP® R/3®, mySAP™, SAP BW, and BEX queries with data from non-SAP systems. All of this data is available to users with a single click. BAPIs, RFCs, SAP Query, SAP ODS/DSO, SAP R/3 TABLES, SAP BW (BEX), iDocs through SAP Extractor—all of these provide data in different levels of granularity and detail. QlikView can integrate all of them smoothly.

- *Tight SAP Data Integration with Business Logic*: No need to create / maintain another extraction layer with a set of custom ABAP programs or middleware like SAP XI. Since all the existing RFCs, BAPIs, OLAP Cubes, BEX Queries, SAP Extractors can be invoked through the QlikView SAP Connectors, there is no need to replicate the logic already existing in the existing programs / components in current SAP setup.

- *Extract Directly into QVDs:* Data from the SAP Tables are directly extracted into the QVD storage, removing the need to maintain another layer of CSV data files. This direct extract supports incremental load of data, and also leverage re-use of business logic implemented already in the SAP system. However, if existing logic implemented poses a heavy load on the SAP backend, then it is preferable to get this logic implemented externally in QlikView.

- *Readymade QVD generator script templates:* Taking the standard SAP implementations as reference, QlikTech provides readily available Extraction template scripts. These scripts automatically pick relevant tables for each module and create the respective

QVDs, which can be used as a quick way of implementing ETL from SAP. This can be further extended to include other tables that are not present including the Y* and Z* tables.

- *Pre-packaged QlikStart templates:* QlikView offers out-of-the-box templates FI, AP, AR, MM, PS, PP, HR and CO—one can gain instant insight from day one. These templates use QVDs generated by the QVD Generators, making the implementation process easier and faster. Using these templates, creation of new QV Applications becomes quicker, expanding existing data Models.

- *Security*: The Connector allows QlikView applications to follow the SAP Security model. Additional field level security is provided by the QlikView platform.

- *Ease of Administration*: Very little administration required. Quick installation and configuration (around half an hour)

Challenges of SAP Connector

Installation of a Transport component on each SAP Server

There is a need to install a TRANSPORT on the SAP Server. The transport is really a read-only feature that allows users to directly connect from the QlikView SAP Connector for extracting data. Sometimes there is an aversion to installing any additional component in the SAP Server. This could be a challenge. However, the Transport is read-only, and does not tamper with the SAP data.

Some Connectors are not intelligent

Since the connector is just like a transparent pipe, there is no intelligence built-in about the data fields / tables and their relationships. Hence the relationship information required to build the data models in an efficient way, needs to be with the data modeler and hence there is a need for an SAP Functional / Technical expert to be available for data Modelling purposes.

Some of this is resolved by the ready-made QVD generators and the ready-made templates, but the need for the SAP experts cannot be avoided when more complex requirements have to be met. With the introduction of Extractor Connector, some challenges are already taken care of. However, need for expertise from the SAP back-end team, both for R/3 and BW/BI cannot be avoided.

Using QlikView with Business Objects

While the Qlikview SAP Connector works with all the R/3 and BI/BW sources, Business Objects (BO) is a very important addition in the SAP BI offerings. While BO has got a whole suite, at core is the Universe.

QlikView can extract data from BO and integrate with other SAP and non-SAP data. The connector available from DataRoket [8] allows BO data to be: a) exported to XML format (scheduled extractions) to specific directories, b) directly extracted into QlikView as a stream.

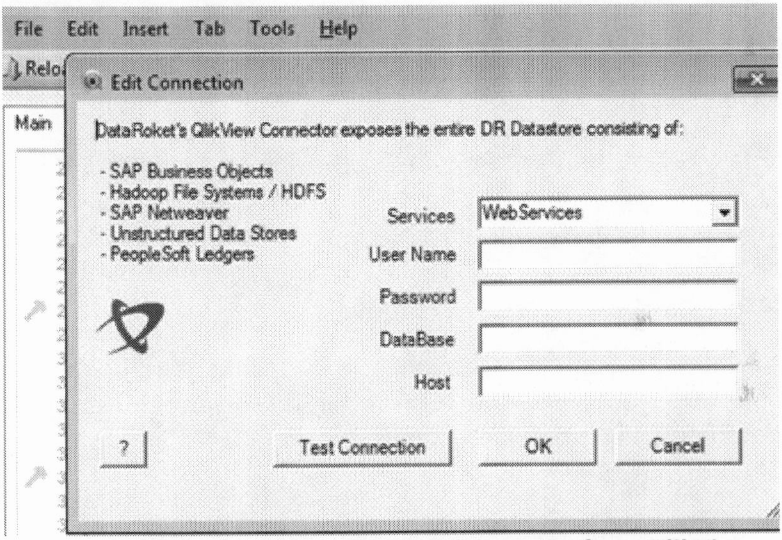

Figure 4: Using Dataroket Connector from QlikView

The Dataroket connector can make following available as data sources:

- Business Objects Universe
- Business Objects Reports
- Multi-BO Domain Document Lists

Some of the interesting features of Dataroket are:

- Automatically adjusts to changes in the universe
- Easily handles millions of rows

- Reads all formulas and schema
- Binds multiple BO Universes
- Accelerates and scales the BO universe for users
- Fully SDK compliant (no unsupported calls)
- Scale the universe without BO
- Component level awareness (BO formulas and objects)
- Streams BO universe data real-time
- Bypass InfoView for access to queries
- Metadata of BO can also be brought to QlikView

Dataroket claims that the extracted BO data looks generic, meaning the user does not have to know BO Universe in order to use the data in QlikView. The power is the ability to associate your BO data with any other data within QlikView.

Distributed Data Extraction

Typically SAP systems in large multi-geography enterprises are installed in a distributed architecture. Data is collected and stored in different SAP servers for different functions / geographies. For analytics with QlikView, there is a need to syndicate data from multiple SAP servers into one place.

There are two approaches possible in such situations: 1) Central SAP Connector + Publisher extracting from all SAP servers, 2) Distributed SAP Connector + Publisher installations for each location extracting data from local SAP servers.

Option 1 is recommended when the amount of data to be extracted in each location is not too large and there is enough network bandwidth available across all locations to support such data exchange.

When the network bandwidth available is less or the amount of data to be extracted is large, Option 2 is used. In such situations, QlikView Connector can be installed in each location separately, along with a local instance of QlikView Publisher. It is also possible to extract in each location using the local SAP Connector + QlikView Developer Clients using Windows scheduler instead of Publisher.

The QVD files created can then be transferred to the remote location for integrating into the Unified Data Repository and then the QlikView User Applications. Since QVD files give a high level of size reduction, transferring QVD files will require very less bandwidth and time to transfer. Added to this, if it is done incrementally, then the bandwidth / time demands are further low.

Using SAP Security with QlikView

QlikView has got a very flexible security model. A detailed discussion of the QlikView security is provided in the next chapter. Broadly, QlikView has Authentication and Authorization components.

Authentication in QlikView happens by using the standard User Identity Management systems like LDAP, ADS etc that exist in the organization. If NetWeaver Identity Management System is used, it can be used to integrate the authentication to create a Single-Sign-On infrastructure.

Authorization is supported by user access permission tables imported into the QlikView section access. These security tables can also be populated with data from SAP security tables. Using the QlikView SAP connectors, security tables of SAP [9, 10] can be extracted and the same model can be re-created inside the QlikView Applications. This information can be used for Authorization.

It is however, important to understand that sometimes access rights in the backend transaction systems are different from what is required in the reporting / analytic systems. If required, centrally controlled user access management tables extracted from SAP, can be updated / changed according to the organizational user access policies required for reporting.

QlikView SAP Templates

The QlikStart Templates included with QlikView SAP Connectors contain two parts for each key functional area: a) QVD Generators and b) QlikView User Application Templates.

The QVD generators have a list of standard SAP tables that are required for the particular functional area. When run they extract this list of SAP tables and write them into a QVD repository. These standard tables are the base tables present in all the vanilla implementations of SAP. If the implementation is customized, the additional tables created (both Y* and Z* tables) need to be included in these QVD extractors.

QlikView User Application Templates import the QVDs generated by QVD Generators, and populate the sample dashboards supplied. The templates added are with limited functionality, and not as exhaustive as a company would need it. However, data model created is re-usable and extensible.

With this data model, the necessary front-end elements can be modified / created very easily, to represent the KPIs needed for the organization. Partners of QlikTech have enhanced these templates for particular manufacturing organizations for readily taking care of all the functions.

Making Best Use of QlikView for SAP

1. Of all the reports and analytics done on top of SAP, some are required for line function decision making in real-time. An example is Open Orders and Available Finished Goods, to decide what available stock item can be dispatched for which open order. This needs to be available in real-time. All such reports need to come from SAP only.

   Except such reports, most other reports are post-facto, which need not run on real-time data, but can be run on data snapshots taken from SAP in regular frequency. Such off-line reports and analytics can be moved away from the SAP system, and can be run in QlikView platform to take advantage of the fast in-memory analytics. Instead of just creating these reports as Static reports and distributed, QlikView can provide these reports, allowing users to get the power of interactive analysis on SAP data.

2. Some tables in SAP get updated by the minute and some other tables get updated weekly, monthly, quarterly or more. Lookups get modified rarely. There is no need to pull data more frequent than their updates. QlikView SAP Connector allows different scripts to be written to extract tables separately. Each of these scripts can be scheduled in Publisher instances to be run in different frequencies so that the related QVD files can be created / updated in sync with

the changes done to the source tables. This will optimize the load on the back-end SAP systems.

3. Using a 4 Tier Architecture for ETL is a good idea. The QVD extractor will be the first layer. The stages explained in the chapters on ETL should be implemented for the most successful long term benefits of using QlikView for SAP.

4. Understanding the existing security model of SAP and deriving the security model required for QlikView is important. Creating a flexible security model will help enable users to get the best benefits from SAP data.

QlikView for SAP will make a significant difference in the way business users get information for decision making, and also the way in which IT experts spend their time servicing all the information requirements. Benefits can be maximized and self-service made more pervasive by appropriate data models created out of the data extracted from SAP, and merging with external non-SAP data.

Conclusions

Investments in SAP can be made extremely useful by unlocking the SAP data with QlikView to provide extensive business value. In a typical SAP installation, most of the users are given an SAP license only for accessing reports and analysis. This adds challenges to the SAP installation, by increasing the query / processing load, due to the various reports that are fired by the report users.

QlikView brings about a major relief for the SAP administrators by taking all these report user loads off the system. In addition, QlikView helps combine data from outside SAP, add new business logic at reporting time without having to develop ABAP code or other customizations.

The relative efforts required to add new reports, provide slice and dice capability are so minimal and the net value derived out of SAP can be manifolds better. The latest QlikView connector gives many ways to make this happen with little effort and takes advantage of already made data and intellectual investments.

References

1. Business Analytics Solutions from SAP – Run Better, SAP.COM,
    [http://www.sap.com/solutions/sapbusinessobjects/index.epx],
2. Data Warehousing Solutions from SAP – Flexible Data Foundations
    for All IT Environments, SAP.COM,
    [http://www.sap.com/solutions/sapbusinessobjects/data-warehousing/index.epx]
3. Platform: Improving Flexibility and Responsiveness, SAP.COM,
    [http://www.sap.com/platform/index.epx].
4. Harness Your SAP Data with User-Driven Dashboards, IDG Connect,
    White Paper,
    [http://www.idgconnect.com/view_abstract/4979/harness-your-sap-data-user-driven-dashboards?region=asia]
5. SAP Reporting Limitations, ABAP Reports, BlogSpot.Com,
    [http://abapreports.blogspot.com/2009/01/sap-reporting-limitations.html]
6. QlikView for SAP, Product Page, QlikView Website,
    [http://www.qlikview.com/us/explore/solutions/data-source/sap]
7. QlikView for Use with SAP – SQL Connector, YouTube Video,
    [http://www.youtube.com/watch?v=c5UqDCiTylY]
8. Business Objects Universe Real-Time Data Connector,
    Dataroket.com,
    [http://www.dataroket.com/index.php?option=com_content&id=303]
9. SAP Security Overview Presentation, October 2010, Gerlinde
    Zibulski, SAP,
    [http://www.sapevents.edgesuite.net/TechEd/TechEd_Vegas2010/Collateral/SCI100.pdf]
10. SAP Security and Authorizations, Book, Mario Linkies and Frank Off,
    SAP Press

CHAPTER 12
DATA MODELLING FOR QLIKVIEW

A MODEL IS JUST A SIMPLIFIED REPRESENTATION OF REALITY AND CAN TAKE MANY FORMS

Introduction to the Chapter

Data stored in multiple data sources are extracted by ETL. After extraction, the data from all these sources need to be stored cohesively in an efficient way to help querying. The way it is stored decides how useful the data can be, and how quickly the answers can be provided to the users. Deciding the structure of data—tables, fields and their relationships—is Data Modelling.

With the evolution of Relational Databases, Data Warehouses and Data Marts over the last many decades, various practices have evolved for Data Modelling. Relational Modelling and Dimensional Modelling have taken shape with all the variations. These methods have been formulated to address the challenges of SQL technology. These concepts are extremely useful for QlikView as well. More technologies like AQL that go beyond the limits of SQL have led to significant evolution in the way data can be efficiently stored and retrieved.

QlikView, with its unique technology, lends data to be stored in optimal ways and derive much better benefits than the SQL based data warehouses and data marts. Hence the principles of data warehousing, data marts and data Modelling have to be amended for the QlikView technology.

Data Model creation is an extremely important part of delivering the QlikView promise of more than static reporting. Modelling needs the expertise of Data Modelers and Architects and then the QlikView

Developers can execute the ETL and Front-End creation using the models. The need is to gain necessary theoretical overview of QlikView data Modelling, a practical Modelling approach for QlikView and best practices to follow on the ground. This chapter attempts to address this.

Starting with a recap of key data Modelling principles, this chapter goes on to create a framework for Data Modelling with QlikView. With QlikView, the need is to have a disk-based storage for all transformed—ready-to-eat—persistent data, and memory-based storage to support associative interactive analytics.

The chapter discusses different Modelling approaches, providing some model templates. In addition, the chapter discusses data Modelling best practices for QlikView and the ETL process required to support such Modelling.

Evolution of Decision Support Systems

Data is a great asset, but it is increasingly difficult to access and make use of it—primarily due to multiple formats, platforms, files and database structures developed by different vendors and sheer quantity of data. Transaction systems store data optimized for handling transaction speeds and are not optimal for querying and analysis performance. For transactional systems, the relational structure based fundamentally on the SQL processes is used. Decision support systems evolved from the same SQL technologies have performance challenges.

Hence, separate Decision Support / Data Analysis systems have evolved to support decision making efficiently without performance penalties: Warehouses are integration / syndication platforms and Data Marts are used to provide pre-processed data subsets to help users do analysis.

Data Warehouses and Data Marts

Data Warehouses and Data Marts are conceptual models used to create decision support systems and allow business users to use them effectively. Some of the books and articles provided in the references section give great overview and details of these concepts and the practices around them. Of Particular mention are "The Datawarehouse Toolkit: The Complete Guide to Dimensional Modelling" [1] and "The IBM RedBook: Dimensional Modelling" [2].

Data warehouse is intended to store all the data from various information sources in the enterprises, to meet the following purposes:

1. Historical and Current data to be available in one place
2. Data to be kept in easy-to-query and fast-to-retrieve form

Since these warehouses get data from all the systems in an enterprise and combine them with integrity, it takes a long time to mature.

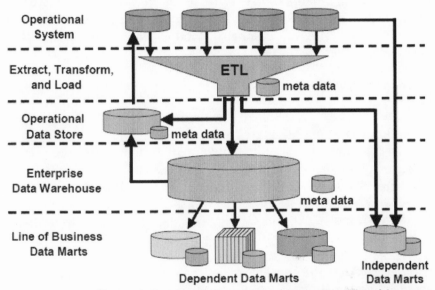

Figure 1: Data warehouses and Data Marts Architecture

Many departments and business are anxious to get the benefits of data warehousing, and reluctant to wait for the natural evolution. The concept of data marts exists to satisfy the needs of these departments. Simplistically, a data mart is a small data warehouse built to satisfy the needs of a particular department or business area. Data mart typically contains a subset of corporate data that is valuable to a specific business unit, department, or set of users.

This subset consists of historical, summarized, and possibly detailed data captured from transaction processing systems (called *independent data marts*), or from an existing enterprise data warehouse (called *dependent data marts*). It is important to realize that the *users and functional scope of the data mart* defines the data mart, not the size of the data mart database.

Influence and Dependency on SQL and Hardware Technologies

As seen in previous chapters, these solutions are implicitly conditioned and driven by the strengths and weaknesses of SQL technology. At the core were the limitations of hardware technologies available: CPUs and particularly memory were very expensive whereas the storage was relatively cheaper. All characteristics of the solutions were shaped by these core factors. Earlier chapters "Comparison of Reporting Technologies", "What is QlikView?" and "QlikView in Depth" discussed this in detail. The key interest was how to make least use of memory and CPU and yet give reasonably good performance to the users performing analysis/reporting.

Data Architectures and Data Models

In spite of such technology limitations, the evolution of Data warehouses and Data Marts created a framework and a large set of best practices in implementing Decision Support Systems. These principles, practices and framework are very relevant when implementing QlikView in enterprises. As the core of all these practices and frameworks, Data Architectures and Data Models are the two important aspects. Data architecture defines the various information layers and data model defines how data will be stored in each of the layers.

The Data Architecture chosen decides the way in which data flows from source operational systems to the business users in the form of reports and analytics. The information pyramid created and referred in the "IBM Redbook" is a good way to understand the possible layers.

Various architectures have been evolved for decision support systems. The key architectures that are popular include the following:

- Enterprise Data Warehouse (EDW)
- Independent Data Marts
- Dependent Data Marts

These architectures can be used in combination as well. The most typical structure is combining the EDW and dependent data marts. QlikView is deployed in majority of the cases as Independent Data Marts. While this is very useful for department deployments, the other architectures can be used in deploying QlikView as an Enterprise Solution (more in chapter on "Deploying QlikView")

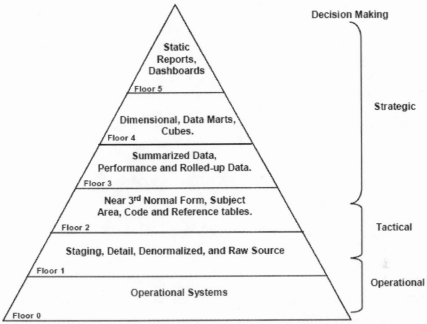

Figure 2: Information Pyramid

Data Modelling experiences in the past many decades can be put to good use, with adjustments to work for QlikView. Next section highlights these key principles & later sections integrate experiences till now and evolve the data Modelling approach and framework for enterprise deployment of QlikView.

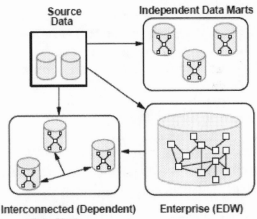

Figure 3: Data Warehouse Architectures

Principles of Data Modelling

Data model defines the structure in which data will be stored in the enterprise information layers. Both in transactional and decision support systems, data need to be stored in a structure which supports the purpose in an efficient manner. Modelling of data storage is a key to enabling this efficiency. Modelling decides data elements and the way they are stored. The chosen model decides efficiency of the underlying systems—most importantly speed of development and performance.

Modelling Approaches

Broadly, most common & popular data model approaches used are Relational Model (also called Entity Relationship ER Models), and Dimensional Model (Star and Snowflake Models). These two different approaches are most commonly used for operational systems and decision support systems respectively:

Relational Modelling: Efficient and fast handling of transaction is the key need. The relational model focuses heavily on normalization of data. Normalization basically involves splitting large tables of data into smaller ones, until every column is independent on any other column, each row consists of a single primary key and a set of totally independent attributes of the object that are identified by the primary key. This type of structure is said to be in third normal form (3NF).

The need is to reduce redundancy of data so that any field needs to be updated only in one place. This ensures efficient transaction processing, with minimal overheads and duplication of updates. This E-R Model data structure is used for transaction systems for the update efficiency.

Relational Modelling evolved from the time SQL was created, and kept improving with the growth in various hardware technologies, particularly storage. However, 3NF form databases are very inefficient for analysts since they need to painfully traverse through multiple tables to find data. Added to that is of course the penalty of joining many tables leading to query inefficiencies.

Dimensional Modelling: Efficient and fast querying and analysis is the key need. Dimensional models focus heavily on de-normalization of data: the need is to reduce the time to retrieve and calculate / aggregate data to produce the reports and analysis that users request to help support their decision making process swiftly.

Dimensional Modelling evolved to remove penalties of SQL (JOIN, GROUP BY) by various innovative ways: Pre-organizing, pre-joining, pre-processing / pre-aggregating. These techniques remove penalty of executing complex queries during user requests for reports / analyses.

However, by joining more tables together into less number of tables, redundancy of data is increased. Hence the amount of data required to be stored in data warehouses is very large, making storage needs more expensive. Also duplication of data requires adequate controls to ensure consistent updates/changes across all instances of the same data.

These Modelling approaches are two ideal references that show two distinct approaches possible using the relational algebra. In real implementations, these models are combined based on the hardware and data size considerations. Later sections discuss how these two models can be used separately or combined in QlikView applications for different purposes.

Models and Schemas

The relationship between all tables in the form of primary and foreign keys is defined as a data model. Once a model is arrived at, definition of the tables and fields in a formal language supported by a data base management system (like Oracle, SQL Server, etc) is called the Database Schema. These are essentially table creation statements along with the integrity definitions. In SQL it is CREATE TABLE statement and in QlikView it is LOAD statement which produces tables. Schema definition is the final destination of all data Modelling activities.

ER schema is found in all transaction systems, however perfect 3NF (total normalization) is not always a reality. There is always some data redundancy in practical transaction systems. Dimensional schema is very easy to understand without having to traverse through many table chains. It typically consists of large table of facts—*fact table*—with a number of other tables surrounding it that contain descriptive data— *dimension tables*.

Fact tables have the following characteristics:

- Contain numerical values which are measured. For example, a fact value of 20 might mean that 20 widgets have been sold.
- Fact tables typically contain a small number of columns.
- Each fact table contains the keys—called foreign keys—to associate dimension tables.

- Compared to dimension tables, fact tables have large number of rows.
- Fact fields are numeric & used to generate aggregates & summaries. Hence the data values need to be additive or semi-additive.

Dimension tables have the following characteristics:

- The dimension tables contain descriptive information about the numerical values in the fact table, i.e., they contain the details or attributes of facts. For example, dimension tables for a marketing analysis application might include attributes such as time period, marketing region, and product type. That, as an example, enables business analysts to better understand the data and their reports.
- Since data in a dimension table is de-normalized, it typically has large number of columns.
- Dimension tables typically contain significantly fewer rows of data than fact table.
- Attributes in a dimension table are typically used as row and column headings in a report or query results display. For example, the textual descriptions on a report come from dimension attributes.
- Dimension tables are also referred to as Master Data, Master Reference Data or just Reference Data. Wiki Page on Reference Data gives an overview.
- Master Data is used across individual system/process, multiple systems/processes, across all enterprises and across the market as discussed in the Wiki Page Master Data.

Dimensional Model Schemas

Depending on how many fact and dimension tables exist in the schema, there are three different forms of dimensional schemas. Any of these schemas can be used.

Star Schema: If one fact table is used with just one level of dimension tables, the design is a star schema. The dimension tables are de-normalized. Star schemas are useful because every property of a dimension can be retrieved with one SQL join from the fact table to the relevant dimension table. This improves query performance, but could possibly increase data volumes.

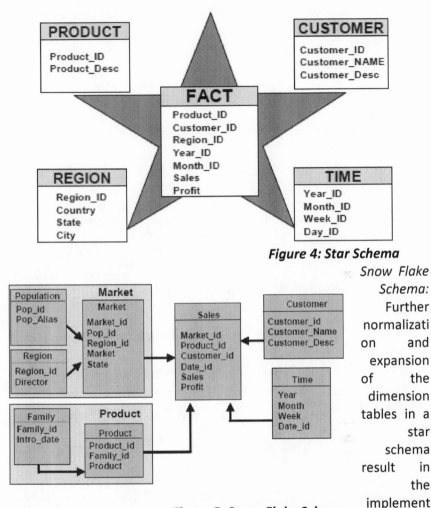

Figure 4: Star Schema

Snow Flake Schema: Further normalization and expansion of the dimension tables in a star schema result in the implementation of a

Figure 5: Snow-Flake Schema

snowflake design. A dimension is said to be snow-flaked when columns with least number of distinct values (low-cardinality) are moved to a separate table and linked back to the original dimension table.

Multi-Star Schema: This consists of multiple fact tables, joined through dimension tables. This model gets formed in practical situations if one is not careful. This could lead to complexities in querying. Instead care should be taken to combine multiple fact tables into one table by using various pre-processing stages combining JOINS and CONCATENATE. All models & their variants are used in actual data warehousing systems.

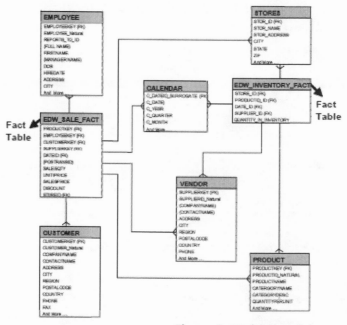

Figure 6: Multi-Star Schema

Following diagram shows typical enterprise architecture for a warehouse. It is interesting to note that, Staging and EDW layers use ER Models. Data Marts use the Dimensional Models.

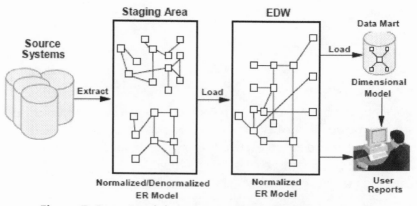

Figure 7: Data Models in Enterprise Warehousing Environment

This understanding is very useful in deciding the data models required when implementing QlikView. The intermediate stores/stages of QlikView need to use ER Models/Schemas whereas the in-memory

Application data model / store need to use Dimensional Models/Schemas.

Data Modelling Process

Keeping requirements in mind, structure & storage for business data should be planned; they should help get answers for key business questions. The process used for arriving at the storage and structure is defined as data Modelling life-cycle and is seen as a three part process:

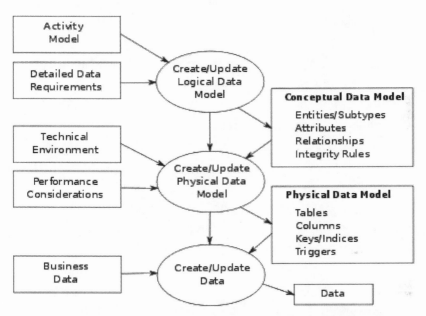

Figure 8: Data Modelling Process

Conceptual Data Model: a high level model to describe requirements in business terms.

Logical Data Model: a skeletal data model describing solutions using business terms.

Physical Data Model: a detailed data model that defines database objects. This is needed to create the physical tables of database for the working solution.

Physical data model defines output required from ETL process to create persistent data, stored in the warehouse or the analytical data mart. This is discussed in detail in the Wikipedia page on "Data Modelling" [4] and in the IBM Redbook "Dimensional Modelling" [2]. All or any of these techniques can be used in implementing QlikView by appropriate use of its relevant capabilities. The entire Modelling process is done to ensure that the final physical model contains all the fields required to meet all the business needs, particularly to monitor and measure efficiency. The following key steps outline the Dimensional Modelling Process:

1. Convert E/R (Transactional) model to Dimensional Model:
   a. Identify Business Processes (by studying the E/R model and user interactions)
   b. Identify Many-to-Many tables in the E/R model and formulate Fact Tables
   c. De-normalize remaining tables into Dimension Tables
   d. Identify Data and Time from the E/R model
2. Identify Grain of the Model—for Facts and Dimensions by understanding business requirements
3. Finalize the Dimensions and dimension tables of the Model—identify various dimension categories and integrate them appropriately
4. Finalize the Fact tables of the Model—identify additive, semi-additive and non-additive facts, design appropriate composite keys and event fact tables
5. Create physical design with techniques of QlikView optimization—use splitting of fields, combining garbage dimensions, aggregate tables, snapshots, back-end processing and hashes. Create multi-layered QVD structure: intermediate stores & dimensional models
6. Change management—changes to data, structure and business

QlikView Data Modelling Approach

The data Modelling for QlikView follows the same principles discussed above. QlikView can work with any schema. The only need is that there should not be any circular reference—any relationship path starting from one table through a key field, cannot connect back to the same table in a circular fashion.

In Figure 6, Multi-star schema shown contains EDW_INVENTORY_FACT and EDW_SALES_FACT tables. These two are connected to each other through four master tables: STORES, PRODUCT, VENDOR and

CALENDAR. Due to this, there are multiple loops formed in the schema. This schema will not work in QlikView as it is.

In QlikView, two data schemas need to be created:
1. Unified Data Model—Persistent Data Storage—equivalent of traditional data warehouse, and
2. Memory Data Store—in each QlikView User Application—equivalent of traditional data marts

Unified Data Model - Persistent Data Storage

The Persistent Data Store is created during the ETL process. While deploying QlikView, as discussed in the Chapter "QlikView ETL" multi-stage ETL requires to be used for ease of an enterprise wide implementation. The Stages 2, 3 and 4 create the QVDs as persistent stores of data tables. This in effect will be the Unified Enterprise Data Model, with all data elements appropriately stored and connected to the rest of the enterprise data.

Collection of all these data tables forms the *Physical QVD Warehouse*, in the QlikView world, which is the equivalent of traditional data warehouse. While in traditional warehouses, an ER schema is created to connect all the tables, in the QlikView Physical QVD Warehouse, it is preferable to create an ER or a Snow-flake schema without any circular references. This becomes a pre-cooked form of data storage, which can be loaded as-is into data models, without any need for further transformations to create the snow-flake in-memory model.

In this Physical QVD Store layer, the transaction data are stored in the form of fact tables, with linkage to all the related dimension tables. In addition to storing the granular data, summaries are also created and stored to facilitate summary level presentations in the final stage QlikView Applications.

This will ensure that the basic and common processing (aggregating, joining, de-normalizing and mapping) that is normally required to be done across all functions is done *just once* and stored. The commonly implemented pre-processes include: a) multiple calendars, b) various dimension hierarchies, c) joining facts with slow and fast changing dimensions, d) aggregation of various fact tables, e) combining various fact tables to reduce number of fact tables, f) pre-calculation of various measures, in and across rows in single and multiple tables and g) pre-calculation of ratios and KPIs for the enterprise.

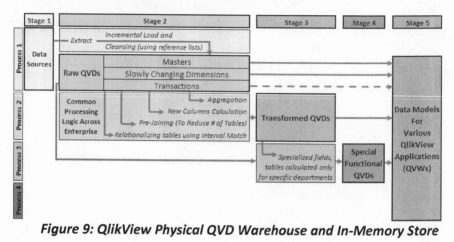

Figure 9: QlikView Physical QVD Warehouse and In-Memory Store

In a nutshell, the Physical QVD Store can be seen as a single large pre-cooked and organized enterprise-wide GENERIC DATA MODEL, connecting all data pieces of the enterprise in an integrated fashion. Hence this could be seen as the UNIFIED DATA MODEL of the enterprise.

RAW QVDs + TRANSFORMED QVDs + SPECIAL QVDs
= UNIFIED DATA MODEL (Physical QVD Store also referred as QV Data Warehouse)

In traditional Data Warehouses, the tables created are all indexed on various fields, partitioned and stored as materialized queries etc., to ensure good SQL performance.

In QlikView there is no need to create such indexes and partitions since there is no SQL involved. This is a huge saving in time, memory, storage and processing requirements.

In-Memory Data Storage—Analytic Data Model

It is important to understand the key difference between QlikView and the SQL Systems. The following diagram is from a presentation by Dan English [3]:

Table 1: SQL Vs. QlikView Model Approach

SQL Data Model Approach	QlikView Data Model Approach
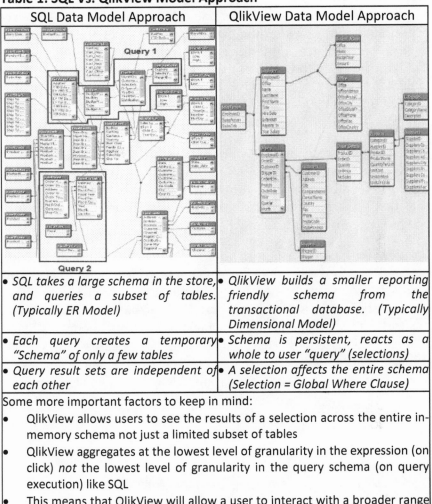	
• SQL takes a large schema in the store, and queries a subset of tables. (Typically ER Model)	• QlikView builds a smaller reporting friendly schema from the transactional database. (Typically Dimensional Model)
• Each query creates a temporary "Schema" of only a few tables	• Schema is persistent, reacts as a whole to user "query" (selections)
• Query result sets are independent of each other	• A selection affects the entire schema (Selection = Global Where Clause)

Some more important factors to keep in mind:

- QlikView allows users to see the results of a selection across the entire in-memory schema not just a limited subset of tables
- QlikView aggregates at the lowest level of granularity in the expression (on click) *not* the lowest level of granularity in the query schema (on query execution) like SQL
- This means that QlikView will allow a user to interact with a broader range of data than will ever be possible in SQL
- Each SQL query can join different tables together in completely different manners. There is only *one* way tables join in any QlikView file. Hence Schema design is much more important in QlikView!
- Since QlikView has only one way to link (equivalent of SQL join) tables in the memory data model, the Physical QVD Repository is essential. This allows multiple QlikView Applications (and hence data models) to be created to link tables in different ways according to the business requirements. This is very useful for the Power Users who can create new applications and perform new analysis on-demand

Interactive aggregations are supported by OLAP cubes—but the possible aggregations are all *pre-calculated* and retrieved on demand. QlikView does it on the fly, allowing more flexible analysis paths. In QlikView, the tables of data related to the topic of interest are loaded into memory and left connected through key fields. Like it was discussed extensively in earlier chapters, in-memory analytics engine of QlikView provides a significant advantage in speed of aggregation and flexibility of analysis, taking advantage of QlikView associative and aggregation engines.

As discussed earlier, real life data models are not pure E-R, Star or Snow-Flake schema. They are all hybrid, and as long as there are no circular references, QlikView In-Memory Associative Engine can deliver analytics. If there are any circular references, QlikView forcibly unlinks one of the connections to break the circularity, at a random point.

QlikView is designed to load transaction level data and provide aggregations on the fly to any level. Sometimes it is good to also load aggregated data and include them in the data model to reduce on-the-fly calculations. This is particularly useful in large data sets (multi-million records) with large number of simultaneous users (in hundreds). Some summary applications, particularly the dashboards for senior management, are generally created using just the Summary Tables. In case they need details, the transaction level applications are transparently daisy chained, to allow drill down to transaction level data. Based on the expressions and the frequency of use of a particular table combination, the data model needs to be organized across summary and detail applications.

For ensuring good performance, the most important guideline to be followed in the in-memory model: Minimize total number of tables by combining them as much. This reduces number of table traversals when any user clicks any field to observe the associated effects on all the objects. The traversals are equivalent to the JOINs across multiple tables, though done quickly in-memory.

In addition to this, the other key QlikView internal factor that affects performance of QlikView applications is the memory used by QlikView fields. When fields contain a large number of distinct values, the amount of memory used by these fields is higher. Minimizing the number of such fields by using various techniques is the key to making the QlikView models efficient and scalable. These techniques are discussed in the Best Practices section later in this chapter, and also in the Chapter "Making QlikView Work" in Part III.

Apart from these basic guidelines, the QlikView Modelling follows some key patterns, based on the types of dimensions and number of fact tables. The following sections discuss the various patterns that are typically used in the data modelling for different applications.

Analytic Model Patterns for QlikView

Data models are flexible and can take any form, based on the business needs. However, there are some basic constructs and real life application data models that contain combination of these constructs. As discussed before, the flaking of dimensions and facts need to be kept to a minimum due to the cardinal rule: Number of table traversals need to be minimal to avoid performance issues as data sizes increase. With low data sizes, up to a few million records, the differences in data schema do not create much difference. But for large data sizes they do create performance problems.

Generally, like other Data Analytic systems, the in-memory model needs to have the following preferred schemas (in the order of preference – highest first):

1. Star Schema with one Fact Table
2. Snow-Flake Schema with one Fact Table
3. Snow-Flake Schema with multiple Fact Tables

DIMENSIONS, FACTS & MEASURES
Dimensions are NOUNS of business. *Facts* record the VERBS of business with NOUNS as subjects (doers) and objects (receptors). *Measures* are ADVERBS describing the VERBS with How, How Much, How Long. They together help businesses answer How Come and How To!

In addition to performance needs, there are certain standard requirement patterns, for which there are well-known efficient Modelling patterns. With these patterns, dimensional Modelling needs to go through a defined Dimensional Model Design Life-cycle (DMDL).

A typical design cycle is very nicely depicted in the Redbook. The same process is useful for QlikView but some of the challenges of SQL systems do not exist in QlikView. Following sections show differences and discuss specific approaches unique for QlikView.

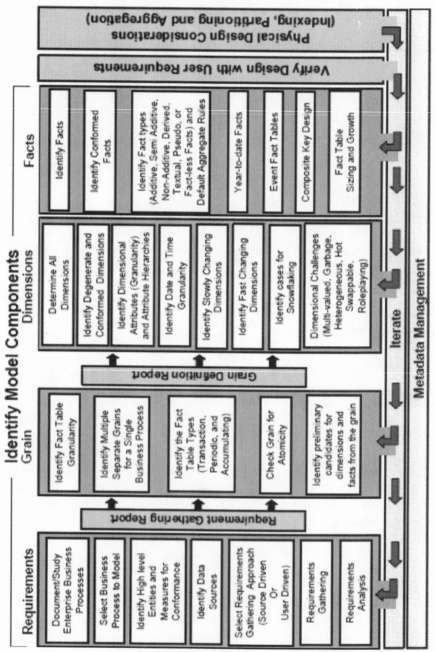

Figure 10: Dimensional Model Design Life-cycle

Dimensions and Their Patterns

Dimensions are generally Master Reference Data as discussed in Wiki Pages on *Reference Data* [5] and *Master Data* [6]. The dimension data comes from Master Data repositories of the enterprises. Capturing, maintaining and administering this Master Data of the enterprise are done by applying Master Data Management Principles: Cardinality (# of unique values), Lifetime (period of validity), Complexity (level of detail stored), Value (worth), Volatility (frequency of change), Reuse (need across enterprise) are the aspects to consider to decide various dimensions. Defining master data and qualifying it is pretty complex. An interesting discussion is in an MSDN article (a must read for data architects): *The What, Why and How of Master Data Management* [7].

Dimensions that qualify for Master Data generally form their own hierarchies:

a. Geography: Street, Area, Zip, City, County, State, Region, Country, Continent, Parts
b. Products: Item, Product Sub-Group, Product Group, Product Category, Industry
c. Customers: Customer Name, Customer Group, Customer Industry
d. Vendors: Vendor Name, Vendor Group, Vendor Industry
e. Employees: Employee, Supervisor, Manager, Senior Manager, Director, etc
f. Time: Minute, Hour, Day, Week / Fortnight / Month, Quarter, Year

Non-Hierarchical Dimensions (also called Lookups) include the following:

g. Ranges of values: Age Group, Price Group, Size Group, Quality Group, etc
h. Status Names and Flags
i. List of Universal Objects: Stars, Body Parts and all Proper Names of other universal objects

Tables of each dimension hierarchy can be joined together into one combined table. Though these dimension hierarchies when joined create an expansion of memory usage, impact of growth is minimal.

Actually the number of records in dimension hierarchy tables is very minimal compared to the number of records in fact / transaction tables.

Values of dimensions are generally taken as a snapshot on a particular date-time, and used as standard master tables – *Static Master Lookups*, which do not change at all. However, there are changes in master data over time. In some business situations the changes can be ignored and only current values need to be considered and in some, the historical changes have to be kept and used. These changes can be slowly changing over longer times, or very fast changing within short intervals. Depending on changes happening over time in all these attributes, they are handled as *Slowly Changing Dimensions* or *Fast Changing Dimensions*. The following sub-sections provide an overview of them.

Static Master Lookups

Simple lookups are part of the non-hierarchical dimensions listed above. These do not change over time and hence are made as standard lists available forever. Such datasets are created in each company separately. Range of Values, Status Names and Flags are generally unique to each company and are generated specific to every company, though there can be industry generalizations.

Names of Universal objects do not change across companies. Particularly, places information does not change with time. Common datasets are readily available for such non-changing entities from various sources.

For example, USPS (United States Postal Service) provides a free Zip code (http://federalgovernmentzipcodes.us/) database for United States. An ambitious project called Freebase (acquired by Google in 2010) provides collection of data (http://www.freebase.com/) on various non-changing people, places and things. Freebase also provides APIs with which the data can be extracted and used.

Many such initiatives are being done online to provide useful standard master data for different domain areas. It will save a huge amount of time to re-use any of these databases wherever possible. Please refer the Wikipedia entry on *Data library* and *Freebase*.

Slowly Changing Dimensions

Normally each dimension is taken as a snapshot in time, but in reality dimension attributes change over time. For example, a customer might be listed as living in Canada, but has only recently moved there from France. Facts that occurred in France cannot be assigned to Canada. Similarly, employees change department, and stores change manager.

To effectively store historical changes to dimension members, slowly changing dimensions (SCDs) are required. This is an area that requires planning to achieve the correct results and an ad-hoc approach is unlikely to succeed. There are three types of SCD in use that cover most historical requirements.

Type 1 SCDs are effectively standard dimensions that allow changes. If an attribute needs to be changed, we simply change it and take no further action. This keeps all records "as-of-date", but does not solve any of the historical problems that were mentioned earlier.

Type 2 SCDs solve the problem of historical changes by creating multiple records for each dimension member when there is a change. For example, if a store manager changes, another record is created that lists the new manager. This creates a duplicate key for the record. Therefore, original key of the store can be stored as an alternate key and a new, unique, primary key is created. The other need with a SCD-2 is to know which record applies to each fact in the fact table. This is achieved by storing start and end dates of each record. Figure shows alternate key, StoreIDAK, and the start & end dates of the manager. It is straightforward to find the current manager because this has a NULL ManagerEndDate field.

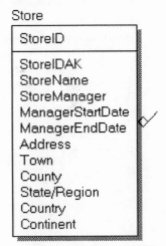

Figure 11: Type 2 SCD

Type 3 SCDs are a compromise between Type 1 and Type 2. We need only know the original and current values of the dimension member. For example, we might want a starting price and a current price. We do not require any other prices, so we do not require the complexity of a Type 2 SCD.

We can simply store original and current values as separate attributes of the dimension and only one row is required for each member. Although this simplifies storage, most real-life models use Type 1 or Type 2 SCDs. A more extensive treatment of Slow Changing Dimensions is provided in the "IBM Redbook on Dimensional Modelling".

Fast Changing Dimensions

A dimension is considered fast changing if any attribute changes frequently and in many rows. Assume a customer table has 10 million rows. If 10 changes occur per customer per year, using Type-2 approach will make this table grow to 100 million rows.

Hence the approach should be different to maintain manageable sizes. The typical attributes which change rapidly are in Table 2.

Table 2: Fast Changing Dimension Samples

Age	Income	Test Score	Rating	Credit_ History_ Score	Customer_ Account_ Status	Weight
18 to 25	$800 to $1000	2-4	8-12	7-9	Good	88
26 to 28	$1000 to $1500	5-9	8-12	10-14	Good	88
29 to 35	$1500 to $3000	10-17	8-12	15-19	Good	88
More	.....	.....	.....	.....	.....	.....

- Age
- Income
- Test Score
- Credit Score
- Customer Account Status
- Weight
- Ratings
- Temperature

The approach used for this is to introduce mini-dimensions. The concept behind this is to force the attributes to take limited discreet values—by converting them into band ranges. The above table shows sample rows for these dimensions. These are the mini-dimensions, which contain fast changing attributes of a larger dimension table. Rows in mini-dimensions are fewer due to the band-range value concept. In QlikView this can be easily implemented by using the MAP ... USING construct during load.

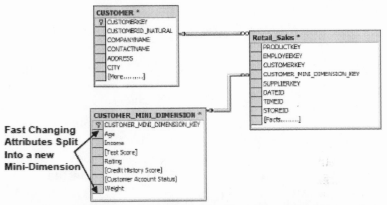

Figure 12: Mini-dimensions for Fast Changing Dimensions

In the data model, the mini-dimensions need to be connected as additional dimension tables directly attached to Fact tables, instead of linking them to large dimension table as normalized snow-flaked tables. The ideal way to use mini-tables is presented in the diagram.

Dimension Hierarchies

All key dimensions are essentially dimension hierarchies: Geography, Product, Customers, Vendors, Employees and so on. Assemblies (sub-assemblies) vs. Components (sub-assemblies) form an items hierarchy in an automobile manufacturing company. Account Group heads vs. Sub-heads vs. Individual Account heads form a hierarchy in Finance. These are important in roll-up and drill-down analytics. Much of rich data discovery is possible using these hierarchies and their relationships.

Hierarchies document the relationship between different levels inside a single dimension and generally fall into one of the following: Balanced, Unbalanced and Ragged Hierarchies.

Balanced Hierarchy is where all of the dimension branches have the same number of levels or consistent depth. Date Dimension is a balanced hierarchy, with the depth consistency across years, quarters, months and day of the month.

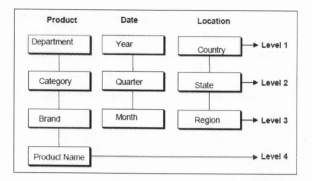

Figure 13:Dimension Hierarchies

For two different years, the hierarchy levels are logically equivalent and can be compared with each other. Typically a PERIOD TABLE can be created with DATE as the Surrogate Key, and multiple date hierarchies can be created in the same (Calendar, Fiscal, Retail Sales, etc) and used for analysis. If there is more than one fact table in the model, then typically this table is created as the COMMON PERIOD and connected to all those fact tables using different Date Foreign Keys. Further discussion on handling dates is given in a separate section in this chapter.

Unbalanced Hierarchy is where dimension branches with varying numbers of levels or depth are present. Typically Parent-Child dimensions are unbalanced hierarchies. Organization hierarchy, product lineage, channel hierarchy are all examples of unbalanced hierarchies. A common example of an unbalanced hierarchy is an organization chart. Employees at a given level may have many reporting to them, while others at same level in a different branch may have few or none. Each employee can be a manager or reportee. A report may require summarizing sales of an employee or manager (including subordinates).

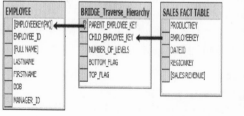

Figure 14:Unbalanced Hierarchy

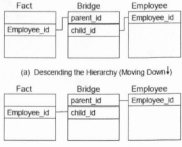

(a) Descending the Hierarchy (Moving Down↓)

(b) Ascending the Hierarchy (Moving Up↑)

Using SQL, the EMPLOYEE TABLE is an ADJACENT NODES (recursive) table, with each employee record having a MANAGER NODE ID. Then typically a BRIDGE table is used, as shown in Figure 14. In QlikView,

Original Table

Account	Parent	Level
1		1
2		2
12	1	12
21	2	21
22	2	22
123	12	123
213	21	213
214	21	214
224	22	224
2241	224	2241
2242	224	2242

Output Of Hierarchy Load

Account	Parent	Level	level1	level2	level3	level4
1		1	1	-	-	-
2		2	2	-	-	-
12	1	12	1	12	-	-
21	2	21	2	21	-	-
22	2	22	2	22	-	-
123	12	123	1	12	123	-
213	21	213	2	21	213	-
214	21	214	2	21	214	-
224	22	224	2	22	224	-
2241	224	2241	2	22	224	2241
2242	224	2242	2	22	224	2242

STANDARD PIVOT IN QLIKVIEW

level1	level2	level3	level4	Amount
1	12	123 ⊞		500
		Sum		500
	Sum			500
Sum				500
2	21	213 ⊞		1000
		214 ⊞		400
		Sum		1400
	22	224	2242	400
			2241	100
			Sum	500
		Sum		500
	Sum			1900
Sum				2400

Figure 15: ETL - Hierarchical Load and Pivot in QlikView

Hierarchy Load takes an Adjacent Node table and automatically expands every row into full hierarchy path. The same table will be loaded with additional fields—one for each level of the hierarchy (named as level1, level2, etc). Once this is loaded, QlikView Pivot table can help present this as a report. This table can now be used to produce various charts and combined with the rest of the tables in a data model, like any other table. This is very useful in all unbalanced hierarchy situations, particularly in electronic and manufacturing related industries, dealing with up to 20 levels of parts hierarchy.

Ragged Dimension Hierarchy contains at least one member whose parent belongs to a level that is more than one level above the child. Ragged dimensions contain branches with varying number of levels. Typically this happens in Geographies, (refer Figure 15) with one level of the hierarchy not applicable in some branches. For Greece, there are no states and hence the value of the state can be kept as "No States". This way the hierarchy can be kept balanced.

Challenging Patterns in Dimensions

In addition, there are various challenges in handling dimensions. These are identified patterns of challenges that occur, and need conscious approaches to ensure they don't become problematic. The dimension patterns that need to be watched for in QlikView Modelling include:
1. Degenerate Dimensions
2. Garbage Dimensions
3. Multi-Valued Dimensions

Figure 16:Ragged Dimension

For each of these known categories of dimensions, there is a need to choose an approach of Modelling in QlikView and also understand the implications of these dimensions on performance and memory usage.

Degenerate Dimensions

The attributes of a transaction, like Invoice Number, Bill Number, Transaction Id, are dimensions, since they are not measures. However, these are typically used to get counts, or for finding individual Invoice / Bill / Transaction totals. These are typically fields that contain very large number of distinct values (high cardinality), and hence tend to occupy a large memory in QlikView models. In QlikView, these are good candidates to be hashed and converted into fields of lower width (fewer bytes).

Garbage or Junk Dimensions

Dimensions that contain very less number of distinct values (low-cardinality) such as codes, indicators and status flags are called Garbage Dimensions or Junk Dimensions. They are not related to any hierarchy. Creating separate dimension tables for each of these dimensions will increase the number of foreign keys, and increase the processing time and memory.

With QlikView, one approach is to include these in the fact table itself. The amount of memory used by these fields

Garbage_ Dim-Key	Customer_Store _Feedback	Customer_ Employee_ Feedback	Payment_ Type	Bag_Type
1	Good	Good	Credit card	Plastic
2	Good	Bad	Credit card	Plastic
3	Good	None	Credit card	Plastic

Table 3: Garbage or Junk Dimensions

is automatically kept to a minimum by QlikView since the fields have low-cardinality. In case there are many such fields, they can be combined into a single table and just one foreign-key will occupy the fact table. For example a system may contain low-cardinality fields similar to the following:

- Customer feedback: Good, bad, and none
- Customer feedback about employee: Good, bad, and none
- Payment type: Cash or credit card
- Bag type to carry goods: Plastic, paper, or both

These fields can be combined to one table as shown. The Garbage_Dim_Key can be used in the fact table. If the number of distinct values of these dimensions grows too large then they must be split to ensure performance. With QlikView, the impact of this is not going to be significant in smaller data sets. However, in larger datasets this is a good approach to reduce total memory used, and the compute load for multiple table traversals.

Multi-Valued Dimensions

There are situations when multiple values for a dimension need to be attached to a fact table row or attach a multi-valued dimension table to the fact table. Typical examples are: a) multiple family members are attached to a single Account which is connected to one or more family insurance policies, with one premium being paid per month by the family for each policy, b) many customers associated with a single bank account (joint accounts) and c) multiple diagnoses are associated with one patient. All of these create a many-to-many relationship that needs to be modeled.

The following typical approaches are taken to handle multi-valued dimensions:

1. *Choose only the IMPORTANT value and ignore others.* Needs to be done very carefully after ensuring that the ignored values are indeed not required
2. *Extend the dimensions list* (record) to include a fixed number of multi-valued dimensions as additional columns. If the number of values is not fixed, then the design may fail and require modifications when the number of values increases.
3. *Use of a Bridge (Link) Tables* helps manage many-to-many relations. Bridge tables help manage Unbalanced Hierarchies & Multi-Dimensional Hierarchies. This is the most preferred

method, though this increases model complexity. This can provide the necessary sturdiness to the model to withstand and accommodate changes required due to business needs.

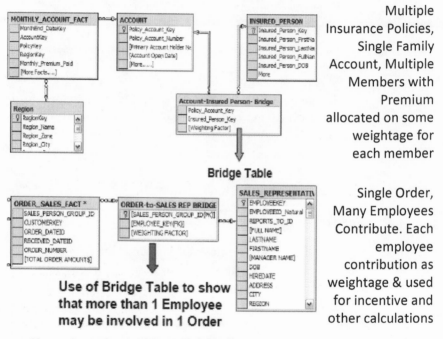

Multiple Insurance Policies, Single Family Account, Multiple Members with Premium allocated on some weightage for each member

Bridge Table

Single Order, Many Employees Contribute. Each employee contribution as weightage & used for incentive and other calculations

Use of Bridge Table to show that more than 1 Employee may be involved in 1 Order

Note: Grain is a single entire Order

Figure 17: Multi-Valued Dimensions Using a Bridge Table

Heterogenous Dimensions

When multiple product lines—like Home and Auto Insurance—are offered to the same set of customers, the need is to maintain a product table that contains both Auto and Home Policy attributes. This is easily taken care of in QlikView by FORCED CONCATENATE. This creates all the attributes (fields) from both Auto & Home for every record, but the memory is used only for attributes having values in for every row. Hence, Home rows will not occupy space for Auto columns & vice versa. This can help build a unified model to handle all products.

A Systematic Approach to Handling Dimensions

- As part of the system study, it is important to make a list of all the dimensions that are being captured in the source systems.

- For each dimension, identify its type: Hierarchical, Degenerate, Garbage/Junk, Multi-Valued or Heterogeneous.

- For each dimension types, choose the approach required based on the discussions above and write down in this list.

- For each dimension choose grain required based on the business needs. Different departments and different levels of business users may need different grains.

- If hierarchical, then the parent level of that dimension needs to be recorded in this list. It helps decide the hierarchy.

- Based on this understanding, decide the number of dimension tables, the fields that would be included in each, and the granularity that will be used.

- This will have an impact on the decision of granularity of fact tables as well.

In *Transaction Systems*, the granularity in which events are executed, monitored and managed, define the level of detail in which of the events recorded in the transaction tables, and the number of tables used to represent all the observed/recorded events of the transaction.

In *Decision Support (Reporting / Analysis) Systems*, the granularity in which reporting and analysis is done can be different from the transaction system granularity. This difference requires that the fact tables are transformed / aggregated / combined based on the necessary granularity and attribute details for the Dimensional Model. The difference between the two needs to be handled by the ETL, in transforming the source tables into the desired Fact tables for the DSS.

Facts and Their Patterns

In Transaction Systems, transaction tables capture events of a transaction and mostly they are kept in multiple tables to handle one-to-many and many-to-many relationships. These are time-stamped records of each event of every transaction.

In Dimensional Models, Fact tables hold the behavior of transaction events over time. Star Schema, considered the ideal form of Dimensional Models, necessitates that there is only ONE FACT table. However, in reality making a single FACT table is possible only if the scope of the Model is limited to ONE simple process. With more than one FACT table, Snow-Flake Schema is used mostly, though it is considered a penalty on performance.

The interest is to combine multiple Fact tables into fewer Fact tables, preferably just one. To understand how, it is required to understand the nature of transactions captured by these fact tables, their characteristics and define the target Fact table structures. For more detailed discussion on various Fact table structures and relationships please refer to the "IBM Redbook on Dimensional Modelling" and also the 2nd edition of Ralph Kimball's "Data Warehousing Toolkit: The Complete Guide to Dimensional Modelling".

The subsequent sections establish a methodology specifically for QlikView in-memory Modelling, to handle most of the common situations. First we need to understand the need (analysis) patterns and their impact on the grain required, structure of typical Fact tables in Dimensional Model and then explore ways of designing the structure of the Fact tables.

Grain Required Based on Types of Analysis

Measures about the event are either over an elapsed time—multiple events—or a point in time—single event. Generally the analysis required by Business Owners, Process Owners and Action/Event Owners are of distinctly different granularities. The following table gives key differences between these types of analyses and the need of granularity of data.

Table 4: Types of Analyses Vs. Granularity Required

Business (Owners) Analysis	Process (Owners) Analysis	Event Owners Analysis
Balance Sheet, Profit & Loss, AR/AP Balance Sheet Trends Trends of Process and Event KPIs Compliance KPIs	Trends of Event KPIs Elapsed Time (TAT) Efficiency KPIs Performance Measures	Counts Sums Top N / Bottom N Capacity / Utilization
COARSE GRAIN NEEDED	*MEDIUM GRAIN NEEDED*	*FINE GRAIN NEEDED*

The grains needed are typically coarser or finer across all the dimensions including time, geography, product, customer, and partner and vendor dimensions. This grain understanding is a key step in the Dimensional Model Design Life Cycle as discussed before.

Fact Table Structure

A fact table typically consists of the following data:

- One or more foreign keys to dimension tables
- Fact Attributes which may be:
- Additive like SALES AMOUNT, QUANTITY (absolute measures)
- Semi-additive like ACCOUNT BALANCES, STOCK (as-of-date measures)
- Non-additive like Textual, Per-Unit Prices, Percentages and Ratios, Measures of Intensity like Temperatures, Averages and Degenerate Numbers like Bill_No
- Pseudo facts (such as 1 and 0 in case of attendance tracking)
- Textual fact (rarely the case)
- Derived facts (formulae like Days Sales Outstanding)
- Time-to-date facts (YTD, MTD, WTD Sales, Incentives, etc.)
- Degenerate dimensions (one or more)

While evaluating various transaction tables to be combined into Fact tables, it is important to list all fields in them and classify each field into above categories. This helps define grains and also the way in which various fact tables can be combined to form an efficient snow-flake schema. In defining the right grain, the *types of analysis* required by business, as discussed above, play an important role.

From all these source tables, various attributes need to be chosen carefully for the business needs. Understanding each attributes in the light of the above Fact table structure is essential. Accordingly appropriate transformations need to be planned to create Fact tables. All these transformed Fact tables are included in the dimensional model, based on various considerations detailed below.

Designing the Fact Tables

The first step is to decide what should come in these tables, next the grain required and lastly, how they can combine into less number of Fact tables to create an efficient Dimensional Data Model.

When deciding how the facts need to be kept in the Dimensional Model (combined or separate) one needs to take into account the following:

- Granularity
- Types of Fact Attributes
- Relationship among Fact Tables

Granularity

The Facts required in the reporting/analysis Systems are either in the level of detail in which the events were captured, which is the highest possible grain or in a summary form where the behavior is represented by an aggregate. These aggregates can be:

1. Aggregates of occurrence (count) or other measures (sum, average, percentile, quartiles, moving average, etc)

2. Across coarse time periods (weekly, monthly, quarterly, etc) and

3. Across coarse grains of other attributes (like Geography: City, County, State, Country, etc. Product: Product Sub-group, Product Group, Product Category, etc. Customers: Customer Group, Industry, etc).

This is decided by the Granularity in which analysis will be done by the business users (event, hourly, daily, weekly, etc). Hence understanding the requirements helps decide granularity.

The granularity in which data is *captured and stored* is the highest level possible for analysis. Any additional level of detail cannot be expected from the attributes captured. In some cases, extra demographic information from other sources, particularly third party data sources or other applications can be included to enrich the data with additional attributes. Such third party data can also not increase the granularity of data, but add more attributes.

Based on the decided granularity that is required for business users, the source data needs to be aggregated (GROUP BY) on the attributes of interest, using SUM, COUNT and other aggregates as required and stored in the Physical Repository of QVDs. Then the relevant QlikView User Applications can use QVDs of required granularity for the intended analysis.

Types of Fact Attributes

The various attributes—measures—in the fact tables fall into one of the following categories: Additive, Semi-Additive and Non-Additive. Depending on the type, these measures can be aggregated and kept in a coarser granularity or Not.

Additive measures can be aggregated (SUM) and kept in a coarse granularity of period or any other dimension by dropping any of the dimensions at any grain that are not important / not relevant for decision making. For example SALES of products can be kept in Monthly Level (dropping days and time), Product Group Level (dropping Product Item), Country Level (dropping State, City, Zip). Then from that level, the values are additive, SALES can be aggregated by any combination of dimensions from that granularity to calculate coarser granular levels.

Semi-additive measures can be aggregated (SUM) and kept in certain dimensions only, and are not additive in other dimensions. Account balances and Stock Quantity-on-hand are semi-additive. Account balances can be summarized across any of the Geography (Branch), Customer (Customer Category), Account (Type of Account) dimensions, but not across the Date dimension. Also the account balances can be aggregated across other dimensions only AS-OF-A-PARTICULAR-DATE. Similarly, Quantity-On-Hand is additive across the Product and Store dimensions, but not across the Date dimension. Such aggregates of Quantity-On-Hand are appropriate only at a given point in time.

Non-Additive attributes are meaningful for analysis sometimes. There are various categories of non-additive attributes and each need to be carefully handled to make good use of them. The following notes help handle these non-additive attributes appropriately:

> *Textual facts*: Adding textual facts does not result in any number. However, counting them may result in a sensible number. In QlikView Models, they tend to use more memory if the number of unique values is large.

> *Averages*: Facts based on averages are non-additive. For example, average sales price is non-additive. Adding all average unit prices produces a meaningless result.

> *Per-unit prices*: Adding unit prices does not produce any meaningful number. For example, unit sales price or unit cost is strictly non-additive because adding these prices across any dimension will not be meaningful. Instead, store Total Price (per-unit cost x quantity purchased), is correctly additive across all dimensions.

Percentages and ratios: A ratio, such as gross margin%, is non-additive. Non-additive facts are usually the result of ratio or other calculations, such as percentages. Whenever possible, such facts to be replaced with the underlying calculation facts (numerator and denominator) so the metric can be calculated in the application. It is also very important to understand that when adding a ratio, it is necessary to take sums of numerator and denominator separately and divide these totals.

Measures of intensity: Measures of intensity such as room temperature are non-additive across all dimensions. Summing room temperature across different times of the day produces a totally non-meaningful number. However, an average of several temperatures during the day can produce the average temperature for the day, which is a meaningful number.

Degenerate Numbers: Degenerate dimensions are also non-additive. Numbers such as order number, invoice number, tracking number, confirmation number, and receipt number, are stored inside the fact table as degenerate dimensions. Counts of such numbers produce meaningful results such as total number of orders received or total number of line items in each distinct order.

Based on the additive/semi-additive/non-additive nature of the fact attributes, and the need for the grain in which analysis needs to be done, the aggregation conditions shall be chosen, to transform the source tables into the Dimensional Model Fact Tables. More details on these are available in the "IBM Redbook on Dimensional Modelling" in the Chapters on "Modelling Considerations and Dimensional Model Life Cycle".

Relationship among Fact Tables

The above considerations help to choose the tables to be used as Facts for the Dimensional Model. Now there is a need to combine as many of these Facts, to arrive at the least number of Fact tables.

Transaction tables record various events—they are essentially time-stamped records of various actions that happen in execution of a business process. Depending on the stages of transactions, and their respective granularity of execution and monitoring in a particular business, the constituent events are recorded in multiple sub-tables, which combine to create the transaction record.

Typically these component tables have following relationships among each other in the E/R Model:

1. *Parent–Child (More Details of Single Event) tables:* Different levels of a transaction segment are recorded in different details. For example, Invoice table has the basic information, Invoice Items table has the list of line-items in the Invoice, and then the Invoice Item Details table has the various attributes of the item and the details of where they need to be delivered, etc.

2. *Sibling (Additional Attributes of Single Event) tables*: More attributes about the same event, typically are stored in separate tables due to the verbose nature of the content, or since these details are not regularly used/updated in the progress of the transaction. Sometimes these tables are an after-thought, though they form an integral part of the transactions, and were added as a separate table without affecting existing table structure of the transaction system.

3. *Event Sequence (Successive Events of Same Transaction) tables:* Events of Multiple stages of same transaction are recorded in different times. For example, issuance of a life insurance policy is made of a series of transaction events: Request for Quote, Quote, Underwriting, Accept/Reject, Issuance and First Premium Collection. This spans into parallel tracks: Continuing Premium Collection, Claims, Claim Settlements, Renewal / Fore-close, Cancellation / Revoke, Change of Address, Change of Policy Terms, etc. Depending on the granularity in which monitoring/analysis needs to be done, these elements are aggregated or considered in detail.

There may be other relationships that are possible among the transaction tables, but these are the most prominent ones found in practical implementations. Efficiently managing how they are used in the Dimensional Models for QlikView is important to ensure good performance and scalability both on data sizes and on adding business requirements.

Combining Fact Tables

With standard combination techniques, these fact table sets can be combined to just one table:

Sibling (Additional Attributes of Same Event) tables

Sibling tables can be combined by simply JOINing to the main table. This reduces the number of tables, and more importantly, duplicate copies of the KEY fields that are common to the tables are removed and just one copy is retained. This frees up large memory in apps.

Parent-Child Fact Tables

All parent-child fact tables can be left to stay as individual tables and just connected (LINKED) through the primary-key and foreign-key of these tables using their natural connections. QlikView in-memory data handling engine automatically takes care of dynamically joining these tables whenever required. Also the individual counts and sums performed on a parent table is automatically performed in the SCOPE of that table itself, thereby avoiding summation and count errors created by one-to-many relationships typical of such situations. This is done without any special effort from developers and users.

This automatic linking is very useful in smaller data sets (up to 20 GB or so raw data) and simpler data models (up to about 25 tables). When it gets heavier, all Parent-Child Fact tables should preferably be JOINED during load; starting from lower most child, LEFT JOIN every parent upwards.

For example, the Invoice Master, Invoice Details and Invoice Details2 tables are connected to each other in a parent-child relationship. Starting from Invoice Details2, Invoice Details is LEFT JOINed and then the Invoice Master is LEFT JOINed to create the combined table. Normally in the SQL world, such joining will bloat the data sizes. However in QlikView, combining these tables does not bloat the data size to the same extent. In fact by joining all these three tables, they would be de-normalized, and all the fields will be available in just one table, but with marginal to negligible data bloating. This reduces, more importantly, the traversals required across the data model for performing multiple calculations.

It is important to understand that, all counts which are required of the non-additive degenerate keys of the parent tables, for example of invoices, can be done in the front-end charts, by using the DISTINCT keyword as a qualifier for the COUNT expressions as is shown here: =COUNT(DISTINCT INVOICE_NO).

When tables are connected in a Parent-Child relationship, the KEYS used to JOIN these tables are typically the DEGENERATE KEYS like Invoice Number, Invoice Item Line No. The date of occurrence of the PARENT is typically inherited by the CHILD records as well. The PARENT and CHILD records may have additional date fields as extra attributes to capture subsequent events associated with those records (like Order Amendment Date either at Parent level or in every individual record level). Generally, the Parent-Child and Sibling tables are of the same time and other granularity since they hold data about the same transaction.

Multi-Stage Transaction Tables (Successive Events of Same Transaction tables):

All the multi-stage sub-transaction tables can be combined by using FLAGS and FORCED concatenation.

For e.g., there are Order, Despatch and Invoices in a typical supply chain scenario. Order details and order parent can be combined using JOINs as discussed above. Same for Despatch and Invoices as well. These three tables can then be combined into a single table by using CONCATENATE to combine them into one, as shown in the diagram. There are some attributes that are common

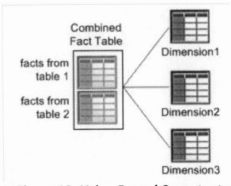

Figure 18: Using Forced Concatentate

to the three of them and there may be attributes unique to each of them. In such a scenario this is called FORCED CONCATENATE.

When a forced concatenate is applied to tables with different set of fields with only a few being common, the following resultant table is created: a) number of records of the resulting logical table is the total of all the records, b) resulting table contains just one copy of all the common fields from all tables. For fields that did not exist in a table, rows from those tables will be filled with NULL for these fields. It is important to note that during this kind of concatenation all the tables should contain non-null data in each of the TIME Dimension fields. As an example, when the grain of the data is up to the DAY, the HR, MIN and SEC should be filled with 23, 59 and 59 to ensure that the data rolls up properly when these fields are used as the group-by columns in any aggregation.

The records from each of these tables can be differentiated by using a FLAG like say "RECTYPE". It can be filled with "Invoice" for Invoice table rows, "Order" for Order table rows and "Despatch" for Despatch table rows.

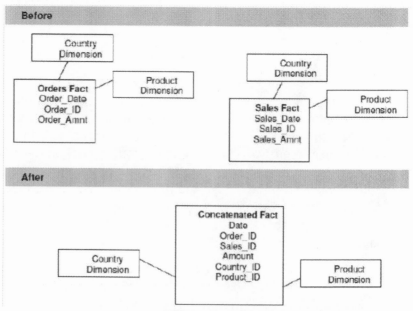

Figure 19: Forced Concatenate Example

This allows maintaining a common date in just one table, making it easier to build a common calendar and manage the period based analysis. When all tables are combined, only one instance of the key-fields like Date, Customer Key, Vendor Key, Product Key, etc., are kept in the combined table. This reduces the memory usage significantly in QlikView.

In case there is a need to calculate elapsed times, from Order to Despatch, Despatch to Invoice, Invoice to payment etc., this will not be easy with the single table created. To handle this, a separate table of dates of Despatches, Invoices and Payments can be created and linked to the Order rows. For example, if Despatch date is required for every Order, then a separate table containing two columns: (Order No, Order Item Line No and Despatch Date) can be created and LINKED to the combined ORDER-DESPATCH-INVOICE table using (Order No + Order Item Line No) as the key. This new table can also be LEFT JOINed to the main table, to include DESPATCH DATE as an additional field for the Order rows. In other rows, the field will be empty (NULL). If other elapsed times also need to be stored, then the field can be named as NEXT EVENT DATE, and using a similar process, INVOICE DATE can be attached to the Despatch rows, and PAYMENT DATE to the Invoice rows of the table. This approach will optimize the memory used by the otherwise extra fields.

Combining Tables: First the Siblings should be joined then the resulting tables should be tested for Parent-Child relationships and joined. Then Multi-stage transactions should be identified and appropriate CONCATENATION / JOINS should be performed. Then again, iteratively look for Siblings, Parent-Child and Multi-Stages, till the time there is no further scope for combining tables together. Lastly, all the fact tables should be identified in the final granular form that is required for business.

When Should Fact Tables be kept separate?

Generally speaking, if the events are independent and have different measures and grains, they need to be in their own facts. Following are the other situations when different fact tables need to be kept separate and connected through a LINK TABLE or BRIDGE TABLE:

1. Events are independent and happen in a business sequence
2. Measures are different
3. Grains (levels of aggregation) are different—on time or other dimensions/hierarchies
4. Dimensions are different
5. Facts have a many-to-many relationship
6. "As was" will have different versions for different points in time and finally one "As is" is cumulative of the entire past

In an earlier section on Multi-Valued Dimensions, bridge-tables were discussed as a way to handle many-to-many relationship between Fact rows and Dimensions. In a similar way, many-to-many relationships between Fact tables also need to be managed by a BRIDGE TABLE (called LINK TABLE in QlikView circles). In most of the cases, date fields along with the primary keys work as the common connection between different tables or as the primary keys of such bridge tables.

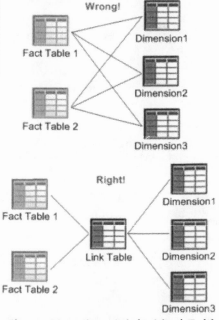

Figure 20: Using Link (Bridge) Table

A Systematic Approach to Handling Facts

Keeping all the above discussions, the following is the recommended process in which facts can be handled while Modelling in QlikView:

- Create a list of all fields (attributes and dimensions) of various source transaction tables
- Identify the fact attribute type of each of these fields—Additive or not, Derived and As-of-date or for-the-period

- Understand the analysis needs (patterns) and the grain of each field required for the analysis
- Based on the grain required & possible, decide the transformations (aggregations) required for each destination fact table
- Identify relationships among Fact tables—Sibling, Parent-Child and Multi-Stage Transactions—and plan for merging these groups of tables as outlined before. Iteratively repeat the sequence as much as possible and minimize number of tables
- Convert all the transformations in one or more ETL QVW Applications, and output the processed LOGICAL FACT tables into the Unified Physical Repository of QVDs

Conclusions - Data Modelling with QlikView

Most of the process steps outlined in the Dimensional Modelling Life Cycle apply to QlikView completely. Physical implementation decisions are uniquely different for QlikView due to the in-memory and AQL technologies. A successful data model will produce a powerful and sturdy application, scalable and gives good performance irrespective of the data sizes. Adding new KPIs and allowing users to do analysis as they want becomes easily possible with a good data model.

In addition to this chapter it is strongly advised to read the QlikView Best Practices documents referred to in the references section [8, 9 and 10]. Success of all the QlikView projects essentially depends on the Data Model. It needs to be designed well to take advantage of all the good capabilities of QlikView in-memory architecture and AQL Engine. A well designed data model gives business users and technical users extreme pleasure in using the applications and extending their functionality.

References

1. The Data Warehouse Toolkit: The Complete Guide to Dimensional Modelling (2nd Edition), Ralph Kimball and Margy Ross, Wiley, ISBN: 0471200247
2. IBM RedBook: Dimensional Modelling: In a Business Intelligence Environment, Authors: (Chuck Ballard, Daniel M. Farrell, Amit

Gupta, Carlos Mazuela and Stanislav Vohnik), ibm.com/redbooks, [http://www.redbooks.ibm.com/abstracts/sg247138.html?Open]

3. Best Practices in Data Modelling (QlikView), Dan English, [http://community.qlikview.com/docs/DOC-1881]

4. Data Modelling, Wikipedia, [http://en.wikipedia.org/wiki/Data_Modelling#Data_models]

5. Reference Data, Wikipedia, [http://en.wikipedia.org/wiki/Reference_data]

6. Master Data, Wikipedia, [http://en.wikipedia.org/wiki/Master_data]

7. The What, Why and How of Master Data Management, Roger Wolter and Kirk Haselden, MSDN Library, [http://msdn.microsoft.com/en-us/library/bb190163.aspx]

8. QlikView Best Practices – Development v0.5, Qlik Community Thread, QlikCommunity, QlikView.com, [http://community.qlikview.com/servlet/JiveServlet/download/188 375-30726/QlikView%20Best%20Practices%20-%20Development%20v0.5.pdf]

9. Best Practices Approach to QlikView Development, A.Rajendran, SlideShare, [http://www.slideshare.net/TBSL/best-practices-qlikview-application-development]

10. QlikView Best Practices, Giles, Quick-Qlear-Qool, [http://www.quickqlearqool.nl/?p=146]

CHAPTER 13
QLIKVIEW SECURITY

KNOWING WHAT TO PROTECT IS IMPORTANT BEFORE TAKING
MEASURES TO SAVE

Introduction to the Chapter

There are many technological advances providing extensive security
solutions to cover from possible threats. On the other hand, newer
exploits are discovered, taking advantage of vulnerabilities that exist
across various systems. The site "Enterprise Security Today" [1] provides
a to-date update on Enterprise Security related information covering all
technologies and products.

With all these, one can get in a paranoid spin to implement complex
information protection measures. However, it is very important to have
a clear idea of *what we are protecting*, and *from whom*. In addition,
should know the *need for protecting* and *what impact if not protected*.

Most of the Enterprise software hold data captured for a specific area /
department / processes. QlikView, being a BI solution, brings data
together from multiple systems, distils them into insights and provides
them so that informed decisions can be taken by the company
chieftains.

Access to this information, if compromised, lands it in the hands of
competitors, such a breach of security could lead to negative
consequences. Protecting *confidential* information is a business
requirement, in many cases also an ethical and legal requirement.

This chapter focuses on various aspects of security that need to be
taken care while developing, deploying and managing QlikView solution
for enterprises. It covers the layers of security: Network, Authentication,
Access and Authorization. Then it walks through each layer and
explores how these layers can be protected to ensure a secure QlikView
deployment.

Network, Authentication and Access layers are typically available in the Enterprise outside of the QlikView platform—they exist in enterprises as a common secure layer to protect all information systems from ERP to BI solutions. QlikView makes use of these layers appropriately, and provides alternatives in the Authentication and Access layers, in case existing layers in the enterprises are not complete. QlikView provides facilities to define who can access which part of data in a QVW file using Section Access—the unique authorization methodology of QlikView.

Finally with a review of Mobile security and Security during development, the chapter covers possible challenges and recommended solutions for both. The chapter then closes with a summary of best practices for implementing QlikView in an Enterprise in a secure way.

Defining the Security Needs

Data/information is many times more valuable an asset than other assets of an Enterprise. Protecting Information is the key purpose of Information Security systems. As highlighted in the Wikipedia article on "Information Security" [2]:

> **Information security** means protecting information and information systems from unauthorized access, use, disclosure, disruption, modification, perusal, inspection, recording or destruction.

Many security advisories and security organizations have put together frameworks and methodologies for implementing security measures in enterprises. Wikipedia article "Enterprise Information Security Architecture" [3] outlines various frameworks which are evolving continuously. With QlikView, or any BI, the concerns of security are more acute, due to the sensitivity of distilled information provided by them. BI systems are an essential component to establish successful Governance, Risk and Compliance (GRC) strategy. It involves both Risk and Regulatory intelligence.

Basically, business has to monitor its internal environment, as well as the external environment the company operates in, for issues, events and risks that can impact the organization. The goal is to intelligently maximize opportunities while mitigating or avoiding negative events.

In BI security domain, this means implementing tools that have the ability to integrate into your environment, monitor changes, collect information, and report the state of security across systems, processes and relationships. Further, these tools need to have content and process/workflow management capabilities to store information and provide processes to evaluate risk.

In addition to these, securing this information and ensuring right people get access to the insights is of paramount importance. Some key articles that throw some light into the significance and concerns around BI security are referred in the references Section for further reading [6, 7, 8 and 9].

Goals of Security

While creating a protection system, it is important to know what is to be protected and have a reference checklist of items that need to be protected. The following are the key items that need to be covered by a protection system of BI:

a) Save enterprise data (like customers, prices, profitability, employees, etc) from competition and from customers as appropriate

b) Ensure only relevant data is available for decision makers and enforce visibility policy of the enterprise among its employees

c) Ensure customer data, particularly sensitive personal data about customers, is not let out in the open

d) Ensure uptime and continuous availability of BI systems to support better decision making as required by the business

e) Ensure that unwanted elements from the society do not get into the enterprise network just to destroy or mutate the data for causing general disruption, or for personal gains

f) Ensure that the unwanted elements do not cause any performance degradation by any form of attacks, viruses, worms or other such forms of efficiency killers

The responsibility is on the BI systems to meet the first four needs. For the last two, security measures available in BI solutions should build on top of the other enterprise-wide security layers existing to provide the necessary protection.

While implementing comprehensive security infrastructure, using reference models ensure every required aspect is covered. There are a few security reference models that are useful. Architects should spend time understanding these and evolve a model, if one doesn't exist already. The key models that could be of use are (provided in the references section):

1. Enterprise Information Security Architecture of Gartner [3]
2. Network Security Model of SAN.ORG [4]
3. Open Security Architecture of OSA [5]

This chapter has drawn from these models and other practical project experiences, and created a framework to discuss all aspects of protection needed in a QlikView Deployment. Further extension can be done with the help of above reference models to address more complex situations.

Overview of QlikView Security

Following are the purposes/goals of Security:

1. Don't Allow Access to Unwanted Intruders. No unwanted outage
2. Allow only explicitly identified (authenticated) users to enter
3. Allow access to only allowed (authorized) content / data to users
4. Ensure continuous availability of Data as and when needed without performance degradation

Any solution, including QlikView should provide features, to use enterprise features available for all the above, or provide own features / solutions, to ensure that these enterprise needs are met.

Enterprise Security and QlikView

Goal #1 (Don't allow access to unwanted intruders) is addressed by the generic *Network Layer*, which ensures that the network, resources inside the network, data stores and applications (hence the data in applications) are protected from unauthorized and unwanted external and internal intruders. Network Security Section below covers this.

QlikView does not add any value on this layer, but just relies on the existing enterprise setup.

Goal #2 (Allow only the explicitly identified) is addressed by the generic *Authentication Layer*, which identifies users as they enter into the network by a challenge response process of up to 3 levels of security. This is to ensure that *the person is indeed what they claim to be*. QlikView provides ways of using existing enterprise Authentication capabilities and also a framework to create a QlikView-specific Authentication setup, in case the enterprise doesn't have an Authentication framework.

Goal #3 (Allow access to only the authorized) is taken care of by the generic *Authorization Layer*. This identifies what is accessible for the users in question: a) in the form of permissions for accessing a resource (an application, a file, or a device) and b) in the form of permission to view/use various parts of the resource (features of an application, sections of a file, or parts of a device). For the access control, QlikView relies on the Enterprise facilities available but also provides a mechanism to implement this in case there is no reliable enterprise facility. For the fine-grained data access control, QlikView provides an infrastructure to restrict data access inside the in-memory QlikView application – allowing only some part of the data/application to be accessed by users, according to the authorization conditions.

Goal #4 (Ensure continuous availability of Data) is covered typically by High Availability and Fail Safe Layer of the organizations. QlikView provides a facility to take advantage of the High Availability and Fail Safe facilities available in the Enterprise (Network Attached Storage or Storage Area Networks, Redundant Physical or Virtual Machines, Load Balancers, etc) and in addition, offers Clustering options for various components of QlikView. These are sometimes considered as part of the Security needs of an organization.

Reference Security Architecture Checklist

The following table summarizes various aspects of Security and the respective layers in which they need to be handled. The goals discussed above are covered among these five layers.

Table 1: Security Layers

LAYER	KEY ELEMENTS TO BE COVERED
Network Layer	Stop Intruders: Allow Users with Permissions, Only allow necessary services (Ports), protocols and tunnel, Access Control Lists. [Goal #1]
Authentication Layer	Establish Identity as they claim to be: password, key, retina/finger print. Verify against O/S, Directory Services or Custom User DB. [Goal #2]
Files Access Control Layer	Inherit USERID from Authentication. Enlist allowed resources: Files and Documents. Access Definitions in NTFS / DMS / External DBs. [Goal #3a]
Authorization Layer	View only allowed content. Sheet, Object, Row, Field and level access. Use USERID or USERGROUP to manage access. [Goal #3b]
Availability Layer	High Availability, Clustering, Fail safe. Load Balancing, Common Storage, Centralized Administration. [Goal #4]

Each of these layers is discussed in the following sections, with details on how QlikView components interact with other Enterprise systems and help implement these layers. Before discussing each layer separately, a review of QlikView architecture is provided from a security point of view. Various layers and components of QlikView are designed to address security concerns in an integrated fashion.

QlikView Products and Security

QlikView uses a tiered approach which forms a best practices basis for deploying QlikView in a secure fashion. The earlier chapter on "QlikView Components and User Roles" gives a detailed overview of the different components in great detail. More comprehensive alternative topologies of the architecture are included in the best practices sections in this Chapter and also in Part III.

The tiered SOA approach is very helpful to design secure implementations, with least amount of possible entry points. Front-end and Back-end are connected only through files saved in the storage. There are no ports required for communication between the front-end and back-end components. Figure 1 provides a simplified overview of the various QlikView layers to understand the security structure in a simplified way.

Backend
(Including Infrastructure Resources)

This is where QlikView Source Documents reside and contain scripts within QVW files to extract a) data directly from the various data sources (e.g. data warehouses, Excel files, SAP, Salesforce.com) or b) the extracted binary data from QVD files.

The main component that resides on the Back End is QlikView Publisher—responsible for data loads and distribution. In the Back End, Windows file system controls the access privileges. The Back End depicted here is suitable for development, testing and deployment environments.

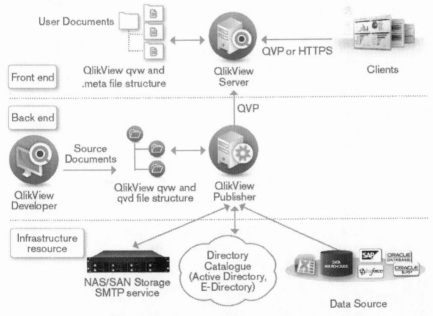

Figure 1: Simplified QlikView Deployment Architecture

Front End

The Front End is where end users interact with the documents and data that they are authorized to see via the QlikView Server. It contains the QlikView user documents that have been refreshed / created via Publisher on the back end. The file types seen on the Front End are QVW, .meta and .shared documents. All communications between clients and server occur here and handled either via HTTPS (in the case of the AJAX client) or via the QlikView proprietary QVP protocol (in the case of the plug-in or Windows client). Within the Front End, the QVS is responsible for client security. Though the diagram does not show, the users actually first connect to a web server—IIS or QV HTTP server—to get a list of all applications allowed for the user. Once the user chooses an application, the QlikView server displays the document through the AJAX client or the IE Plug-in.

From a security standpoint, it's important to understand that the Front End does not require any open ports to connect to the Back End. It does not send any queries to data sources on the back end, nor do any of the user documents (QVW's) contain any connection strings to data sources located on the back end. End users can only access QlikView documents that exist on the Front End.

QlikView Services, Ports and Protocols

QlikView uses a Service Oriented Architecture and each of the components run as services listening on defined port numbers. In general the components in each of these tiers communicate with other components in the same tier. The components that connect to both the front-end and back-end are QlikView Directory Services and QlikView Management Console that use the QMS API available on the Server, Access Point and the Publisher. All the communications use specific protocols, with appropriate security built into them. The adjoining table provides port numbers used by various QlikView components.

Table 2: Ports used by QlikView Components

QlikView Service	Ports	Tier	Protocol
QlikView Server	4747, 4774	Front-End	QVP (A variant of HTTP) or AJAX
QlikView Distribution Service	4720	Back-End	HTTP or HTTPS
QlikView Web Server (or IIS)	4750, 80, 443	Front-End	HTTP or HTTPS
QlikView Management Service	4780, 4799	Back-End	HTTP or HTTPS
QlikView Directory Service Connector	4730, 4735, 4731 (SNMP)	Back-End	HTTP or HTTPS

Of these only the Front-End services need to be accessible for the users who access the QlikView applications. Hence these ports [4747, 4774, 80 and 443] need to be (open) allowed on the Firewalls that separate the Front-End and the users.

The other ports are all required to be open on any firewall that separates the back-end services from one-another. Also, the ports required to connect to the data sources should be open in any firewalls that separate them from the Publisher.

With this broad overview of the QlikView architecture following sections discuss the five layers mentioned above, and discuss how they work with QlikView.

Network Layer

Anyone coming in touch with an enterprise, either from inside or from outside, connects to the various resources through the network. Hence the network layer should be constructed with enough controls and restrictions, to ensure the following:

1. Stop unwanted intruders from entering into the network
2. Identify allowed users by their source (based on IP address or domain name of the machine)
3. Allow only services that are permitted to be accessed for the user
4. Stop stealing of data during transmission

Various network layer components ensure these requirements are met. Key elements of network layer are Firewalls, ACLs, VPNs and appropriate network topologies created with them.

Firewalls

Firewalls are the bastions in the entry points of an enterprise network, to control who can enter and what gets transmitted to and from network resources. They protect networks from unauthorized access while permitting legitimate communications. There are three broad types of firewalls: a) Packet Filter, b) Stateful and c) Application Firewalls in increasing order of sophistication.

The common method of control is to maintain which source IP addresses are allowed to access which services (ports) on which internal destination server IP addresses. Every packet is inspected to find if the source, destination IP and ports are in the allowed list, and then pass the packets that match. Other packets are just dumped without any further action.

Almost all routers and firewalls have packet filtering capabilities which are deployed by default. "StateFul" and "Application" firewalls include packet filtering features and have additional capabilities that are useful. Microsoft ISA and Bluecoat are some examples of advanced firewalls, which allow much more sophisticated controls. These are useful when we want to implement integrated SSO using 3rd Party SSO solutions (Authentication section below).

ACLs—Access Control Lists

ACLs are rules defined in the Firewall, used by the Packet Filters to decide what should be allowed and what not. Packet filtering firewalls, in general, do not worry about the identity of the user who is accessing, but just focus on the rules at the packet level, and provide the basic safety required for the enterprises. Typically all services are blocked on the Firewall as a start, and explicit packet filtering rules are setup to allow legitimate communication. When implementing QlikView, the need is to get the necessary ports open for communication. Such ports are allowed by setting appropriate ACLs (see "QlikView Services, Ports and Protocols" above).

DMZ and other Network Sections

There are two internal firewalls and one external firewall creating a rigorous security setup in large organizations. A sample comprehensive topology of such a rigorous network is provided in Figure 2. The space between the external firewall and the first internal firewall is called the DMZ (De-Militarized Zone) [14]. The external users from outside the organization are allowed to reach pre-defined services (ports) on designated servers kept in the DMZ. Typically, the machines that run Front-End QlikView Components are all kept in the DMZ for external users to reach through External Firewall.

Some of the QlikView components that are allowed to connect to other internal servers, like the Publisher, Directory Services Connector, Management Console, are all run inside the Internal Server Section of the network, between the first internal firewall and the second internal firewall. All the internal users are allowed to connect to the various services from behind the second internal firewall. Explicit rules are set in the second internal firewall to allow users to reach services in the DMZ and not have access to the Server Section which typically contains all the internal enterprise application, mail and database servers.

VPNs

Many key internal users travel outside the premises, and they need to have access to the QlikView applications. For all such users, there is a need to make them connect into the enterprise network from wherever they are and get treated as if they are "inside" the network. QlikView access can be given by allowing access to the IIS or QV HTTP server kept in the DMZ. Sometimes, the sensitivity of the data is so much that even this cannot be allowed.

In such situations, the need is to run a VPN solution, which allows the traveling user's machine to connect and authenticate against the internal identity server. On authentication, one client-side VPN program runs connecting to the VPN server, which transparently makes the client machine a part of the internal network through a secure network layer, establishing a connection over the public internet in an encrypted path.

Once this VPN connection is established, the user machine acquires the IP address and credentials to connect to the servers inside DMZ. Using a browser, user can now connect to the Access Point and login to access QlikView applications as is done from inside the premises.

Choosing the Right Network Topology / Physical Architecture

The key decisions to take are what components of QlikView will be run in what sections of the network. The various practical considerations used in defining this QlikView topology are presented here, for each possible section of the network. There are many ways in which corporate networks can be "Zoned" to ensure security. Some references on this topic are included in the references section [10, 11, 12 and 13] (particularly the paper on Secure Network Zones is a good introduction).

Figure 2 shows a typical number of practical zones in a Network Topology, and this is used as a reference for the discussions below.

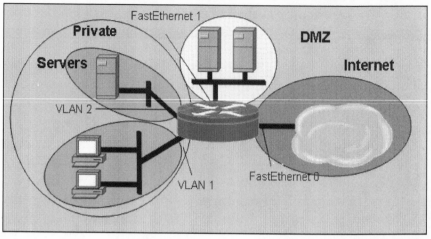

Figure 2: Network Zones

Refer to this article on Cisco site for more information: "Zone-Based Policy Firewall Design and Application Guide" [11]. Not all zones may exist in each company, and understanding the current network topology is an important starting point to decide how QlikView should be deployed. Though a particular topology is chosen in the beginning, it is not very difficult to redeploy QlikView with a different topology as security demands change.

Particularly with QlikView 11, enterprise administration of all QlikView components are done with Management Console, making it easy to re-configure the deployment as required.

Access Point in DMZ

QlikView Access Point (QAP) is deployed in the DMZ between External Firewall and Internal Firewall-1, on Windows IIS (Internet Information Service) or QlikView Web (HTTP) Server. Multiple Access Points can also be deployed to handle heavier web server load, and all of them can be placed in the DMZ in a load-sharing configuration, behind a load balancer. Access points are involved in the Authentication process, and provide the authenticated credentials to the QlikView Server during user access (more details in the section on *Authentication Layer).*

QlikView Server in Application Server Zone

QlikView Server (QVS) is typically deployed in the *Servers Zone*. In some less stringent security environments, QV Server is deployed in the DMZ itself. And in more stringent security setups, QV Servers are deployed in a separate *Application Servers Zone*, the data base servers are kept in a separate *Database Server Zone*.

QlikView Servers receive the User Credentials (User ID) from the Access Point or other custom Front-Ends developed using QlikView WorkBench. Then QVS connects to the enterprise ACLs (NTFS, LDAP, etc) to retrieve the Access Control (File) permissions. On allowed documents, Authorization (data access) for the user is retrieved from the SECTION ACCESS portion of data model to decide what part of the data/application the user can view and interact (more details in later section on "Authorization Layer").

QlikView Publisher in Database Server Zone

QlikView Publisher is known as QlikView Distribution Service (QDS) and typically deployed in the Application Server Zone, isolated from database servers to ensure more data security. Sometimes Publisher is deployed along with the Databases in the Database Server Zone as well. There may be other variant topologies as well.

Multiple Publisher instances are deployed as a cluster in situations where more capacity is required to run multiple parallel tasks of reload. The way in which Publisher handles security is explained in the section on Authorization Layer.

External Users (Traveling Internal Users or Extranet Users)

All users from outside the enterprise network, who have access to the QlikView application can access through a Browser. After appropriate authentication on the web server (discussed in section on "Authentication Layer"), access is given to the list of QlikView applications allowed for the user. The need is to open these port numbers on the external firewall: 80 (HTTP protocol for the Access Point) and 4747 (QVP protocol to connect to the QlikView Server to open QlikView applications). In more security demanding situations, users connect to Access Point and QlikView Server through a secure VPN, after authenticating into the enterprise network.

In some scenarios, port number 4747 cannot be opened on the external firewall. Then tunneling is enabled on the Web server so that all the interactions with the QlikView Server are encapsulated over HTTP protocol from user browser to the Web Server; the web server converts this into QVP protocol through Port Number 4774 with the QlikView Server instance (this port is to be allowed on the firewall between Web Server and QlikView Server).

Internal (Intranet) Users

Intranet users from inside the network, access using their browsers, and connect to Access Point in the DMZ as a normal deployment. It is also possible to keep a separate Access Point (or a cluster) just for the internal users, to separate internal and external user loads.

Port numbers 80 and 4747 are required to be open for access. Using tunneled QVP protocol for internal users is also seen as a practice in large enterprises—the Web Server connects to the Server using port 4774 (again this port needs to be allowed on firewall between Web Server and QlikView Server).

In extra-ordinary security governance situations, an internal DMZ is also kept between Application Server Zone and internal users, with the Access Point placed in the internal DMZ. Authentication is done by the internal Access Point as well—more often with SSO integration, so that the users need not enter another set of username / password (credentials) to login into QlikView applications.

Deciding the right network topology

With all the above choices possible, it is important to decide the right topology for any enterprise in consultation with Network and Security teams of the organization. The choices made for the network topology lay the foundation for the security of the entire deployment. As mentioned earlier, the choice that is made need not be used forever, but changes can be planned and implemented fairly quickly with the integrated management console. However, the need is to carefully plan and decide the topology to avoid frequent changes.

As a common error this is not done early enough in projects. Doing this early during the planning phase gives enough time to get necessary hardware, security clearances and appropriate ports opened. The decisions should of course include the Authentication and Authorization requirements as well, so that the security plan is comprehensive. If started late, this can delay project go-live significantly.

In smaller organizations, recommendations should be based on what they have or what they can afford. The least that is required is a software firewall to prevent any intrusions if there is a need for allowing users from outside the network. Once the basic network security concerns are taken care of, the Authentication and Authorization become the next important considerations.

Authentication Layer

Authentication is the mechanism whereby systems may securely identify their users. Authentication systems provide answers to the questions:

- Who is the user?
- Is the user really who he/she represents to be?

Authentication systems may be as simple (insecure) as plain-text password challenge (found in some old FTP servers) or a complicated challenge-response across multiple systems like the Kerberos.

Authentication Basics

All computer systems require some form of authentication before users can use them. In all cases, authentication systems depend on some unique bit of information known (or available) only to the individual being authenticated and the authentication system—a shared secret. Such information may be:

- What the User *Knows*—a classical password
- What the User *Is*—some physical property of the individual (fingerprint, retinal vascularization pattern, etc.), or
- What the User *Has*—some derived data (as in the case of so-called smartcard systems).

In order to verify the identity of a user, the authenticating system typically challenges the user to provide his unique information (his password, fingerprint, etc.). If the authenticating system can verify that the shared secret was presented correctly, the user is considered authenticated. Using two of these secrets—one a Password and two a Physically Available Key like a Smart Card, Physical Token, or One-Time Password (OTP) (a Key sent as an SMS in real-time to the phone of the user) is called *Two-Factor Authentication*. Adding more such pieces is *n-Factor Authentication* in general.

Single Sign-On (SSO)

There are times that, after users authenticate to an individual system, they need resources on a second system. To help users authenticate only once, but avail resources and services running on other systems without authenticating again and again, centralized authentication solutions are used – known as Single Sign On.

Kerberos (developed by MIT) is the common technique used by the Active Directory Services, to implement this in an all-windows organization. In many medium and large organizations with heterogeneous systems, this is accomplished via a sophisticated Single Sign-On (SSO) infrastructure.

Implementing SSO across all Web Enabled Applications is relatively easy, by implementing a reverse proxy or an ISAPI Filter, using the Basic or NTLM Authentication methods using the HTTP headers of the requests. Implementing SSO across heterogeneous applications—web-enabled and non-web-enabled—running on different platforms, with their own authentication processes can be very complex. There are different solutions available in market to implement SSO in simple and complex situations [15]. A typical SSO solution includes three key components to perform the following:

- *Identity Stores or Directories*: Active Directory, LDAP, OpenID and Custom Databases.
- *Federated Authentication*: Kerberos, ADFS, ForeFront, SiteMinder, WebSeal, Ping Federate, FreeIPA, OneLogin, Imprivata OneSign, OpenAM, etc. These authentication engines can make use of Two-Factor or n-Factor Authentication.
- *Feed Identity to Applications*: Mechanisms for conveying the user identity established to the individual applications in the network—

Basic and NTLM Auth, HTTP Header Injection to mimic Basic/NTLM, web-scraping to transparently auto-fill form values by posing as a user and lastly agent libraries to be included in the applications. Agent library based solutions require the application to be modified at code level to add the necessary authentication agent library calls.

Based on the security needs, Care should be taken to understand the current setup, and plan for integration of QlikView into them, in discussion with security team of the organization.

Authentication and QlikView

QlikView is a network resource that can be used by multiple users from all over the network. Although QlikView can be configured to allow anonymous access, the majority of implementations require that users be authenticated.

QlikView relies on the authentication to be performed prior to accessing QlikView, and some token of Identity is transmitted to, and trusted by, QlikView. By default QlikView is SSO enabled, relying on the NTLM / Kerberos authentication that is available in the enterprise.

The various common authentication scenarios when implementing QlikView are:

Single-Domain, Trusted Multi-Domains and Workgroup Scenarios

1. Anonymous Access – no authentication
2. Standalone Windows Desktop Authentication
3. Standalone QlikView Customer Users Database
4. QlikView Server with Integrated Windows Authentication (IWA)
   Multi-Domains without Trust Relationship
5. QlikView Server with External SSO Package
6. QlikView Server with Custom Ticket Exchange (CTE)
   Other Authentication Scenarios
7. QlikView Server with QlikView Custom Users Database
8. Combining Multiple Authentication Mechanisms

Each of these scenarios is discussed below.

Single Domain, Trusted Multi-Domains and Workgroup Scenarios

When the users belong to a single domain, the level of trust across users, servers and client machines is relatively high. In such scenarios, authentication is tightly integrated with the common infrastructure in the form of an ADS or an LDAP, implemented at the organization level. In case the setup is small, then there is no domain, & just the work group based authentication is good enough. Sometimes no authentication is used in smaller setups.

Anonymous Access – No Authentication

Internet deployments where applications are allowed to be accessed by everyone over the web, authentication is not required. Example: http://demo.qlikview.com.

Typically in all customer situations, during initial phases of development, testing and evaluation, user based access is not implemented. Applications developed are made accessible to everyone, either through Local QlikView Clients or QlikView Server. In these scenarios, when the user opens an application, the user's NTNAME is automatically passed on to QlikView Application (on Desktop or Server), and the application can still use it for deciding what to allow and what not (Authorization).

While this is good to have a quick start, if applications would eventually need user based restrictions to access applications, it is better to have the appropriate setup done sooner. Developers can perform access tests during the development itself for final deployment.

Standalone QlikView Custom Users Database

Inside QlikView, there is a facility to add an authentication section, using two fields USERID and PASSWORD. When these two fields are present in the Section Access (discussed later in this chapter) QlikView automatically prompts for the USERID and PASSWORD. This USERID can preferably be the NTNAME or any other OS USERNAME of the current user. However, if it is different, every user who will access the application needs to be given a unique USERID and PASSWORD (could be different from the regular AD or NT PASSWORD). This is not a preferred method since this leads to managing another password.

However, this could be a useful approach for highly confidential applications, meant to be accessed only by a select few, like HR apps or secret/confidential project analytics.

Standalone Windows Desktop Authentication

When QlikView Local Client is installed in a Desktop, the current user credentials— NTNAME and NTDOMAINSID—are automatically picked by the application. These two fields can be used inside the QlikView Application in Section Access (discussed below) to define what is accessible for which user.

The use of NTDOMAINSID is a very important security measure—it ensures that the application cannot be opened, from a different domain other than the domain on which the NTNAME belongs to. There is a facility in the Local Developer QlikView Client to insert the DOMAIN SID in the section access code (more in section on "Section Access"). Though same user NTNAME and NTDOMAIN names can be given in a fake setup, the local NTDOMAINSID will be unique for that setup, and hence the authentication will fail. This protects from an outside user who gets access to the application unofficially.

QlikView Server with Integrated Windows Authentication (IWA)

On a local area network, Integrated Windows Authentication (IWA) is most common, and most suitable for recognized Windows users on a LAN. Also on a WAN, where trust relationship is setup across domain controllers, the IWA can be implemented.

The user is authenticated when logging into the workstation. On connecting to the QlikView Access Point or QlikView Server through a browser, this identity is automatically passed on by the browser to the server using the Kerberos or NTLM. This solution will provide single sign-on capabilities right out of the box. In case the authentication exchange fails to identify the user, the browser will prompt the user for a Windows user account name and password.

To make use of this authentication credentials for Authorization, applications are developed using NTNAME and NTDOMAINSID as fields in section access table (see "Section Access").

Some versions of NTLM are considered unsafe for deployment even in a trusted domain setup. Kerberos is considered a better solution wherever possible. The browser and server (IIS or QlikView) negotiate to identify what can be supported by both, and that is used as the protocol to complete the authentication mechanism.

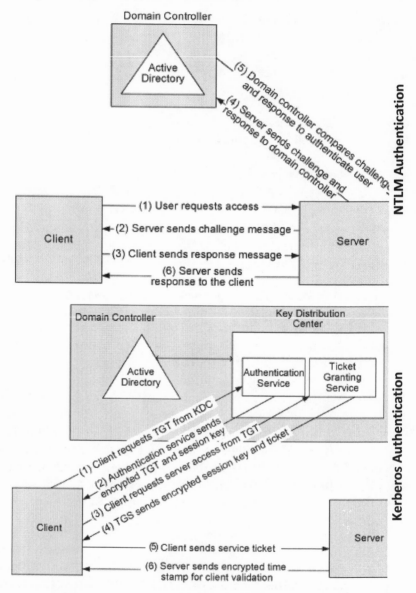

Figure 3: Integrated Windows Authentication Mechanisms

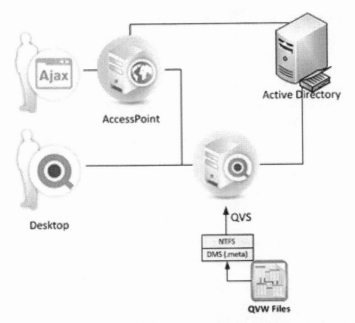

Figure 4: QlikView Active Directory Authentication

Figure 3 is an overview of QlikView authentication with Active Directory:

Local Desktop Client using QVP:

Desktop sends the NTNAME to QVS. QVS communicates with AD and authentication is purely handled by Windows natively.

Web Clients:

User reaches Access Point using Browser. User NTNAME is sent by the browser to Access Point. Access Point connects to AD and receives Group Info for the user. Access Point sends the User/Group Info to QVS to receive document list. When the user opens a document, the User/Group Info is sent to the QVS to receive a ticket. Depending on the client, the ticket is either linked to the Session ID (AJAX Clients) or sent to the client to be attached to the QVP protocol (Plugin).

Multi-Domains without Trust Relationships

When the client machines and users belong to a different domain, and server belongs to another, there is no trust relationship between the domain of the workstation and the domain of the server, or when users access the servers across a reverse proxy. This is a multi-domain environment. In a multi-domain environment, the internal company network IWA cannot be used.

The approach used is to authenticate the user against a central Identity Management Solution, and then expose this authenticated identity to QlikView. The choices are External Single-Sign-On (SSO) or use the QlikView Custom Ticket Exchange (CTE) solution. In both cases, the user credentials are verified against external user identity repositories in the form of LDAP, AD, Custom Databases, etc.

Typically, when multiple domains exist within the boundaries of an enterprise, then an existing external SSO service can be used. When multiple domains exist beyond the boundaries of an enterprise, then QlikView Custom Ticket Exchange can be used.

Third Party Single-Sign-On (3P SSO)

There are many different ways to implement Single Sign On and multiple techniques have been used by various implementation vendors. (Refer List of Single-Sign-On Implementations in the references section). QlikView supports the HTTP Header Injection Method—to use the already existing Basic / NTLM authentication used for Web Application Authentication.

In environments where SSO infrastructure already exists (e.g. CA SiteMinder, IBM WebSeal, or Oracle Oblix), QlikView can utilize the HTTP header injection method of single sign-on provided by these software packages right out of box. These can be configured as follows:

- Repeat users get access: After already signing into the SSO's authentication page, a user requests access to QlikView, the SSO package will transparently pass on their credentials to QlikView. If the user is present in Section Access of QlikView, user is granted access.
- New users log in: If the user does not have an existing session with the SSO package they will be redirected to the SSO package's login page. After logging in they will be redirected to the original URL they requested.

In both cases, if the user has properly authenticated to the SSO software, the username gets injected into an HTTP header and the QlikView server accepts it as the user's authenticated identity. Figure 4 provides an overview. Use caution with the HTTP header injection method. Note that unless SSO software is properly implemented, this method should not be used—HTTP Headers can be easily spoofed. All of the SSO software packages named above provide protection against this type of spoofing attack if they are the only path that users can use to access the content.

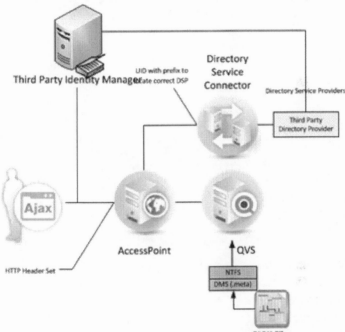

Figure 5: QlikView SSO with HTTP Header Injection

This is highly suited to extranet deployments wherein the users may not exist in the internal Active Directory, but are available in a central identity management directory service.

A typical deployment is to put a reverse proxy (IBM WebSeal, Microsoft ISA WebProxy, BlueCoat ProxySG, OpenSource Squid Proxy) or ISAPI filter as the *only* entry point for all the web applications. This will ensure that communication between users and Access Point / QlikView Server happens only through this single path, so that any unauthorized access by misusing HTTP Header injection is not allowed. Authentication is performed by the reverse proxy or ISAPI filter that intercepts the end user attempt to interact with QlikView content. Reverse-proxy or ISAPI-filter is set to connect to the 3rd Party Authentication Infrastructure.

A typical complex authentication setup using HTTP Header in non-trust scenarios is provided in the diagram below. In this the Third Party Authentication Authority Authenticates the user, passes the NTNAME to the Web Server and QlikView Server (QVS). Then the Web Server and QVS connect to the appropriate User/Group lookup, to find the list of applications and the content that the user has got access to. Directory Services Connector (DSC) is used for looking up the Groups.

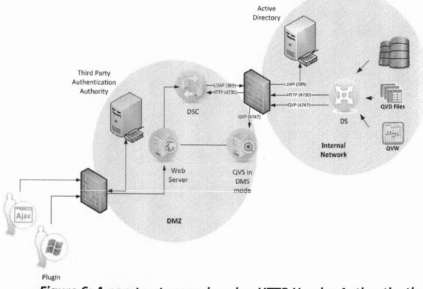

Figure 6: A non-trust scenario using HTTP Header Authentication

Currently QlikView supports only HTTP Header Injection based SSO. It would be good to see SAML support on QlikView to enable it to make use of Federated Identity solutions like Ping Identity and Cloud Identity infrastructure like OpenID.

The Reverse Proxy based HTTP header injection solution ensures that the session continuity and security is maintained, and offer protection from session stealing. Every request that passes back and forth between QlikView Server and Client Browser needs is inspected for being part of a valid session.

QlikView Custom Ticket Exchange

Following unique situations can occur in an enterprise where QlikView is to be rolled out:

- Multiple identity solutions exist but without an SSO, for eg., internal users are on Active Directory and external users are authenticated using a) a custom user database table typically for extranet/partners, or b) an external cloud application like Salesforce or Google Apps, or using OpenID (Facebook, Gmail, Yahoo, Microsoft Live ID, etc)—typically for Internet—users.
- No centralized identity management solutions implemented – not even an Active Directory, but each application is authenticating using its own credential data store.

Solution created in these situations involves following three key parts:

First, the user needs to be authenticated against respective identity data store where the user data exists. This is typically taken care of by using different landing pages for different users. If a single landing page needs to be used, then additional information is taken from users to decide their class. Along with username/password, domain names from complete mail ids, options like Customer/Employee, are used to identify the user class. The landing page then performs the authentication with appropriate authentication mechanism to establish the credentials of the user according to the user class.

Second, once the user is authenticated against these respective identity stores, the session needs to be secured directly between client browsers and the QlikView Server during interactive analysis. This is implemented by the use of Custom Ticket Exchange. If not secured well, the system can be compromised using false impersonations by session stealing.

The typical way in which QlikView CTE infrastructure works is:

1. The user opens the relevant landing / login page on the Web server. Server authenticates user against the relevant identity store.
2. The IIS or third-party system is granted the privilege and responsibility to request an authentication token (called a 'ticket' in QlikView) from the QVS on behalf of that system's authenticated user. It is that third-party system's responsibility to only request a

ticket for a user who has properly been authenticated (e.g. QVS has no knowledge of the user's authentication status).

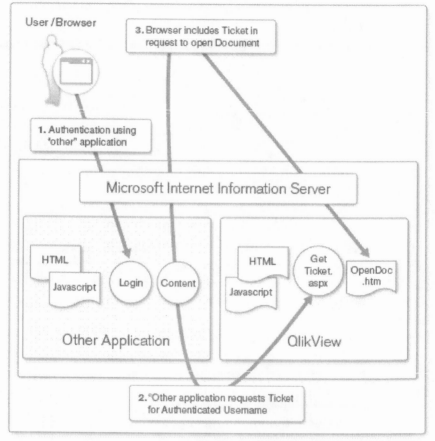

Figure 7: QlikView CTE Authentication

3. This system then passes the authentication token to the user who then utilizes it in their request to open a session with the QVS.
4. QVS validates that the ticket is valid and then opens a session for the authenticated user.

Ticketed authentication is most applicable to embedding QlikView content in third-party applications and portals, and rarely used for providing general access to QlikView. Typically a small amount of custom development is needed to implement the request and passing of this ticket for the Custom Ticket Exchange method to work. See the article on "Using QlikView Tickets" by Jay Jakosky [16]. There are many threads on the QlikCommunity to help with the specifics of creating the custom code required to use the tickets, and a detailed description of the ticketing process in the QlikView Server Manual. After authentication is established and a Ticket is created, the user session gets established—QV Server remembers the USERNAME associated with the session. With this user identity, QV Server needs to get their Group membership information for authorization.

If it is available from one central store—typically an Active Directory—it can be implemented using the NTLM mode of QV Server. If this store does not exist, the need is to maintain a separate Authorization data store as part of the QV implementation using the DMS mode of QV Server (more on this in the Authorization section below).

Other Authentication Scenarios

Not all but two important situations are covered here: a) Completely separate user database dedicated only for QlikView and stored inside QlikView, b) Combination of multiple methods of authentication listed above, or their variants, to take care of the variety of authentication needs that exist in a large enterprise.

QlikView Custom Users DB

All the above methods use some form of single sign-on, where the userid and password of the users is stored external to the QVS and an external entity is responsible for the authentication. What if the organization does not have an external store of users or an authentication mechanism?

There is a facility to store the user credentials in QlikView Server environment itself, though less commonly used. This uses the Custom Users functionality in the QlikView Publisher. In this case, the users and their passwords are defined and stored within the QlikView environment, in the Custom Directory, accessible through the Directory Services Connector. All users need to be created in the Custom User repository using the Publisher User Management interface.

The web tier of the QlikView Deployment is responsible for the forms authentication, typically using a login.htm entry point. Credentials entered by the user are validated against the DSC, and on authentication, the users are given access to the QVS.

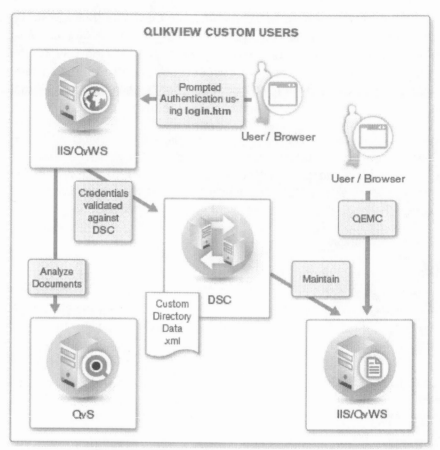

Figure 8: QlikView Custom User Database Authentication

This solution is suitable for smaller, standalone QVS deployments, and should not be used in environments where the user definitions need to be available to multiple systems. In environments where definitions should be available on multiple systems it is highly recommended to use one of the three single sign-on solutions described earlier.

Combination of Multiple Authentication Methods

In most enterprises, the user databases are distributed among various Identity Stores, and also there are different Authentication Infrastructures available for different services. For example, while mail and intranet portals may be connected tightly with the AD Infrastructure, the SAP / Oracle / other ERP solutions, or CRM solutions like Salesforce on Cloud, all may have their own way of authentication.

The choice is to use different authentication mechanisms implemented in different entry points (login pages) for each segment of users. Each form of authentication may require a distinct WebServer instance. Even if all users enter into a single entry point, they can be automatically redirected to different Web server entry points—transparently—based on some additional attribute of users (domain name, department, IP address of the client, user type (vendor/employee/customer), GPS location and user client (browser / mobile, etc).

Several WebServers can forward User Requests to the same QVS instance(s). In such a scenario, using Custom Ticket Exchange approach to connect to the QVS becomes a good choice. The access permissions for the respective applications still need to be managed carefully, and this is discussed in detail in the Authorization section below.

Authorization Layer

After using any of the authentication methods, the user credentials are established. Authorization essentially manages the rights of the user: What are you allowed to see? What are you allowed to do? Authorization defines and implements the Access Control. Formally, "to authorize" is to define access policy. During operation, the system uses the access control rules defined to decide what is accessible for the user who was just authenticated.

Once a user has been authenticated (i.e. the system knows who they are), the first step in assigning their security privileges has been completed. The next step is to find the authority or rights the user has to use QlikView Resources: Applications, Data and QlikView Administrative Rights.

For regular users, first is to identify the list of QlikView Applications, the user has access to. Then identify what data, within each of those User Documents is allowed for the user. Both are part of the Authorization process in QlikView. Access to web-based QlikView Enterprise Management Console is restricted to Windows Users who are a member of a particular local Windows Group.

The Authorization Layer which implements the Access Control process can be divided into two phases: 1) Policy Definition phase where access is authorized, and 2) Policy Enforcement phase where access requests are approved or disapproved.

During the initial setup, an administrator will populate an Access Control List (ACL) with a list of users and/or groups and what they should have access to. When the time comes for a user to request access, the system looks up the user's authenticated identity in the ACL and verifies if the administrator has granted the user enough privileges to do that.

Document Level Authorization—Access to QlikView Documents

Direct access to the QlikView Document using QlikView Desktop is always governed by Windows NTFS File Security. For users coming over the network, through the Web Interface, once a user has been authenticated the QVS typically handles authorization on its own. The QVS offers the choice between storing the ACL information as Windows NTFS privileges (applicable only when the user is authenticated using a Windows user identity) or storing the ACL information in QlikView's own internal repository (called DMS or Document Metadata Service). The choice of NTFS or DMS affects access to all documents on the QVS— they cannot be mixed in a single instance of QVS.

NTFS VS DMS

As a default, QVS uses the Windows file system's own NTFS privileges to store authorization information. When in NTFS authorization mode, QVS controls access to a given QlikView document by determining if the authenticated user has NTFS privileges to the underlying QlikView Document file (.QVW file). When using just the QlikView Server without the Publisher, the privileges of the authenticated user are configured by a server admin using standard Windows Explorer functionality via directory properties. With Publisher, the permissions are assigned on the Publisher Admin pages or in the directory service used.

As an alternative to Windows NTFS, QlikView can use its own ACL called the Document Metadata Service (DMS). Unlike NTFS, this allows non-windows users and groups to be authorized to access applications and data. DMS integrates fully with the existing Directory Service Provider (e.g. Active Directory, other LDAP) where Group Membership has been assigned—this is a mechanism by which QVS can re-use existing enterprise accounts and group structures. The permitted Users or

Groups are recorded in a *"meta"* file that resides beside the QlikView Document, and is managed on QlikView Management Console.

NTFS is the default document authorization model and is suitable when all users and groups are identified in Active Directory or locally on the QVS host. The NTFS permissions may be inherited from the directory that the QlikView documents are in (when just the QlikView Server is used without Publisher), or may be assigned using QlikView Publisher distribution tasks (when Publisher is used).

DMS is required if the authenticated user identity is not a Windows User Account. The DMS permissions are explicitly assigned using the QlikView Management Console, or may be assigned using QlikView Publisher distribution tasks. All the DMS permissions are stored in metadata files associated with every document - <QVDOCUMENT.meta>

Access Permission to Documents

The access permission of any user to any document is decided by the explicit permission for the USERID or by the effective permission of the GROUP the user belongs to. Normally, documents are given access to groups, rather than individual users, since the users may be very large in number. The users are then made as members of the groups. This USER – GROUP relationship is maintained in one of the user identity systems.

The QlikView 'Directory Service Connector' (DSC) is used for interaction with whichever repository containing the Group Membership. QlikView provides several configurable 'Directory Service Providers' (DSP) and also an API for development of a custom DSP.

The following are the types of directory services QlikView supports.

- Active Directory: QlikView provides built-in support for users in the same domain as the QlikView Server. It also supports users in any domain trusted by the QlikView Domain.
- Local Windows Users: QlikView supports Local Windows users for environments where no Domain controller is available.
- LDAP: QlikView allows you to configure a connection to directories such as Novell, OpenLDAP, ADAM, SunOne LDAP.
- ODBC: QlikView Users and Groups may have been created in a database. This DSP is expected to be most relevant when QlikView has been embedded in an OEM product, and rarely used otherwise.

- Custom (QlikView) Users: QlikView allows administrators to create users in QlikView, side-stepping the need to set up users in Windows or Active Directory.
- Custom Directory Service Connector: QlikView provides the ability to write a custom connector to authorize against other user repositories (e.g. SalesForce.com, SAP)

By using the Directory Service Connector, the QlikView server identifies the membership of a user in any group. Then the access to the documents is found using the GROUPS, and hence the user's access rights are found as effective rights for the documents of interest.

Anonymous Access

When users are typically authenticated on the IIS using a custom form authentication, the IIS Auth Mode would be set as Anonymous. The IIS automatically assumes the user to be IUSR_<IIS_MachineName> (of the machine that runs the IIS server).

Instead of using Windows Authentication or DMS authentication, QVS can be setup to use Anonymous access. In this situation, QVS should be run as user IUSR_<IIS_MachineName>, and this ID must have the access rights to the documents requested by any user.

This will work using the Custom Ticket Exchange approach, where the actual Ticket Request is done using USERID, and the Token gives the access permission. However, all documents should be accessible for the IUSR_<IIS_MachineName> user (using the QV Server console).

Data Level Authorization

Once a document is accessible for a user, within that QlikView File, only a part of the content inside the document can be given access to the user, using the Data Level Authorization. For example an organization might have a single application covering worldwide sales transaction data. However it may want to limit country managers to view data only pertaining to their own country.

This data-level security can be further refined to both row-level and field (or column)-level data access. QlikView provides data-level security using Section Access within the QlikView document, or by using

Reduction/Distribution performed by QlikView Publisher or some combination of the two.

Section Access (aka Dynamic Data Reduction)

'Section Access' is a QlikView technology that allows QlikView to control which users have access to specific data (or 'sections') in a QlikView application. Because the document contains all data, and the rules that restrict data access are enforced when an authenticated user interacts with the document it is also referred to as Dynamic Data Reduction.

Section Access uses a security table, called "Section Access Table", to determine what data users can access, and applies security based on an association between users and data.

In Section Access tables, user ids can be the external user logins or created internally within the application. Section Access security table with usernames and passwords, can be stored either within the QlikView document itself (in a password-protected script section) or in a separate database or file that resides in the QlikView Server.

Whenever the user's identity is supplied to QlikView after any authentication (Integrated Windows Authentication, Header, Ticketing or Custom) this is exposed to the QlikView Document in a field called NTNAME. If the NTNAME is associated with data restriction rules in the document then there is no need to record or validate any further password within the QlikView Document. In case this NTNAME does not exist in the internal user table, then the QV Server may throw a dialog to enter Username and Password for authentication.

User-Role-Data associations or restrictions can be re-used among many QlikView documents if they are stored in a commonly accessible location such as database tables or using the User Management feature of the QlikView Management Console.

During setup, an administrator needs to supply only 3 parameters for each user intended to use the application:
1. Role (User or Administrator): that affects the Users capabilities when opening the QlikView Document file using QlikView Desktop.

2. Identity: a) NTNAME, or b) Username and password
3. Reduction field: Additional reduction fields optional

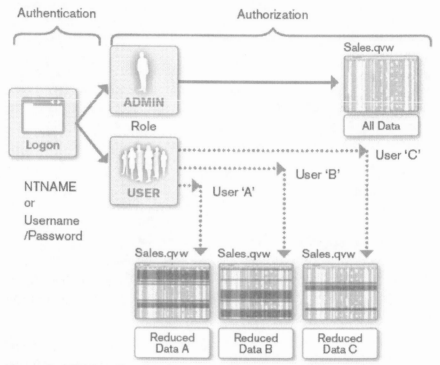

Figure 9: QlikView Section Access – Dynamic Data Reduction

Row Level Security: Reduction field is a field that determines which data a user can access. For example, if users should see only data associated with a specific department, the reduction field could be "Department", and users who have been granted access to the data associated with a specific department will be limited to access this data only.

Field Level Security: In addition, field (or column) level security can be applied using Section Access. Individual users or groups can be denied or permitted access to fields by invoking the 'OMIT' keyword in Section Access script. OMIT keyword is a reserved keyword in QlikView script to determine which users will be granted access to specific field-level data.

Even if document authorization (NTFS/DMS) permits a user to see that a document exists, if Section Access rules excludes from seeing any data, user can't open the document. Also, on a standalone Local QlikView Client, users assigned with ADMIN role in Section Access definition are not subject to Dynamic Data Reduction, they get to see all the data, rows and fields in the application.

Using Binary Load, an existing QlikView document (QVW file) can be loaded as a data source in another QlikView document by any user. A binary load will cause the access restrictions to be inherited by the new QlikView document. A person with ADMIN rights to this new document may change the access rights of this new document by adding a new access section. A person with USER rights can execute the script and change the script, thus adding own data to the binary loaded file. A person with USER rights cannot change the access rights. This makes it possible for an administrator to control access rights also for users accessing derived QlikView documents with binary loaded QVW files.

Reduction / Distribution / Splitting (Static Data Reduction) with QDS

For larger deployments and/or those needing centralized control of authorization capabilities, the QlikView Server/Publisher products are used. Often, a department or function has a 'master' application containing all relevant data covering all their analysis needs. This master document needs to be separated ('reduced') according to the intended audience's needs and access privileges.

QlikView Publisher reloads the QlikView document with available data, refreshes the Section Access tables and can split the large QlikView document into many smaller documents based on values of a particular field. This "Reduction and Distribution" allows for a file containing many data fields to be broken up by the contents of a field and distributed to authorized users or groups according to their access privileges.

An Administrator can use the QlikView Management Console to create tasks on source .qvw or .qvd files to accomplish this. At a basic level, the steps are as follows:

1. On the source document (either .qvw or .qvd), apply data reduction criteria (e.g. choose field name on which to reduce the data)
2. Apply distribution criteria to newly created (reduced) files.
   a. Assign authorization privileges to users
   b. Choose type of distribution (e.g. qvw files or pdf report)
   c. Choose location for newly created files

3. Apply notification criteria for completion of task (e.g. email notification)

The newly created files will only contain the data that a user or group is authorized to see because the data has been 'reduced' from master document according to reduction criteria set out. This is why the process is 'Static Data Reduction'. Therefore, there is no chance of an unauthorized person viewing data because only authorized data exists in each file.

Publisher tasks run to reload each document based on the schedule defined. The administrator configures the ADS/Windows GROUPS/USERS who have access to each application. For each document after reloading the data, if the LOOP & REDUCE option is enabled for the document, the list of users who have access to the document is identified by querying the enterprise AD/LDAP. Based on the settings mentioned above, the users will get a notification about the newly available files that they can see. In case of PDF, the output files can be directly mailed to the individual user mail boxes.

Combining Section Access and Split Distribution

It is often desirable to merge the capabilities of Section Access and the Reduction/ Distribution capabilities from the central server. This gives a flexible way of protecting the information. An example may be the distribution of Country or Division specific data to a collection of remote users (using static reduction), who can then see only their local State / City within their Country that they are individually permitted to see (dynamic reduction).

Using the two techniques, both row and field level security can be accomplished for the master document. Row-level security can be accomplished using Reduction/Distribution on the server side. For example, a source document might contain a field containing 3 unique geographical regions.

This can be reduced to produce 3 new files containing data pertaining to each region respectively. Field-level security can then be applied by invoking a Section Access script at the file level, restricting any given user (or group) to specific fields.

Mobile Security with QlikView

Mobile devices have become a very important part of the enterprise infrastructure. QlikView provides a robust means of using mobile devices, particularly iPads, and leverage the entire security infrastructure of a typical QlikView enterprise deployment. With the touch-enabled Ajax client support, any device including iPad can be easily integrated into the QlikView infrastructure [17].

From a security standpoint, the weakest links in a mobile deployment can be one of the following:
• Device
• Transmission
• Authentication and Authorization

Device Security

The most common problem with devices is that they could be lost, or accessed by others very easily. The Ajax client ensures that there is no information stored locally. Data resides only on the QlikView server, with the implemented access controls. This ensures that the device insecurity is covered properly.

Transmission Security

Another possible challenge is that data can get intercepted during transmission between the mobile device and the enterprise. Particularly the concern is because the devices not only use 3G or 4G channels, but Wi-Fi is also used from public places. Most of the advanced mobile clients, e.g., the iPad client, for example, support VPN connections where communication between client and QlikView server are encrypted.

In addition, the QlikView deployment can support encrypted communication between browser and QlikView Web Server using secure HTTPS/SSL protocols. Typically, HTTPS and Secure Sockets Layer (SSL) are used with server certificates installed on the Web Server.

Authentication and Authorization

For the mobile devices, before the regular user authentication, a first authentication is done using digital certificates, to establish the *credentials of the user/device* first to connect to the corporate network. Typically a web server, like IIS in the DMZ is setup to provide one-to-one certificate mapping. When a user first connects to the site, the user is prompted for a certificate. The certificate already created on iPad is presented and its public key is submitted to the IIS Server.

Using this public key, the user's identity is established, and then the user is allowed to connect to the QlikView application. All communications from IIS to the client will now be encrypted using the public key of the client. The client can decrypt with the private key it has, and the communication starts.

This is an additional layer of security for mobile devices. QV Tunneling is also enabled between the IIS and QlikView Server, to use encrypted communication between the two. This also removes the need for opening port 4747 for the mobile client to communicate with QlikView Server directly. Beyond this, there is no difference between the Desktop Clients and iPad Clients.

High Availability and Clustering

Ensuring the availability of information is part of the security mandate. An important aspect is to ensure that hardware or software failure in any of the components of QlikView deployment does not bring the entire system down. The business becomes heavily reliant on the information provided by QlikView over time. If at any point this becomes unavailable business can get adversely affected.

To ensure the continuous availability of QlikView applications to users, the need is to look at every possible single point of failure and ensure continuity of availability in those points by appropriately creating fall back mechanisms.

QlikView provides such availability options for Access Point, QlikView Server and Publisher servers. Multiple instances of each of these components can be added to ensure that failure of any of them will not affect the overall availability of the information for the users. More detail on this is provided in the chapter on "Deploying QlikView".

Development Security Best Practice Checklist

The Chain is no stronger than its weakest link. While extensive efforts are taken to implement best network security & high availability infrastructure, administration of authentication and authorization for all business users, development environment can become the weak link.

The following checklist provides a list of various "links" in the QlikView development and administration environment. Any of these links becoming weak can affect the overall security of the system. It is important to ensure the following aspects are taken care of during the initial design of the architecture and processes. On an on-going basis, the compliance to these should be measured to ensure that the security is not compromised at any time. Please refer "QlikView Security Overview" [18] and videos [19] for a background and approach discussion.

Backend Security

File Security

QlikView Data Files: The QVD files do not have any security whatsoever, inside them to protect reading by anyone who has a QlikView Local Client. The only protection that can be used is the operating system file permissions set on the QVDs. Maintaining correct read/write permissions of QVD files is the most essential security measure in every organization.

QlikView Source Documents: The source documents should be accessible only to the QlikView Administrators and QlikView Modelers.

Folder Structure for QlikView files: Design and document a folder structure for QlikView source files, depending on your customer needs.

Security Structure (Access Permissions): Design and document a security structure for your QlikView source files based on folder structure. Domain security groups should match source document file structure.

File System Security on Server: If DMS Authorization is not set on the Security page in Management Console, QlikView Server will only make a QVW document available to a connecting client that has an identity with operating system file access rights to that document. When using QlikView Server without Publisher, each user must be given read permissions to both document folders and the documents themselves through Windows file permissions; these permissions are automatic when used with Publisher.

Scripts

Relative Paths: Always use relative paths in QlikView scripts.

Use Common Libraries: Keep all standard variables, functions in common include files with permissions for all developers / modelers to use, it's a good practice. QlikView Components (QVC) created by Rob Wunderlich on Google Code is a great place to start.

Common InLine Tables & Variables: Use include files

Template Based Development: Create a QlikView Document template with your graphical company profile, with predefined include files with variables in the template.

Data Sources

Secure all connection strings: The Connection strings used to connect to backend data sources should all be stored in a separate $Include file. Always use include files for data connection strings (ODBC/OLEDB), placed according to the folder structure guideline: $(Include=..\include\DBserver_database.txt).

Write Permissions for Includes: Only QlikView Administrator Group and Publisher will have the rights to read and write the connection strings in the respective include files.

Additional QVD security Layer: One can create a folder structure containing QVD loaders for various databases. The final cleansed QVD files can be copied to the QVD Files repository in each department that needs these QVD files.

QlikView Service Accounts and Groups

QlikView Administrator Group: This is a domain level group that has access to all groups, distributed documents and the services. In each of the servers, this should also be a member of the QlikView Administrators group. The members of this group can administer the Enterprise Management Console. They should also be a member of the local administrator group on all the servers running QlikView components – Server, Publisher, Directory Services Connector and Web Service (IIS or QV HTTP).

QlikView Power User group: This has the rights to administer Publisher tasks but can't change any settings. It is optional to use this group.

QlikView Supervisor group: This applies to AccessPoint resources. Supervisor is a user that can see all data in an AccessPoint resource.

QlikView Service Account: This is a domain account that needs to be a member of QlikView Administrator Group and the local QV Admin Group. This account needs to have access to: File systems, Active Directory and Databases (for SQL SSO). Though very rarely, if not on domain, this user needs to be created as a local account in each of the servers (Access point, QV Server, QV Publisher, QV Directory Service), with explicit permissions given to access the above resources.

QlikView Multiple Environments (Dev / Test / Prod)

Folder Structure: The document folder structure in each of the servers should be identical with the same permission structure. As a good practice, developers should not have permission to write into the production folders; this should be reserved only for Administrators.

Different Connection Include files: When moving applications from one environment to other, QlikView documents should automatically connect to different data sources depending on the connection string in the include folders. (Test and pre-prod should have same structure as Production databases).

Front-End Security

QlikView User Documents

QlikView User Files: QlikView files are safe only behind the QlikView Server. Allowing QlikView downloading is a potential threat. Allow only if extremely essential.

All QlikView documents are scrambled which makes the information unreadable with viewers, debuggers etc., but they can be read by using QlikView Desktop Version, if there are no section access restrictions inside the application.

Section Access in All Documents: Every document created preferably should be implemented with a section access where only users of the Domain can open and view the application.

This can be done by including a code like the following:

```
Section Access;
LOAD * INLINE [
    ACCESS, NTNAME,
NTDOMAINSID, OMIT
    USER, *, S-1-5-21-
xxxxxxxxxx-xxxxxxxxxx-
xxxxxxxxx, ];
Section Application;
```

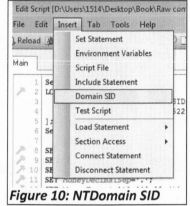

Figure 10: NTDomain SID

The NTDOMAINSID should be the ID of domain, which can be inserted from the INSERT menu of EDIT SCRIPT Dialog of QlikView Local/Developer Client. By doing this, if the file is copied into any domain other than this original domain, the file will not open. This can be set as the minimum regular practice for all QlikView files created.

Security settings inside the Document: In the QlikView Developer Client, there are three possible security settings that can be used on individual QlikView documents:

- Settings -> Document Properties -> Security tab
- Settings -> User Preferences -> Security tab
- Settings -> Sheet Properties -> Security tab (comes only for ADMIN)

In these tabs, there are many settings for ensuring security and stop unwanted access to data or applications. Fine grained controls are provided to define what should be allowed and what should not be. This can be set at every document level. When the document is deployed on the server, or edited on the client, these settings decide the behavior.

It is important, as part of the QlikView Security policy for the Enterprise, these items should be explicitly mentioned and choices made to allow or deny each of them for different document types. More details about these options can be seen in the QlikView help file to formulate the policies for these features.

Macro Security: When using macros in the front-end (VBScript or JavaScript), the settings in the Edit Module can define whether the document is to be run in Safe Mode (no system or application access outside of QlikView), or in System Access Mode. If in System Access mode, the end user will be prompted when opening the document to approve system access (Allow System Access) or disable all macros in the document (Disable Macros) or allow only macros without system access (Safe Mode). To suppress the macro-security dialog on QlikView documents, and set one of the options as a system default behavior, some settings in the windows registry can be used in older versions— refer to Stefan Walther's blog on "Suppressing Macro-Security (Module Security) Dialog" [20]—this is applicable to Windows Standalone & Plugin Clients. From Version 10, these settings are moved out of the registry into settings.ini file.

Securing QlikView Applications: There are situations the QlikView application scripts should not be accessible / editable for any user to whom it is sent. This is needed if the script contains some algorithms that are proprietary (Intellectual Property) or confidential (Some scoring algorithm with parameters to be kept confidential). To secure the script, in general HIDDEN SCRIPTS with passwords, and separate Module Password to protect MACRO SCRIPTS can be used. Read article: "How to secure QlikView Applications" [21]. In addition, in the Publisher Distribution Settings, it is recommended that the option should be set to clear the script when distributing the QlikView Applications.

Securing Connection Strings: Documents that are distributed through Publisher (including Loop and Reduce) contain no explicit reference to source data (e.g. a database connection string) in their script area. Therefore, if a user is interacting with the document via the desktop client, they will not be able to see the location of the source data. All of the data pertinent to their needs is contained in the document.

Communication Security

QVP Protocol: The communication between a QlikView Server and a QlikView Windows client is encrypted.

AJAX with HTTPS/SSL: With AJAX client, the communication is not encrypted by default. This can be encrypted by using HTTPS/SSL. The

QlikView Server Manual explains this process clearly, and QlikCommunity Thread#45326 [22] is also a great help.

Audit Trails

Setting up right security infrastructure forms the core of secure implementations. However, even authorized users could misuse access and perform activities that could cause damage to business. The logging of all user accesses, in as much granularity as possible, is another important element of implementing security.

The knowledge that user activities are being recorded and any mistake would be traced back to them deters misuse in the first place. Any stated rules of usage, with a note that all the activities are being logged, heightens alertness and reduces occurrence of mistakes.

Log Files: Alerts from QlikView Server will appear in the Windows event log. More detailed logs for sessions can be found in the logging directory specified on the QlikView Server Settings, Logging tab of the QlikView Management Console. Keeping a backup of all the logs, and performing log analysis to measure against set norms is a very important process. In addition, Audit Log facility can be enabled for fine grained usage analysis.

OpsMonitor.qvw – A QlikView document designed to load data from the log files and support analysis is provided on the default installation of QlikView Server. It is a good tool for reviewing / analyzing the log files created by various components of QlikView. Data size trends, reload times, usage of applications and performance indicators logged by Publisher, Server and Management Console are all provided in an integrated fashion in this application.

Depending on the organizational control procedures, this application can be modified to keep track of security / performance indicators and pro-actively administer the QlikView installation.

Concluding Remarks on Security

For any enterprise software solution in production, security is an absolute requirement and IT professionals from a DBA all the way to the CIO are tasked with ensuring that

a. Unauthorized access to data never occurs

b. Data is made readily available to those who need it

Implementation of these twin goals can often be at odds with each other and it is important that software vendors and implementation partners provide clear and accurate information related to how their solutions adhere to any organization's security standards.

QlikView provides robust means of securing data utilizing industry standard technologies such as encryption, access control mechanisms, and authentication methods. It easily integrates with authentication methods via standard directory services, allows administrators to choose between the creation of user-defined ACL's or utilizing Window's ACL's for file authorization and has a range of capabilities for data-level security at both the file and the server level.

QlikView has provided many features that are necessary and sufficient to ensure security in all the enterprise implementations. The key challenge is to ensure that these features are understood thoroughly and used in the most optimal way, in accordance with the enterprise needs in each implementation. This chapter has been an attempt to provide all of them in one place, so that architects, security specialists and administrators can make use of them.

The key step in ensuring security in any deployment is deciding the appropriate architecture, taking into account every challenge that is expected, and ensuring the right solution elements are integrated for the actual implementation. To help in such planning a reference architecture is provided, in the Chapter "Deploying QlikView" in Part III.

The second key step is to ensure that the decided Architecture is actually implemented on the ground. The risks of not deploying the actually decided architecture are many. Particularly with reference to security, the extent of auditing done before approval of the roll out is very low in most implementations. This is due to absence of a checklist & a process for validation.

The third key aspect is the processes that are set up to ensure the architectural norms and guidelines, particularly in security, are not diluted along the way, due to lack of monitoring and enforcement. Security policy audits should be done with thoroughness to ensure that the implementation is continuing to be in desired good health. This is to identify the possible vulnerabilities that are being introduced by the changing business dynamics, and fix them with appropriate changes in the security architecture, if required.

Security should be built into the architecture and the core processes so that there are no options to by-pass the security "wish-list". This is one of the most difficult things to do, particularly with an extremely flexible product like QlikView. However, since this is one of the serious concerns expressed by the hard core security professionals in the enterprises, the processes should become more rigorous. More discussions on best practices and architecture are provided in Part III.

References

1. Regular Security Updates, Enterprise Security Today - Online Magazine, [http://www.enterprise-security-today.com]
2. Information Security, Article on WikiPedia, [http://en.wikipedia.org/wiki/Information_security]
3. Enterprise Information Security Architecture, Article on WikiPedia, [http://en.wikipedia.org/wiki/Enterprise_information_security_arch itecture]
4. Network Security Model, SANS Institute, [http://www.sans.org/reading_room/whitepapers/Modelling/netw ork-security-model_32843]
5. Open Security Architecture, OpenSecurityArchitecture.org, [http://www.sap.com/platform/index.epx].
6. Business Intelligence Security Considerations, William McKnight, Tech Target Article, [http://searchbusinessanalytics.techtarget.com/answer/Business-intelligence-security-considerations]
7. Mobile Enterprise: Security Threats and Business Intelligence, Marisa Peacock, CMS Wire, [http://www.cmswire.com/cms/enterprise-20/mobile-enterprise-security-threats-and-business-intelligence-009762.php]

8. Privacy and Security Issues in BI, RoseIndia.Net,
   [http://www.roseindia.net/technology/business-
   intelligence/privacy-and-security-issues-in-BI.shtml]

9. Mobile BI brings more than security concerns to the table, Nicole
   Laskowski, TDWI Research,
   [http://searchbusinessanalytics.techtarget.com/news/2240114634/
   Mobile-BI-brings-more-than-security-concerns-to-the-table-TDWI-
   says]

10. Zone-Based Policy Firewall Design and Application Guide, CISCO,
    [http://www.cisco.com/en/US/products/sw/secursw/ps1018/produ
    cts_tech_note09186a00808bc994.shtml#topic4]

11. Secure Network Zones, Peter Kai Wimmer, AtSec.com,
    [http://www.atsec.com/downloads/pdf/ISSE_2009-
    Secure_network_zones-Peter_Wimmer.pdf]

12. Security Zones, IBM Tivoli Software pages, IBM.COM,
    [http://publib.boulder.ibm.com/tividd/td/ITIM/SC32-1708-
    00/en_US/HTML/im460_plan46.htm]

13. Network Zoning (The Zone), Practical Tactics, Oct 2011,
    [http://practical.wordpress.com/2007/10/15/network-zoning-the-
    zone/]

14. DMZ_Computing, Article on Wikipedia,
    [http://en.wikipedia.org/wiki/DMZ_(computing)]

15. List of Single Sign On Implementations, Wikipedia List,
    [http://en.wikipedia.org/wiki/List_of_single_sign-
    on_implementations]

16. Using QlikView Tickets, Jay Jakosky, AndPointsBeyond,
    [http://andpointsbeyond.com/2008/05/13/using-qlikview-tickets/]

17. Technical Security Brief – QlikView on Mobile, Whitepaper,
    QlikView.com,
    [http://www.qlikview.com/us/~/media/Files/resource-
    library/global-us/direct/datasheets/DS-Technical-Brief-QlikView-on-
    Mobile-Security-EN.ashx]

18. QlikView Security Overview, Whitepaper, QlikView.com, [http://www.qlikview.com/us/explore/resources/whitepapers/qlikview-security-overview]

19. QlikView Security Video Series, QlikView.com, [http://www.qlikview.com/us/landing/security-video-series]

20. Suppressing Macro-Security (Module Security) Dialog, Stefan Walther, qlikblog.at, [http://www.qlikblog.at/523/qliktip-19-suppressing-macrosecurity-module-security-dialog-qlikviewserverqlikviewdocuments/]

21. How to Secure QlikView Applications, QVApps Blog, [http://blog.qvapps.com/2010/04/23/how-to-secure-qlikview-applications/]

22. SSL in QlikView 11 with QV Webserver, Em Vau, Qlik Community Thread, [http://community.qlikview.com/thread/45326]

PART III

HOW TO MAKE BEST USE OF QLIKVIEW?

Introduction to Part III

MAKING BEST USE OF INVESTMENTS IN QLIKVIEW TECHNOLOGY AND PRACTICE

"Never invest in a business you cannot understand"
- Warren Buffet

"Let us not look back in anger or forward in fear, but around in awareness"
. – James Thurber

Understanding business and constantly being aware of its pulse and movements in every part is the key to run the business efficiently and profitably. QlikView can provide this continuous business visibility, and once such visibility comes, the business owners, leaders and managers become completely dependent on such insight source for running the business day-to-day.

Once QlikView becomes such a key resource for the business, the need is to ensure that it is implemented in the most robust manner, with no outages, no breakdowns. In addition, like with any production system, come up with monitoring, measuring and managing processes and systems, to ensure that the benefits continue to add up.

Part III discusses various ways in which QlikView can be deployed robustly, and made to work consistently in a production setup. There are extensive experiences of various customers – over 20000 – around the world. They have learnt by mistakes and arrived at what works and what does not.

These nuggets of experience have been presented in many places as Best Practices for QlikView implementation.

In addition to these, the author and his team have gone through over 150 hands-on deployment situations, and gained a lot of personal experience. The chapters put together a framework, where learning from all over can be put to use, as a checklist. Best practices are never a substitute for actual learning, however the learning can move in the direction where much time is not wasted.

The approach is to set a framework of options, based on which the particular architecture, integration and processes around the deployment of QlikView can be formulated. Every organization is unique, and these experiential notes could help in shortening the time required to create a wonderful and sustained QlikView experience for the organization.

The overall intent of this Part is to help layout a direction in which the deployment can be taken forward, so that the chances of success are increased. Success in a QlikView implementation not just allowing all the wonderful capabilities of QlikView get expressed and allow users to experience the quick, dynamic insights flooding into one's brains. Success truly happens when business users get great insights, and the necessary detail to take the right decisions around those insights, with a complete conviction to act on those insights. QlikView can change the way businesses work and increase their Analytics Quotient manifolds, leading them to the path of profitable excellence.

CHAPTER 14

DEPLOYING QLIKVIEW

GOOD MATERIALS, GREAT ARCHITECTURE AND EXCELLENT
CONSTRUCTION MAKE A GOOD HOUSE

Introduction to the Chapter

QlikView is "Good Material". Right "Architecture" and Right
"Construction" are important to make sure good business intelligence /
decision support system is created. Not to mention, Right
"Maintenance" is important to keep it good and useful all the time.
QlikView provides a rich set of components, features to handle variety
of enterprise situations. In practice, the need is not just QlikView
components, but integrating them with other infrastructure and
software that are already present, or being added. There are multiple
points in which such integration needs to be planned.

Typically development teams focus only on connecting to data sources,
developing applications and deploying them on QlikView servers. But
the actual deployment involves multiple environments, integrating
access, user management and security, defining the processes and
integrating them all into the regular IT management processes. This
chapter walks through key aspects of deployment and provides
reference templates/checklists for real-life deployments.

First the focus is on architecture: Reference architecture is discussed,
which can be adapted for various types of deployment. Individual,
Departmental and Enterprise wide deployment topologies and settings
are discussed, with different scenarios, including distributed
deployment. Sizing, Scalability, High Availability and Load Balancing
solutions of QlikView are discussed next to supplement the various
scenarios discussed. Disaster Recovery is discussed and some broad
pointers to implementing DR are provided. Finally a sub-section on High
Volume Reporting / Publishing is discussed and various possible
solutions are compared.

The second topic covered is Enterprise Integration, with focus on various aspects including: making data available in other repositories, integration with enterprise monitoring solutions like Tivoli etc., Virtualization and its impact on QlikView, Integration of Advanced Analytic Applications like R and finally QlikView on the Cloud.

The third aspect is about creating processes around the implementation of QlikView—before, during and after development. These processes connect the threads throughout the implementation, making it successful. From requirement documentation, common definitions, data dictionary, to managing metadata, all aspects of implementation process are discussed. Finally, the regular usage monitoring and related processes for sustaining good performance, smooth flow of all the information to business and license planning are covered.

The discussions are an attempt to syndicate information available on these topics from various sources together in one place, and to provide the experiences of the author in the real life implementations. As more large enterprise deployments of QlikView are done, the product will evolve further, and more scenarios can be supported with relative ease.

Solution Architecture

Planning and designing a deployment is an extremely important first step of any real-life deployment of any system, more so for BI solutions with QlikView. Taking various possible situations in mind, it is important to create a detailed architecture for deployment, with a roadmap of initiation architecture to the end-point architecture.

Checklist for Solution Architecture

Architecture should define the following key items before the implementation - these are all typically schematic representations of how the various QlikView components will inter-operate among themselves and also with other enterprise components in the following four layers: Data, Software, Security and Network/Physical.

1. *Data Flow Architecture*: Data Flow from various sources to the users (information consumers) with necessary intermediate stages
2. *Software Architecture*: Logical block diagram of QlikView components & other software with connectivity and flow

3. *Security Architecture*: Security Components and Plan—Network, Authentication, Authorization and Failsafe/High Availability

4. *Physical Architecture*: Physical Server, Software and Network layout with routing plan

5. *Bill of Materials*: Servers, Storage, Software licenses, Network Equipment, Load Balancers and data connectors (existing and new)

Creation of these documents, keeping in mind all the needs of the organization, is the key output of Solution Architecting. Individual or collective team expertise and experience in these layers are essential to ensure right solution. A *Solution Design Document (SDD)* needs to be prepared at the end of the Solution Architecting exercise, combining all the above documents, to be used as detailed guide by the implementation / deployment team.

Roadmap for Phased Roll out

Another important factor to keep in mind is: Most implementations will start small, and grow to be larger. Based on the scope, #users, risk appetite and possible investments, implementations will go through a few phases. The phases will progress toward the final setup that will meet all expectations / needs of the organization. Creating this roadmap is also an important part of solution architecting.

Requirements Understanding for Architecting

Every organization has a unique situation, and based on the stage of information evolution they are in, the needs of the organization will be different. Their constraints in terms of predefined collective notions and particularly the already made investments will be an important factor that decides what solution would work for them, and in which progressive phases. For each phase, the various needs could be different, as well as budgets. It is important to keep all this in mind and document them, so that the solution architecting process is done to meet their needs.

While the *Business Requirements Document (BRD)* gives the business needs of the enterprise, there are other factors that help arrive at the final QlikView Solution Architecture including the following:

- Business Constraints – existing hardware, new investment potential, risk appetite
- Security Needs / Guidelines
- Deployment Scale – Data Size, #Users, Refresh frequency
- Performance Considerations - Response Times, Reload windows, Concurrent usage
- Need for Multiple Environments for Dev/Test/Stage/Production/DR
- Need for High Availability, Failsafe, Load Balancing, Clustering
- Bulk / Volume Static Reporting Requirements
- Current Hardware/Software, Network Topology, Security, Data Center, Storage, etc

A *Solution Requirements Document (SRD)* summarizing these needs should be created, as an addendum to the BRD. Only with a complete understanding of these items, the right solution can be architected. And importantly, these needs can be different for different phases.

Reference Architectures

Based on the needs set out in the above analysis, the actual design of each phase should be decided. Deciding the Data, Software, Security and Physical arrangements for each phase is important, keeping in mind their needs. For each of these layers, there are reference architectures, which can be used as the ideal deployment methods. Based on constraints and difference in requirements, these reference architectures can be adapted, for any particular deployment.

Data Architecture: Figure 1 shows some possible data architectures. As a best practice, it is good to try and use the 5-stage data architecture discussed in the chapter "QlikView ETL". Even if it is a small deployment, following this structure makes future scaling effortless and synchronized. In a bid to do things faster, if this structure is not followed, it provides only marginal savings in time. Later, it will require rework to create enterprise wide deployment architecture.

Security Architecture generally follows the various Network, Authentication and Authorization layouts discussed in the chapter "QlikView Security".

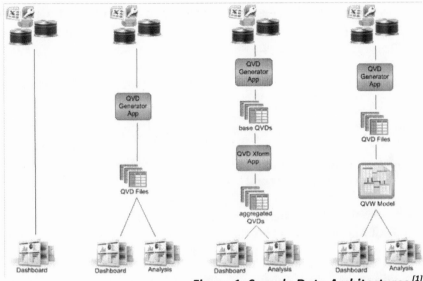

Figure 1: Sample Data Architectures [1]

Figure 2 provides the inter-relationships between various QlikView components from a security perspective.

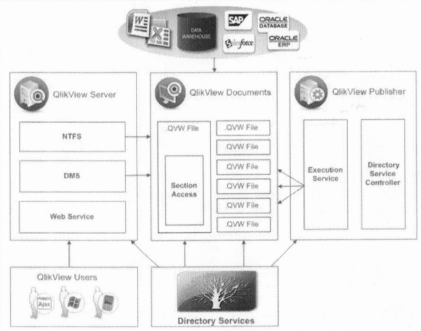

Figure 2: Security Architecture

From QlikView 11, the security architecture can be changed pretty easily by reconfiguring the settings in the unified QlikView Management Console and by introducing more servers. Earlier QlikView versions had multiple management interfaces for different components of QlikView, and it used to be difficult to make changes in the deployment plan.

Software Architecture sub-section provides a reference architecture, which needs to be used as a guideline for QlikView deployment.

Physical Architecture is essentially a more detailed view, where Security and Software layer elements are combined. It is with additional information about networking equipment like routers and switches, VLAN, combining everything into one detailed drawing. This, along with the Bill of Materials, provides the necessary inputs for the infrastructure folks to put the pieces together and provide the setup required.

This entirely depends on all the investments that the enterprise has

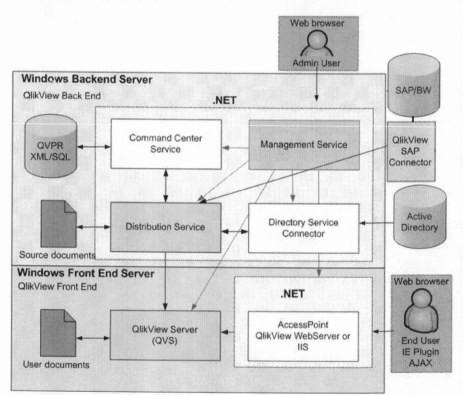

Figure 3: QlikView Product Architecture - Components relationship

made already, its preferred vendors and products they prefer or already procured (Servers/Storage/Routers/Software).

QlikView Software Architecture

QlikView has different components and they have a tight relationship with each other. The detailed information about what each component does is presented in the chapter "QlikView Components and User Roles". The Figure 3 gives the relationship of QlikView components with each other.

The Access Point, Server and Publisher layer can be scaled by adding multiple instances. Each of these layers can be a cluster of that layer. Each layer can thus scale independently, by adding more servers horizontally scaling into a cluster, or by vertically scaling with additional CPUs, Memory and Network Bandwidth. As mentioned before, a single QlikView Management Console can allow cluster configurations to be created, modified and managed very easily.

Patterns of Deployments

Real life requirements can be various subsets of this reference architecture. Generally based on every company setup, the deployment pattern chosen is different. Some of the sample deployment patterns are provided here for reference.

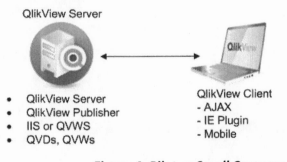

QlikView Server

- QlikView Server
- QlikView Publisher
- IIS or QVWS
- QVDs, QVWs

QlikView Client
- AJAX
- IE Plugin
- Mobile

Figure 4: Pilot or Small Company

Pilot Projects or Smaller Clients: This is typically a starting point for pilot projects and smaller clients who only have one server to utilize for their initial deployment of QlikView.

During pilots, based on the size of the hardware, appropriate subset of data needs to be chosen to ensure good performance.

Departmental Deployments: This pattern can be employed when a large (but not massive) number of users need to hit several small-to-medium sized applications and only two servers are available. The assumption here is that the load on Publisher is either small enough or isolated to overnight hours when usage of the servers is low. The use of Load Balancer is to help the users reach one IP address/URL, and automatically the right QlikView Server is allotted to respond to user.

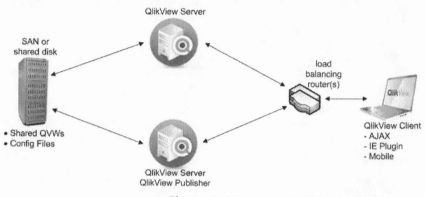

Figure 5: Departmental Deployments

Mid-Sized Enterprise Deployment: *Scenario Description:* This pattern can be employed when a large (but not massive) number of users need to hit several small-to-medium sized applications and the Publisher load is heavy enough to warrant its own server.

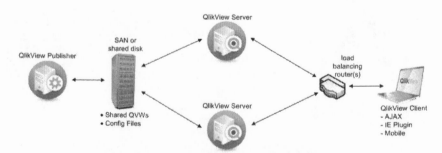

Figure 6: Mid-sized Enterprise (few departments) Deployment

The Publisher Server can also help with development and testing, as developers will be able to perform unit or test loads of applications with the Publisher server which do not impact the production QlikView servers. This is assuming that the Publisher server does the production reloads in overnight hours only, after the end-of-day processing on the source systems.

Mid-sized Enterprise-wide Deployment: This pattern can be employed when a large number of users need to hit several small-to-medium sized applications and only a few servers are available to load balance.

This is scaled for peak performance across applications. The number of applications & growth in data sizes can demand for scaling in Publisher layer also.

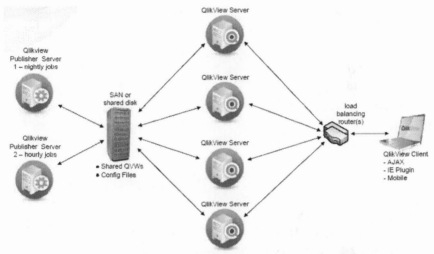

Figure 7: Mid-sized Enterprise-Wide Deployment

Large Enterprise with Multiple Large Departmental Groups: This pattern can be employed when there are multiple large departmental user groups that need high performance and do not want to share bandwidth and applications. This will provide separate production environments but retain a single "portal" for the customers to come in through.

The portal can control which Qlikview access points can be accessed based on user rights. Though the diagram does not show, scaling on Publisher can be done by adding more publisher servers like the previous pattern.

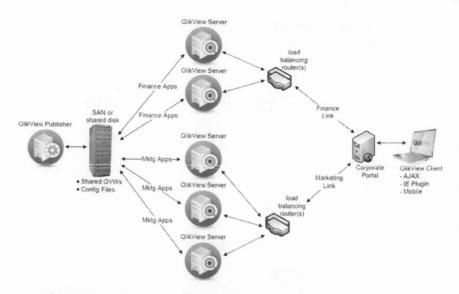

Figure 8: Large Enterprise with Multiple Large Department Groups
An Enterprise with Internal and Extranet Users: This pattern can be employed when there are multiple large departmental user groups, including external (public) users.

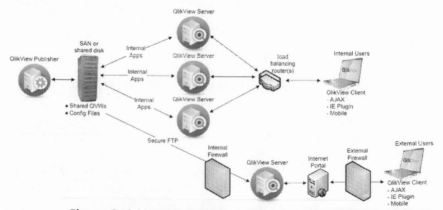

Figure 9: A Large Enterprise with Internal and Extranet Users
The internal applications are loaded on to an internal cluster of QlikView servers while the external users hit QlikView server in the "DMZ" between the external and internal firewalls. QVWs are secure FTP transferred each night from the internal SAN to the external QlikView Server so that there is no inward communication from that server to get these files.

Global Deployments with Remote User Centers: This pattern depicts a global deployment, where a central data center pushes reloaded QVDs to distributed user centers.

Each user center has QlikView servers to accommodate the high traffic and heavy usage of the applications. In order to better utilize the servers in each center, load balancing is used to pool them.

Please note that in all these situations discussed, the Access Points themselves can be made as the load balancing routers on clustered QV Servers. In situations where Access Points are clustered, the load balancing routers are required.

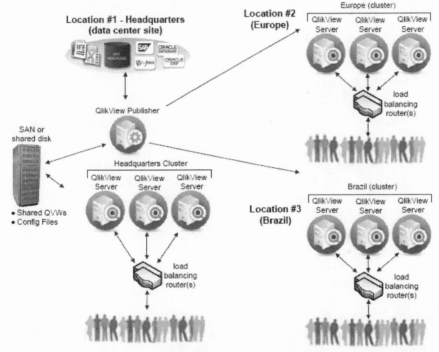

Figure 10: Global Deployment with Remote User Centers

Global Deployment—Remote Data Centers: This pattern depicts a global deployment, where multiple data centers are located in global sites. Users are located mostly in a central location.

Size of data extracted from remote data centers necessitates distributed reload servers depicted in Figure 11.

Based on the budget, #users and scope of requirement in any phase, a deployment pattern has to be decided for each of the phases.

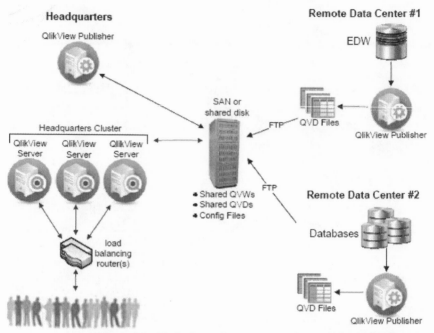

Figure 11: Global Deployment with Remote Data Centers

Care should be taken to ensure that the pattern of one phase should naturally evolve into the pattern of the next phase, by appropriate addition of items in each of the component layers of the complete architecture.

Multiple Environments and Version Management

While deploying any pattern, another aspect that needs to be kept in mind is the need for multiple environments: Development, User Testing and Production.

There are four possible environments that may be required: Development, Test, Pre-production and Production.

Depending on the rigor of practices in any company, the necessary environments are used. Typically, Development, QA/Test and Production environments are used.

When such multiple environments are created, the following necessary conditions should be maintained:

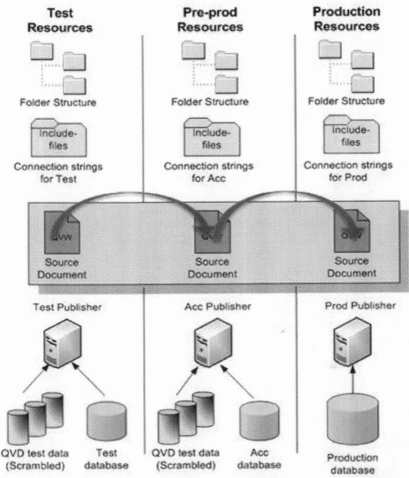

Figure 12: Multiple Environments – Dev/QA/Prod

- Document folder structure in each environment should be identical.
- Servers in the environments do not need to have the same hardware specs. VMs can be used as needed.
- When moving applications between the environments QlikView documents will automatically connect to different data sources depending on the connection strings in the include folders.

- This procedure will require that the databases for test and pre-prod are equivalent to the production databases.
- In lack of good test data a work around is to create scrambled QVD's from production & use for test. Use include-files for QVD loading.

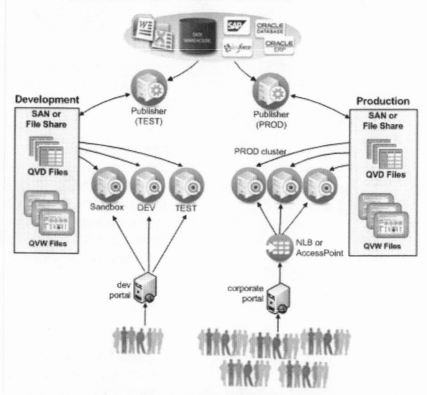

Figure 13: A Complex Sample of Multiple Environments

In large organizations with complex setups, multiple user groups and multiple development cycles, the setup can be even more complex. The adjacent diagram gives an approach that can be used for such complex scenarios. Additional environments can be added similarly, for Test or for Pre-Production as may be required.

The key aspect of this approach is the set of processes that are defined around the inter-operation of these environments. The way in which the applications are moved from one to another has to be managed using appropriate controls, version management and code management practices.

Source Control and Version Management

For the development environment, Version 11 supports integration with existing version control solutions like VSS. The modelers, developers and administrative users can check-in and check-out from the VSS to maintain the versions. The Source Control feature available in QlikView 11 is very useful for the purpose. The Source Control section of the QlikView Reference Manual provides more information on this: *Microsoft Source Control Plug-in API (MSSCCI) version 1.2 is the provider used for this function.* There are many MSSCCI provider DLLs that enable integration with different source control systems and are available for downloading. The functionality of the Source Control feature is provided in the manual.

The chapter on "QlikView Components and User Roles" highlights the various categories of users who would work in a QlikView deployment. All these users should be given definite job responsibilities, and should form part of various administrative and developmental processes that will form the QlikView solution management. The section on "Process" gives a more detailed view of the various aspects that need to be taken care of on an on-going basis. The source control features can be weaved into those processes to create an approval based development, testing and production deployment process.

Extranet Deployment

A key need in large deployments is to provide access to users from outside the internal network. This could be for internal employees traveling outside, field force or even extranet users – vendors / customers / partners. In all such situations, the need is to allow external access but protect the internal network from any unwanted breaches from unwanted sources outside. The chapter on "QlikView Security" discussed various measures taken for ensuring this protection.

One approach was discussed earlier in Global Deployments with Internal and External users: Keep a separate QlikView server located in the DMZ which is allowed to be accessed by users from outside. However, there are situations where this would not completely meet the need to provide access to the internal users traveling or extranet users who need more than just one application.

To take care of this need, alternative is to use Reverse Proxy setup.

- A reverse proxy is either a proxy server or network appliance.
- Typically, they are used in front of one or more Web servers.
- All connections from Internet are routed through them.
- They provide another layer of defense masquerading web servers behind the proxy.

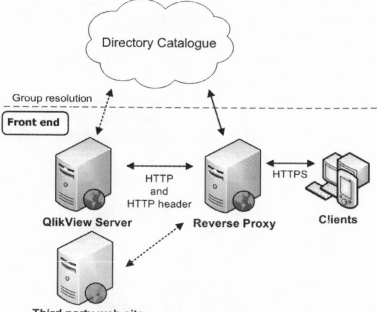

Figure 14: Extranet Access through Reverse Proxy

- Reverse proxies can also provide Application firewall features, to protect against common web-based attacks.
- Reverse proxies can provide Secure Socket Layer (SSL) connection from clients to itself, and the individual servers need not have SSL support.

The reverse proxy can also be configured to get users authenticated with the enterprise directory services like an AD or LDAP server as well. With reverse proxy, the authentication using NTLM or Basic Authentication can also be implemented using HTTP Header Injection method as discussed in the chapter on "QlikView Security".

Enterprise Scalability and Availability

When QlikView gets deployed in critical business decision support, the availability of the solution is extremely important. Also, with the growth of data sizes, the application response has to be consistently good, without any reduction in user response speeds. Hence the availability requirements are of two parts:

1. System response being good (within prescribed limits) always and
2. System not going out of service at any point in time, due to any failure in the system

Scalability

To ensure response speeds to be consistent as data grows, the scaling can happen horizontally – by expanding into more servers or vertically – by increasing memory, CPU and network bandwidth on the same server.

Horizontal Scaling: QlikView has various components inter-connecting with each other as explained earlier in the sub-section "QlikView Software Architecture". First level of horizontal scaling happens when the various parts of QlikView are expanded into different servers.

Second level of horizontal scaling happens when the same component of QlikView is run in multiple instances on more servers. This allows more users to use more applications, without reduction in response times, by moving some applications into other servers.

Horizontal Scaling is used typically when the number of users increases or the number of applications increases. This is used in conjunction with the Static Reduction (Splitting) of applications based on Section Access. The various deployment patterns given above are all ways of horizontal scaling.

Vertical Scaling: This is done by beefing up the servers with additional RAM, CPUs and additional network cards/bandwidth to support higher throughput. Memory is typically added when the data size increases and splitting into different applications is not possible. Also when such monolithic applications need more users to be supported, then additional CPUs are added. Sizing methodology of QlikTech should be used to decide how much memory / CPU should be added.

High Availability and Load Balancing with Clustering

When doing horizontal scaling, the multiple instances of the different components can be configured to work together, as a single instance of each component. The users should not need to choose which servers – Access Points and QlikView Servers - they need to login to use the services effectively. The need is to provide three important functionalities to support efficient enterprise deployments:

Load Balancing: The need is to have a mechanism which will automatically and transparently allocate user requests to the free/available instance of the application. This ensures that not one server is unduly loaded, giving skewed performance experiences to the users.

High Availability: Increase availability of applications, with the best response times. This is an effect of load balancing ensuring either automatic or manual distribution of applications.

Failsafe: In addition to these, even if one server fails, all requests are served by other server instance(s).

QlikView Clustering

The QlikView Clusters allow all the above three needs to be met. All the various deployment patterns provided earlier in this chapter may to use the Clustering capabilities of QlikView. Clustering is configured using the QlikView Enterprise Management Console. Please refer the Technical whitepaper: Clustering QlikView Servers [2].

QlikView Servers in a cluster support load sharing of documents across multiple physical or logical computers.

Common Storage: All servers point to the same physical location for the files. QlikView Server will create and maintain additional files to store load sharing data. These files will have a file type extension of .pgo (Persistent Group Object), and they will be located in the *Qlikview Server Root folder*.

This common storage can be in either NAS or SAN. This common storage will also store all associated files of users as well—Server Bookmarks, Shared Collaboration objects and Annotations— .shared files.

A detailed discussion on whether to use SAN or NAS is provided in the "Technical Brief – SAN vs. NAS" [3].

This sharing includes ability to share in real time, collaboration objects, automated document loading and unloading (through DMS), and user license CALs. Special cluster licensing is available to enable multiple server instances to share the same license number.

Managing Cluster Configurations: All the cluster configurations can

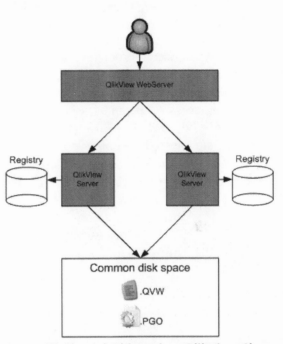

Figure 15: Shared Objects in a QlikView Cluster

be managed through the Enterprise Management Console. In earlier versions individual admin interfaces of respective components, were used for cluster configurations. The QlikView Server Manual provides extensive information about how to setup a cluster. In addition the "Technical Whitepaper: Clustering QlikView Servers" provides more detailed information. There are other references provided in the References Section for further reading. There are many QlikCommunity threads that discuss about Clustering of QlikView in addition to these.

Clustering of Publisher and Directory Services Connector: Both Distribution Service and Directory Services Connector can be clustered, like the Access Point and QlikView Servers. In order to cluster QlikView Distribution Service, the services will need a common disk area on a NAS to save the configuration file. The Directory Service Connector can employ load sharing and only when running Custom Users does it need a common disk area on a NAS for the different services.

Clustering Licenses: Clustering with QlikView requires separate licenses. This licensing allows the server licenses and user CALs to be shared. Also common storage of configuration and shared information can be shared through a common storage.

Load Share Clustering Approaches - Software and Hardware: Load sharing setup can be done for all the QlikView server components, each of them requiring an individual approach. For load sharing on QlikView Servers, the Access Point can be used as the Load Sharing – load allocation engine – *Software Based Clustering* setup. For QlikView Servers the clustering/load balancing can happen only through Access Points. However the Access point can be put behind hardware load balancing equipment to distribute the incoming requests across the two. Since authentication is involved in connecting users to Access Points, the sessions established once with one access point cannot be changed in the middle of the session to another. This needs to be ensured by the external load balancer.

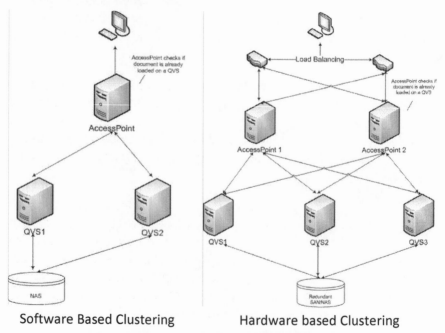

Software Based Clustering   Hardware based Clustering

Figure 16: Clustering Approaches

Publisher load sharing happens by appropriately configuring the tasks in a shared mode, and keeping a shared storage to handle the tasks. The

Enterprise Management Service will automatically allot different tasks to different Publisher instances keeping in view the current load conditions on each instance of the publisher. Directory Services Connectors just sit behind an external load balancing equipment, and receive requests that are sent to each instance by a round-robin allocation algorithm, much similar to the DNS servers.

Enterprise Volume Reporting with QlikView

QlikView is envisaged as an interactive analytic tool with excellent Data Discovery capabilities. However, in any organization, many users require information delivered to them for the purpose of transactional decision making, deciding which action should be done. These are typically reports and scorecards provided as every day reports/updates. If at all any interactivity is required, they are all pre-defined drill-down hierarchies without the need for true data discovery. Most of the times, there is no need even for this interactivity and the information is presented in a static report format - such information needs to be sent to the consuming users in the form of a mail, or placed in a directory so that they can access it through a portal / document distribution mechanism.

Static Report Distribution: The QlikView solution to provide these static reports / outputs is the PDF Distribution. This is a separate licensed feature that works on top of the Publisher. PDF reports can be defined in the actual QlikView application as part of development / updates. From the PDF distribution console, any report of any application can be chosen for distribution.

When distributing PDF reports to multiple users, Publisher can honor the Section Access definitions. For every report, the recipient users can be defined as the first level of access restriction. As the next level of control, the Publisher allows definition of what is referred as Loop, Reduce and Distribute capability. With the Static Reduction discussed in the chapter on "QlikView Security", PDF reports are also subjected to Section Access restrictions with the use of Loop, Reduce and Distribute settings.

The tasks of PDF distribution should naturally be scheduled after all the tasks belonging to the various stages of ETL. The Loop and Reduce (L&R) and Loop and Distribute (L&D) features require fields that would act as the filters for them. Typically, L&R and L&D tasks should be part of the same job. Actually there is no need to write any code for implementing this, since Publisher supports both these task types. Ideally, once the necessary loop filter fields are defined in the application, a QV Administrator should be able to take care of the administration of user-application mappings.

The PDF Publisher uses the QlikView PDF Printer driver that is given free of cost by QlikTech. BullZip and other PDF printer drivers can also be used to get the same effects.

Apart from the PDF Publisher option of QlikTech, there are 3rd party solutions from NPrinting and Team (Q-Reporter) which provide similar functionality. Particularly with older versions of QlikView, the PDF Publisher was not available and these solutions were quite useful. Also, in situations where complexity is low and cost is a pressure, solutions for publishing as PDF can be built using the APIs and Macros/Actions/Exports. Such custom developed utilities can also support export of these reports into Excel, Text and XML for further feeding into other downstream software.

Limited Interactivity Reports: When the true data discovery is not required for a set of transactional users, the current licensing of QlikView may get very expensive for large organizations with a large number of information consumers. The need could be for a limited interactive report. Currently there are no solutions available from QlikTech to meet this requirement. It is either full interactivity or no-interactivity in information consumption. Using the various APIs, it is possible to create an application that could export the data and wrap it into a flash based or excel based pivot table and such. This is currently a time consuming exercise, and probably some companies would come up with a 3rd Party Solution sometime soon. One such solution available is QVExcel (http://www.qvexcel.com). Alerts in QlikView are another reporting option, and is discussed more in page 405.

QlikView as an ETL + another reporting front-end: Another radical approach is to push the Stage 3 QVDs after ETL into an open SQL platform (SQL Server, Oracle DB, Informix, DB2, MySQL, etc.) as a star / snow-flake schema based Data Warehouse (DWH). In this approach, QlikView functions as an extremely efficient and cost effective ETL tool for the enterprise data processing. The other approach could also be to push all the tables of the QlikView User Applications into these open SQL platforms and keep them as separate Data Marts to address needs of each of the departments/user groups using this data set. Then using existing tools like MSRS, 1Key, Microstrategy or BO etc., which the enterprise has already invested in, the necessary reports can be provided to meet the need for limited interactivity for the users who need, at an affordable cost. While these workarounds may be required for some more time, QlikTech is expected to come with a solution for this purpose sometime soon, to counter similar solutions available from Business Objects and others. This opening out of data from QlikView, to be used by other tools would be a great step forward towards democratization of data, driven by QlikView.

Performance Considerations

Performance of QlikView applications is impacted by following factors:
Inherent QlikView Characteristics
1. Amount of Data
2. Number of concurrent users at any point in time
3. Number of calculations / KPIs done in all the screens being accessed by the users at any time

External Characteristics
1. Size of hardware – 32/64 bit, number of CPUs and Memory
2. Network bandwidth – from users' browser to the Access Point and QlikView Server

For the inherent QlikView characteristics, there are many best practices available for improvement of performance: Load Scripts, Data Model and the Visual Application front-end. The Load Script and Data Model best practices have been discussed extensively in the chapters on "QlikView in Depth", "QlikView ETL" and "QlikView Data Modelling" in Part II. The clustering features discussed earlier in this chapter also help extensively in handling these aspects.

The Application front-end best practices are not covered in this book, though some discussions around it and a checklist are present in the chapter "Making QlikView Work". There are extensive discussions, documents available in the forums and in QlikTech website to help learn best practices for QlikView Application Development. Starting with QlikView Reference Manual, the most interesting readings around this are provided in the References section. This book aims to address all the other aspects except the actual front-end development which is very evident and naturally the most understood. With the online tutorials and training material, and the intuitive nature of the product, development is learnt very quickly and with limited class room training.

The hardware and network factors play a key role, and it is important to ensure the impacts of the choices made here are well understood. One is to ensure that the right hardware is deployed, and the other is to understand how QlikView is equipped to make use of better hardware.

Memory: This is a very important factor for the good functioning of QlikView applications. The necessary amount of memory is easily identified by using QlikView Optimizer application. By generating a .MEM file from the application, and then loading this into the Optimizer application, the amount of memory required for the expected number of simultaneous users, can be found out. This is very useful to get an initial understanding of how much memory is required - sizing sub-section later in this chapter dwells more on this.

CPU: 64 bit processors are becoming more common, and they are naturally much better than the 32 bit counterparts. One of the most important factors is the amount of memory addressable in a 64 bit processor is much higher. QlikView Server is available for Windows 2003 Server for 64-Bit Extended Systems (x64). 64-bit memory addressing eliminates the 2-3 GB per task virtual memory limitation, and provides for access to up to 512 GB of virtual memory in a Windows 2003 64-bit Datacenter Edition Server OS, with a theoretical limit of 512 Petabytes. This will eliminate memory bottleneck completely.

In addition, improved multi-threading of the internal memory manager has led to significantly higher utilization of multiple processor cores in environments with many users and documents.

Network Bandwidth: The bandwidth can pose problems in two areas:
   a) ETL – while extracting data from the various data sources, and while transferring data to be consolidated in one or various places as required.

b) User Access – while users access the applications from their browser front-ends.

With ETL processes, it is important to get the data extracted in distributed centers onto a local QVD extractor instance. Once the data is all saved as QVDs, the size is reduced significantly, and from there, the QVD files can be syndicated into the places where they are required. The amount of data reduction is as high as 60 to 90% depending on the type of data. This can lead to significant savings of time and bandwidth usage to transfer data across the enterprise for reporting purposes.

With User Access, the typical bandwidth required for each user is in the range of 2 kbps per user for interactive analytics on an average in a typical implementation. The data stays in the QlikView server and all the processing is done in the server. The information about the visual display refresh is sent across the network to the local browser client, and the browser now completes the rendering of the visual front-end. This is more like Citrix though it is more sophisticated than simple screen refresh. Many of the front-end renderings are taken care of by the browser client – either plug-in or Ajax.

Depending on the number of interactive clicks on the QlikView applications by a user, data is transferred from server to the browser and vice versa. The amount of data that is transferred is very low and that's why about 2 kbps bandwidth is required. If there are large number of data points being updated in the individual charts, and more charts are present in a single page/sheet, the response over the network could get slow.

ETL Process Performance: Earlier versions of the Publisher used to load the QVW applications for every value of the filters set for Loop and Reduce/Distribute. This used to take a lot of load/unload time for completing the ETL. Now with the Version 11 Publisher, the document is loaded once into memory and the various Loop and reduce/distribute steps are done in one load without having to load and unload. This shall reduce the load due to the publisher jobs. Also, the ability to chain tasks in a complex fashion now can help implementing complex dependency tree based reload sequences, to reduce the overall time taken by the ETL processes.

Managing Data Growth Issues: When the data size grows continuously, the performance gradually degrades, given the same application and number of users. There is a need to optimize how much data is required for the actual analysis. Various techniques including Telescopic Summarization can be deployed, and in many situations unwanted data need not be included into the QlikView applications. Proactively using such measures ensures that the performance does not become a problem and frequent upgrade of hardware is not required. For more information on this, refer to chapters on "QlikView ETL" and "QlikView Data Modelling".

Enterprise Integration of QlikView

QlikView offers a variety of integration points to meet the many needs of enterprise deployments. The previous chapters have discussed about each of the following integration points. This diagram summarizes all the integration capabilities in a single casual snapshot.

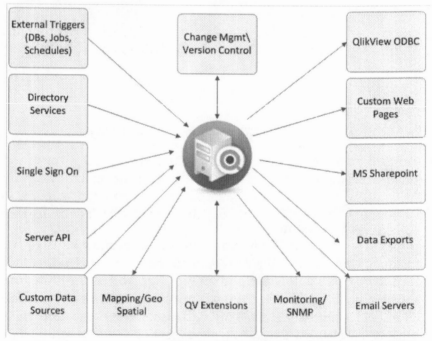

Figure 17: Integration Features of QlikView

Several tools can be used as inputs to feed into QlikView to drive security, scheduling, single sign-on and API functions. There are also two-way integrations with mapping tools and the new QlikView 11 extension objects, as well as integration points outward from QlikView to accommodate portal integration, downstream systems, monitoring and communications. New APIs to manage QlikView Server environments are available with QlikView 11. These enable a finer control and automation than ever before and allow enterprise ETL schedules to be integrated with QlikView ETL schedules with seamless coordination. Features are grouped into five integration categories:

ETL Integration: Custom Data Sources (QVX, SAP Connector, SFDC Connector, etc), External Triggers (EDX - DBs, Jobs and Schedules) and Data Exports. QlikView ODBC existed in older versions up to 4.03 to allow other programs to read data from QlikView Files (QVW). This will be a great integration point if supported and evolved further.

Security Integration: Directory Services Connector and Single-Sign-On (Custom Ticket Exchange)

Front-End Integration and Extensions: Custom Web Pages (Workbench), MS Sharepoint (Web Parts), Mapping / Geo Spatial, QV Extensions (Extension API), Automation API, OCX API and AJAX Javascript API

Server Integration: Server API (QMS), Monitoring / SNMP, Email Servers and Collaboration (Annotation) features

Development Integration: Version Control and Change Management

Integration features have been improved from version 8.5 onwards and remain to be a major focus for QlikView. As more enterprises push QlikView deeper within their organizations and to broader audiences in & outside their organizations, integration needs will continue to expand.

The real integration capabilities are taken advantage of, primarily by the OEM Customers across the world, who have integrated QlikView seamlessly as an integral part of their offerings. Large enterprises can benefit greatly by taking advantage of these integration capabilities. The extent to which their productivity can be improved, and their information availability can be extended would be mind boggling, if all the features are put to good use.

Integrating Advanced Analytics and QlikView

QlikView provides an excellent way to slice and dice the data, in any order or hierarchy sequence. It gives a great way to get insights into the past by exploring various possible associations. However, understanding patterns of behavior is still a manual exercise, trying to correlate between data across selection sets and understanding the semantic patterns in data. In addition to slicing and dicing of the past, QlikView provides to some extent the ability to project into the future, but using standard mathematical extrapolation equation – this is implemented using "What-if Analysis".

There are many statistical and mining techniques, which automatically help identify the semantic correlations and higher-degree relationships in a given data set. Statistical Analysis like Clustering, or predictive Modelling using algorithms like Bayesian or Decision Trees Analysis are certainly extremely useful techniques to make more use of available data. In a nutshell, such algorithms generate data that don't already exist in the dataset, by labeling patterns, or using trends to predict unknown values for select fields.

Applications like R, SAS and other statistical analysis and data mining tools provide algorithms to perform these advanced analytics. Such algorithms provide derived characteristics to the existing data, which allow us to group them in different intuitive ways, using the new data that is created. The clustering algorithm can create a new CLUSTER label for each data row.

Decision Trees can predict values of fields like "CHURN" with a probability of churn, by learning from already churned data. Most of these Statistical Analysis / Data Mining tools do not have a great data discovery front-end, nothing to match the capabilities of QlikView.

With the Extension API, QlikView allows integration of such advanced analytics and use the analysis results seamlessly inside the QlikView application itself. QlikView technical brief document "Integrating QlikView with R" provides an in-depth view of how integration can be done using the Extensions API, and COM interfaces of R package. Example integration has been done to demonstrate this capability and presented in QlikView Technical Brief "Integrating QlikView with R" [4].

The integration requires installation of all StatconnDCOM Server, RCOM and rscproxy. Once these are installed, Visual Basic script is used to call

R from QlikView application and perform the desired R functions on the selected QlikView data. The following screenshot is taken from the example application: Cluster Analysis.QVW. The sales data is available at order level, and contains zip codes. The example uses the R clustering algorithm (K-Means Clustering) to segment the zip codes by order frequency, average order size and customer count metrics.

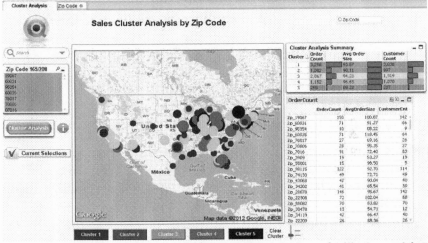

Figure 18: Integration of QlikView with R

Clustering is an advanced statistical method which is the task of assigning a set of objects into groups (called clusters) so that the objects in the same cluster are more similar (in some sense or another) to each other than to those in other clusters. Clustering is a main task of explorative data mining, and a common technique for statistical data analysis used in many fields. In this example, R is used to achieve clustering of selected zip codes into 5 groups based on similarities of order count, average order size and customer count. This data does not exist in the source data, but needs to be created by using the Cluster algorithm.

With some VB Scripting using the features of Extension API, the following steps are done:

- The data that is selected table is placed in the clipboard
- R functions are called to do the following:
- Read table data from clipboard
- Run K-Means function on the table

- Get the cluster result into QlikView as an array
- Update the array values back into the table that was sent as source data using UPDATE

The technical brief gives a step-by-step process to integrate R with QlikView. While this example discusses integration with R, it is possible to integrate any application that provides a COM bridge very easily. In case there is no COM bridge, then data files can be used to send data from and receive data to QlikView during run-time using Extension API. As an aside, it is interesting to see how R is competing with SAS - read the discussions on the LinkedIn discussions: SAS vs. R [5].

QlikView & the Cloud

Any enterprise wanting to run QlikView on an off-premise "Cloud" infrastructure can do so by using the QlikView image available on Amazon EC2 cloud. This can allow enterprises to create off-premise, often distributed deployment of QlikView. In essence, running QlikView on Amazon EC2 is very much like running QlikView in-premise. The licenses for QlikView are required to be purchased. The software distribution need not be installed on the Amazon EC2, but a ready-made image of QlikView already available on the Amazon can be chosen and deployed in no time. Refer how QlikTech uses Amazon to run the Demo environment [6].

The key aspect is, like any other cloud deployment, data stays in cloud. Where enterprises have their current data in the enterprise data center, then moving the data to the cloud could become a bandwidth intensive exercise. Extraction of data into QVDs from their source, and transferring QVD files over to the cloud server is a good way to optimize bandwidth and storage usage. Even if applications like CRM etc. are already in cloud, they exist in separate service providers, and the data still needs to be transferred to the virtual server where QlikView is running. Bandwidth will still be used for the same amount of data.

Following are some key situations when an enterprise can look at cloud:

1. Quick pilot to be done, without waiting for infrastructure additions
2. Do not want the upfront capital costs for server hardware
3. Need a flexible quickly scalable solution

4. Relatively less amount of incremental data being generated
5. As for security, the features of security discussed in chapter "QlikView Security" are relevant in the cloud deployment as well. Integration with data sources and portals are all the same as the in-premise deployments.

Some of the benefits in using cloud deployments include:

- Zero infrastructure requirements - Elastic scalability
- Instantly available - Users are up and running in 15 minutes
- Standard QlikView user license pricing (licenses can be moved from and to cloud)
- Shifts expenses from capital expenditures to operational expenditures
- Platform neutrality - Available through Amazon's fast and reliable Elastic Compute Cloud (EC2) Web service

Currently, most organizations cannot move completely to cloud, but need a coexistence of in-premise and cloud infrastructure/solutions. QlikView can also be implemented in a hybrid fashion, to take advantage of the cloud benefits. QlikView is not available as a "Saas" or a "PaaS" offering at the moment. OEM offering of QlikView allows OEM customers to custom license QlikView and deploy on a multi-home/multi-tenant servers to offer pay-per-use services. For more information, refer to QlikView Blog: "QlikView and the Cloud - Have it your way" [7] and QlikCommunity discussion "QlikView in the Cloud" [8].

Processes around QlikView Deployment and Maintenance

As discussed earlier in this chapter, the key aspects of deploying QlikView successfully include: Architecture, Integration and Processes during and after the deployment. This section focuses on the processes that are required. The chapters in Part I focused on setting the base for the various methodologies and processes that are required to be used at various stages of QlikView deployment.

This section summarizes some of the key elements and discusses on establishing some processes for regular upkeep and maintenance of QlikView to be productive and successful in an on-going basis.

The processes around QlikView can be defined in three parts: a) Planning and preparations for QlikView Deployment, b) Deployment Processes and c) On-going Processes to make sure QlikView is successfully used in the enterprise.

Planning and Preparations: The planning and preparations were discussed in Part I, in chapters on "What should be the QlikView Strategy for my Company?" and "What benefits can be expected from QlikView?"

Three most important factors include: a) Detailed Business Requirements understanding and b) Defining the Data Dictionary with every data element identified – primary dimensions and measures and secondary / derived dimensions and measures, c) Common Definitions of all the metrics that are used inside the enterprise, to measure and compare performance of every aspect of the business.

Once these definitions are created, the important need is to create the entire data definition in a format which can be used in the data lineage application in QlikView. QlikView allows Metadata to be managed in an easy and efficient way, rather than using complex metadata control systems.

As a part of on-going maintenance of QlikView deployment, metadata is an important part, and is discussed in detail in a later sub-section. Creation of the data dictionary was discussed in detail in the chapter on "QlikView ETL" as well.

Preparation of following key documents forms the completion of Planning and Preparation stage:

1. Business Requirement Document (BRD)
2. Solution Design Document (SDD)
3. Enterprise Data Dictionary (EDD)
4. Common Enterprise Definitions (CED) for metrics

Once these are prepared the deployment can start, on the arrival of all the items in the bill of materials (BOM) as a part of the Solution Design Document (SDD).

Deployment Processes: The various documents that are created as part of the Solution Design Document (SDD) require to be implemented. Each design finalized - Physical Hardware and Networks, Data Flow, Software and Security – need to be discussed with appropriate authorities in the enterprise, and implemented on the ground.

Test acceptance processes for each of this need to be created and later followed and audited certificates of acceptance need to be provided to further progress on a production release of the systems. Generally, these processes are part of the organization IT compliance processes. Involving the right people in the right times is the key to completing the deployment.

On-Going Processes

While the other processes have been outlined elsewhere in this book, the on-going QlikView maintenance process is the focus of this section. The key aspects that need constant attention and execution include:

- Publishing workflow
- Metadata understanding and management
- User Classification, Identification and Management
- Usage Monitoring and Management
- License Planning
- Performance Audit and Improvements

Each of these items is extremely important for a healthy upkeep of QlikView and its constant value improvement. If these processes are constantly followed and managed strictly with complete adherence, the enterprise will receive exceptional value from QlikView. These are the basis for the famous Land and Expand strategy of business intelligence deployments.

Publishing Work-Flow

In the chapter on "QlikView Components and User Roles", the QlikView application development process was divided into three parts: QlikView Modelling, QlikView Application Development and QlikView Administration.

The QlikView Modelling and Development are done when the first time the application is created or when there are improvements / changes done on the same application – with new versions being released. The QlikView Administration role manages the remaining life-cycle of the application using a process like the following:

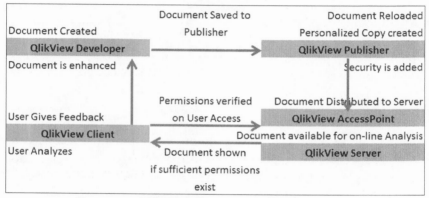

Figure 19: QlikView Document Life-Cycle Process Overview

The QlikView Administration involves the following aspects:

a. Deploying the application for testing and then on production server

b. Setting up the section access and schedules for Reload

c. Performing Loop and Reduce and create personalized applications - Reducing data by looking up security from AD via DSC

d. Adding security entries to the personalized application

e. Distributing the application on QlikView Server—distributing to QVS (port 4747) or by file copy to the shared storage location—QVS sets security right given by QDS and saves the document

f. Monitoring usage of the application, collecting statistics and making necessary changes

Defining owners, approval processes if any, for managing these processes is extremely important. Appropriate communications to every stake holder is important for the QlikView eco-system inside the company to work seamlessly.

Bridging the Metadata Gap

QlikView is a tool that can democratize data and allow everyone in the organization to get insights by the excellent data discovery capabilities it provides. QlikView can literally make all the fields from all the tables across all the systems to be available in the hands of all the interested users. However the practical challenges include:

Business Users esp. Analysts need to understand:

1. Which field means what?
2. Where does the data of any field come from? (Ability to trace)
3. What are the pre-processes done for this field while populating?
4. The common accepted definition of each of the metrics / KPIs
5. The formula used for various calculated columns

IT Administrators need to understand:

6. Who is using which data?
7. Whether the data is being used the right way?
8. Know who all will be affected if some change is done to a data element in the source

Developers need to understand:

9. Know what re-usable components are at their disposal

This is essentially the Metadata gap that needs to be filled to improve the effectiveness of the QlikView applications. The need is to have Metadata that should be able to answer all these queries, so that the context of analysis is understood properly, and data can be appropriately used by the data users. Preferably this metadata should be available as part of the applications, or next to the applications, so that referring this data becomes easy and quick. The QlikView Metadata White Paper lays the foundation for the approach [9].

QlikView takes a pragmatic view of metadata, balancing the speed of deployment, with oversight and control. QlikView handles three forms of metadata: Descriptive, Administrative and Structural. The glue that binds all these information together is the QlikView document.

As administrators, developers or business users look at the descriptive data for a QlikView document, they can also see the administrative and structural metadata.

With QlikView metadata capabilities, the key differentiators are:

a) Metadata Management is optional and pervasive,

b) The focus is on QlikView itself, within itself and

c) Developers & administrators can introduce metadata over time.

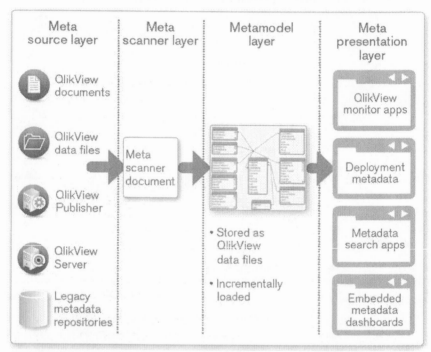

Figure 20: Architectural Overview of QlikView Metadata Model

The Metamodel of QlikView is presented in the diagram here. In this model, no additional tools are needed — just QlikView. The Meta Scanner QVW collects all the data from the various components of QlikView. This data is stored in a set of QVDs that form Metamodel layer. The blog of Erica Driver, "QlikView's Pragmatic Approach to Metadata" gives some good insights [10].

Using this Meta QVD model, different presentation layers can be created, to make use of the data collected from all the sources. The log files, the lineage information, the usage and performance data, can all be used to administer and manage the QlikView implementation effectively.

There is a sample application created by QlikTech, provided along with the QlikView installation – OpsMonitor.QVW. This application provides very useful information out of the box. The application screen shot is provided here for reference.

The Metascanner application and the MetaMonitor application are provided for download in the QlikCommunity threads [11, 12].

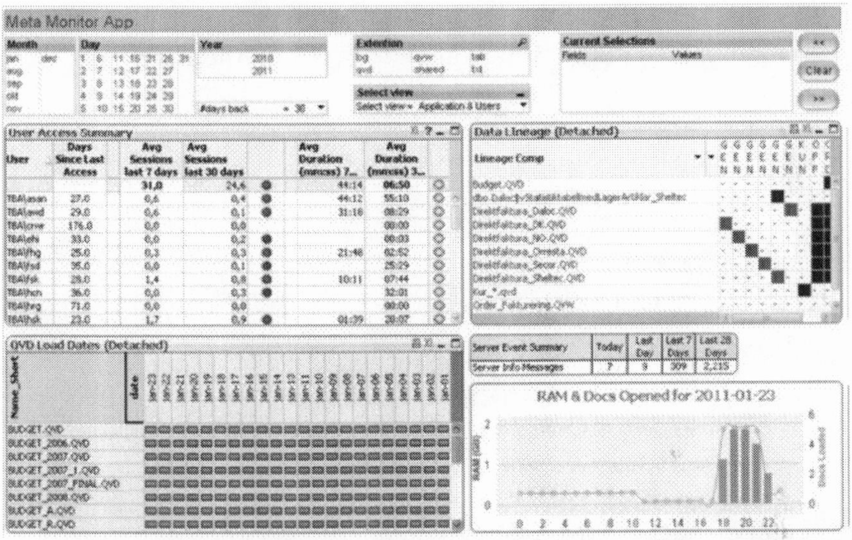

Figure 21: Meta Monitor Application showing all three metadata

The data lineage is required for business users. Administrative and structural information are required for the IT professionals for handling the regular QlikView processes. It is a good idea to create separate Data Lineage applications and deploy along with the other applications. Another approach is to integrate data lineage information into each application, so that the information is available in the context of usage itself, with the necessary access control.

User Management

Every user who has access to information from the QlikView setup needs to be added in the user database. As seen in the chapter on "QlikView Security", the user data can reside in any of the user identity authentication repositories and access authorization repositories.

1. Authentication Data: Adding / Modifying / Deleting users, managing their passwords to protect their identity is normally done in the Authentication / Identity repositories. These are typically in the ADS or LDAP in most cases. In some of the SAP driven companies, the SAP ID is used as the identity for the user across all the applications. For extranet users, the identity information could normally stay in custom SQL databases.
2. Access Authorization Data: The authorization information is stored either in the file system (NTFS) or in the DMS service of QlikView. In addition, the user's membership in various groups is stored in AD servers or other LDAP solutions as well. The combination of the two is required for the implementation of Access Authorization.
3. Section Access Authorization Data: In addition, the section access requires definition of which user has access to what information inside the allowed applications. This also needs to be done as part of the Authorization for the users.

The processes around these three change management points are important along with appropriate approval mechanisms. Normally, this process is integrated with the HR processes so that any changes in the life-cycle of the user can be reflected easily. When large numbers of users are present, particularly from the extranet side, the need is to update their credentials in the DMS. This could be a daunting task if done manually. There are different ways to populate the DMS:

- Enter manually in the Management Console
- QlikView Publisher writes DMS users and groups via QlikView Server. This is done by the Directory Service Connector (DSC) and DSP plug-ins for directory sources.
- Programmatically using API's (DEMO)

Based on the enterprise user management process, any of these approaches could be used. The need is to have a defined process to be followed systematically since this will be a key element of successful QlikView deployment and usage. Definition of the user management process is an integral part of the Solution Architecting process.

User Classification on Information Needs

The information needs of the organization are of four categories:

1. Flexible Interactive Analysis – Data Discovery – Dashboards and Slicing & Dicing – QlikView Named and Document CALs are meant to serve this purpose.
2. Limited Interactive Analysis – Combination of Session and Usage CALs are meant to serve this purpose. The other approach is to export data to XLS and send for consumption. Third alternative is to have data pushed into an open SQL system and allow use of other front-ends.
3. Static Reports – Fixed format reports on PDF – Detailed Reports – PDF Publisher is the solution from QlikView for this. For light-weight needs, custom reporting is also possible using the Automation APIs/Macros/Actions.
4. Static Short-Message (summary / current status) Consumers – Scorecards – Alerts from QlikView can be used for this.

Users have needs for all these forms of information. The matrix below gives a summary view of typical needs in a typical company.

Table 1: Typical User Needs of Any Company

User Category	Data Discovery & Collaboration	Limited Filtering	Static Reports	Short Updates
Top Management	Yes	Yes	Yes	Yes
Senior Managers	Yes	Yes	Yes	Yes
Analysts	Yes	Yes	Yes	Yes
Line Managers		Yes	Yes	Yes
Executives		Yes	Yes	Yes
Occasional Users			Yes	Yes

The need is to identify the various user needs and plot them in this matrix as appropriate for the enterprise. This will give a deep understanding of the needs of the organization, and set the priorities for what should be done when, helping in defining phases of deployment. Typically, in all QlikView implementations, Data Discovery and Static Report needs are covered very well. The Limited Filtering and Short Update needs are not given the necessary attention and hence the solution architecture is generally wanting in these two areas. Generally, in a data-driven company, the need for Static Reports (Scorecards) and Short Updates (Sales Flash, etc) are required to reach the largest population. Any solution/architecture that does not address these two requirements, do not do justice as Enterprise-wide Information Systems.

License Planning

In addition to this, the number of QlikView applications that each person should have access to in the Data Discovery and Limited Filtering categories—will decide who should be given Named CALs, Document CALs, Session CALs and Usage CALs.

User Licenses: Lowest frequency users (few times a month) will generally require Usage CALs. Medium frequency users (few times a week) will be able to use Session CALs. Frequent users (many times a day) with just one or two QlikView applications would be right fit for Document CALs. Power users who require access to many QlikView applications (many times a day) will require Named CALs.

Static Reports for users can be provided by the use of PDF Publisher. Short Updates can be provided by use of Alerts defined in the applications, triggered at the time of reloads. Users that receive information in these two methods need not be licensed on an individual basis for QlikView access. PDF Publisher is a server license and Alerts can be sent to anyone whose email ID is known.

For large extranet users, who are occasional users, there is a special Session CALs option available.

Server Licenses: Typically, in a full-blown implementation, licenses are required for QlikView Server(s), QlikView Publisher(s), PDF Publisher, Test Server, Cluster License and Sharepoint Web-parts. Directory Services Connector, Access Point, QlikView HTTP Server and Management Console come with no additional licenses. If extranet QlikView applications need to be deployed, like Dealer Performance, etc., Extranet Server is required.

Other QlikView Licenses: Workbench and SAP Connector are external licenses required based on the requirements. Workbench is required when custom QlikView front-ends need to be created, particularly for extranet applications or for public internet applications.

Usage Planning, Monitoring and Usage Management

Usage of the QlikView applications by nature takes a hockey-stick trend – initial excitement that slows down due to gaps in data, presentation and implementation. Then once these are fixed and depending on the change management effectiveness, the usage ramps up. Sometimes the ramp up is so fast that the resources allocated are not enough to deliver. Then QlikView enters into an "its-not-as-easy-as-you-said" phase and gets caught in rough weather. They key to solve this is the usage planning, with fair prediction of load and needs.

Planning: Based on above combination of users / applications / analysis-types sizing of hardware, number of licenses and security measures should be done. This planning is many times difficult, needing inputs from various quarters of the enterprise. However, if the architecture is done without this, the solution is likely to break in its seams more often than not. The usage planning should also involve response times, periods of usage, geography of usage, simultaneous users and data growth projections, and should be included as part of the Solution Requirements Document (SRD).

Monitoring: As with any other systems, the usage of QlikView needs to be monitored on a constant basis to achieve the following end-results:
1. Understand which users are using and how much. Who are not?
2. Applications most used, and least used. Including which parts of the application.
3. Performance of applications – user response and reload times.
4. Data growth trends and identifying useful windows of data inclusion.

All these information are captured in various log files, and the OpsMonitor provides the syndication of these log files, and allows these trends to be monitored regularly.

Management: A set of processes should be defined for monitoring these. Most importantly, threshold levels for each metric should be defined, so that any measure that crosses alarm levels should be identified. In such situations, a sequence of corrective measures should be triggered as part of the process. This management is an essential part of making a QlikView implementation a success. The criteria for success are the usage of the system, and this management process will continue to focus on successful usage and improve it.

One of the important steps to drive success of QlikView deployment is to monitor the trends of usage. Focusing on the low volume users and providing what could increase the value they get from QlikView is important. Also, continuously understand new needs of the best users, and providing those is important.

Constant Monitoring and Re-allocation of Licenses: The OpsMonitor allows monitoring usage of QlikView Applications by various users. In spite of all the initiatives to provide additional value to all users, some users tend not to use at all, due to their lack of interest or other pressures. Identifying these users and releasing their licenses to be used by other needy / interested users is an important step, to constantly drive value – a better ROI on QlikView.

Performance Audit and Improvements

Regular monitoring and management processes focus on user traction and meet their functional needs. During this monitoring, performance degradations happening in the system should also be identified.

Whenever any such degradation of the system is visible, requiring additional hardware or software to beef up performance, the need is to have an Audit done by expert QlikView professionals. Such Expert Service Audits look at the complete QlikView application life-cycle, and identify the weak links of the current deployment. They also identify what could be done in the current deployment to improve the overall performance, and prevent further degradation.

QlikView is fundamentally an agile implementation product, allowing quick and easy changes to meet new requirements relatively quickly. However, because of this, erroneous methods may be introduced to produce the required right results. Though the requirements are met, over time, the unwanted deviations in process/practice, may lead to degradation of performance. Without affecting the speed of agile gratification to the users, the performance deviations should be kept under check, by periodic audits and health checks. This ensures continuous health, without affecting the nimbleness of the solution.

Based on such audits, the expert services teams from QlikTech and other experienced partners like Team, Climber, etc., can suggest improvement methods & implement the same. A process should be defined in each implementation to have such Quality/Process Audits and Performance Reviews done periodically. It could be as frequent as every quarter in complex multi-departmental deployments, to once a year in relatively slowly changing environments. Keeping the QlikView eco-system nimble and highly responsive is an important element to delivering the promise of BI, and QlikView in specific.

Concluding Remarks on Deployment

Generally deployment is seen as a project to get the QlikView components up and running, along with the first few applications, as part of the first deliverable. But in reality, deployment has a starting point – when the solution is procured – but there is no end to it. From one stage of evolution, the solution keeps evolving to continually help address more information needs and support more decision making. Also, every application created will go through changes as the decision making process gets refined and gets more data driven.

Deployments need to evolve and grow along with the business in a synergistic mode. Good QlikView deployments can change the fundamental way in which a business is run, and change the culture of the organization. Like the Sloan MIT – IBM study highlights, the data-driven culture highly correlates to high-performance of companies with better profitability and growth trends. QlikView is a great tool to enhance the data-driven cultures, by not just making data available easily, but allow insights to come easier than most other solutions available. Hence, QlikView can play a very important role, if used well, in increasing the inherent value of the organizations. Appropriate architecture, leading to a fitting deployment and continuous management of the deployment, are key aspects of this success.

The key purpose that QlikView will help achieve is – the Analytical Quotient of the enterprise will be increased. This one single outcome can increase the likelihood of the organization to be more profitable and grow sustainably [13, 14].

References

1.   QlikView Data Architectures, Presentation from QlikCommunity,

2.   Technical White Paper: Clustering QlikView Servers, Dec 2010, QlikView.com, [http://community.qlikview.com/servlet/

JiveServlet/previewBody/1883-102-1-
1867/Clustering%20QV%20Servers.pdf]

3. SAN vs. NAS – Technical Brief, QlikView.com,
[http://www.qlikview.com/us/~/media/Files/resource-
library/global-us/direct/datasheets/DS-Technical-Brief-SAN-NAS-
EN.ashx]

4. Integrating QV with R, November 2011, Technical Brief,
QlikView.com

5. QlikView and The Cloud: Have it your way, The QlikView Blog, Dec
2011, [http://community.qlikview.com/blogs/theqlikviewblog/
2011/12/21/qlikview-and-the-cloud-have-it-your-way]

6. QlikTech Case Study: Amazon Web Services,
[http://aws.amazon.com/solutions/case-studies/qliktech/]

7. SAS Versus R, Linked In Group, Started by Oleg,
[http://www.linkedin.com/groups/SAS-versus-R-35222.S.65098787]

8. QlikView in the Cloud, QlikCommunity Group, QlikView.com,
[http://community.qlikview.com/groups/qlikview-in-the-
cloud?view=discussions]

9. QlikView Metadata White Paper, April 2011, Brad Peterman,
QlikCommunity, [http://community.qlikview.com/docs/DOC-1782]

10. QlikView's Pragmatic Approach to Metadata, Erica Driver, Mar
2011, The QlikView Blog, QlikCommunity,
[http://community.qlikview.com/blogs/theqlikviewblog/2011/03/1
0/qlikview-s-pragmatic-approach-to-metadata]

11. Metascanner Application Download, Qlik Community Thread,
QlikView.com, [http://community.qlikview.com/docs/DOC-1783]

12. MetaMonitor Application Download, Qlik Community Thread,
QlikView.com, [http://community.qlikview.com/docs/DOC-1836]

13. Outperforming with a higher AQ (Analytics Quotient), IBM, IT
ToolBox,
[http://businessintelligence.ittoolbox.com/research/outperforming-
with-a-higher-aq-24853]

14. What's your AQ (Analytics Quotient), IBM, IBM.COM, [http://www-01.ibm.com/software/analytics/aq/] **(Must Read)

CHAPTER 15

MAKING QLIKVIEW WORK

THE INTERESTED WILL DO WHAT'S CONVENIENT. COMMITTED WILL DO WHATEVER IT TAKES

Introduction to the Chapter

Products with rich and diverse capabilities, like QlikView, can keep organizations busy for a long time, even without meaningful outputs and still give a sense of achieving something. Many people can be engaged doing seemingly meaningful and exciting work. However, success is not defined by features, the exciting technological achievements or the time spent in implementing. These lead to disappointments in most situations and that's why the successful BI implementations are a low percentage.

Also what is success for one company or person may not be success for others. Every organization is in some stage of information evolution with different Analytics Quotient. Depending on the current stage, the ability of the organization to use information is different and with that the needs change. Hence making QlikView work for each organization will vary due to these factors. Identifying and ensuring QlikView is put to right use in each organization is a key to making it really useful.

After identifying the right use, the use cases, the need then is to focus on deciding the right steps, and doing them all right. Numerous companies have spent time in deploying QlikView and have gone through a learning curve, along with the product maturity, and found ways of making it work better. Some of these learning can be used successfully by others and such expensive learning can be minimized. The chapter summarizes some of the "best practices" which are a combination of process and technology aspects.

Non-technology process aspects form an important part of best practices. These are discussed as well. The most important aspect is the organizational culture of using data, reviewing and taking decisions driven by data. Like it was seen in Part I, this is what makes a company move towards excellence and demonstrate consistent growth and move towards success. The final section focuses on this and gives examples of how some organizations have improved their Analytics Quotient.

Defining Success

Deployment of QlikView can mean different things to different people in various layers/roles. Efficiency improvement of IT processes can be success for IT Department. Availability of data in the right times by itself can be a success for the Data Analysts. Being able to arrive at a few actionable recommendations can be success for Business Analysts and Business Advisors. Actually seeing change on the ground in improved business profitability can be the success for the Business owners.

Each layer/role may have some objectives of their own, with some budgets allocated for achieving them. QlikView could be used to meet any of these objectives. However, the scale of deployment and impact of success increase as these layers move up towards Business Owners.

For a successful deployment of QlikView, understanding the needs of these layers is important, along with their constraints. The chapter on "What Benefits Can Be Expected from QlikView?" elaborately sets various ways in which QlikView can be put to good use.

Short-lived Exclaimed Reactions

Most of the times, during Proof-of-concept exercises and initial short projects using QlikView, customers give extremely positive responses, with following exclamatory observations:
1. Wow, you were able to do this dashboard so quickly!
2. Fantastic Slicing & Dicing!
3. Great looking dashboard!
4. Such a reduction of data sizes – up to 90% lesser size!
5. Quick reloads – ETL. It takes ages for us with our older solution!
6. Did not know we can handle such a large data set! 1 TB!

All of these are immediate knee-jerk reactions from IT and Business, seeing the capabilities of QlikView. Of the over 300 companies for which proof of concepts have been done by the team led by the author in the last 6 years, every one of the companies have jumped out of their seats and said WOW, this is fantastic. The sales guy would walk out, chest up, head high, saying the sale is done. However, experience has taught that these are short-lived success indicators.

In the next couple of meetings, the reaction from the senior management and business users is: "What can this actually do for our business? We do not see how this can add business value to us". The real question is, "How can we put this to use in our company, to support business growth and our strategic objectives?"

So the key definition for success with QlikView is: "What business problem was solved using the increased insight / visibility that QlikView provided, to manage the business better?" Conversely, if these outcomes are not envisioned right in the beginning, and the objectives set clearly, the implementation of QlikView is not likely to create a sustainable success.

Key Steps to Success with QlikView

With this understanding, the following are the key steps that need to be done, carefully step-by-step, to ensure success. This spans across the time from before QlikView is bought, to way beyond the time when QlikView implementation is completed and handed over to internal members to use it for business:

1. Defining Achievable Goals—specific needs definition
2. Understanding all constraints—technical, skill, commercial, process—including current status
3. Designing the solution—technical, process, commercial, people skills, usability
4. Verify solution against best practices and ensure they are followed
5. Implementation as a project
6. Maintain and use as a production line
7. Review criteria and review process—technical, usage, commercial and process
8. Verify periodically if needs are all met and set new goals/needs

Of all these, points 3 and 4 are specifically skills associated with QlikView technology and its understanding. Around these two points, there are best practices which are very useful in ensuring these two steps are done in the quickest and easiest way, with the best quality, right in the first time. The first three articles in references provide further thoughts on gaining success with QlikView [1, 2 and 3].

Development of QlikView Applications

Though the scope of this book does not cover the development of the front-end application, this section just touches upon some pointers. There are many online resources and reference material available from QlikTech to quickly learn QlikView application development. Once the fundamentals of QlikView development are understood, creating useful applications for the enterprise is easy. Best place to start is "New to QlikView" forum on QlikCommunity [4].

Another great place to start is the free online QlikView training page [5]. One can learn development, relatively quickly and easily. Particularly with prior database and excel knowledge, the learning is rather quick. In addition, the whole blogosphere that talks about QlikView is constantly covering in detail, the how-to's of development.

With every new release of the product, the "Whats New in QlikView version xx?" is an interesting place to start understanding the changes and improvements. The release notes on product also are very helpful. Community Blog: *"Top 11 Resources for QlikView 11"* [6] is a good example of such information in one place to help migrate to a new version.

QlikTech offers training—both online and class-room—directly and through partners across the world in different geographies and their schedule is given in their website. They also organize on-site training programs through partners. Train-the-trainer option is also available which can help create many developers internally. Some partners provide workshop-style training to enterprise customers with their own data sources and people, to enable quicker learning in the context.

More and more trained developers are now available in the market, though availability is still scarce and cost of resources is on the higher side. With the increase in number of partners and investments into training, the cost of resources should come down. Many organizations are providing off-shore development & support to help reduce TCO particularly for mid-size and large customers.

The eco-system around QlikView is quickly building up, especially after the high-visibility IPO in 2010. The movement of QlikView into the Leaders Quadrant of the Gartner Magic Quadrant shows the trend. The larger system integration giants like TCS, CTS, Wipro, etc. are all jumping into providing QlikView services, showing the movement of the product beyond the chasm on life-cycle. Customers who have invested in QlikView for initial projects have found good returns and are expanding into other larger projects across the enterprise. The need now is to consolidate all the efforts, give an enterprise-wide strategy and approach. Setting the ground for such strategic thinking is the purpose of this book, helping the eco-system not to just focus on the easy and quick first wins with the QlikView technology, but to think and engage into making it a viable long term strategy for large enterprises equally.

Best Practices

Past many years of QlikView usage has led to many best practices contributed by many practitioners of QlikView. A lot of these Best Practices documents have been put together by the QlikView experts around the world. Most of them are available through the QlikView contacts, Partners and through the QlikCommunity website. Experienced partners like Team and Climber have their own standards and special practices, owing to the large number of implementations they have done. More partners are moving in this direction.

Discussed in earlier Chapters

All the chapters in this book have discussed various best practices in different areas, and some are quickly summarized here:

Identify Needs / Objectives: The Part I chapters focus entirely on understanding what should be aimed, and how to consolidate the needs / objectives in pre-defined buckets of expectations. Completing these in a systematic way, including every stake holder in the system is the most important success criteria. The best practices include: a) Collective business requirement understanding to create a Business Requirements

Document (BRD), b) Understanding the business and technology constraints to create a Solution Requirements Document (SRD),

Design/Architect/Deploy: Based on the BRD and SRD, making a Solution Design Document (SDD) detailing the deployment architecture, Integration points and processes is a very important step. This stage requires interaction with the various stake holders as described in the chapter on "QlikView Deployment".

ETL – Data Architecture: The data architecture decides the sustainable stability of the solution, with the flexibility to include new functional areas, with ease of development and manageability. The chapters on "ETL and Advanced ETL" discuss at length the various details of the data architecture and the best practices around it – including the reference 5 layer architecture. The ETL also includes the setting up of the Publisher tasks. Using Loop and Reduce and integrating with other enterprise wide ETL tasks using triggers is a best practice. Rob Wunderlich's tutorials on Publisher are very useful, among the other Qlik Community articles and the QlikView Publisher manual.

Security Architecture: Security architecture lends the credibility and robustness for an Enterprise deployment. The best practices of QlikView security are discussed in the chapter on "QlikView Security". The essential need is, the security considerations should be included in the architecture design stage itself, so that every step done falls into a structure and makes best possible use of the security framework offered by QlikView.

Change Management / Training / Services: Getting QlikView up and running the first time is the quickest possible thing to do – typically in a few weeks, any complex application can be created and set up. However, this approach is useful only for initial evaluation or very urgent requirements. For a sustainable QlikView usage in an organization, the need is to set up a comprehensive Change Management / Training / Services setup. This will lead to the best use of QlikView to address more and more business needs—leading to better return on investments—and get into "Expand" after the "Land". Most of the times, customers are left to fend for themselves in this space. The best practice would be to have an internal or an external organization setup, either on-site or remote, to be available for supporting the setup on a continuous basis, to cover Change Management / Training and Support Services needs. Partners (like Team) have started providing these services at affordable prices for customers across geographies.

App Development: Application development in QlikView has three major parts—ETL Scripting, Data Modelling and Front-end Application development. ETL architecture is extensively discussed in the chapter on "ETL and Advanced ETL". The actual scripting is the first learning that is required. The output of ETL is the data model, and the Data Modelling has been discussed extensively in "Data Modelling for QlikView". The Front-end application development have not been discussed in this book, but there are excellent resources available as discussed earlier – in many online resources – mentioned in the previous section. A search on Best Practices in the QlikCommunity brings up a lot of discussions around this topic. Another important aspect is, during scripting, use of standardized frameworks, like QlikView Components (QVC)—the open source project run by Rob Wunderlich—is a great idea. This brings portability and continuity of support for various projects. Collective contribution to the QVC project by everyone will increase the speed of development without the need to do extensive testing of new code every time. QV CookBook available from Rob's website [7] is also a great point to start QlikView development with best practices.

Migration to latest versions of QlikView: Every major QlikView version release comes up with new features and improvements. Many patch releases, known as Service Releases come out periodically, primarily for bug fixes. These patch releases have the same major version number. Service Releases do not require any migration effort they are just installed on top of existing installations. Moving from one major version to another typically requires migration process. QVD and QVW files are all binary compatible. The files created with older versions work as it is on the newer versions, while the files from new releases may or may not work as expected in the older versions. New features of later versions can be added to older files—open and edit once in new QlikView Developer client and save.

Actual challenges in migration are faced with Macros, Publisher tasks, Bookmarks and other shared server object files. They require a careful migration process to ensure proper functioning in the new version. Most of the large partners provide this service, after trying out migrations in their internal labs. Best practice of migration is to move the applications to a new Test/QC Server, ensure the complete operations, and then perform the migration to the actual production server.

Migration of OEM applications, and custom developed integration elements in an enterprise are typically a major point of concern. The best practice is to generally try and use the SOA architecture, making communications happen over API interfaces and standardized data exchange mechanisms.

Other Critical Best Practices

Apart from technological aspects of QlikView development and deployment, there are other areas in which it is important to use others' experiences, to ensure the success is not just technological but an all round business success.

Commercial – User License Planning: Various components of QlikView and their licensing are relatively simple and easy to understand. User CALs: The classification of the users and their needs is an extremely important step to decide the appropriate license investments in different CALs. Periodically reviewing the usage of QlikView by various uses, and re-allocating licenses is an important step to optimize the ROI. This is discussed in chapter "Deploying QlikView".

Performance & Server Deployment: Though initial deployments are generally simplistic, with lowest possible investments to ensure ROI, the best practice is to have multiple environments for Development, Testing and Production. In some situations, there are pre-production / staging environments required for transitions to be smooth with no possible points of failure. In addition, based on performance metrics, horizontal scaling should be planned periodically, and clusters should be used. The chapter "Deploying QlikView" has discussed multiple environments and clustering. Some publisher deployment tutorials are found on Rob's website [8].

Project Management: Implementing QlikView in a company needs to be planned systematically, and executed with appropriate project management methods. QlikTech has presented / recommended a project management framework for this purpose as a starting point:

S.A.F.E.   [http://www.qlikview.com/us/services/consulting][9].   This method as is given, or a variant of this, is used by most of the partners and trained consultants [10], as well as the professional services division of QlikTech. S.A.F.E methodology documents can be received from QlikTech representatives and their partners on request. The providers like Team and Climber have evolved their own implementation methods around this process. Team particularly has a CMM Level 3 certified process used across all the implementations. TCS, CTS, Deloitte and other partners will certainly strengthen these processes with their own learning from across other BI technologies as well.

Visual App Design – Usability: QlikView helps create some of the best looking dashboards, following the recommendations of Stephen Few and other visualization experts around the world. Shima Nakazawa [14], Donald Farmer and many others at QlikTech share great ideas for the best practices for QlikView application design and usage. Shima's "Design and Functionality Best Practices" document [13] is a great guide. The Designer course offered by QlikTech provides a great way to learn good practices, based on scenario-based presentation design.

There is no single best way to design an application, but using standard templates for the company, and making all applications follow some common layout theme, is a great practice. This allows the users to naturally know where to find what, and what colors mean what, which charts should be read / interpreted in which way. Among the QlikView developers, who come mostly from programming background, there is a lot of stress given in understanding the scripting, Modelling, expression writing and automation. The importance of visual impact is not fully understood and practiced. Evolving enterprise visualization guidelines, particularly for data, and creating an enterprise template layout is a very important best practice approach.

Demo site of QlikView.com (http://Demo.QlikView.Com) [16] is a great resource site to find great applications, and "borrow" some of the ideas/layouts and methods. Apart from that, the references section provides some links to cool consultant sites talking about best practices of app-design / presentation with QlikView [11, 12, 17, 18 and 19]. Some great work connecting principles of design/presentation, with the capabilities of QlikView, giving some clear suggestions on how this can be applied in customer situations is being done by Rob and others.

Enabling right use of QV: Asking the question, "Is this a right problem to solve with QlikView?" is a very important best practice question. While almost any information need can be serviced using QlikView, there are situations when QlikView is not the right solution and there are situations when the problem is not the right one for QlikView. For example, trying to provide QlikView front-end for users requiring pixel-perfect reports on QlikView, or real-time reporting are straight forward examples of wrong use-cases.

Other bad uses of QlikView, or for that matter any BI solution, is to choose wrong KPIs, wrong representation of data and—more difficult to identify—applying on problems that do not add any business value to the company, while there are other extremely important problems that need to be solved with QlikView. Having a set of criteria defined to select problem areas and use QlikView to help solve those problems is very important.

Review process & metrics: The chapter on "Deploying QlikView" presented the monitoring and management of QlikView. It is a best practice to define parameters that need to be monitored on a constant basis to ensure the health of the complete QlikView deployment, end-to-end, including the benefits that users get by using QlikView.

Key indicators that measure the health of QlikView deployment are:
a. reload times for various stages of ETL
b. size of QVDs and QVWs and their trends
c. memory and CPU used by applications
d. usage of applications: Number of accesses, clicks etc - patterns
e. response times for users for every click on various sheets/objects
f. availability of applications
g. extent of collaboration in the applications: sessions, bookmarks, annotations

With these measures, and associated 'healthy' range set for each metric, the health of the QlikView deployment in all aspects can be monitored. Whenever any trend towards 'unhealthy' state is observed, corrective measures can be setup to ensure it is corrected.

For example, in one of the implementations, when the Usage of Applications dropped below an expected minimum value, the CEO of the company started calling various dashboard users with their dashboard open in front of him, and started discussing numbers based on the dashboard. This increased the usage of QlikView, which increased possibility of taking informed / better decisions.

When the Memory and CPU usage of applications increases beyond thresholds, and the response of QlikView to users become sluggish, the need is to revisit the architecture, data model, data periods, formulae, and so on, to ensure the application is made slick and useful again. QlikView, due to its ease of development and use, allows an agile methodology enabling incremental improvement in functionality and performance. Because of this, the aspects that are not taken care of in the initial development due to prioritization may come up as challenges subsequently. Hence, audits should be done periodically, to ensure overall system health and usefulness of QlikView for the enterprise.

QlikTech and other experienced partners offer Expert Services to perform audit, identify the problem areas and fix them. Such audits and performance improvement activities should be periodically repeated to ensure that QlikView produces the necessary benefits for the business.

Business and Performance Reviews with QlikView: One of the most important and most rewarding best practices is to use QlikView for regular business reviews inside the enterprise. Instead of taking static reports out of QlikView in the form of Excel, Powerpoint or PDF outputs. QlikView should be projected live in the management meetings and performance reviews.

The insights and dynamic understanding of root-causes and causal relationships between various data patterns, gives a powerful mechanism to collectively and collaboratively appreciate trends and correlations. This helps leaders and managers to take informed decisions together, on the spot, without having to meet again with analysis results and observations.

One of the important effects is—the quality of data at all levels will get validated—"Familiarity with data improves quality of data". The organizational pressure that comes naturally to cleanse and keep right data in all levels becomes very high. This is a creative pressure for improving the organization continuously.

Also, newer metrics and measures are created to push the organization to higher levels of excellence continuously in such meetings. Thanks to the ease with which QlikView allows new measures/metrics to be created and applied for decision making.

Concluding Remarks

Performance improvement is an important agenda for enterprises, to maximize profitability, efficiency and market share. Constant *inspection with trust* is considered the mantra for moving towards profitable excellence. Constantly setting goals and measuring the difference between target/budget/efficiency goals, and the achievements is the prime mover—creative pressure—that pushes organizations towards excellence.

Increasing visibility and providing metrics—in the form of balanced scorecards, dashboards and reports—is only one part of enabling this inspection and data-driven management style. What is more important is the ability to understand what causes the gap, explain the variances and identify root-causes. Only then will the corrective measures pop-up in the minds of the management—driven by experience, knowledge and imagination—and the action decisions are born.

QlikView is a great instrument to help gain these insights to action. Hence the use of QlikView should be primarily in areas where these data-discovery led insights will make a huge impact in the move of the organization towards excellence.

Once this is done, all levels of the organization gain a higher Analytics Quotient and use data to take informed decisions. The accuracy of data, availability of QlikView and performance become very important for the enterprise, making this a mission-critical application. In such a situation, use of best practices in all the aspects is important. This chapter focused on integrating all the discussions across the book, to have them as a checklist of practices in every deployment. This checklist should be used to verify / audit the QlikView implementation, and take it to the next level. This helps push the organization to higher levels of business excellence.

QlikView changes the culture of any organization, and helps it become a high-performing organization, if implemented in the right way. The responsibility of QlikView consultants and the partners is to carry this sincerity, and ensure that the organizational evolution towards higher excellence is supported by deploying QlikView—not just for technically deploying QlikView or even worse, just to meet the quarterly quotas!

Fortunately, the partners and customers of QlikView around the world are very passionate. Such a checklist driven approach will make QlikView implementations a pleasure not only for technologists and analysts, but also for business users and all the stake holders!

And lastly, best practices themselves are not the end, they are just the beginning. A great insight from Barry Diller helps plan the next steps: "Don't give me best practices, they are yesterday's news. Give me emerging practices, they are tomorrow's news".

References

1. A Conversation with QlikView Architect Hakan Wogle, Nov 2011, Erica Driver, The QlikView Blog, [http://community.qlikview.com//blogs/theqlikviewblog/2010/11/11/a-conversation-with-qlikview-architect-h-229-kan-wolg-233]

2. The Underlying Technology of QlikView, June 2010, Curt Monash, DMBS2, [http://www.dbms2.com/2010/06/12/the-underlying-technology-of-qlikview/]

3. Busting 5 Myths about QlikView, April 2011, Dmitry Gudkov, BI review, Blogspot.in, [http://bi-review.blogspot.in/2011/04/busting-5-myths-about-qlikview.html]

4. New to QlikView, QlikCommunity Section, [http://community.qlikview.com/community/new-to-qlikview]

5. Free Training, QlikView Web Site, [http://www.qlikview.com/us/services/training/free-training]

6. Top 11 Resources for QlikView 11, QlikView Community Manager Blog, QlikCommunity, [http://community.qlikview.com/blogs/communitymanager/2011/11/23/top-11-resources-for-qlikview-11]

7. QV CookBook, Rob Wunderlich QlikView Consulting, [http://robwunderlich.com/downloads/]

8. QlikView Publisher Tutorials, Rob Wunderlich QlikView Consulting, [http://robwunderlich.com/tutorials/]

9. SAFE Project Method, Thread on QlikCommunity, [http://community.qlikview.com/message/84497#84497]

10. Start your QlikView project the right way, Steve Dark, Quick Intelligence, [http://www.quickintelligence.co.uk/start-your-qlikview-project-the-right-way/]

11. QVDesign, Blog Posts of Mathew Crowther, Visual Analytics, [http://qvdesign.wordpress.com/]

12. QlikView Best Practices, Gilles Pol, Quick-Qlear-Qool, [http://www.quickqlearqool.nl/?p=146]

13. Design and Functionality Best Practices, 2007, Shima Nakazawa, [http://www.scribd.com/doc/60672520/Design-and-Functionality-Best-Practices]

14. Shima Nakazawa's Stuff, Qlik Community, [http://community.qlikview.com/people/sna?view=overview]

15. Best Practices for QlikView upgrade from v8.5 to v10, Innoppl Technologies, [http://innoppl.com/best-practices-for-qlikview-upgrade-from-v8-5-to-v10/]

16. Qlik Demos, QlikView Demo Applications, QlikView Website, [http://demo.qlikview.com/]

17. QlikView Optimization Best Practices, 2007, Qlik Community Resource, [http://community.qlikview.com/docs/DOC-1882]

18. QlikView Data Model Best Practices, Qlik Community Thread, [http://community.qlikview.com/thread/31709]

19. Best Practices Approach to QlikView Development, A.Rajendran, QlikView Practice Group, Team Computers, [http://www.slideshare.net/TBSL/best-practices-qlikview-application-development]

EL FIN

MILES TO GO BEFORE WE CALL IT THE END; IT'S THE
BEGINNING.

Running businesses better is the unquestioned need of all enterprises across the world. Better is defined differently, for example, by shareholders as profitability, by managers as efficient and by governments as compliant. Making the company better in each of these ways, is the need. Information plays an important role in this aspiration of companies. Visibility of this information, provided in an un-interrupted and unlimited fashion is the pre-requisite for making this happen.

Through various chapters, this book explored how QlikView can be used to serve this purpose of better visibility. Access to information when we want is one level of liberation in this direction. Being able to slice and dice, without limits, is another level of liberation that QlikView brings. QlikView is a disruptive technology, which removes the barriers of hierarchical analytics—providing Associative Analytic experience to the business users—enhancing the natural capability of the human mind to find associations between different elements, intuitively.

QlikView has many aspects that offer solutions to challenges of technology, psychology of human analytical capabilities and to use tactile associative visualization (click and view) as an added tool to help increase the strength of mind. Various benefits that QlikView can bring were explored in Part I.

Understanding the tool in depth, and appreciating the way it works, provides a strong confidence to take advantage of its capabilities and nuances. With new technologies and approaches that QlikView uses, it is refreshing to look at how it works, and understand what traditional problems of business intelligence it can solve. Part II explored all the innards of QlikView and provided an inside view of its capabilities.

Part III focused on establishing a process, methodology and architecture to make best use of QlikView. The introduction of QlikView brings about a disruptive change in the way in which some of the senior managers and the discerning analysts think and act. Channelizing this disruptive capability into a constructive force and enabling the company to draw from the strengths of this force is the focus of this last Part.

Generally a discussion about QlikView revolves around the front-end capabilities, how to build an application, and how various aspects of business data can be presented using the different visualization components. This book was intentionally kept outside of that discussion, to focus more on the non-visual and abstract parts of QlikView. The key interest was to create the conceptual framework, integrating it into the larger enterprise software framework, and defining the points of connectivity of QlikView with the rest of the enterprise.

A picture is equal to 1000 words. An interactive picture is an entire book. QlikView allows us to read businesses as a rich interactive book with the freedom of choosing the twists and turns as we desire!

ACKNOWLEDGEMENTS

I take this opportunity to express my gratitude to everyone who has walked along with me, guided me or provoked me with their questions—customers, colleagues, partners and team members, and my family above all for their constant support. You are all the reason for what I am today!

At the outset I would like to thank all the customers who have made the journey with QlikView possible, and gave opportunity to create value. The first order we got from Primus Apparels (@Value Stores) in Bangalore in 2005 set us in sail - thank you Balaji Bhat. The second order from Apollo Tyres strengthened our sail, thanks to Dheeraj Sinha and Jitendra Mahanna. The vision of Mohan Chandrasekharan at Reliance Life, Pramod Krishnamurthy at Fullerton India Credit (now at Birla Sun Life), Sanjay Rao and Sayan Ray at Shriram Fibres, Shikha Rai at Canon India added to the real experience in large enterprise settings - can't thank them all enough. After that every customer has added great experience and value to us - Shashi Kumar Ravulapati of Reliance Consumer Finance, Sriram Naganathan of Reliance General, Shyam Sundar of Royal Sundaram General, R.V.S. Mani of SBI Life, Mayank Bathwal of Birla Sun life, Krishnan of L&T Finance—over 160 customers and I wish I can mention everyone's name. I thank every one of you with whole heart.

Of customers in US, ASG (now of ICICI Group) gave our entry into the US market - thank you Rahul Basu and Arjun Mitra. California Casualty Management Company is a leading-edge full cycle deployment of QlikView—thanks to the vision of Satish Ranganathan, Vasu Kadambi and Michael Cochran—it made us get recognized in the US as a strong player—thank you all. The experiences we have had with Bloomberg, Cisco, Autodesk, Pacific Biosciences, KLA Tencor, Applied Materials,

PlaySpan (Visa now), Enphase Energy have all added to the evolution of our enterprise understanding and made us grow in the US market.

The joy of creating an entity, making it grow and deliver to customers is immense. I am grateful to my friend and colleague Ranjan Chopra, for creating Team as a platform where we have built an organization that truly cares to create value for customers—across technology and products—solving their information pains. Along with him is Sudhir Rao, who steered us in the vision for providing information insights and set the ship in sail—thank you Sudhir and I love your philosophy of *Enterprise Care* similar to Health Care. Thank you, CV Prakash for laying the foundation for all that I have done and being the emotional super-charge for many. Thank you, Deepak Rai, for being the critical eye of it all, pushing us to see things in different perspectives to create sustainable growth.

Johan is very special—he was the first person at QlikTech whom we reached out to start the relationship of Team Computers as a Master Reseller in India. From then, the way he walked us along has been wonderful, and we share a lot of excellent moments of success in bringing QlikView to customers in India and in the US. Thank you, Johan for your constant inspiration and now the *Foreword*—it means a lot.

Many people in QlikTech have made it possible for the practice to flourish and my personal learning to grow: Shima's influence on our thinking, through her training in 2006, Frederick Uhno's visit providing insights to everyone in the team. Was an excellent experience having Les Bonney in some of the early customer meetings and getting specific insights to approach the market. John Teichman with his certification visit to Delhi, made a strong impact on our consultants and raised the quality awareness. I really appreciate the guidance and contributions of Rabah Krouchy, Peter McQuade in establishing the market. When QlikTech became present in India, contributions of Paul Rajesh were extremely helpful, particularly his unique combination of technology and friendly approach—thank you Paul. I want to thank all of you, and give my gratitude for all the help and support to our team. Earlier Raghunathan, and now Ramendra Mandal and the team in QlikTech India have led the growth and I thank them all for their support. Particularly, Mehul Desai who has shown the way for a collaborative market approach—thank you Mehul.

In the US, I want to thank Michael Johnson, Jon Wolken and Sean Hughes for their constant support and encouragement, when we started the presence. Many friends in US operations were so supportive and particular thanks to Brad Copeland, Michael Booth, Lisa Stifelmann Perry, Ellen Lehr, Susan Osorio and Quinci Cubiburu—thank you.

My Team—I have been lucky: every one of the entire team of over 200 QlikView consultants, who have been part of the Team at various stages, was a great reason for my learning constantly—every session of teaching / sharing with all of them, every time they brought a problem from a customer location, it added to my personal learning. Of special significance are my core team members: Jatin Sawhney, Sanjay Madan, Abhishek Ranjan, Shalendra Daga, Vijay Kumar, Ashwini Bhatia, Rameen Dhall, Muruganantham, Sangeet Patil, Parag Naik and Prashant Momaya, who constantly add strength to the organization and me personally. The extended management team including Mahesh Tomar, Kaushik, Rana, Ravi Dutt, Prakash Pal and Pranab have added strength to this growth like invisible manure. I should mention the passion and support extended by Valan Arasu, Lakshminarayanan, Srinivas Rao, Pooja Chatrath, Manish Bhandari and Ponnanna Uthappa for their solid contributions to the growth. And every one of the team members in India and US: Thank you all. It's a great journey and I relish every moment. The colleagues in the US operations provided a great support and want to thank every one of them—Manu Jerath, Amanda Carson, Arjun Ganjoo, Rashmi, Gayathri and other friends. I want to thank John Brooks, John Horner and Mathew Feyling for their support. It is a pleasure working with Rob Wunderlich on training programs and other process improvement initiatives—thank you Rob.

There are very few days in the past 7 years that I have not travelled. I owe the world to my family, for allowing me and supporting me to invest all the time in my passion, in building this practice and spending time with customers. My wife Meena has taken the complete load on her shoulders and supported me—thank you my love for being you.

The joy of being the father of an understanding daughter is one. It went to a greater height when she came up to help with the book, and became the most demanding editor—making me go through multiple revisions of editing. I am not sure if anyone else would have been able to convince me so strongly and win my acceptance. My daughter Mahashree has been a great support and a light. Thank you my dear.

It is not just a few people, and it would not be possible to mention everyone, in India, in the US operations, in QlikTech, in Customer places, there have been so many who have helped me in this path of understanding and appreciating QlikView and its uses.

I take this opportunity to thank everyone in the extended family who has been a great support at various times -parents, parents-in-law, brothers, sisters-in-law, sisters, brothers-in-law, friends, colleagues and everyone who have made me what I am!

I have not taken all the names of every one of you I wish to thank but I thank each of you with the whole of my heart. I am grateful to nature, for having this chance to stand up and appreciate everyone's contribution. Not every day we get such a chance!

Thank you all!

Warm regards,
Rajendran Avadaiappan
29 April 2012

Made in the USA
Lexington, KY
18 February 2013